Acclaim for Willie Morris's

NORTH TOWARD HOME

Willie Morris

NORTH TOWARD HOME

In addition to *North Toward Home*, Willie Morris was the author of *My Dog Skip, My Cat Spit McGee, New York Days*, and many other books. As the imaginative and creative editor of *Harper's* magazine he was a major influence in changing our postwar literary and journalistic history. He died in 1999 in Jackson, Mississippi, where he lived with his wife, JoAnne.

BOOKS BY WILLIE MORRIS

NORTH TOWARD HOME

NORTH
TOWARD HOME

Willie Morris

VINTAGE BOOKS
A Division of Random House, Inc.
New York

FIRST VINTAGE BOOKS EDITION, AUGUST 2000

Copyright © 1967 by Willie Morris

Portions of this book appeared in *Harper's, Commentary, The New Yorker, The
New Republic,* and *The Saturday Evening Post.*

"When I Buy Pictures" is reprinted with permission of The Macmillian Company
from *Collected Poems* by Marianne Moore. Copyright 1935 by Marianne Moore,
renewed 1963 by Marianne Moore and T. S. Eliot.

Grateful acknowledgment is made to Edwin M. Yoder, Jr., for permission to use
the introduction to the 1982 edition written by him, published
by Yoknapatawpha Press, Inc.

Library of Congress Cataloging-in-Publication Data on file.

Vintage ISBN: 0-375-72460-5

Author photograph © David Rae Morris

www.vintagebooks.com

Printed in the United States of America
10 9 8 7 6 5 4 3 2 1

For Mamie and my mother,
two Mississippi people

The past is never dead. It's not even past.
—Gavin Stevens
in *Intruder in the Dust*

CONTENTS

INTRODUCTION

by Edwin M. Yoder, Jr.

Recently, on a chilly Virginia night, I returned a bit apprehensively to Willie Morris's *North Toward Home* after fifteen years. Rereading a special book is risky, like a rendezvous with a long-unseen old friend. It is a relief to find the remembered intimacy unwarped by time.

My worries about *North Toward Home* were needless. From the opening description of that highway plunging from the hills into Yazoo City to the last page, it remains compelling. I recall, as if it were yesterday, reading the first excerpts from it in the old *Saturday Evening Post*, and never since then have I doubted that it will endure with the great American autobiographies.

Americans—and not only Americans, for that matter, or Southerners or Mississippians—will be reading it many decades hence—appreciating its emotional honesty, its fidelity to the experiences of a young man with a genius for experience, its sensitivity to transformations that, like a great flood, devastate some familiar landscape and yet leave it recognizable under the sediment.

The mid-1960s, when Willie Morris was writing the book in a sunless New York apartment, may have been the last moment when a memoir of American provincial life could strike most readers as more than a museum piece. Willie Morris's generation, of the 1930s and early 1940s, was perhaps the last to escape the homogenization that he describes in his brief, bleak account of Palo Alto, California—"mile after mile of chrome and asphalt horror, slicing through the debris of this American age: the used car lots, the hot-dog stands, the drive-in movies, the jumbled-up shopping centers, the motels . . . streamlined abominations that looked as if they would be lucky to last twenty years." Those of us whose early lives predated the chrome and asphalt age often came from small Southern, Midwestern or New England towns, not unlike Yazoo City if you set aside a few degrees of longitude or latitude. We grew up on the same books, the same Protestant hymns, the same popular tunes and radio programs. We, too, heard the ceaseless family talk that Morris describes so well. More crucially, perhaps, we luckily escaped television: silencer of conversation, brutal processor of mass-minded sensibilities.

Maybe the world as we had known it did not "break in two" between our age and that of our children, but it seemed so. Often these days one reads of people going back to the land, or small towns and villages, in search of values, landscapes and folkways too casually discarded in the rush to the Big Cave (as Morris calls New York). Many of us had our Big Caves, all right, and discovered their dimness as he did. But the past is never recapturable, not the self-contained and self-sufficient world of Yazoo City or Jackson as they were in Morris's boyhood, with their certitudes, stable traditions and familiar faces and houses. There seem to be fewer grandmothers like Willie's Mamie, with her vivid and particular memories of the old time; fewer grandfathers like Percy, with his special idiom, his dedication to baseball, the building of model steamboats and other boyish pursuits.

In 1967, when *North Toward Home* first appeared, there was also a special curiosity about Southern books. It was a time of interest in the South as a place, in Southerners as people. It, and they, were marked. The great social changes in which Southerners had participated seemed then a triumph of will, promising some limitless capacity for social redemption. For a Willie Morris, who described with such self-searching honesty the complexities and ambiguities of Southern experience, even warily cynical New York has a sympathetic ear. Editors who now complain of having been conned by Southern writers were printing all they could get from the Morrises, the Styrons and others. Indeed, Morris's book was published in the same week as William Styron's *The Confessions of Nat Turner*.

So it was a special moment, a crossroads, and a book like *North Toward Home* was there to seize and cross it. I wrote then that the book was a study in three violent societies—Mississippi, Texas and New York City: a judgment that now seems to me embarrassingly callow. Reread after fifteen years it is less striking in that way than in its remarkable fixation of a special personal experience.

The South remembered by Willie Morris was, he says, "the old, impoverished, whipped-down South," with other stock figures all of us remember well: the Protestant God, "anthropomorphic and quick-tempered, a natty beard on his Anglo-Saxon face"; a Negro doctor who had by ageless custom to enter a white house by the back way, even when a child's life hung in the balance. Morris had boyhood friends, otherwise amiable enough, who slew their mothers and grandmothers in the fine old Gothic way; and there were neighbors who could reveal an ugly streak when the racial order seemed threatened. But it was a pleasant world, too, of ordinary boyish things—high school football and American Legion baseball; playing the trumpet at military funerals; precocious dogs and eccentric great-aunts; moonlight trysts on the delta and dancing the Memphis Shuffle with your blond plantation girl; trekking the great woods where water sprang up in every spongy footprint.

It isn't clear, even to him, why Willie Morris, so happy and accomplished on this familiar stage, left it abruptly to go off to school in Texas—except that his father told him he must "get out." In Texas he would attend a big state university, edit the student paper, wrangle with deans and regents about its freedom, win a Rhodes Scholarship, and return after four years in Oxford to edit an insurgent weekly. He writes: "Mississippi would lurk forever in the heart; Texas was where I reached maturity. There it was politics, the ambivalent and exposed world of the politician, that taught me about the complexity of human affairs, about the irrelevance of most dogmatic formulas, about loyalty and courage and devotion to human causes." And, he might have added, about colorful and brave people, for it would be hard to improve his evocative portraits of figures like Maury Maverick Jr., Ronnie Dugger, Bob Eckhardt and other fellow Texas insurgents.

Later, drawn to try his fortunes as a writer and editor in New York, he would encounter impersonality, raw snobbery and casual indifference to suffering. More to the point, for a writer, "there were temptations to be not merely careless, but dishonest, with the most distinctive things about one's self."

And is this not, in fact, the single greatest threat of modern American life to the soul? Willie Morris's resistance to those temptations is, I think, the ultimate theme of *North Toward Home*. It is full of wonderful and funny stories—who could forget the kitchen overhanging the subway tracks?—but it is also a story of endurance and survival. Willie Morris displays his rings here, like an ancient tree trunk. The layers of his life as a man and a writer enclose, never conceal, the earlier ones and together they tell a story of growth. And it is a growth of integrity: the integrity of seeing life steadily and seeing it whole. In a time too given to formulas, jargons, ideologies, systems, attitudes, stereotypes—all of them ways of evading human experience and guarding one against the task of coming to terms with it—Morris manages to be gloriously free of screens and poses and evasions.

Two passages, of many that could be cited, seem to me to sum up the theme. On his brief West Coast sojourn Morris is watching a baseball game at Candlestick Park, San Francisco, when a home-run ball strikes a bleacher and bounds back into the outfield. He sees the great Willie Mays trot over and toss the ball "across the fence to the boys who had been deprived of a free baseball," and finds in it a memory-stirring "fine aristocracy." Elsewhere, Morris describes his friendship in New York with two Southern-born writers, both black, Ralph Ellison and Albert Murray. In that special South-against-the-world spirit born of an immutable transracial heritage, they share his determination to resist the brittle intellection that fills the air of literary New York. "They knew the evils of the South—as Negroes, much more intimately that I ever had.

". . . Yet they tried to reduce their experience, not to polemicism but to metaphor."

In Willie Morris one finds that "fine aristocracy" of gesture, that fierce will to view life in the round and in pictures and metaphors, that he finds in others. His story, in other words, is the most familiar yet the most difficult known to any writer—the search for a language capable of containing without cheap falsification the rich freight of human experience. *North Toward Home* has the wit, wisdom and prophecy that only uncommon courage, a clear eye and a good heart can wring out of one's own life and locales. Like other fine autobiographies it is the vehicle of more than mere self-regard. It can be read as the memoir of one especially sentient American provincial, but also as the universal story of anyone who has known the same "love for a small, inconsequential place." That "inconsequential" is irony, to be sure. No place, or places, that inspire a book of such humor and poignancy can be inconsequential. They are, on the contrary, of mythic proportions.

Alexandria, Virginia
January, 1982

PART ONE

Mississippi

1

HALF AN HOUR north of Jackson on U.S. 49, not far beyond the Big Black River, the casual rolling land gives way to a succession of tall, lush hills, one after another for twelve or fifteen miles. In spring and summer the trees and underbrush are of an almost tropical density, and the whole terrain is grown over with a prolific green creeping vine, right up to the highway, and sometimes onto the concrete itself when the highway workers have let up a day too long. On a quiet day after a spring rain this stretch of earth seems prehistoric — damp, cool, inaccessible, the moss hanging from the giant old trees — and if you ignore the occasional diesel, churning up one of these hills on its way to Greenwood or Clarksdale or Memphis, you may feel you are in one of those sudden magic places of America, known mainly to the local people and merely taken for granted, never written about, not even on any of the tourist maps. To my knowledge this area of abrupt hills and deep descents does not have a name, but if you drive up and down them once on a fine day and never see them again, you will find them hard to forget.

Beyond these hills, if you follow the highway as it forks north and slightly west, the hills suddenly come to an end and there is one long, final descent. Out in the distance, as far as the eye can see, the land is flat, dark, and unbroken, sweeping away in a faint misty haze to the limits of the horizon. This is the great delta. Once it was the very floor under the sea; later knee-deep in waters and covered with primordial forests — a dank shadowy swampland, fetid and rich. There will not be a hill or a rise now until just below Memphis, 180 miles away. In a fast car a man can almost make it to Tennessee on automatic pilot, driving the straight, level road in a kind of euphoria, past the cotton fields and the tenant shacks, the big plantation houses and the primitive little Negro churches, over the muddy creeks and rivers, through the counties with the forgotten Indian names — Leflore, Coahoma, Tallahatchie, Tunica.

The town where I grew up sits there on the edge of the delta, straddling that memorable divide where the hills end and the flat land begins. The town itself was half hills and half delta, only forty miles from the Mississippi as the crow flies. One afternoon when I was ten years old, lounging in front of the Phillips station on the street which came hell-bent out of the hills as the highway, I watched a man and his wife emerge from a Buick with Illinois plates. The woman smoothed out the wrinkles in her dress with her palm, paused for a second to look at the drab vistas of the downtown, and whispered, "My God!"

Its name was Yazoo City, from the river that flows by it from farther up in the delta — a muddy winding stream that takes in the Tallahatchie, the Sunflower, and God knows how many less ambitious creeks and rivers in its southward course before it empties itself into the greater River a few miles north of Vicksburg. "Yazoo," far from being the ludicrous name that others would take it, always meant for me something dark, a little blood-crazy and violent. It is, in fact, an old Indian name that means "Death," or "waters of the dead"; the Indians who once inhabited the region as fighters and hunters had died by the scores of some horrible disease. Stephen Foster at first meant his song to be "Way Down upon the Yazoo River," but it was rumored he found out about the meaning of the word, and felt he had been tricked. Hence the town was "death city" to its detractors, and to my contemporaries when I left the place later for college, I was called "Yazoo," such was the spell the very name exerted on you long after you had left it. When the Greyhound out of Jackson stops at some dilapidated grocery store covered with patent medicine posters to pick up a few Negroes, or a solitary traveler waving a white handkerchief in the middle of nowhere, the driver will ask "Where to?" and the passenger will say "Yazoo," with the accent on the last syllable, rich and bass like a quick rumble of thunder.

In the nineteenth century the cotton growers, adventurous younger sons and brothers, came here from the older South where the land had played out, seeking the rich alluvial earth. Later the merchants came to exploit the commerce of the Yazoo River, where the old river boats were stacked ten and fifteen deep in cotton bales, and steamboats with names like the *Hard Cash*, the *City of Greenwood*, and the *Katie Robbins* plied their trade from the upper delta to Vicksburg. Keel- and flatboats laden with flour and apples started out on the Yazoo River, then entered the Mississippi and went all the way south to New Orleans. These early settlers had names like Beatty, Adams, Bull, Clark, Gray, Howard, Little, Robertson, Sparks, Taylor, Thompson, Walton, Whitehead, Young. The slaves had the names of the masters, and for years the tax lists of the place suggested the old Anglo-Saxon blood-source. Later others came to this lower delta — Italians, Irish, Jews, Syrians, even Chinese — to produce a curious melting pot, black, yellow, and white, and all the gradations known to man.

For a white boy growing up in the 1940s it was a pleasant old town; many of its streets were unpaved, although most of them in the white neighborhoods would be sooner or later. Broadway, the street that came swooping out of the hills, was the most unusual of all. Its angle was so steep, and its descent from the top so long, that ever so often the driver of some doomed car or truck would discover that his brakes were not nearly sufficient to deal with this reckless terrain. His path to death would be an agonizing one, as he whipped 80 or 90 miles an hour out of those hills, usually crashing into another car or truck where the ground leveled off at the intersection with Main Street. Once, as we were told it later as children, a truckful of Negro cottonpickers got out of control coming down that street and crashed into a big pecan tree at 70 miles an hour; the dead and dying were thrown for yards around, even into the broad limbs of the pecan tree.

The main street, stretching its several blocks from the Dixie Theater at Broadway down to the cabin that housed Western Union at the bend of the river, was always narrow and dingy, so that the gaudy colored postcard of the "business district" on display in the drugstore seemed more like another place altogether; and out along the highways where the town began there was that raw, desperate, unsettled look, much like towns I later would know in West Texas and the red-clay parts of Louisiana. But down in the settled places, along the quiet, shady streets with their pecan and elm and magnolia and locust trees were the stately old houses, slightly dark and decaying before the descendants became prosperous enough to have them "restored," which usually meant one coat of white enamel. Even the names of the streets suggested they might have been there for a while: Washington, Jefferson, Madison, Monroe, Jackson, Calhoun, and, of course, College, which ran by the high school.

All this was before the advent of a certain middle-class prosperity, before the big supermarkets and the neighborhood "shopping centers," back when the game laws were the only device protecting Republicans, both New ones and Old. Then it was a lazy town, stretched out on its hills and its flat streets in a summer sun, a lethargic dreamy place, green and lush. all year except for those four stark months at the end and the beginning, heavy with leafy smells, at night full of rumblings and lost ghosts — the Yankees in the sunken gunboat down in the river, the witch in the cemetery who burned down the whole town in 1904, Casey Jones crashing headlong into that unfortunate Illinois Central freight. So isolated was the place that when a big passenger plane mistook the few lights of the dirt airport for Jackson, circled around town and finally came to a skidding halt in the mud, everyone who heard the motors drove out to the airport before the lost plane landed, and a representative of the chamber of commerce put up a stepladder and said to each passenger climbing down, "Welcome to Yazoo." All over the town, everywhere, the Negro sections surrounded the white, and in that curious fractured pattern which Northerners have never quite comprehended, many Negro and white houses sat side by side. But in the larger, unbroken Negro sections — on Brickyard Hill, in the river bottom with its shacks on stilts, around the town dump and the Cotton Club honkytonk where all the killings were said to take place Saturday nights — even in these a white boy would wander about any time he felt like it, feeling that damp adventure and pulsing of blood of walking through niggertown alone. I have a vivid image of myself as a child, on the first day the "city bus line" opened, riding all one afternoon in the only bus they owned, paying a nickel every time the rickety old vehicle turned around at the end of the line. We rode in great excitement and pride, having never had a bus line before, down Grand Avenue and Canal to Main, then turned around at the old Western Union station, headed up Main and Canal again and along the rim of Brickyard Hill over the same route: these were the limits of my world.

Somewhere I once saw a roster of the prominent people the

place had produced. General Pershing's aide-de-camp. Senator John Sharp Williams, a friend and advisor of Woodrow Wilson. Hershel Brickell, a literary critic in New York, who died the day I finished my last examinations in high school. Who remembers them now, who knows much about them or cares? And who knows, for no one has any records, what Negroes came from this common place, moved to Chicago or Harlem, and remembered in pleasure or anguish what they had left behind? As a boy Richard Wright lived on a tenant farm not far from the town. Once, many years later, when I was full grown and twenty-two, I found myself in Paris; I got Wright's phone number and called him, saying I was a white Yazoo boy. "You're from Yazoo?" he asked. "Well, come on over." We went out to an Arab bar and got a little drunk together, and talked about the place we both had known. I asked him, "Will you ever come back to America?" "No," he said. "I want my children to grow up as human beings." After a time a silence fell between us, like an immense pain — or maybe it was my imagining.

•

When I was slightly less than a year old, in 1935, I almost died. I lay in a crazy fever in the back room, shook with convulsions, and gave every indication of a precocious death. My doctor could not be found. My parents tried to telephone every white doctor in town. Finally, as I was told it later, they called Dr. Miller, the Negro doctor. He came right away and saved my life.

"Which door did he come in?" I asked my grandmother, who had been there, many years later.

"What do you mean, which door?" she asked.

"I mean, was it the front one or the back one?"

"I declare," she said, pausing to remember . . . "I believe he came around back."

The child Dr. Miller saved, having come in to him through the back door, was a child born into certain traditions. The South was one, the old, impoverished, whipped-down South; the Lord Almighty was another — anthropomorphic and quick-tempered, a natty beard on his Anglo-Saxon face; the Negro doctor coming around back was another; the printed word; the spoken word; and all these more or less involved with doom and lost causes, and close to the Lord's earth.

My father was a native of those sulphurous hills south of Nashville who had come to the Deep South, of all places and at all times, during the Great Depression; he had come to work for Cities Service. He was thin and gaunt, a hunter and a fisherman, an indomitable country baseball player whose nickname was "Hooks" for the way he could hook-slide; his own father had served in the Tennessee Senate with Cordell Hull. To my father the swamp-bottom was a more civilized place than the Rotary Club, Wolf Lake when the white perch were biting beat any church, and the firemen, the mechanics, the bootleggers, or the prosperous "Syrians" who were not allowed into the Country Club, were likelier company than almost everyone of the respectable bourgeoisie. He was *country*, in the way that he was tuned to its rhythms and its cycles; he and his Tennessee people were simple, trustworthy, straightforward, and good as grass.

My mother's people, on the other hand, the people who captured my imagination when I was growing up, were of the Deep South — emotional, changeable, touched with charisma and given to histrionic flourishes. They were courageous under tension and unexpectedly tough beneath their wild eccentricities, for they had a close working agreement with God. They also had an unusually high quota in bullshit.

Most of them had come to Mississippi when it was the frontier, in the nineteenth century, and they had played a prominent role in the state. My great-great-great uncle, Cowles Meade, was the first acting territorial governor of Mississippi, who tried unsuccessfully to catch up with Aaron Burr when Burr took off down the Mississippi River on his curious scheme to conquer the territories belonging to Spain. His magnificent estate on the Natchez trace was burned and completely destroyed by Grant's army. But another uncle by marriage, Henry S. Foote, was my true family hero, ever since the day in my childhood when I saw him looking fiercely down at me from his portrait in the state museum in Jackson.

Henry Foote was one of those authentic nineteenth-century Southern-Americans, a fighter for the Union, an uncompromising enemy of the Southern extremists. For a time he edited a newspaper called *The Mississippian*, published first in Vicksburg and then in Jackson, until the outbreak of the Civil War one of the most influential Democratic papers in the state. He was one of the most exciting politicians and stump-speakers on the national scene in mid-century America — an erratic, courageous bantam of a man who had the unequivocal good judgment to hold Jefferson Davis in low esteem. He and Davis, the two U.S. Senators from Mississippi in the 1840s, were more than rivals in power; they loathed one another and had once exchanged blows.

As a United States Senator, Foote was one of the most outspoken of the Southern moderates; his Mississippi enemies branded him a *pacifist*. As early as 1850 he clashed in the Senate with John C. Calhoun, who held in debate that secession was the only legitimate remedy for the slaveholding states; in reply Foote defended the Constitution and "the good old Union, the fruit of the sage counsels of our immortal ancestors." On the Fourth of July, 1850, when sectional feeling was running strong,

he was chosen to deliver the conciliatory address at the base of
the unfinished Washington Monument. He exhorted all sections of America to "dwell together in harmony," after which
President Taylor, who was in the audience, collapsed under the
sun and soon died, perhaps from the heat generated by Uncle
Henry Foote's fervid rhetoric, which one detractor called "a
diarrhea of words." Once, in another stormy Senate debate,
he drew a pistol on Senator Thomas Hart Benton of Missouri
right on the floor, but a colleague managed to snatch the gun
away while Benton was inviting my uncle to go ahead and
shoot. This was a widely published fiasco which the American
minister to London called "extremely humiliating" to those
who represented the young Republic overseas, everyone apparently overlooking the fact that Senator Benton deserved
shooting.

In 1851 Foote defeated Jefferson Davis by a thousand votes
for Governor of Mississippi, where he continued to fight the
secessionists, sometimes bodily, more often with his blistering
ridicule on the stump. In the presidential campaign of 1860,
the year the Democratic Party split into its Northern and Southern wings, he traveled all over the lower South speaking for
Douglas and the Northern Democrats as the last hope of the
Union. Yet when secession came, trapped in it along with so
many other Southern moderates, he stayed with the Confederacy, serving for a period in the Confederate Congress where he
continued to make life difficult for his old rival who had become President.

My mother's family were the Harpers; they had settled in
Virginia and founded places like Harpers Ferry, then scattered
throughout the state and fought for Washington and the Revolution. One of my Harper uncles, Captain John, crossed the
Delaware with Washington and fought at Trenton, Monmouth, Princeton, Brandywine, and Germantown. Another

Harper uncle, Captain William, went with his artillery company in 1793 with Washington to lay the cornerstone of the United States Capitol; then they all retired with Washington to the Harper house, Rose Hill, for a "sumptuous feast." With his company at Mt. Vernon, this particular Harper fired the minute guns at Washington's funeral. Out in these mythical reaches of the family there was enough intermarriage with the Biddles, the Washingtons, the Monroes, and the Lees to make Virginia one large family sharing the same corpuscles.

Many years later, when I returned to America after four years in Oxford, England, and was driving south from New York to Mississippi, I stopped off in Harpers Ferry to look for the grave of one of the Harpers who had started that beautiful and blood-stained village on the banks of the Potomac. I discovered he had gone back to England in his old age and had been buried in Oxford all that while; the Harpers had always been elusive like this for me. But I felt in those Virginia foothills what must have been their great contrast with the raw, unsettled frontier to which my land-poor branch of the family departed in the first half of the last century. It must not have been easy to leave the Old Dominion for Mississippi, but there were many departures in that day, and the linkage between the two states was a direct one; Virginia was the uncle of us all.

My great-grandfather, George W. Harper, came south as a young man; he met my great-grandmother for the first time in the Mississippi Governor's Mansion when her Uncle Henry was governor. George W. Harper was editor of *The Hinds County Gazette* in Raymond, a thriving town near Jackson. He fathered sixteen children, whose births ranged from 1853 to 1878; my grandmother, Mamie, the youngest of the sixteen, was, in 1967, the last one living. She, of course, was the one who was the repository of those valiant tales and vanished troubles, who made that old time come alive for me. The family Bible recorded the births and deaths of the Harper children; when I was a child, reading that interminable list, I loved the sound and texture of the names: Gordon Sims, George William, Samuel Dawson, Henry Winter (named for Henry S. Foote), Sarah Virginia, Thomas Moffet, Anna Moffett, Margaret Caroline, Frank Gardner, Susan Gibbs, John Hubbard, Ella Meade, Robert Goodlog, George William III (the second George William having died in infancy, so they tried again with another) and finally Marion, the one who became "Mamie" to me.

No less than four of the Harper children, my great-uncles and great-aunts, were born during the Civil War. It was not a propitious time for them, because when Sherman's troops came through Raymond they searched out George W. Harper's newspaper office, even though he had opposed secession. They threw his printing presses in the town well, and he had to turn to one-mule dirt farming. During the Civil War, as I was told it as a boy, the family cow disappeared; my great-grandmother, with seven mouths to feed, went to the captain of the federal troops and complained in great agitation that his soldiers had stolen her cow. "Find this lady a cow," the captain ordered his staff, and then graciously escorted her home. "Mamma said he was such a nice man," my great-aunts would say to me as late as the 1940s, sitting in their dark parlor on North Jefferson Street in Jackson, "such a nice honest man who *cared*," but when the original cow wandered home the next day and the herd increased to two, Yankee chivalry was not rewarded with the return of the merchandise. The Harper legacy in such cases would teach me a great deal about how to roll with the punches.

Later, during Reconstruction, my great-grandfather served in the Mississippi legislature. There was an old picture of the state legislature of that period, and when I looked at its faded images I saw my great-grandfather Harper — a white face surrounded by black ones. After the withdrawal of federal troops in 1876, some of the old Bourbons asked him to stand for Governor; he said he was tired and refused, and lived just barely into the twentieth century as an impoverished newspaper editor and town druggist.

When he died, this is what they wrote about him in his paper:

> When grim visaged war burst in all its tremendous fury upon the fair southland, the gallant major entered the confederate service and was actively engaged in the commissary department until the close of the struggle, an affliction of the eyes from which he had suffered from youth rendering him unfit for fighting in the ranks. After grim visaged war had smoothed his wrinkled front, Major Harper returned to the *Gazette* office, allied himself with the Democratic Party, which had absorbed the old Whig organization, and through the dread days of reconstruction, when the furies of peace were worse than the terrors of war, he advocated conciliatory measures and a peaceful acceptance of the terms of surrender. In 1875, when the black vampire of radicalism was choked from the neck of this commonwealth, Major Harper was a member of the impeachment committee taking a leading part in the events which brought about the abdication of Republican Governor Adelbert Ames and the restoration of the State to the control of the whites.

One day in the 1960s a local lady in Yazoo City, who had just returned full of fire from a convention of the Women for Constitutional Action in Dallas, turned on my grandmother Mamie, the last of the Harpers, and said, "Your trouble is that you're just not a good enough *American*." My grandmother replied: "Not American? I'll have you know my father was on the committee that impeached Adelbert Ames!"

•

My father had met my mother in Jackson, and when I was six months old, in 1935, they moved the forty-two miles to Yazoo. My mother cried over leaving the big city for a bedraggled place like Yazoo, where most of the streets were gravel and where they still talked about the Great Flood of 1927, that catastrophic breaking out of the Mississippi which Faulkner would one day describe in *The Old Man*, when weary prisoners like the tall convict had worked desperately to bolster the inadequate levees with sandbags; the waters, muddy and infested with snakes, had inundated the houses on the street where we were to live, forty miles from the River. There would be watermarks on many of the walls of the older houses, and in one vacant field near the house we were to occupy the water moccasins, as a neighbor was to tell it, had been so thick they were wrapped around each other, and there were bloated carcasses of horses and cows, and floating dogs and telephone poles. Even the Yazoo River, in the 1930s and 1940s, would play tricks on the town, coming out of its banks almost every spring to flood part of the business section and leave the streets and roads covered in ooze and filth sent down to us from Minnesota, Illinois, and Missouri.

At first we lived in a small frame house with a front porch shaded by great oak trees, next door to a little girl who carried me around on her back and would one day be "Miss Mississippi" and runner-up for "Miss America." We lived with "Aunt Tish," not our aunt at all but an ancient old lady, born in the 1840s or 1850s, whom everyone, in the Southern fashion of that day, called "Aunt." It is Aunt Tish whom my uncertain memory tells me I saw first; back in some old mist a swing broke and crashed to the floor, an awful crying was to be heard at close range, and an old lady picked me up and started humming a tune. The night was still except for the katy-dids all around, going "katy-did, katy-didn't, katy-did, katy-didn't," and for some reason this collection of rusty molecules and second-hand corpuscles chose that instant to take notice of the planet.

I remember the cold, quiet nights and the stifling hot summers, starched summer suits and the smell of talcum, sweet-
smelling black people in white dresses who could be adoring
and gentle and then impatient and demanding — tugs at my
hand, and a high rich voice telling me, "If you don't behave,
boy, that police gonna put you *under* the jail." There were
three big birddogs named Tony, Sam, and Jimbo, warm tongue-
licks and rasping barks, the feel of their bodies in front of a
black stove, the taste of gingerbread and hot corn on the cob,
and the whispered words, "God please bless everybody and
me." God blessed with affection and comfort, three birddogs,
and the little girl next door.

My father had a huge green truck — so large I had to sit on a
box to see out its windows — and from the back came
the heady smell of Cities Service gasoline. There was a gas station to play in, and somewhere down a wide street and beyond
a railroad track a place with tanks, platforms to jump from, a
cool warehouse with dirt for a floor, and room for the dogs to
run and bark in the tall grass on a hill.

Later there would be long rides with my father in the green
truck, on hot dusty roads over rivers and creeks, out to the edge
of the world: to little towns scorching in the sun, ugly unpainted houses with tanks in front and mud everywhere, and
big places with white bushes and porches that ran all around
the house. Colored men would pat me on the head and say,
"That's enough, Mr. Ray," and my father would take the gas
hose out of the tank and the man would give him money. And
then the long ride back, on the quiet flat land, past the dark
woods and the little shacks, up to the town where the hills
started again.

One day my father said, "I'm going to take this boy on his
first hunt." We started out the way we always went, down the
steep hill and onto the level land; my father was dressed in

khaki clothes with his gun next to him, and in the back seat the dogs whined and shivered. It started raining and my father stopped in an open place in the middle of the woods; the dogs sprang out and started running in circles. My father said, "You wait in the car, I'm going in here for a minute to see what's there, and then I'll come get you." There was something smoky in the air, a rain mist, and I was frightened. I got out of the car and looked into the woods, but no one was there. In the ditch next to the road was a big stream of muddy water; I jumped and landed in the water. Suddenly my father came out of no-where and lifted me out, put me in the car and wrapped a blanket around me. "Now that wasn't smart, was it?" he said. The dogs gave me a lick and I clung to them for warmth. Back home they put me under some sheets, and my mother came in and said, "He's not going to take you hunting until you're *water*proof." I went to sleep with the sound of raindrops on the roof.

We moved down Grand Avenue to our own house, set in a big yard with walnut, elm, and pecan trees. Just behind it the houses were ugly and unpainted, and there was a honky-tonk with loud music every Saturday night. One day all the grass and weeds in the back yard caught fire. My father fought the fire with a blanket and water, and a colored man walking down the sidewalk saw the fire and ran back to help. When the fire was out my father paid him. I went in the house, to the dresser where I kept pennies, and rushed out and caught up with the man and gave them to him. "Thank you, boy, thank you," he said, and later I heard a neighbor tell my father, "He gave that nigger all his pennies." I would go back across the alley to the unpainted houses and play with the colored children. Their houses smelled musty and sharp, and there was always food — gingerbread, cornbread, biscuits, and buttermilk, which we all ate under a big chinaberry tree. One afternoon my mother came and got me and yanked me home. "Don't ever play back here again," she said. "But why?" I asked. "Just you hear me. Just you don't."

My mother taught older children to play the piano. It was a large black piano which took up half the space in our front room, and on late afternoons when it began to get dark, I would sit in my room and listen to the music from the front. It was not the music they played over and over, up and down the scale, that I liked, but the things my mother would play when she told the children, "Now I'll play your piece all the way through like Mr. Mozart would want it played." I can sometimes hear her music now, after thirty years — and remember the leaves falling on some smoky autumn afternoon, the air crisp and the sounds of dogs barking and train whistles far away.

•

When I was five my mother took me by the hand into the two-story brick school on Main Street and left me in the care of Miss Bass, a stern old lady who looked as if she would bite. Someone was supposed to get me after the first day was out but failed to come. Bubba Barrier, who was in my room, and I were intimidated by the prospect, but finally we walked hand-in-hand, along the "Bayou," up Grand Avenue to home. Such adventure befitted one's stature as a first-grader in the free public school system of Yazoo County, Mississippi.

The school was a graceful and imposing old structure with white columns, iron fire-escapes, and tall old-fashioned windows. It was set in a triangle plot of ground that covered three or four acres, with the public library ("the oldest in Mississippi," the teachers would tell us) at one end and at the other, in the farthest corner of the grounds, the gray Confederate monument. On top of the monument, about thirty feet from the ground, were statues of a lady holding the Confederate flag in front of her and a soldier with a rifle in one hand, his other hand slightly extended to accept the flag, but a little reluctantly, as if he didn't want to go around all day holding both a flag and a gun, particularly with a ten-inch bayonet attached. The inscription on the side of the stone read:

1861–1865

As at Thermopylae, the greater glory was to the vanquished. This monument is erected to perpetuate the memory of the noble courage, constancy, and self-sacrificing devotion of the women of the Confederacy and the patriotism and heroic valor of the Confederate soldiers and all who fought on land or sea for the country and the cause they loved so well.

By
Jefferson Davis Chapter,
United Daughters of the Confederacy . . .
And the sons of the Confederate veterans and people
of Yazoo County. Dedicated July 8, 1909

Inside, the school building was all long, shadowy corridors, smelling faintly of wax and urisol. On the wall near the front entrance were portraits of George Washington and Jefferson Davis. Downstairs was a large basement, where we congregated to wait for the bell to ring on rainy days and where, at noontime, we took our lunch. It was a dark, forbidding place, symbol and apotheosis of a dismal childhood claustrophobia. I would have a recurring nightmare of those years: I am trying to climb out of this sunless basement, through a small, narrow window to the yard outside. The window is not big enough. I am caught in it, nothing can budge me. The bell rings and everyone goes upstairs, and I am left alone. Waiting on some gray morning in the autumn solstice in that concrete chamber, with the single lightbulb in the peeled ceiling casting its grotesque shadows, I could hardly bear the time until the bell rang. The room was attached to the boys' toilet, and from it came the echoes of toilets flushing and the smell of urine. Off to the side, in a kind of wired-in compound, was the lunchroom, where lunches went for a dime apiece, and where the teachers would exhort us with shouts and occasional slaps to finish all of our weiners and sauerkraut, or our bologna and blackeyed peas. It was our small contribution to the war effort, to eat everything on our plate. Once the third-grade teacher, known as the cruelest in the school, stood over me and forced me to eat a plateful of sauerkraut, which I did, gagging and in tears, wishing I could leave that crowded underground vault and never come back. When the bell rang we would march in long lines, boys and girls together, through the toilet up the stone stairs to our classrooms.

All this was in 1940, and '41 and '42, with the war on to defend democracy, as our teachers told us; they told us we were in school to help democracy, to strengthen our country and our God, and to learn enough so we could make good money for ourselves. In the assembly hall upstairs, where we marched in every Friday with the music teacher playing the March from Aida on the spinet piano, with the American flag on the right of the stage and the Stars and Bars on the left, the speaker would tell us of the man he once knew who could have been President of the United States, except that when the time came for him to be chosen, some of his friends felt honor-bound to tell the authorities he had been a lazy worker, lied a great deal, and had taken to alcohol when he was young. Or the preachers would come regularly to speak to our souls, and remind us of our obligation to the one who had died in agony for every last one of us.

Those of us from the town's middle class probably sensed we would make it through all right, and someday in the far-distant future be sturdy citizens of the place — planters or store owners or druggists or lawyers. One of the secrets was to stay on the good side of the teachers. Trapped in the same room with twenty or twenty-five other children for a whole year under your teacher's unchallenged dominion, you learned to respond to her every whim and eccentricity, laughed when she laughed, gave her something at Christmas, and had your parents invite her to supper. Your mothers phoned her to see if you were being "good" and "working hard," and paid sly compliments to her, making up nice things you had never said about her. There were six or seven of us in every room who read faster and better than the slower children of the families from "out in the country." The red stars on the bulletin board were always next to our names, we got the A's and the 1's on our conduct reports. We knew we were the teachers' favorites; we knew that the stirring challenges they laid down were secretly meant only for us.

But within our own breed of whites and Protestants (we would never have given thought to the possibility of any other variety being there with us) that school was a democracy, a seething, turbulent cross-section of rural and small-town humanity. Each day the black-and-yellow school buses, with "Yazoo County Public Schools" written on their sides, lined up on Washington Street to discharge their cargo. The daintiest daughters of prosperous plantation owners and the meanest last sons of the most downtrodden sharecroppers came in together. In the town itself the banker's boy from the big white mansion walked down along the "Bayou" to school each day with the skinny little girls who lived in the three unpainted shacks — nicknamed Faith, Hope and Charity by our elders — which sat incongruously in the middle of the "good" section of town near Lintonia Park. These girls did not salute the flag; I would see them on Main Street on Saturdays selling their religious newspapers.

And there were the "redneck" boys — not called redneck by

us, and not anything at first except "the boys from Graball Hill." They were as distinct a group as any in the school. They wore faded khakis or rough blue denim and heavy torn shoes; their teeth were bad and their hair was never combed. I would notice them at lunchtime, gathered in a large group near the Confederate Monument. Some of them would go across Main Street to Spell's Grocery to buy a nickel Moonpie or a Baby Ruth bar, and wash their lunch down with water from the cool green fountain by the door; some would not eat any lunch at all. I particularly liked one of these boys, the gentlest one from Graball. His name was Bo. He was the slowest reader in the class, and he wore the same clothes every day. Once, after Christmas, when our teacher polled every child in the room about what he got for Christmas, he said: "I didn' get nuthin'. I ain't studyin' toys."

Almost all of them were rough and open, and you learned early to treat them with a diffident respect; they were bigger and often older, from failing a grade or from having to stay out of school, sometimes for days at a time, during picking season. Their habits ran to violence of a general kind, and they performed unique acts on an instant's whim. Sometimes when there was no teacher around three or four of them, in concert, would piss on the floor of the upstairs hall; one afternoon late, having missed their bus home, they crawled through the window to the principal's office and shit on the rug. Next day the teachers were looking for answers, and appealing to school pride if not school sanitation, but there were no takers.

They suffered from strange maladies, like sleeping sickness and diarrhea, which would keep them home longer than the cotton-picking. One of them almost died from having been bitten by a black-widow spider while sitting on a woodpile. They fought hard and long, especially among themselves. Pity

the poor colored child who walked past the schoolhouse when
they were outside. There would be cries of "coon" or "nigger
baby," followed by a barrage of rocks and dirt clods. When I
was a grown man, and saw the deputy sheriffs and the mobs
pummeling Negro demonstrators on television, I needed no one
to tell me they had been doing the same thing since the age of
eight. One afternoon — I remember the terror of it as if it
were yesterday — Millard Fillmore of Graball Hill beat up Erp
Windley, one of the town boys, for a distance of twelve blocks;
he used fists, feet, and whatever sticks and rocks were handy,
and ended by stuffing a handful of cow shit down Erp's
throat. A preacher lady in a car, seeing this, stopped and said,
"You should be ashamed of yourself, you big bully," and Millard replied, "Go fuck yourself, you ole bitch," something that
must have seldom been said to a preacher's wife, at least in
anger.

We had violent games of football at recess and at noon, bone-
jarring rituals where you got your first test in physical courage.
Sometimes an arm was broken, and one of our friends got a
brain concussion from a flying tackle that sent him almost
up against the reference to Thermopylae on the monument. I
still have a scar on my left ankle from the day Millard Fillmore
knocked me into a fire hydrant which served as coffin-corner.
After the first ten minutes of this bloodletting, however, I
learned I could run circles around the Graball boys. They
tired easily and began panting like hounddogs on a long hunt.
Only later did I recognize that this came from a simple lack of
nutrition. Only one of them, to my knowledge, "made it." He
got through high school as a football star (once knocking a ver-
tebrae in my back out of joint when we were fifteen, so that I
had to see the town chiropractor for a month before I could
walk without a limp) and ended up as left tackle for the Ala-

bama Crimson Tide. But as for the others, I sometimes wonder what became of them, if they are still hoeing the impoverished red earth on some forlorn hill, or picking the same scraggly cotton deep in the Mississippi backwoods.

2

TERROR lurked for me in that school. The name *Miss Abbott* brings back long dreary afternoons, weary recitations, secret
rage, and wounded bafflement over my own unexpected failure.
She was my fourth-grade teacher; I was nine, and for the first
time my grades were erratic and my conduct report question-
able. My own mother, who had pushed me onward as the nic-
est and brightest boy in the county, predicted I would never
work out, and began blaming the social effects of Radical Reconstruction, always an ominous sign.

Miss Abbott had a pink nose and came from a small town in
South Mississippi. She pronounced words like "night," "bright"
and "sight" with the "i's" prolonged and nasal, a sure sign of
hill-country origins. The only book she read through and
through, she told us, was the Bible, and you lived to believe her,
and to rue the day she got hold of that book. I myself had my
own private relationship with God, which embraced the good
old hymns and quiet mumbled prayers and holy vengeance
when it was really deserved, and in that town and at that age
you took God so much for granted that you knew he was keeping a separate ledger on you simply as a matter of course. But

Miss Abbott's religion was Christianity by fear and by rote —
so tenacious it got you by the extremities and never let go; it
was a thing of interminable monologues, crazed soliloquies;
she wanted you to believe she herself was in radio contact with
the Deity, and had hung the moon for Him on day number six.
When she talked about the time she had been saved, a moist
glint began creeping into her eyes, which invariably meant the
sermon was on its way. She learned to play a little plastic lute,
the kind you could get in Woolworth's for a quarter, and she
would play us rousing hymns and Christian marches, heedless
of the saliva trickling down that instrument onto the floor.
After the music she would preach us on sin and redemption,
there being more of the former than the latter, or what the Old
Testament said about niggers or Japs, or why we would all end
up in hell if God caught us in a backfire. She would not drink
Coca-Colas, she said, because of their alcoholic content. Sometimes she would lapse into a sweet, unexpected silence, and
gaze out the nearest window for endless minutes. Her features
would be bathed in gentle peace. Then I knew Miss Abbott
was praying to herself.

Twice a day, in the morning when the class convened, and
in the afternoon after lunch, she would call on each of us to
pray. We would all begin by blessing our soldiers and then
ripping into the Germans and the Japs. Once Bo, from Graball
Hill, began his prayer by saying, "Dear Lord, thank you for the
bombs that ain't fallin' on us," and then stopped. "What's
wrong?" the teacher asked, and Bo said, "I just can't think of
nuthin' else to say." The worst tortures were the Bible verses.
Two hours each morning she had us recite the verses she had
assigned us to learn by heart; when we forgot a verse, she would
rap our palm with a twelve-inch ruler. Then out would come
that lute again, and if she caught you drowsing, while she
piped away on "Onward Christian Soldiers," or scratching at

your weary tail, she would go to her "conduct book," and with a slight little flourish, write down a "5."

I made the mistake of correcting her one day, during one of the rare intervals in which we were doing schoolwork. The capital of Missouri, she said, was St. Louis. I held up my hand.

"What is it, Willie?"

"Miss Abbott, the capital of Missouri is Jefferson City."

"No, it's St. Louis."

"I bet it's Jefferson City," and then immediately regretted it, because of the scriptural attitude on gambling.

"Kay King," she snapped, "look in the book and show him it's St. Louis."

The little girl looked in the book and turned red. "Well," she said, "it says here Jefferson City," but obsequiously, like everyone in that ill-fated class, she added, "But Miss Abbott ought to — "

"We'll see," Miss Abbott snapped, and changed the subject. Later, during "silent study," I caught her glowering at me. Why couldn't those people in Missouri have settled on St. Louis?

At noon recess that spring, while the teacher sat on the grass with a group of fawning little girls around her, fetching things for her and scratching her back when it itched, giving her little compliments and practicing their Bible verses, holding her hand and looking for four-leaf clovers to put behind her red ears, we were playing softball nearby. Honest Ed Upton hoisted a lazy foul that went high into the air behind third base; from shortstop I watched its slow descent with interest, with an almost fanatic regard, as it drifted earthward and smacked Miss Abbott on the head. She sprawled on the ground, with a moo like a milk cow's — out cold. *Oh joy of joys!* The other teachers picked her up and carried her away in a car. In our room later, supervised by the principal, all the little girls cried — silent little bawls — and even Honest Ed Upton shed tears. The boys scratched their heads and fiddled with pencils; such was the tyranny in that room, they dared not look into one another's eyes. Except Bo — he caught a glance of mine and puckered his lips, and before long a penciled note came over from him — "*i wich the old bich got hit with a hardbal insted.*" I prayed that she would die.

But back she returned, risen on the third day, and on a Friday afternoon, when she had stepped out of the room, I made a spitball and threw it two rows over at Kay King. "*William!*" The sound of Miss Abbott's voice sent terror to my soul. Each afternoon during that incomparable spring I had to "stay in" — two hours a day for six weeks, working long division. Miss Abbott would sit at her desk, reading the Bible or *Reader's Digest,* while the shadows got longer and the sound of boys' voices wafted in through the open window. And when that year ended, with the C on my report card in math, I had crossed, swum, waded the Sea of Galilee, and joyously entered the city limits of old Jerusalem.

•

The Main Street Elementary School was not all divine retribution. There were trips in the late afternoon to the town library, a cool and private place, where I would sit in a quiet corner and read the latest serials in *Boys' Life* or *Open Road for Boys,* or examine the long rows of books and wonder what was in them and why they were there. On Sundays the town boys would go to the cotton gin, a sprawling tin structure with bales piled almost to the roof, perfect for hiding and climbing. We would take long hikes up the "Bayou," which had been dug deeply into the earth to bring the waters down, two miles or more, from Brickyard Hill and the cemetery, through the white residential section, past the cotton gin and niggertown into the Yazoo River. At some times in the year, when the water was coming out of the hills, the Bayou would be crawling with hundreds of crawfish. Under its bridges it was dark and foul, full of dead fish and bugs. We would walk under one bridge after another, following the source of the water until the Bayou itself ran out, and then on into the hills where the colored shacks were, descending only when the lights of the town twinkled on far below.

In the spring and summer we would go to the political rallies in some vast and dusty clearing in the middle of the woods. The barbecue and yams and corn-on-the-cob and biscuits were stacked on long tables and served up by country Negroes; we would sit on the grass with this steaming feast on our laps, lazily eating and listening to the preachers and politicians. The preachers would bless the barbecue and then bless the politicians. We would sit there and bathe in all that florid rhetoric; you could get a sun-tan just listening to those politicians. At one of these country rallies I first heard Senator Bilbo, a little man with a broad sweaty forehead, as he waved his arms and shouted his wide-ranging denunciations. "It's a miracle," my father said. "He'll carry Yazoo County and get elected, but nobody ever votes for him." After the star attractions, we would hear all the candidates for sheriff and the board of supervisors. Once Pearl Hanna, a shriveled-up old lady who rode in a black carriage and acquired her name from her pearl-handled pistol which she wore at her side, got up to announce her candidacy for sheriff of Yazoo County. She said, "My platform ain't but one thing, and that's to clean up the jail. If you ain't never been in there you should. It's a mess, the floors ain't been swept and the toilets ain't flushed. I intend to get it cleaned out or die tryin'."

We were close to growing plants, to the earth, and to nature's wilder moods. In the Mississippi delta there was nothing gentle about nature — it came at you violently, or in a rush, by turns disordered and oppressively somnolent. In the spring, when the muddy waters overflowed the Yazoo into the town, and the nigger shacks on stilts in the bottoms were sometimes covered over, we would see the open trucks with the Negro convicts crowded up in the back, their black-and-white stripes somber under the ominous gray sky. Or a tornado would twist down and do strange tricks to the things it hit, carrying someone fifty yards and leaving him barely hurt, or driving straws into car tires like needles, or sending our garage across the alley into a field of weeds. One afternoon a tornado hit while we were watching a movie in the Dixie Theater; we heard the hailstones on the roof, hitting in steady torrents. A few minutes later, right on Main Street, I watched a giant rat caught in the water where the gutter was, carried by the strong current closer and closer to the sewer that would transport him into the river, his mouth opening and closing in desperation as three little colored boys pummeled him with rocks and crushed open his head. Then one of them fetched him from the water, held him by the tail in his death throes, and said, "You ain't goin' nowhere, Mr. Rat."

·

There was something in the very atmosphere of a small town in the Deep South, something spooked-up and romantic, which did extravagant things to the imagination of its bright and resourceful boys. It had something to do with long and heavy afternoons with nothing doing, with rich slow evenings when the crickets and the frogs scratched their legs and made delta music, with plain boredom, perhaps with an inherited tradition of contriving elaborate plots or one-shot practical jokes. I believe this hidden influence, which will explain much that follows, had something to do with the Southern sense of fancy; when one grew up in a place where more specific exercises in intellection — like reading books — were not accepted, one had to work his imagination out on *something*, and the less austere, the better. This quality would stay with one, in only slightly less exaggerated forms, even as a grown man.

So it was, at Christmastime one year, when my feelings against Miss Abbott were running strongest, I went looking for the biggest, darkest, foulest dog turd I could find. I took it home in a paper sack, and when no one was around I put it in a small box and gift-wrapped it in beautiful red paper. I put this box, containing its Christmas cheer, in a larger box and gift-wrapped that one, in fine green and white paper — then a larger box still, then two or three others, each one more elaborately wrapped and ribboned. When I had finished, I put all six boxes in wrapping paper and, using my left hand, I wrote out Miss Abbott's address. Then I took the parcel to the post office and mailed it. I felt good for days.

When Bubba Barrier and I were ten years old, we found out where the Women's Society of Christian Service was holding its Wednesday afternoon meetings. One morning, following the recipe in a cookbook, we baked two dozen oatmeal cookies, using every ingredient just as directed, and then for good measure we added a mixture of castor-oil, milk of magnesia, and worm medicine for dogs. When the cookies were cool we gift-wrapped them and pasted on a card which read, "To the Women's Society of Christian Service from the People of Yazoo City." Then we sneaked through the bushes to Sister Craig's house and deposited the gift inside the screen door. Later we peered through the window off to the side as Sister Craig served the cookies and Coca-Colas. The first guest who bit into our oatmeal cookie chewed on it for a moment, her jaws working politely, but with a purpose, then spit with such exuberance that the crumbs landed at a point six feet away, spraying three other guests with the ruinous matter.

Once I gift-wrapped a dead rat, labeled the package "perfume," and left it in the mailbox belonging to an adult whom we did not admire. At various times I gift-wrapped sheep-droppings, used contraceptives, six-month-old moonpies, live crawfish, grubworms, and hot bacon grease. When we were old enough to learn that in Mississippi, despite its being a dry state, you could order liquor and have it delivered anywhere at any hour of the day, we had a case of Jack Daniels sent to the Tuesday meeting of the Baptist ladies, and watched from the shrubbery while Harry, of the Top-of-the-Hill "Grocery," was berated, stampeded, and torn apart by the ladies when they caught sight of his cargo. "You . . . you . . . Get out of here!" the president cried, and Harry, more frightened of physical injury than fearing a waste of good sour mash, swooped up the case and escaped in fast order.

When we were eleven, Bubba and I started borrowing his family's car. Bubba had learned to drive when he was quite young; early at night we would sneak into the garage where they kept their grand old sedan and drive up Brickyard Hill and through the colored section — up hills and narrow dirt roads, down through the cemetery, anywhere that white adults were not likely to spot us. The Negroes loved the sight of two little boys driving a big Ford. They would shout and wave and come over to look in at the dashboard, and we would sit on the steps of some ragtail Negro grocery store and eat candy bars while they stood around and examined that car right down to the whitewalls. Then back down the hill we would go and sneak the car into the garage, and walk away nonchalantly as if nothing had happened at all.

We took also to spending long hours in the cemetery, the coolest place in town and in some ways the most sensible. Death in a small town is a different proposition from death in a large city; in a small town one associated death with landmarks, with the places people had lived or the places they spent most of their time, so that I connected certain graves with specific houses, or stores. One day when I was ten or eleven, I made a count of all the houses on my street as I walked home, and to my horror discovered that someone I had known or knew about had died at one time or another in more than half of them. Death in a small town deeply affected the whole community. For weeks or even years the physical presence of the dead person would be missed in specific places; his funeral itself would touch closely upon the life of the town. Years later, when I would go to small funerals in non-denominational funeral parlors in New York City, I would be appalled by the cramped impersonality of natural death. The service itself would be hurried, as if they wanted to get it over with as soon as possible; and outside, on the crowded streets, people would never give a thought to the meager little procession. But when I was a boy, and the hearse and dozens of cars weaved slowly through the streets of the town toward the cemetery, people would stop and say: "There goes Mr. Baskin," or "look at that line of cars for Mrs. Scott," or "that Mr. Davis, he sure was popular."

The cemetery itself held no horror for me. It was set on a beautiful wooded hill overlooking the whole town. I loved to walk among the graves and look at the dates and words on the tombstones. I learned more about the town's past here, the migrations, the epidemics, the old forgotten tragedies, than I could ever have learned in the library. My favorites were the graves of two of John Hancock's grandsons, who had died of some colorful disease many years before while passing through Yazoo. They lay here now in the sunshine, side by side and a long way from home. Sometimes we would bring our lunch, ham sandwiches and Nehi strawberry, eating in the shade of a big tree near the Hancock boys. On other days we would come

and play until late afternoon, until the lightning-bugs came out
and the crickets started making their chirping noises. Or in
broad daylight we would wander through the Negro graveyard
nearby, a rundown, neglected area, fierce with weeds and insects, joined together by a rutted dirt road that ran intermi-
nably up another forlorn hill. Exploring this place one day, we
discovered a Negro grave that was badly sunk in because of
the heavy rains. Wordlessly we began digging at it with sticks,
for thirty minutes or so, until one of us struck something made
of hard metal, let up a terrible shriek, and we ran away from
there as if Death himself were after us.

We contrived an elaborate hoax that summer against a little
boy named John Abner Reeves. We told him we would give
him a quarter if he would walk alone, carrying a flashlight, at
nine o'clock one night, halfway through the cemetery to the
"witch's grave" — the demon who had burned down the town
in 1904 and whose resting-place was marked now with a heavy
chain, with one link missing where she had escaped. John Abner
Reeves consented: two of our conspirators promised to accom-
pany him to the gates at nine and send him alone up the road.
At eight-thirty "Strawberry" Alias and I went to the cemetery.
It was a still, moonlit night in early June; the light of the
sun was just going out on the horizon, giving the evening a wonderful tranquil glow before the coming of the dark. "Strawberry" stationed himself ten yards from the witch's grave in a
clump of bushes. He had a long stick, with a white pillowcase
attached to the end; I had only my silver trumpet, and I hid
behind some trees on the opposite side. As we waited for our
victim, I spotted a colored man walking up the road about
fifty yards away, taking a shortcut up to Brickyard Hill. I signaled to Strawberry to be still and took out my trumpet. Pressing the valves halfway down, I played a long, ghastly moaning
wail, as loud as the horn would go. The man gave a little hop-

skip-and-jump, listened again, and then took off at a steady gait
up into the woods, while we doubled over and all but rolled on
the ground with joy.

Soon we heard the faint sound of footsteps on the gravel, and
there was John Abner, a frightened little boy walking stealthily
through the trees, looking all around and flashing his light in
every direction. When he got within a few steps of the witch's
grave, Strawberry all of a sudden stuck the stick out from the
bushes, and waved the pillowcase. Then I blew a solemn high
note on my trumpet, and descended to the same moan I had
used on the Negro. When we looked out, all we could see was
a wisp of dust on the road, and we heard the echo of small feet
moving fast.

Sometimes these energies were exerted in more constructive
causes. Every Saturday morning at ten o'clock there was "the
Kiddie Matinee" at the Dixie Theater. On the screen would be
the latest chapter of an adventure serial and a full-length western — Roy Rogers or Gene Autry or Lash Larue or Don "Red"
Barry. Many of the country people, including the sheriff candidate Pearl Hanna, would bring their lunches in paper sacks
and stay all day, right until sunset, watching Roy or Lash over
and over again, joining the town children in cheering the scene
in which the hero would dash across the range on his horse at
the speed of sound to rescue his friends from torture and slow
death. The theater would always be crowded, noisy, filthy, full
of flying objects; one of the Coleman boys from Eden had his
eye put out when somebody threw a BB. In the morning, first
thing, there would be a talent hour, where you could save the
admission price of ten cents by giving a performance. Almost
every Saturday Honest Ed Upton, Bubba Barrier, and I would
sing a trio — "The Marines' Hymn," which we dedicated to all
the Marines at San Diego; "The Caisson Song," to the Army in
North Africa; "Anchors Aweigh," to the sailors in the Pacific;

or sometimes, for the hell of it, "Dixie," though that war seemed increasingly remote. We led the drive to collect coathangers and tinfoil for the war effort, and got to see "Spy Smasher" adventures free for our acts of patriotism. Yet we compromised our loyalties by carrying out a lively black-market trade in chocolate bars and bubble gum, the two most flourishing status symbols to my generation in that time of temporary deprivation.

The war itself was a glorious and incomparable thing, a great panorama intended purely for the gratification of one's imagination. I kept a diary on all the crucial battles, which I followed every day in the pages of the *Memphis Commercial Appeal* and the *Jackson Daily News*, and whenever the Allies won one of them, I would tie tin cans to a string and drag them clattering down the empty sidewalks of Grand Avenue. We never missed the latest war film, and luxuriated in the unrelieved hatred exercised for the Germans and the Japs. How we hated the Japs, those grinning creatures who pried off fingernails, sawed off eyelashes with razors, and bayoneted babies! The Germans we also hated, but slightly less so, because they looked more like us, and because Erich von Stroheim bore an uncomfortably close resemblance to the Methodist preacher. And the English (with whom we shared a "common tongue") and the French and the Russians, they were good fellows, and the Chinese were curious but friendly, and the Italians (the accent on the first "I") were cowards, but in captivity lovable, full of song, and willing to change sides. We worked in victory gardens and looked into the skies for any sign of Junkers or Zeroes, whose shapes I had memorized from twenty-five-cent books on enemy aircraft. Because of the Southland Oil Refinery a few miles from town, and the flow of commerce on the River, Yazoo had been chosen by Berlin as a prime target, and when we noticed a blanket hanging on the clothesline behind a house in niggertown with a swastika emblazoned on the cloth, we sent a letter to the sheriff warning of Nazi agents around the town dump. Only later, and with undisguised disappointment, did I learn that the swastika was an Indian symbol on an old Indian blanket. I resolved to myself that if Yazoo County were ever captured, I would never give in. I would retire to Brickyard Hill and the cemetery as a guerrilla fighter, and if ever caught and put before a firing squad I would yell: "Long live America!"

Bob Edwards had lived in the big white house next door. He had enlisted in the army when he was seventeen. We exchanged V-letters; once he sent me pictures of his tent, full of bullet holes, and told me, "Sometimes I want to stick my leg out of a fox hole and let them shoot it so I can come home." I had no idea what he meant. One day a big package came from France, with a real German helmet, and the name of the soldier — "Willy" — carved inside it, and a German belt, with its engraving "Gott Mit Uns," and an iron cross, and German money, and postcards of SS troops, all wrapped in German newspapers filled with page after page of crosses and death notices.

Tolbert, the Negro man who often did handiwork about our house, was fascinated with that German helmet. Sometimes I let him wear it home, and he would walk off down the alley in an exaggerated goosestep, then turn and wave at me, snapping his heels and giving me the "heil" sign. I wore the helmet, the iron cross, and the belt down Main Street one Saturday afternoon. All the country boys standing on the corners came to look these over.

"Gott Mit Uns," one of them said. "Now what does that suppose to say?"

"God be with us," I replied. "That's a German saying."

"Yeah? Well I'll be damned. Now ain't that sumthin'? 'God be with us.' I'll be damned. You reckon they really mean that?"

One day my mother, my grandmother Mamie, and I were

driving to Jackson; there was an army ordnance plant in Flora, and we stopped to pick up two soldiers who were hitchhiking. I was wearing the German helmet and belt. The conversation for a few miles was about the helmet and belt, then about the ordnance plant, and about the Dutch fliers who were stationed in Jackson, and about army life in general. Soon my grandmother asked the boys where they were from.

"I'm from New York," one of them said, "and my buddy here, he's from Massachusetts."

At this point my mother and grandmother exchanged a look and began talking about the Civil War, about how "your people" threw George Harper's printing presses into the well, and about what the Yankees did during Reconstruction. "Oh, you treated us awful," my grandmother said. "You just don't know how awful you treated us, lettin' the niggers run wild, not givin' people enough to eat, stealin' silver, burnin' down houses." The soldiers were silent, looking out the window at the rolling country, and I began to wonder which side they were on after all, and if they bayoneted babies during Reconstruction. Could Yankees be loyal to America during this war? I asked my mother this question. "Oh, we're one country now," she said. "We're united. But it wasn't that way always."

Dominating this good old time was the image of FDR — his voice on the radio, his face with the dark rings under his eyes on the newsreels. FDR was the war itself to me. My father, at the breakfast table reading the *Commercial Appeal*, would whisper, "That damned Roosevelt!," or, later, taking a ten-cent piece from his pocket with FDR on it, he would say, "Well here's another destroyer dime." Once after having seen FDR on the newsreels in 1945 with his face so gaunt and tired, my father said, "He won't live another month." And when he died, after having heard all the bad things about him, and the neighbors talking about "Eleanor lovin' all the niggers," I came home

and said, "I guess it's a good thing old Roosevelt's dead," and
my mother told me that wasn't a nice thing to say at all. "He
may've done wrong," she said, "but he was our *President*."

The day the Japs surrendered, I was in the house with Tolbert, who was supposed to be hanging wallpaper. We waited
all day for the announcement the radio said was coming. Tolbert was unable to get much work done because of the excitement, so we threw the baseball in the yard for a while, and
shelled pecans, and shot a few baskets, while the radio blared
out at us from the bedroom window. Then Truman came on
and told what had happened, and Tolbert and I shouted and
danced around, and hugged each other, and Tolbert said,
"That's the end of them ole Japs! We whupped them Japs!"
and we whacked each other on the back and shouted some more,
and got out a whole six-pack of Double-Colas to celebrate.

3

THERE WAS a war on also for my salvation. It was less global
in nature, less straightforwardly masculine in its inducements,
but it did not entirely lack in drama. Its battleground was my
soul, a treacherous entity full of ravines and inherited pot-holes,
and by the time I was eight I knew it was up for grabs. Before
I turned twelve, I had been "saved," not once, but at least a
dozen times. I had played, at various times in church pag-
eants, kings, wisemen, angels, shepherds, camel-drivers, Joseph,
and Jesus. I had given away enough frankincense and myrrh

to stock the cosmetics counter in a modest-sized nickel-and-dime store, and I had tried to get into so many inns where there was no more room that I would have done better to take out a long-term American Express Credit Card acceptable at all hostelries in the Middle East.

I would remember best of all the revivals, when a visiting preacher and his singers would arrive and hold services for a week or more in the First Methodist Church, twice a day, in the mornings and at night. There would be a restless excitement in the air; the singing would be better than usual, and since the hometown preacher probably had hit the bottom of his repertoire and would be repeating himself in his weekly sermons, the imported preacher would be sure to bring a new stock of stories, sly jokes about the Baptists, and new and different appeals for getting saved all over. The talent was invariably more professional. Miss Abbott's proselytizing was all gray and boondocks, but this was something high-class. At the end of his sermon the preacher would signal to the organist and the choir to do one of the more stirring hymns, but quietly, as background accompaniment, and in a subdued voice that would stir around at the bottom of your soul he would ask all of us who felt the call of Jesus Christ to come to the altar and re-dedicate ourselves in His image, to live a better and more fruitful Christian life, and to assure ourselves of an advance reservation in Beulahland. I could seldom resist; the mileage I chalked up going from pew to altar would have done justice to one of Jimmy Brown's best seasons; and afterward I was so full of peace and benevolence, however temporarily, that I would be tempted to embrace the first person I saw in the street, white or nigger.

When there were no revivals on, there was regular church, and Vacation Bible School in the summer, and Sunday School every Sunday morning. I began Sunday School when I was four; my Negro nurse would bring me at nine-thirty in the morning,

and wait out back with the other nurses while our teachers told
us stories about the Bible, or helped us make religious posters,
or led us in singing.

> Jesus loves me! this I know,
> For the Bible tells me so;
> Little ones to him belong;
> They are weak, but He is strong.

Later as we grew older there would be more sophisticated Sunday School sessions, when we would sit in small circles and
talk about religion and how we could get the children who
had not showed up that Sunday more interested in it. We would
hold hands and pray, and whisper the benediction, and dream
up projects to make our class the most active in the whole
church and how best to help out the preacher in his many
duties. We would read Bible verses and discuss their hidden
meaning. One morning in our ten-year-old class our teacher,
the wife of the town veterinarian, read us a long passage from
Psalms which included:

> Thy people shall be willing in the day of thy power,
> in the beauties of holiness from the womb of the
> morning: thou hast the dew of thy youth.

Jerry Walker asked, "Teacher, what's a womb?"
"What's a what?" the teacher replied.
"That womb there. What's a womb?"
The teacher paused. "Yeah," she said, and then kept right on
reading, while the little girls laughed and squirmed, and Jerry
Walker, not knowing what the joke was, got madder and mad-
der.

Our brand of fundamentalism was so much a part of us that
its very sources, even its most outrageous gyrations and cir-
cumlocutions, went unquestioned. It was the faith of our fa-

thers, the rock of ages, the thing that abided with you, the kindly
light that led; it involved walks with Jesus in secluded gardens,
sweet bliss and tender joys. By turns it could be humble and
contrite, and then righteous and terrible, a martial summoning
to make life miserable for those who had not heeded the call.
In its small-town context it was a middle-class affair, and at
least moderately contained. The town Baptists were both
more numerous and more aggressive, given to wilder exercises,
inured to a form of baptism calling for heads to go under the
water (the Methodist joke being, "I have nothing against the
way the Baptists baptize, except it should last forty seconds
longer.") and, as a body, not so solidly middle class as the town
Methodists; when they had a revival you could hear the sounds
of their singing for blocks, for their lungs were powerful and
they tended to equate volume with devotion. Next up the scale
from the Methodists were the Presbyterians, who had more
"prominent" people, and more dues-paying members of the
country club; at the top of the scale, smaller and more exotic
and more willing to mix a cocktail, were the Episcopalians, who
rivaled the Presbyterians in money, and surpassed both the
Methodists and Baptists in respectability if not in numbers.
The farther one got from the center of town, the more off-
shoot and contorted the white Protestant churches became;
near Graball Hill the little frame churches were places to roll
and shout, and as you got farther from the sources of civilization, out in the backwoods or the red hills, it was rumored that
even rattlesnakes were solicited as honored participants in the
devotionals.

And there was the Catholic church, a big, damp, ominous
place not far from our church. It was a frightening place for a
child, and when you walked by it, even in broad daylight, you
always felt the compulsion to walk a little faster. They even
said the priest, Father Hunter, had drunk a whole beer right

out of the can at a ceremony to raise money for a new convent. One afternoon three of us, working up our courage through dares, walked right into the Catholic church, peered down the long aisle and saw the statues in that brooding darkness, smelled the sweet foreign odors, and found the whole secret business so awesome that the common Puritan dread hit us simultaneously, and there was a mad running away such as you never saw. Yet we came back, not only to the Catholic church but to a Catholic funeral; for one day we had been playing football with our friend Strawberry Alias, and in a few days he was dead, from complications which developed from a blow on the head playing with us — and as I sat in the pew watching those strange rituals and hearing those solemn litanies, I was full of such terror I could hardly stay there, terror not only for Strawberry's death but for a God-in-death so different from mine that he had to be serving another constituency altogether.

My God looked like the king on the cards, and could be talked to without such extra paraphernalia. "I was glad when they said to me," the sign outside my church read, "Come let us go unto the house of the Lord." My church was not secret and damp, but plain and airy, full of room to play musical chairs or quiz games in, and all right too for the more private miracles. A little girl named Theo was in the church by herself late one afternoon, to fetch her Bible which she kept there, and on the portrait of Jesus in her Sunday School room she suddenly saw the halo shine and twinkle! Her story was told from three Protestant pulpits the following Sunday, and everybody kept going up to the same portrait at twilight, but the trick never worked again.

What I liked most of all was Yazoo at Christmas, in the clear, cool air. We would go Christmas caroling with our church group, and watch the path of the star, it must have been *the* star, as it moved across the heavens from around Belzoni out in the delta, up over Brickyard Hill and beyond. Sung on such a night, the Christmas carols were the most comforting and peaceful blessings in all the world. We would take Christmas baskets to poor Negro families living in shabby little cabins in the hills, and feel glad that our families were not in such bad straits. On Christmas Eve my parents and I would drive down Main Street and look at the bustling crowds, the whites and Negroes, and the Christmas decorations; then out into the white residential section to see the Christmas trees in the windows. The town seemed expectant, all laid out and still under the clear Christmas skies.

•

But as a boy gets older, unless he has special inner resources, or a tailbone made of sheet-iron, or unless he gets saved by Billy Graham at twilight in a football stadium, the simple small-town faith starts wearing thin. One cannot move along at a crisp rate on a steady diet of salvation. With me the old-time religion gradually began to wither not as a result of the exercises of brain cells, or the enlightenment of civilized discourse, for I would not have known what this was, but from plain human boredom.

The Sunday sermons, interminable, inexorable, became the most trying part of the faith. "What does he get so *mad* for?" I would ask my mother, after the preacher had finished a ten-minute stretch of extraordinary shouting and fist-banging and then shifted gears, for no logical reason, into a mood of sweet tranquility. By the time I was thirteen I had reached my quota on preachers who had gone to the Holy Land, subsidized by the congregation, and had returned with innumerable notes, trinkets, Kodak slides, sand from the desert, bones, second-hand garments, rocks, dirt, jars full of water from the Sea of Galilee, and more inside knowledge of the place after a two-week vacation than Moses got in a lifetime — all this stretched out over three or four Sundays in a row. They would give minute-by-minute descriptions of meals they had eaten, excursions they had taken, conversations they had exchanged with fellow preachers from Alabama or Arkansas, prayers they had prayed on seeing some natural wonder, remarks their wives had made, exact hours of arrival and departure and retiring and awakening. No, I never want to hear another lecture about the Holy Land again, and at the age of thirteen I had already promised myself I would never go there, no matter what the inducements or how exceptional the circumstances.

There were two stories making the rounds of the Methodist churches in the 1940s which, by the time I reached puberty, I must have heard at least fifty times each, from two-score different preachers behind two dozen different pulpits. My guess is that they are still being used in Mississippi, and that there are wretched boys now, like myself then, who can feel these stories coming twenty sentences away, and who can spot the symptoms of them from pure instinct.

One of the stories had to do with the two-mile race at a track meet. It could be told with certain variations, but usually there were about ten participants, and as one after another crossed the finish line, the men in charge were about to announce the official times and give the trophies, when all of a sudden they noticed, way on the other side of the track with a good three-quarters of a mile to go, a small trail of dust; it was a little crippled boy. Since all the other runners had finished, he was going to be the last one anyway, but that did not seem to discourage him. He kept puffing away, his face red in agony, his blood vessels about to pop open, dragging his lame foot behind him as he churned around that track. Finally, after about fifteen minutes of this torture, as the spectators and officials watched in awe, the little cripple came down the home stretch, the most miserable, beaten-down creature you ever saw. He might at this point be dripping blood, depending on how the preacher sensed the mood of the congregation, but as he crossed the finish line he would collapse in one great pathetic inanimate heap. The officials would come over to him and, bending down, ask, "Why did you do it? Why? You knew you were going to be last anyway?" And the little cripple, in a voice peaceful and benevolent, would reply, *"Because I was all my school had."* This story could be used to illustrate almost anything, but in eight out of ten instances it was employed to urge the members of the congregation to be as good Christians as possible, even if they didn't amount to much to begin with.

The second story concerned three laborers who were lifting heavy stones at a building site. A man walking by became interested in the building that was going up. He went up to the first worker and asked, "What, sir, are you doing?" The man replied, "I'm liftin' this heavy old stone to carry it right over yonder."

Then the man went up to the second worker and asked, "What, sir, are you doing?" And this worker said, "I'm liftin' this heavy old stone which will be put in that wall, which will be part of a church we're buildin'."

The man went up to the third worker and asked the same question. The third worker replied, "This heavy stone I'm liftin' is more than just a heavy old stone. It is going to be a small but necessary part of the wall we're buildin' over yonder, and that wall is going to be a small but necessary part of a great and beautiful church, the most beautiful church in the world, so that when it's finished it will be a fitting monument to the God of us all, and it will sit on this hill so majestic that all men will come into its sanctuary when they are troubled or in need." This story was used to illustrate the fact that even the smallest job in religion is worthwhile just so you realize the bigger picture, although on several occasions I heard preachers use it for no particular reason at all, because they had to say *something*.

After a while I would notice that some sermons had been used on me before, perhaps by some different preacher from another province, and sometimes by the same preachers who must have been running extremely low on material. I heard at least a half-dozen different preachers, making some humorous remark about the Baptists, conclude, "But I don't have anything against the Baptists. Why, I love 'em so much I *married* one," and the wife in the front pew, as if on cue, would turn all red and girlish, and the members of the congregation would giggle and laugh; by the tenth time I had heard this old saw (having read in my civics textbook something about business economics) I wondered why no one ever thought to bring in the anti-trust laws. Student preachers who had not yet got their degrees were imported to practice on us, and these were usually the most entertaining of all; sometimes the student would forget what came next, and would stand there, turning red and scratching at his crotch, until he had the presence to make us believe he was right in the middle of a silent prayer; then he would start up again as soon as he got his next lines straight.

One of the preachers at a church at the edge of town, Brother L——, gave a sermon one Sunday entitled, "Why Do We Wear Clothes?" His point was that we wear clothes to keep from being naked and ashamed, because our bodies are shameful and should be hidden. He got so hacked up on this subject, beating the pulpit with his knuckles, rolling his eyes to the ceiling, that I began worrying as I sat as a good visitor in his church if my own wardrobe was sufficient to last out the winter. A few weeks later Brother L—— was mysteriously dispatched to another town, and his church got another preacher ahead of schedule. No one said why. It took me three years to find out that several church ladies had caught Brother L—— with a schoolteacher laid out on a table in the Sunday School basement late one night. He must have felt shameful, because as I heard it neither Brother L—— nor the teacher had on a stitch. But although the parson left, the teacher stayed on in the town — teaching in the same school, going to the same church. As I grew older I wondered what inner hell she must have endured everywhere, but especially in the presence of the righteous middle-aged matrons of Brother L——'s congregation. I came to respect her for this act of bravery, to stay in the face of the horrific gossip of a small town, and to feel a mere disdain for the preacher, who had used the pulpit as a bare-faced old hypocrite, and had left town as soon as the getting was good.

My father came to church once a year, on Easter Sunday, looking trapped in his necktie and suit. He would sit back in the farthest corner of the church in order to make a speedy exit during the benediction. For a long time, I was ashamed of this behavior; other fathers not only came to church, they took up collection or even sang in the choir. I imagined other men as my own father, and secretly wished they were. My mother would say, "Ray, now why don't you come to church this mornin'?" This would get my father going with a diatribe against hypocrites. He gave us the names and numbers of the pious old men who took up collection on Sunday, while during the week they made their living gambling or selling whiskey or gouging the Negroes with 50 percent interest on loans. Every time he saw them taking up the collection plates on Easter Sunday, he said, it made him sick. He preferred to stay home Sundays reading *True Detective* or *Field and Stream*, or listening to a recording of last night's Grand Old Opry from Nashville, or playing dominoes at the firehouse, or when the weather was right going squirrel hunting at Panther Creek or fishing at Wolf Lake or Five-Mile. Whenever he saw a preacher getting out of his car in front of our house, he would scramble out the back door and hide in the garage, or in the tall weeds by the alley, because if the preacher ever got you in the parlor, you would end up on your knees praying, and maybe giving five dollars to the new church annex. I would go out in the weeds and find my father sitting there in a clump of Johnson grass smoking a cigarette, and say, "Daddy, he's gone."

•

One week when we were in the sixth grade, a clubfooted Baptist preacher roared into town for a revival at the Baptist church. This was at an age when we were getting curious about the girls. We would run races against them, give them Hershey bars, and take them to war movies, and rub up against them playfully when they weren't looking, being by turns gentle and sweet and then, for no earthly reason, mean as could be, sometimes clouting them in the midriff or across their tails to show them who was stronger. Lust at that age is general and undirected, much like an eight-month-old male dog's; if you watch a dog at this age, you will see that he had just as soon fondle the leg of a table or a tree as a female, since he has only the most generic notion of her uses.

The clubfooted preacher by the end of the week had everyone in a state of terror, especially the little girls. His mission was to convince the young people in the town that the opposite sex was corrupt and never to be trusted, and that for the girls to play around with the boys, no matter how tamely, was an act underwritten by Satan himself, and perhaps even by the Roman Catholic hierarchy. Consequently, everybody felt dirty for at least a month.

Far from limiting his message to the First Baptist Church, the preacher went into other churches, and he made two speeches at our school assembly. He wore big horn-rimmed glasses, with the lenses tinted a slight greenish color, and the

sole on the shoe of his abbreviated foot looked to have been
eight inches high; he traveled at a forty-five degree list. Some
preachers, the ones we liked the best, would occasionally
smile, or tell a joke or two to get us in a friendly frame of mind,
but this one was a walking apotheosis of deprivation. His narrow ghoulish features turned so grim as he talked about the
sorrows of the flesh, his eyes got so wild behind his green lenses,
that I was in some doubt as to whether I should ever touch
myself, much less anybody else. We were especially vulnerable
in Mississippi, he told us, because of the way the slavewomen
had done everything in their power to corrupt the white men
many years ago, and according to him this tradition had not
only lingered, it had spread out. Liquor also played a big part.
For a girl to let a boy kiss her before marriage, he said, was a car-
dinal sin, and to hold hands was almost as bad, different only
as to degree.

At a revival service in the Baptist church, on his last night
there, he got hold of this subject with such tenacity, setting
forth the purposes of the Devil with such flamboyant authority,
that when his call came at the end of the sermon for all the
young people who were there with the Royal Ambassadors, the
youth group, to come to the altar and be saved, he was assured
of a record redemption. As the organist played "Stand Up,
Stand Up for Jesus," every boy and girl there walked down, in
groups or singly, until only one was left, a twelve-year-old of my
acquaintance named Buford. Buford remained in his pew all
by himself, sweating and looking desperate, while the clubfooted preacher continued to exhort salvation. The adults
would glance over impatiently at Buford, sitting so alone and
unredeemed, and even some of the young people kneeling at
the altar turned their heads to see what had gotten into Buford, or perhaps what had *not* gotten into him. But Buford
wouldn't budge, even when two or three of his friends at the

altar motioned gingerly to him to come on down and get it over with. There sat the lonely twelve-year-old sinner, unafraid of his sins; he lasted that preacher out.

Later, long after the preacher had departed, Buford told me, "I just didn't like the way he talked. I wasn't in the *mood* to get saved." So, as these things go, Buford became the center of some attention, a minor hero of sorts, and not long afterward we noticed the boys and girls in high school were mingling with each other again; and as the months went by, one's doglust became less general and more specific. I think the imported preacher with the lame foot had played no small part in this evolution. It is an axiom of human nature that if you hear how easy and sinful something is, and if you hear it long enough and frequently enough, and you are warned not to think about it, your thoughts will head that way just of their own volition.

•

In a small town the church is as much a social institution as it is an instrument for winnowing the righteous from the doomed. This was especially true for the children. When I was thirteen I was an important officer in the "MYF" — the Methodist Youth Fellowship. It was both a religious and a social organization, and our adult leader was a reformed alcoholic who ran an ice-cream stand on Mound Street, the center of the Negro business section. He had a rich bass voice and would break out in a hymn on the merest excuse, a fine hearty fellow who had once been a radio announcer in Jackson before the bottle took hold of him, and for this reason he organized a weekly Sunday afternoon radio broadcast at the local station. We would troop down there with him to sing hymns and make stirring testimonials. The local announcers, often country boys working at $30 or $35 a week, were mystified by his professional signals,

especially the way he cut across his throat with his index finger when he wanted the microphone dead, although I think
they were impressed by the manner with which he would begin
a program with his vivacious, *"Hello out there in radioland!"*
Every Sunday, while he read the first part of his script, we would
sing our theme song in the background —

> Living for Jesus a life that is true,
> Striving to please him in all that I do;
> Yielding allegiance, glad-hearted and free,
> This is the pathway
> Of blessing for me.

Then Honest Ed Upton would read from the Bible, or I
would play "The Old Rugged Cross" on my silver trumpet, or
the girls would sing a rousing trio, and all the while our advisor
would be signaling to the country boys in the control room,
who were desperately trying to figure out what the gestures
meant.

Once a month all the Methodist youth groups in the county
would get together at one church for a picnic, singing, and
praying. We would travel out with our radio announcer leader
to the little country churches in the hills, usually one-room
frame structures set under some fine old hickories or gums, with
the graveyard inevitably nearby; we would play games with our
country brethren, and sit together on a hillside and watch the
sun go down in some dense and wooded dale. This would give
the local preacher an ideal chance to disturb the urban compla-
cencies of the children from Yazoo with tales of the way God's
vengeance worked out beyond the city limits. Then his wife
would bless the peanut butter and jelly sandwiches and the
cold Nehi, and after eating we would go into what they always called the "sanctuary" for another round of speaking and
praying. The country preachers always were gravelly-voiced

and seemed meaner than their colleagues in town, but what they lacked in verbal sophistication they made up in their closer knowledge of God's will as it pertained to humankind.

After one of these sessions the local people had organized some square dancing out on the lawn beyond the church; the record player was hooked up with a long extension cord under the trees. Right in the middle of the dancing a booming voice interrupted. "What's going on here?" The music stopped, and everyone caught sight of the preacher from a neighboring church, one of the dingiest in the county. Then he came and took his daughter by the hand and, leading her away, said, "I won't have my girl doin' all this dancin'!" An embarrassed silence struck us, and we watched as his old Ford sped off down the hill, leaving behind it a thin trail of dust. A big dusty moon had appeared beyond the ridge, and it was one of those still heavy Mississippi summer nights meant for nonsense and whooping up, but that preacher had broken up the party, and all that was left to do was to join hands and sing "Jacob's Ladder" and go back to town.

One night we were all sitting in one of these country churches for a special Thanksgiving service. The preacher had delivered an inspiring prayer, then everyone had prayed silently, and the lights were dimmed as the pianist played "Ivory Palaces." One of the local ladies, the director of the choir, stood up to sing, and her contribution turned out to be one of the loudest, highest songs in the Methodist hymn book. I was sitting close to the aisle in the back, and out of the corner of my eye I noticed the three old hound-dogs that one of the country boys had brought with him and had left outside. They were walking down the aisle, all bunched together and smelling each other, twisting around and walking on the top of their toes, the way dogs will do when they are in good spirits. The choir lady was at that moment in the hymn when the notes get higher and higher, and end up in a massive crescendo. The three dogs stopped, lifted their ears in unison, and looked up at the lady. One of them started whining, and that set off the other two; they howled like mad dogs, and then ran back up the aisle onto the porch and into the yard, and you could hear them howling out there for another fifty yards, until the hymn was over and the sermon began. And the preacher said: "Them dogs got the old-time religion."

There was another one of these meetings, when we were thirteen, at the little church off the gravel county road between Benton and Bentonia. Before we retired to the "sanctuary," all of us went off romping into the woods, hiding and scaring one another with shouts and hoots in the twilight. We ran across a rattlesnake and killed him with a big stick, and then both the boys and girls worked up a fine sweat playing softball. Later we reluctantly filed into the church, which was crowded to its capacity with both adults and young people. We sang a country hymn, and then the local preacher took over. The adult leader of the whole county youth organization was moving to Memphis, he said, and the time had come to elect another one. It has been my observation that the longer a country preacher talks, the more pious his voice becomes, so that by degrees, simply in talking about the most pragmatic matter, this one began making everyone feel that the election of a new adult supervisor was the most important event since the Resurrection. "We must have a fine upstanding responsible Christian person for this crucial position," he said, and talked on some more, and then opened the floor for nominations. There was a silence for about thirty seconds, as all the adults sat thinking about their choices. Then a shrill little voice from the back of the quiet sanctuary shouted:

"I nominate Willie Morris, who just killed a five-foot rattlesnake."

The voice belonged to "Mutt" Lewis, age ten. I crouched down in my seat, while all of my contemporaries laughed and shouted, stamping their feet in support of Mutt's nomination. The preacher, turning red with bafflement and anger, pounded the pulpit and demanded order, but it took the most vengeful expression he could muster, which was considerable, to get it. A responsible adult was duly chosen, but this was the closest thing I ever saw in those years to a revolt of the young against the institutional righteousness of that church. It would not have been prepared to withstand a revolution, but in our docility and fear of retribution who would have started one?

•

Mississippi was a dry state, one of the last in America, but its dryness was merely academic, a gesture to the preachers and the churches. My father would say that the only difference between Mississippi and its neighbor Tennessee, which was wet, was that in Tennessee a man could not buy liquor on Sunday. The Mississippi bootleggers, who theoretically operated "grocery stores," with ten or twelve cans of sardines and a few boxes of crackers for sale, stayed open at all hours, and would sell to anyone regardless of age or race. My father could work himself into a mild frenzy talking about this state of affairs; Mississippi, he would say, was the poorest state in the union, and in some ways the worst, and here it was depriving itself of tax money because the people who listened to the preachers did not have the common sense to understand what was going on.

Every so often there would be a vote to determine whether liquor should be made legal. Then, for weeks before, the town would be filled with feverish campaign activity. People would quote the old saying, "As long as the people of Mississippi can stagger to the polls, they'll vote dry." A handful of people would come right out and say that liquor should be made legal, so that the bootleggers and the sheriffs would not be able to make all the money, and because the state legislature's "black-market tax" on whiskey, a pittance of a tax that actually contradicted the state constitution, was a shameful deceit. But these voices were few, and most of the campaigning was done by the preachers and the church groups. In their sermons the preachers would talk about the dangers of alcoholism, and the shame of all the liquor ads along the highways in Tennessee and Louisiana, and the temptations this offered the young people. Two or three weeks before the vote, the churches would hand out bumper stickers to put on cars; in big red letters they said, "For the sake of my family, vote dry." An older boy, the son of one of the most prosperous bootleggers, drove around town in a new Buick, with three of those bumper stickers plastered on front and back: "For the sake of my family, vote dry." And when the time came to vote, the result was of course a foregone conclusion.

•

The preachers, the revivals, the prayers, and especially the good old hymns my mother would play on the organ in the church — these are still so real to me that when I hear church bells on some lonely, cold Sunday morning on Manhattan Island, I feel a touch of guilt, and the remorseless pull of my precocious piety. Then I recall our own church, its big sunny rooms and my own quiet prayers, and the simple unquestioning faith of a young child who loved the Lord and walked in the company of Jesus, back before his tailbone got weary and the preachers lost their grip on perfection. "The leave-takings of the children of faith," Thornton Wilder wrote, "are like first recognitions."

Many years after all this, when my father lay in the hospital in Yazoo dying of cancer, I sat next to his bed, talking with him about baseball; the Methodist preacher came in, and the two of them recited the Lord's Prayer. When the preacher left, I tried to work up my nerve to say, for such was our relationship that I could not have said it easily, "If I ever have a boy, I'll name him after you." I couldn't say it. But my father said, "When you got what I've got, and know it, you do one of two things — you either blow your head off with a shotgun or you become a Christian." He took to listening to the church services on the radio, and the last time I saw him before I had to leave again for Texas, he turned his head away from me and said, sitting hunched-up on the edge of the bed, "No matter what happens, boy, I'll always be watchin' out for you."

Two weeks later, at his funeral in our church, the preacher's eulogy was simple and quiet, and at the end the choir sang the finest hymn of them all:

> Abide with me:
> Fast falls the even tide;
> The darkness deepens;
> Lord, with me abide,
> When other helpers fail,
> And comforts flee,
> Help of the helpless,
> O Abide with me.

4

SEVERAL TIMES every summer I went the forty-two miles to Jackson, to the brick house on North Jefferson Street, to stay with my grandmother Mamie, my grandfather Percy, and my

two great-aunts. In Jackson I did not have to go to church unless I was foolish enough to volunteer; I could remain a
heathen there for days on end. There was a big magnolia in
front of the house and several fig trees in back, and the Number 4 bus came past every fifteen minutes if I wanted to go to
Capitol Street or Battlefield Park or Livingston Lake or the state
museum. When my visits to Jackson were over, they would take
me to the Greyhound Station, and the loudspeaker would always say, "Delta Local Coach now loading on platform 5, for
Pocahontas, Flora, Bentonia, Little Yazoo, Yazoo City, Eden,
Thornton, Sidon, Greenwood, Clarksdale, Tunica, and . . .
Memphis-town!" and the ride back home would always be
oppressive, because in the summertime home could never put
on the kind of show I got in Jackson.

Mamie, the youngest of the sixteen Harper children, kept that
curious household going. She had been born in 1878, two years
after the federal troops pulled out of Mississippi, and she told
me that when she was a baby, riding with her mother in a carriage near Raymond, whenever another carriage approached,
her mother would hide her in the back seat, such was her shame
on having sixteen children. When the preacher came to have
Sunday dinner with the Harper family, Mamie always got the
neck and the wing, because that was all that was left when the
plate got down to her corner. Invincible, courageous, a fount
of unquestioning lore and humor, she would have given away
the last neck and wing in the world to the first person who
asked, white, colored, or Jew.

Percy, my grandfather, worked in the place on Lynch Street
that made potato chips. Every afternoon at four he would
come home smelling of potatoes, and fetch from his satchel two
big bags of chips, crisp and hot from the oven. Sometimes he
would take me to work with him, and I would watch while he
put on his greasy white apron, carried the great sacks of peeled

potatoes to a machine that cut them into thin slices, and then transferred them to the prodigious black oven that heated up the finished product. We munched on potato chips all day, from nine to four, and came home so full of salt and potato grease that we had to have five or six glasses of ice water apiece at supper.

In the garage behind the house Percy built for me a dozen replicas of steamboats, the names of them written in careful block-letters across the "Texas," names like *The Robert E. Lee* and *The Delta Queen*, and he told me about the steamboat races he saw on the Mississippi when he was a boy; one of his uncles had been a full-fledged Mississippi steamboat pilot. He let me shave him with his own razor whenever I felt like it, or scrape the dandruff out of his hair with a comb, and he would take me riding on the city bus all over town, two and three hours at a time, sometimes almost as far as Clinton to see the German prisoners working on a chicken farm. On one of these excursions a little girl, sitting next to Percy, leaned over and vomited all over him; Percy went "*Hot*-damned!" and cleaned himself with his handkerchief, and we kept right on riding, for nothing would get in his way when he and "my grandboy," as he introduced me, were out on the town.

To me Percy was old, older than almost anyone I had known, and indeed he had been born during the Civil War, in Bastrop, Louisiana; but he never let on that my pace might be more than he had bargained for. He would do anything I wanted, from climbing the fig trees to marching down the street beating a dime-store drum. Two or three times a week in late afternoon we would go on the bus out to Livingston Lake for a swim, and when Percy would come out of the bath-house in his trunks, the skinniest, most gnarled-up creature you ever saw, the people on the beach would sit and stare and wonder what principle was operating that kept the flesh and bone all in one piece. I would be a little ashamed of the spectacle he caused, and would go on out into the water; Percy would follow me, and dunk his head under the water to get the feel of it, and when he emerged again on the beach, walking out ever so slowly, he looked like some old sea-animal coming up for air, scarred by innumerable rusty harpoons and seventy-five years of fish-hooks. Then we would lie in the sun while Percy rolled a Bull Durham and talk about steamboat races and Percy's trips to Dallas when he was a boy, and catch the bus back in time for a sack of potato chips before supper.

Often Percy would take a quarter out of his old black coin purse and hand it to me, saying, "My name's Jimmy, I'll take anything you gimme." An honest man was "honest as the day's long." When somebody was drunk he was "drunk as a judge." When I complained about something he would pat me on the shoulder and say, "Don't give up the ship." On especially hot summer days, when we sat on the front porch watching the traffic go by, he would say, "I'm sweatin' like a nigger at a free election," or suddenly, for no reason at all in his slow shy drawl he would whisper, "Willie Morris, the man of the hour" or "Boy, you can do anything you want to, if you just set a mind to it." When I tried to explain something unusual that had taken place in Yazoo, he would nod his head ponderously and say, " 'I see,' said the blindman." Whenever a beaten-up and forlorn old car parked in front of the house and some grim character in khakis got out to go to the Jitney Jungle across the street, Percy would say, "There goes Mr. Filthy McNasty, the dirtiest man in Hinds County."

Once he invested in a South American banana plantation he had seen advertised in a pulp adventure magazine. Every month for seven years he sent $10 to the address in New York City, and then he began writing letters to see if the bananas were ripe, and the letters came back "addressee unknown."

My grandmother would tell me about this, and ask me not to mention the subject to Percy. There was a big white envelope marked "Burial Insurance" on the mantel in the parlor, and I would see Percy put a dollar bill in it every now and then. Once a month, on the same day at the same hour, the man from Wright & Ferguson Funeral Home would come to the front door, and Percy would empty the contents of the envelope and give the dollars to him. When Percy told me stories, he inevitably returned to one about the poor little boy who was not invited to the birthday party down the street, and watched through the picket fence while the rich children ate ten flavors of ice cream and an enormous chocolate cake. That little boy never did get invited in to those parties, and once even got his neck caught between the boards in the fence. One night I asked, "Percy, who was the little boy?" and Percy said, "He was *me*, honey."

Mag and Sue Harper, my grandmother's outrageous old maid sisters, were challenges to Percy's simple existence, although he was always sweet and gentle to them until they got his nerves to the breaking point; then he would say, "*Oh, Pshaw*," and retreat to the garage to work on a steamboat. Only once in all those years did I hear him raise his voice to those unusual old ladies. Mag turned on him and said, "Why don't you just get out of here and don't come back. You don't make enough money off those old potato chips to amount to nuthin' anyway. We own this house and you *know* it." Percy sat saying nothing for a while, then motioned to me to come outside, and he held my hand and we walked around the block without saying a word. Then he walked back inside the house and said to Mag, "Just to *hell* with you," and that ended the episode.

Sue had been born during the Civil War in Raymond, and Mag came along two years later, in 1866. They seemed older by decades than Percy, and now they are like specters to me,

their features blurred and almost forgotten, for they were unreal even in reality. My grandmother told me they never married because of the shortage of eligible young men in those days.
Mag had been the postmistress in Raymond, and Sue had worked
for the Coca-Cola Company, putting the caps on the bottles;
the day after her retirement she took the Greyhound by herself
to Virginia to see the places where our ancestors were buried.
One day she went to Harpers Ferry, and she found the address
of a Harper in the phone book, and went to the house. She
knocked on the door two or three times, and she heard a window being raised on the second floor.

"Hello!" she shouted up. "I'm a Harper."

And someone replied, "So what? So am I!" and slammed
down the window.

Neither Mag nor Sue could see or hear too well, and they had
practically no sense of time, getting me confused with one of
their brothers, or with Miss Ann Sills who died in 1905, or
getting the dates so awry that tomorrow could be 1865 or last
week 1978. Still they had great hidden reserves of energy. In
the afternoons they would sit on the gallery and talk with anyone who passed, white or black, for as long as they could squeeze
out a conversation. They would perambulate inside the house
and around the little yard all day long in their fantastic flowing
dresses, running into doors and trees, knocking things off tables;
occasionally they would bump into each other in these ceaseless explorations, and say "Excuse me," then push off again in
opposite directions for some other destination. One day I saw
Mag trying to strike up a conversation with the garbage can,
and soon after that Sue got caught in some sticker-bushes and
I heard her screams for help and managed to rescue her intact.
They took turns going to the toilet, about two or three times
an hour, and they were constantly gnawing on a bread crust
or an old chicken bone. Once I made the mistake of agreeing

to go with Mag into town to buy some shoelaces, and as we walked the several blocks home along State Street she kept stopping at the big old houses and asking the owners, "Can I please borrow your bathroom?" No sooner was one meal over than they were ready for the next, and they would come up to my grandmother and ask how much time there was before supper, and she would say "Only an hour left" or "twenty-five minutes is all, just you wait." I was playing with some children in the yard next door, one afternoon at about three, and Mag came out on the gallery and shouted, "Come home now, son. It's bed-time!" Those kids looked at me as if the whole household were insane; I did not have the presence of mind to suggest it often ran on Greenwich Mean Time.

At night, as Percy and I lay half-awake in bed, I would hear their voices — Mamie's, Mag's, Sue's — from the parlor. My great-aunts' world was unexpectedly clearer at this hour, and I loved to lie in the next room, in that lulled awareness just before sleep, and hear the tick-tock of the old clock and the quiet, aimless talk: about "Momma" and "Poppa," or the other brothers and sisters long dead, or the one brother who went to New York at the turn of the century and was never heard from again, or the family house in Raymond, sold those many years. Percy would groan in his half-sleep, and recite "Oh to be a child again just for tonight." It was like shifting gears, from boyhood's concerns and the war with the Japs to a different world filled with Yankees, poverty, and death, and the dreadful passing of time. Later, if I woke up in the middle of the night, I would hear snores of such a variety and intensity as were never heard before — tenor and contralto from the back room where Mag and Sue slept, playing to Percy's staccato bass, and moans, and sleep-talking into the early hours.

My two great-aunts were ideal victims. When I was eight, I sent off for a mechanism described as an "ultra-mike" in a merchandise catalogue. It cost two dollars, and must have been the best investment I ever made. It looked like a cheap version of a regular radio microphone, and all you had to do to break into a radio broadcast was to clamp a hook on a wire to any kind of electrical outlet — a lamp would do, or a fan, or a refrigerator. Then you would talk into the ultra-mike, and your voice would come out of the radio as if it were the usual program.

I would hook up this instrument in the back room while Mag and Sue sat listening to the radio in the parlor. Then I would say, "We interrupt this program to bring you a special announcement. *The Yankees are coming! They are ten minutes away from Raymond!* I repeat: the Yankee soldiers are on their way!" Then Mag and Sue, holding their dresses above their knees for better running, would leap out of their chairs and dash to my grandmother: "Marion, Marion, did you hear? They're comin'! They're on their way!"

"*Who* is comin'?" my grandmother would reply. And they would repeat, "The Yankees, that's what the radio said!"

"Oh, that's just the boy," my grandmother would say, "foolin' you again. That was a long while ago anyway."

"Oh, that boy!" my aunts would shout, and go sit down again. But they were such good material, in two or three hours you could try the same thing all over again, and more often than not it worked.

Eventually I discovered that even the "ultra-mike" was not necessary. I would be sitting quietly in a corner of the parlor, between the bookcase and the wall, while Mag and Sue sat rocking and fanning themselves against the afternoon heat. I would say, just in my own voice, but emphatically: "Here come the Yankees! Down the road! Look at them horses! Look at them guns!" and up would jump my aunts and tear back to my grandmother with the news.

We would take long walks, the five of us, down shaded streets, past the mansion of the man they told me had stolen all the money from "the state" in the 1920s and departed for Chicago, and on to the State Capitol to look for envelopes with foreign stamps on them in the big refuse bin where they threw things away. We would go inside the Capitol and browse around in the Confederate museum, examining those countless battle flags and regimental banners, dull and shriveled with age, or the Indian mummy in ceremonial dress in her coffin. Then the slow walk back home in the dusk, holding Mamie's hand and talking about what we would do tomorrow. We would sit drowsily on the porch, and Mamie would tell me stories, such as the one about "Momma's favorite uncle," Henry Foote, and how he was "a little too radical for most folks then." She told how her own mother, Anna, was Henry Foote's "favorite niece." And she recounted for me an incident in the 1850s which her mother had described to her. Her mother, then a little girl, was at Cooper's Wells, a resort near Raymond, and someone ran in excitedly and said, "The Governor's coming!" Everybody looked to the front door as Foote came in; without looking to the right or the left he spied my great-grandmother, put his arms around her and said, "Anna, my favorite girl." She saw that he looked tired. When she asked him what was wrong he said, as Mamie told me, "Sometimes there are disappointments that are more than a governor can bear." At that point, as the story was passed on to me a century later, my great-grandmother "saw a mist in his eyes."

Best of all were the baseball games, the ultimate joy of my childhood summers. The "Senators" were in the Southeastern League, and they played in the state fairgrounds, against teams from Meridian, Vicksburg, Pensacola, Montgomery, Selma, Anniston, and Gadsden. I remember their names now, my heroes of the 1940s — they were Duke Doolittle, Tommy

Davis, Bill Adair, Vern Bickford, Leo Grose, Lou Flick, Dave Caliente, Jim Rivera, and many another who stuck there, not quite able to make it past Class B. Class B, however, was good enough for me. I read about them avidly in the papers, sometimes making notes to myself on their biographical data; I sent them fan mail and donated quarters to the "nights" they had for them. Only Percy appreciated all this, and became a baseball follower along with me; for the others the game might just as well have been ice hockey, or water polo. One night, when Percy was sick, I took Mamie and Mag down to the fairgrounds to see a game. Both of them went to sleep; Mag woke up in the eighth inning and asked what the score was. "It's nuthin' to nuthin'," I said. "Nuthin' to nuthin'?" she replied. "Why, ain't either one of 'em any good?"

It was torture waiting out the long summer day until five-thirty, when Percy and I would set out on the walk to the fairgrounds. Several times I got on my knees and prayed, during bad weather, that the game would not be rained out. Our route to the ballpark is so vivid in my memory I can recall almost every house along the way: down Jefferson to North Yazoo Street, then our shortcut through niggertown, and our first glorious glimpse of the ballpark lighted up through the dust. We got to the gate just when it opened, in time to watch both teams take batting practice and infield. And the smells of that baseball park! The peanuts and the sizzling "Pronto Pups," the fresh green grass in the outfield, the resin — and the echoing crack when the bat hit the ball, the lazy outfielders casually drifting under a tall fly, or waving goodbye when a ball went over the fence. When the game got tense, Percy and I would hold hands in our fear that something might go wrong. And when Tommy Davis hit a home run to break up a game, Percy and I would embrace each other in joy, and hurry home to talk about it with my grandmother, who would be waiting with a midnight snack of shrimp and chicken and cold milk and potato chips. "When Tommy hit that home run," Percy would say, "they wanted to tear the grandstand down and *give* it to him right there." "Sure 'nuff?" Mamie asked, "was it a curve or a fast one?" for we had coached her to ask such questions. Lying sleepily in bed that night, Percy and I would talk more about the game. "I'll sleep good tonight after what *Tommy* did," Percy would say. The next morning I would write Tommy Davis and tell him that surely was the best home run ever hit.

·

The day my aunt Sue died, when I was in the third grade, they took me out of school, and we drove to Jackson for the funeral. I stood in front of the open coffin and looked down at her for a long time, even when no one was in the room. I gazed into her face and spotted, under her eye, a mole I had not noticed before. I said to myself, I have to memorize what she looks like so I won't forget her. I stood there for a long time, until the men came and said, "We have to go now," and took the coffin to be buried in the family plot, in the old section of the cemetery in Raymond, where I saw the crumbling tombstones of the Harpers, my great-grandfather and great-grandmother and their sons and daughters, all enclosed by the iron fence that was beginning to rust. We got in cars and came back to Jackson, and Percy took me by the hand to Woolworth's, to buy me whatever I wanted. He told me, "Now don't you be sad." That day I remember I promised myself that if *Percy* ever died, I would shoot myself, with the pistol my father kept under his mattress at home. But I knew that Percy would never die.

5

A FEW WEEKS later, as a kind of consolation prize against death, I got the most unusual dog I ever owned, shipped from a kennel all the way from Springfield, Missouri. I had never been without a dog for more than six months at a time; this one had been promised to me ever since I behaved myself at my first funeral.

I came across a faded photograph of him not too long ago, his black face with the long snout sniffing at something in the air, his tail straight and pointing, his eyes flashing in some momentary excitement. Looking at a photograph taken a quarter-of-a-century before, even as a grown man, I would admit I still missed him. We had had a whole string of dogs before, first the bird-dogs and then purebred English smooth-haired fox terriers like this one, and I got to know all about dogs — their crazy moods, how they looked when they were sick or horny, when they were ready to bite or when their growling meant nothing, what they might be trying to say when they moaned and made strange human noises deep in their throats.

None of those other dogs came up to this one. You could talk to him as well as you could to some human beings. He would look you straight in the eye, and when he understood what you were saying he would turn his head sideways, back and forth, oscillating his whole body like the hammer on a clock. Before going to bed at night I would say, "First thing tomorrow

I want you to get your leash, and then come get me up, because we're gonna get in the car and go out to the woods and get some *squirrels*," and the next morning he would wake up both my father and me, get the leash, walk nervously around the house while we ate breakfast, and then lead us out to the car. Or I could say, "Bubba Barrier's comin' over here today, and we're gonna play some football," and his face would light up, and he would wait around in front of the house and pick up Bubba's scent a block down the street and come tell me he was coming. Or, "Skip, how about some catch?" and he would get up and walk into the front room, open a door in the cabinet with his improbable nose, and bring me the tennis ball.

Every time I said "*Squirrel!*" Skip would head for the nearest tree and try to climb it, sometimes getting as high as five or six feet with his spectacular leaps. This would stop traffic on the street in front of our house. People in cars would see him trying to shinny up a tree, and would pull over to the curb and watch. They would gaze up into the tree to see what the dog was after, and after a respectable pause ask me "What's he got up there?" and I would say, "Somethin' small and mean." They seldom recognized that the dog was just practicing.

This exercise had nothing to compare with football games, however. I cut the lace on a football and taught Skip how to carry it in his mouth, and how to hold it so he could avoid fumbles when he was tackled. I taught him how to move on a quarterback's signals, to take a snap from center on the first bounce, and to follow me down the field. Ten or twelve of us would organize a game of tackle in my front yard. Our side would go into a huddle, the dog included, and we would put our arms around each other's shoulders the way they did in real huddles at Ole Miss or Tennessee, and the dog would stand up on his hind legs and, with me kneeling, drape a leg around *my* shoulder. Then I would say, "Skip, Pattern 39, off on three";

we would break out of the huddle, with the dog dropping into the tailback position as I had taught him. Bubba Barrier or Ralph Atkinson would be the center, and I would station myself at quarterback and say, "Ready, set, one . . . two . . . *three*"; then the center would snap the ball on a hop to the dog, who would get it by the lace and follow me downfield, dodging would-be tacklers with no effort at all, weaving behind his blockers, spinning loose when he was cornered, sometimes balancing just inside the sidelines until he made it into the end zone. We would slap him on the back and say, nonchalantly, "Good run, boy," or when we had an audience: "Did you see my block back there?" Occasionally the dog would get tackled, but he seldom lost his grip on the ball, and he would always get up from the bottom of the pile and head straight for the huddle. He was an ideal safety-man when the other side punted, and would get a grip on the second or third hop and gallop the length of the field for a touchdown.

"Look at that dog playin' football!" someone passing by would shout, and before the game was over we would have an incredulous crowd, watching from cars or sitting on the sidelines. The Negroes especially enjoyed this curious spectacle. Walking down the sidewalks in front of the house, they would stop and let go with great whoops of astonishment: "Man, that's *some* dog. Can he catch a pass?"

When I was twelve or thirteen and started driving our old DeSoto, I always took the dog in my trips around town. He rode with his snout extended far out the window, and if he caught the scent of one of the boys we knew, he would bark and point his way, and we would stop and give that person a free ride. Skip would shake hands with our mutual friend, and lick him on the face, and sit on the front seat between us. Cruising through niggertown, I would spot a group of Negroes standing around up the road. I would get the dog to prop himself against the steering wheel, his black head peering out of the windshield, while I crouched out of sight under the dashboard. Slowing the car to ten or fifteen, I would guide the steering wheel with my right hand while Skip, with his paws, kept it steady. As we drove by the Blue-Front Cafe, I could hear one of the colored men shout: "*Look at that ol' dog drivin' a car!*"

At night he would go to sleep curled up in the bend of my legs; when it was cold he would root around and scratch at me to get under the covers. First thing in the morning, after he had gone outside for a run, he would bound back into my bed and roust me out with his cold nose. Then he would walk halfway to school with me, and then turn around at the same spot every morning and go back home.

He was the best retriever we ever had. I would throw a stick as far as I could, and then hide in the bushes or under the house. Skip would come tearing around with the stick in his mouth and, not finding me where I had been, drop the stick and look everywhere. He would jump onto the hood of the car and look inside, or sniff at the trees, or even go into the house to see if I was there. This game backfired one day. Bubba Barrier and I threw a stick for Skip and then climbed up the elm tree in the back yard, hiding far up in the branches among the leaves. It took the dog half an hour to find us, but when he did he became extremely angry. He refused to let us out of that tree. We tried everything; every time one of us descended he snapped at our legs with his long white teeth, and since no one was around to come to our rescue, we were trapped up there for over two hours until Skip dozed asleep, and we missed the biggest Cub Scout baseball game of the season.

His favorite food was bologna, and we devised an established procedure with my Negro friend Bozo, who worked behind the meat counter at Goodloe's Grocery Store down the street. I made a small leather pouch and attached it to the dog's collar;

I would say, "Skip, go on down to Bozo and get yourself a pound of bologna." Then I would put a quarter in the leather pouch, and Skip would take off for the store, bringing the package back in his mouth, with Bozo's change in the pouch. Bozo enjoyed entertaining his friends with this ritual. They would be standing around, talking baseball or some such, and when Bozo heard the dog scratch at the front door, he would open the door and tell his friends, "Here's ole Skip shoppin' for a pound of his favorite *foodstuff*," and with a great gesture would negotiate the transaction.

Later, when I first joined the Boy Scouts and began working on merit badges, I discovered that not a single member of the Yazoo troop had Dog Care. I determined to set a precedent but I needed to have my certificate of authority approved by a veterinarian. I made an appointment with the town vet, Dr. Jones. I went to his office and he said, "Since I've never been asked to do this before, I'll just ask you some questions about your own dog." He asked me about age, weight, breed, and training habits, and then said:

"What about fleas?"

"What about 'em?" I replied.

"Does your dog have fleas?"

"He's got plenty, yessir."

"How do you rid him of fleas?"

"Well, I pick 'em off him one by one and throw 'em on top of the heater."

This apparently discouraged the doctor. He started in on another line of questioning.

"Do you feed your dog a good diet?"

"Yessir, I sure do."

"How many times a day do you feed him?"

"Oh, I guess about seven or eight."

"*Seven* or *eight*?" the doctor said. "Don't you know you're

only supposed to feed a dog once a day?" Then, shaking his
head, he signed my certificate, making me the first in Yazoo
County to get Dog Care.

•

One autumn afternoon my father and I had Skip out for squirrels, in the woods at the delta end of the county. There was a
slight rustling in the underbrush. The dog suddenly froze, then
took a neat bounding leap, crashing in after the sound. Almost
as suddenly, he emerged, the most woebegone dog in the world.
A skunk, his dignity intact, strutted out into the opening and
down the trail. The dog had the foul yellow stuff all over him,
and smelled so putrid we had to put handkerchiefs to our
noses; even his eyes looked sick. We walked back to the clearing
and wrapped him in a blanket, and took him home and bathed
him, not once but twice, in tomato juice. We did not want to
lay our sights on him again for days, and until the odor wore
off he was the most listless and unenthusiastic creature I ever
saw.

Our first dogs were the big ones — Tony, Sam, Jimbo; then
we trained the little English fox terriers to go into the woods.
Skip was the best of all, for he trampled the woods with an in-
born sense of the impossible. The delta woods, when I was a
boy, were a living thing for me. There were stretches, in the
dank swamp-bottoms, that stayed almost wholly dark, even on
the brightest of days. The tall thick trees were covered with
vines and creeping plants, and on a gray December afternoon
the silence was so cold and impenetrable that as a small boy I
would become frightened, and stayed close to my father. He
taught me how to note landmarks the deeper we went into the
woods: one hickory had a gnarled limb, like a broken arm, or
the ash next to it was split in two, probably by lightning. Sometimes he would make his own marks, with paper or empty shot-

gun shells, and he always kept an eye close to his compass. Three or four times in my memory, men had gotten hopelessly lost in these hidden places, and someone would have to organize search parties, or get the sheriff and his deputies to circle round and round in the woods in search of footprints or empty shells or the sign of fires. As we walked along the thin trail, fighting the mosquitoes that swarmed at us despite the ointment on our skin, the sun would suddenly open up some half-clearing, and giant spider webs would shimmer and toss in the light. My father would stand dead in his tracks, gesturing to me to be still, and he would point to a deer farther down the path, looking at us a brief instant before scampering away into the trees. We never hunted deer; my father was against it, and mainly we came to these woods to shoot the wild squirrels, gray and red and sometimes black, and the squirrel dumplings my mother would make, even if we had to spit out the buckshot while eating them, was always worth the hardest day's walk.

On other days we would rise before dawn, and drive out the flat roads past the dead cotton stalks in the fields, making it to the woods just as the sun was beginning to show. Then we could catch the chatter and rustling of all the birds and beasts, and the dog would be ready to tear a muscle to get in and see what was there. In the bottoms the ground was so sloggy that our shoes would make faint oozing sounds, and our footmarks would slowly fill up with water as we walked. And there were days when the air would be so thick with mosquitoes in that raw wilderness that we had to give up, and either try to find someplace else or go home.

These woods were so accessible to us, only a thirty- or forty-minute drive from the town, that I grew up taking them for granted. Only later did I realize that they were the last and largest of the great delta forests, that it was only at the bottom of that ∇ of the delta, where we were, that the remnants of the old primordial wilderness had been left intact. It was to this country (only closer to the Mississippi River), as I would read it many years later, when these woods had ceased to have much meaning for me, that Uncle Ike McCaslin came on his last hunt, having to drive "two hundred miles from Jefferson when once it had been thirty."

My father and I were in one of these places on December 7, 1941, when I was seven; I can remember the day by the news that greeted us when we went home. And we had been there many times before then. At first I used a .22, though my father once let me shoot his 12-gauge, out of nothing but maliciousness, because after I squeezed the trigger that gun knocked me for a twisting nosedive into the mud. One afternoon, when I was nine, we were walking through a stretch of swamp-bottom with Owen McGinty, one of the town firemen. All of a sudden Owen shouted "Jump!" just as my foot hit something soft and wet, and I leaped with all the enthusiasm I could muster. "Look at *that*," Owen said, rolling out the *"that,"* and my father went *"wheew."* There was a rattlesnake that must have been eight feet long, right in my path. "Let the boy shoot him," Owen said, and I aimed my .22 and killed him through the head. Owen pulled out his knife and cut off his rattlers and handed them to me. The next day I took the rattlers to school, and the Graball Hill delegation gathered around and said, "He was a *big* 'un." But Miss Abbott, my teacher, found out about it and made me take my trophy home. If the dust from the insides got in your eyes, she said, I would be blinded for life. My father said Miss Abbott got that from an *old wives' tale*. On my twelfth birthday I got a shiny new 16-gauge smelling richly of oil, and the next time we went into the woods I wasted a whole box of shells out of sheer exuberance, and the dogs thought I had gone insane.

Several times in the woods around Panther Creek we ran

across a man my father knew — a "hanger-on," he called him. The man lived right in the middle of the woods, in a little wood shanty he had made for himself. He had a scraggly black beard and wore beat-up khakis and a slouch hat; in the back of his shack was a small vegetable garden. The game wardens ignored him, and he lived off the animals he could kill, and made a little money now and then guiding the deer hunters. My father always asked him how the hunting was going, and later he told me that the man would eat anything just so it wasn't alive, and even then he might eat it if the gravy was good.

Later, when I lived in England, I saw places that the English called "woods," but compared with the delta swamp-bottoms of that boyhood time they could have been grown in the shop of a florist. Similarly, the lakes where we went to fish, compared with the "man-made" lakes I would see later in Central Texas, were real lakes, of a piece with the raw heavy earth that enveloped them. Their waters were murky and oppressive, and the worst death I ever heard about took place at one of them, when a water-skier got tangled in a school of water moccasins.

We did cane-pole fishing, both to save money and because it was lazier, for we seldom exerted ourselves on these trips to Wolf Lake or Five-Mile. The most work came the night before, when we hired a couple of Negro children at a quarter each and went back to the town dump to catch the roaches for our bait. We had a big wire basket with a lid on top, and we would spot the roaches with our flashlights, trapping them in our hands and dropping them into the basket. The next morning, very early, we would drive out into the same delta country, only not so far, rent a boat from a Negro sharecropper, and spend the day drifting around the water. When the biting was good we might bring home twenty or thirty white perch or bream or goggle-eye; when it was bad we would simply go to sleep in the boat. Whenever we caught a small fish my father would say, "Throw him back. Only the niggers take the little uns, and they eat him bones and all." We would stop at some crossroads store on the way back to stretch and have a cold drink, and talk about the fishing with the men who sat out front whittling and chewing Brown Mule, spitting between the cracks of the porch floor and talking all the while. When we got home we would clean the fish on the back steps and eat them fried, with a crust as delicious as the fish itself.

I remember one of these afternoons — one of the last, because by that time I was sixteen and had just about lost interest, and then my father would have to go out alone. But on this spring day the weather had taken turns between sunshine and a light rain, and we caught more fish than we had ever caught before. I barely had time to get the line into the water before I could feel the pulling and tugging, and out would come a fish big enough for a feast. The gars were jumping and making splashes all over the lake, and the turtles were diving off their logs, and the fish kept biting away; clearly something was going on under there. Then the wind rose and the rain came down in heavy drops, and we paddled to land as quickly as we could and made it to a deserted Negro shack just in time. The drops made little clouds in the dust until the dust itself was wet and muddy, and the rain blew in gusts and rattled hard on the tin roof. We waited there for a long time, until the rain suddenly stopped. Then the sun came out again, and the whole earth was wet and cool: the trees heavy and glistening in the sun, and the rich delta land humming and making its grand noises. Then my father said, "We better be gettin' on back. If there're any fish left, we'll let 'em alone to grow."

6

ONE SUMMER morning when I was twelve, I sighted a little Negro boy walking with a girl who must have been his older sister on the sidewalk a block from my house. The little boy could not have been more than three; he straggled along behind the older girl, walking aimlessly on his short black legs from one edge of the sidewalk to the other.

I hid in the shrubbery near the sidewalk in my yard, peering out two or three times to watch their progress and to make sure the street was deserted. The older girl walked by first, and the child came along a few yards behind. Just as he got in front of me, lurking there in the bushes, I jumped out and pounced upon him. I slapped him across the face, kicked him with my knee, and with a shove sent him sprawling on the concrete.

The little boy started crying, and his sister ran back to him and shouted, "What'd he *do* to you?" My heart was beating furiously, in terror and a curious pleasure; I ran into the back of my house and hid in the weeds for a long time, until the crying drifted far away into niggertown. Then I went into the deserted house and sat there alone, listening to every noise and rustle I heard outside, as if I expected some retribution. For a while I was happy with this act, and my head was strangely light and giddy. Then later, the more I thought about it coldly, I could hardly bear my secret shame.

Once before, when I had been a much smaller boy, I had

caught a little sparrow trapped on my screen porch, and almost without thinking, acting as if I were another person and not myself, I had fetched a straight pin, stuck it through the bird's head, and opened the door to let him fly away. My hurting the Negro child, like my torturing the bird, was a gratuitous act of childhood cruelty — but I knew later that it was something else, infinitely more subtle and contorted.

For my whole conduct with Negroes as I was growing up in the 1940s was a relationship of great contrasts. On the one hand there was a kind of unconscious affection, touched with a sense of excitement and sometimes pity. On the other hand there were sudden emotional eruptions — of disdain and utter cruelty. My own alternating affections and cruelties were inexplicable to me, but the main thing is that they were largely *assumed* and only rarely questioned. The broader reality was that the Negroes in the town were *there*: they were ours, to do with as we wished. I grew up with this consciousness of some tangible possession, it was rooted so deeply in me by the whole moral atmosphere of the place that my own ambivalence — which would take mysterious shapes as I grew older — was secondary and of little account.

One fact I took for granted was that Negro adults, even Negro adults I encountered alone and had never seen before, would treat me with generosity and affection. Another was some vague feeling for a mutual sharing of the town's past. (I remember going with one of my friends and her parents to take some food to an old Negro woman who lived alone in a cabin in the woods. The old woman told us about growing up in Yazoo, and of the day she saw the Yankee soldiers coming down the road in a cloud of dust. "I looked out the window," she said, "and there was the War, comin' at me from down the road.") Another assumption was that you would never call a Negro woman a "lady" or address her as "ma'am," or say "sir" to a Negro man.

You learned as a matter of course that there were certain negative practices and conditions inherently associated with being a nigger. "Keeping a house like a nigger" was to keep it dirty and unswept. A "nigger car" was an old wreck without brakes and with squirrel tails on the radio aerial. "Behaving like a nigger" was to stay out at all hours and to have several wives or husbands. A "nigger street" was unpaved and littered with garbage. "Nigger talk" was filled with lies and superstitions. A "nigger funeral" meant wailing and shouting and keeping the corpse out of the ground for two weeks. A "white nigger store" was owned by a white man who went after the "nigger trade." There were "good niggers" and "bad niggers," and their categories were so formalized and elaborate that you wondered how they could live together in the same town.

Yet in the midst of all this there was the ineluctable attraction of niggertown, which enclosed the white town on all sides like some other world, and the strange heart-pounding excitement that Negroes in a group generated for me. I knew all about the sexual act, but not until I was twelve years old did I know that it was performed with white women for pleasure; I had thought that only Negro women engaged in the act of love with white men just for fun, because they were the only ones with the animal desire to submit that way. So that Negro girls and women were a source of constant excitement and sexual feeling for me, and filled my day-dreams with delights and wonders.

Whenever I go back there and drive through niggertown, it is as if I had never left home. Few of the old shabby vistas seem changed, and time has not moved all these years for me: the strong greasy smells are the same, and the dust in the yards swirling around the abandoned cars, and the countless children with their glazed open eyes on the porches and in the trees and

in the road. The Negro grocery stores, the ones my dog and I
drove past in the summers, are still patched and covered with
advertisements, and the little boys still wait in front for a white
man with his golf clubs to drive up and shout, "Caddy!" The
farther one goes into niggertown, up Brickyard or down nearer
the town dump, the more dank and lean-to the structures: at
first there will be the scattering of big, almost graceful houses,
wholly painted or partially so, suggesting a slightly forbidding
affluence as they always had for me — but back along the
fringes of the town there remains that dreadful forlorn impover-
ishment, those dusty and ruined wooden façades which as a
child would send me back toward Grand Avenue as fast as I
could get there.

In a small town like this one in the lower South, where the
population ran close to half and half, one of the simplest facts
of awareness was that Negroes were everywhere: they ambled
along the sidewalks in the white neighborhoods, they mowed
the grass and clipped the hedges in the broad green lawns, they
rode down the streets in their horse-drawn wagons, they were
the janitors and cleaning-women in the churches and schools
and the laundry-women coming to the back doors for the week's
wash. On the main street especially, on Saturdays, the town
was filled with them, talking in great animated clusters on the
corners, or spilling out of the drugstores and cafés at the far end
of the narrow street. Their shouts and gestures, and the loud
blare of their music, were so much a part of those Saturdays
that if all of them had suddenly disappeared the town would
have seemed unbearably ghostly and bereft. The different
shades of color were extraordinary, for they ranged from the
whitest white to the darkest black, with shades in between as
various and distinct as yellows and browns could be. One
woman in particular, whom we saw walking through the crowds
on Main Street on Saturday nights, could have passed for a

member of the women's choir in the white Baptist church. "There's that white nigger again," someone would say. "I wonder what the *others* think of her?" Not until I was fourteen or fifteen did it begin to occur to me to ask myself, "Are we *related?*" And it was about then that I began hearing the story of the two white men who had Thanksgiving and Christmas dinner every year with three Negroes, who were the white men's half-brothers.

•

There was a stage, when we were about thirteen, in which we "went Negro." We tried to broaden our accents to sound like Negroes, as if there were not enough similarity already. We consciously walked like young Negroes, mocking their swinging gait, moving our arms the way they did, cracking our knuckles and whistling between our teeth. We tried to use some of the same expressions, as closely as possible to the way they said them, like: "Hey, *ma-a-a-n*, whut you *doin'* theah!," the sounds rolled out and clipped sharply at the end for the hell of it.

My father and I, on Sundays now and then, would go to their baseball games, sitting way out along the right field line; usually we were the only white people there. There was no condescension on our part, though the condescension might come later, if someone asked us where we had been. I would say, "Oh, we been to see the nigger game over at Number Two."

"Number Two" was the Negro school, officially called "Yazoo High Number Two" as opposed to the white high school, which was "Yazoo High Number One." We would walk up to a Negro our age and ask, "Say, buddy, where you go to school?" so we could hear the way he said, "Number *Two!*" Number Two was behind my house a block or so, a strange eclectic collection of old ramshackle wooden buildings and bright new concrete ones, sprawled out across four or five

acres. When the new buildings went up, some of the white people would say, "Well, they won't be pretty very *long*."

Sometimes we would run across a group of Negro boys our
age, walking in a pack through the white section, and there
would be bantering, half-affectionate exchanges: "Hey, Robert, what you *doin*' theah!" and we would give them the first
names of the boys they didn't know, and they would do the
same. We would mill around in a hopping, jumping mass, talking baseball or football, showing off for each other, and sounding for all the world, with our accentuated expressions and our
way of saying them, like much the same race. Some days we
organized football games in Lintonia Park, first black against
white, then intermingled, strutting out of huddles with our
limbs swinging, shaking our heads rhythmically, until one afternoon the cops came cruising by in their patrol car and ordered
us to break it up.

On Friday afternoons in the fall, we would go to see "the
Black Panthers" of Number Two play football. They played
in the discarded uniforms of our high school, so that our school
colors — red, black, and white — were the same, and they even
played the same towns from up in the delta that our high school
played. We sat on the sidelines next to their cheering section,
and sometimes a couple of us would be asked to carry the first-
down chains. The spectators would shout and jump up and
down, and even run onto the field to slap one of the players
on the back when he did something outstanding. When one of
the home team got hurt, ten or twelve people would dash out
from the sidelines to carry him to the bench; I suspected some
injuries might not have been as painful as they looked.

The Panthers had a left-handed quarterback named Kinsey,
who could throw a pass farther than any other high school passer
I had ever seen. He walked by my house every morning on the
way to school, and I would get in step with him, emulating his

walk as we strolled down to Number Two, and talk about last Friday's game or the next one coming up. We would discuss plays or passing patterns, and we pondered how they could improve on their "flea-flicker" which had backfired so disastrously against Belzoni, leading to a tackle's making an easy interception and all but walking thirty yards for a touchdown. "Man, he coulda *crawled* for that touchdown," Kinsey bemoaned. Once I said, "You got to get another kicker," and Kinsey replied, "Lord don't I know it," because in the previous game the Yazoo punter had kicked from his own twenty-yard-line, a high cantankerous spiral that curved up, down, and landed right in the middle of his own end zone. But this was a freak, because Kinsey and many of his teammates were not only superb athletes, they played with a casual flair and an exuberance that seemed missing in the white games. A long time after this, sitting in the bleachers in Candlestick Park in San Francisco, I saw a batter for the New York Mets hit a home run over the center-field fence; the ball hit a rung on the bleachers, near a group of little boys, and then bounced back over the fence onto the outfield grass. Willie Mays trotted over and gingerly tossed the ball underhanded across the wire fence to the boys, who had been deprived of a free baseball, and that casual gesture was performed with such a fine aristocracy that it suddenly brought back to me all the flamboyant sights and sounds of those Friday afternoons watching Number Two.

On Friday nights, when the Yazoo Indians of Number One played, you could see the Number Two boys, watching with their girl friends from the end-zone seats, talking plays and pointing out strategy. One night my father and I went to the hot-dog stand at halftime and saw Dr. Harrison, the Negro dentist who refereed the Number Two games, standing on the fringes of the crowd eating a hot-dog. My father drifted over his way and said, "How're you, Doc?" though not shaking hands, and they stood there until the second half started, talking about the virtues and shortcomings of the Yazoo Indians and the Yazoo Black Panthers.

•

Co-existing with all this, in no conflict, were the hoaxes we would play on the Negroes, who were a great untapped resource. We would hide in the hedges in my back yard and shoot Negro men who were walking down the sidewalk, aiming BB's at their tails. We would throw dead snakes from the trees into their path, or dead rats and crawfish, or attach a long thread to a dollar bill on the sidewalk and, when the man stooped to pick it up, pull it slowly back into the bushes.

I took to phoning the Negro undertakers, talking in my flawless Negro accent, and exchanges like this would take place:

"Hello, this the undertaker?"

"Yes'm."

"This here's Miss Mobley, from out at Bentonia. I got me a problem."

"What's that?"

"Well, my cousin just died, and I wonder if I can bury him under the house."

"Bury him under the *house?*"

"That right. He never amounted to much to us, and we just want him out of the way quick."

"You can't do it. It's against the *law.*"

"But what if we don't tell nobody? Ain't nobody gonna miss him noway."

"Naw, you can't do it. You got to get a death certificate and things like that."

"Well, we still gonna put him under the house. Is Johnson's Baby Powder a good thing to sprinkle him with?"

"Johnson's *Baby Powder?* Lord no!"

"But it says on the can it's good for the body."

"Lady, you got to have your cousin buried *right*." So I would give the undertaker the address, and then we would dash to the corner and watch the big black hearse come by on the way to Bentonia.

Or I would pick a Negro number at random from the telephone book, and phone it and say I was Bert Parks, calling from New York City on the Break-the-Bank program. Their number had been chosen out of all the telephones in the United States, and if they could answer three questions they would win $1000. "But I must warn you, Mrs. McGee, you are now *on the air*, and your voice is going into every home in America. Mrs. J. D. McGee, of Yazoo, Mississippi, are you ready for *question number one?*"

"Yessir, an' I hope I can answer it."

"Question number one! Who was the first President of the United States?"

"Why, George Washington was."

"That's absolutely correct, Mrs. McGee," as my fellow conspirators applauded in the background. "Now for question number two, and if you answer it correctly you get a chance to answer our big break-the-bank question. What is the capital of the United States?"

"Washington, D.C. is."

"Very good!" (applause) "Now, Mrs. McGee, are you ready down there in Yazoo for the big jackpot question?"

"Yessir!"

"Here it is. . . . *How many miles in the world?*"

"How many miles in the *world?*"

"That's right."

"The whole thing?"

"All of it."

"Oh Lord, I'll just have to guess. . . . One million!"

"One million? Mrs. McGee, I'm afraid you just missed! The correct answer should have been one million and three."

•

Several times I recall my father saying, when I was a small boy, "I don't know why they treat these niggers so bad. They pay taxes just like everybody else. If they pay taxes they oughta get to vote. It's as simple as that. If they don't get to vote they ought not to have to pay any taxes."

But one day the police finally caught Willie Johnson, a Negro who had broken into a number of white houses on our street and stolen everything he could carry away with him. He stole my mother's engagement ring from our house, and several pieces of family silver that the Harpers had buried in the dirt floor of their smokehouse before the federal troops had arrived in Raymond. The police brought Willie Johnson to the city hall for questioning, and telephoned all the men whose houses had been broken into to come down and question him. My father took me with him.

It was a stifling hot summer day, so hot that all you had to do was walk into the sun and your armpits and the hair on your head would soon be soaking wet. The room at the city hall was a small one; it was crowded with white men, and several others peered through the open door from the hallway. The police chief was sitting behind a desk, and when he saw my father he shouted, "Come on in and let's talk to this boy." I found a place on the floor next to my father's chair, and then I saw the Negro, sitting in a straight chair, trussed up and sweating as much as I was. The other white men were looking at him, glowering hard and not saying a word. The police chief asked the Negro a few questions, and as I sat there taking it all in I heard a man I knew turn to Willie Johnson and say, in a strangely subdued voice, sounding not at all like himself: "Nigger, I just want to tell you one thing, and you better get it straight, because I ain't gonna repeat it. . . . If I so much as see you walkin' down the sidewalk in front of our house, I'll blow your head off."

A young boy grew up with other things: with the myths, the stories handed down. One of them concerned one of the town's policemen, a gnarled and skinny old man by the time I was growing up, who had shot a Negro on the sidewalk on the lower end of Main Street and stood over him with his pistol to prevent anyone from taking him away while he bled to death. Whether it was apocryphal or not was almost irrelevant, for the terror of that story was quite enough; we saw the policeman almost everyday, making his rounds of the parking meters. "Don't fool with ol' ——," someone would say. "He'd just as soon shoot you as *look* at you," and then recount the legend in gory detail. There was the tale of the white planter, who owned one of the big plantations in the delta. When one of his Negro hands looked too closely at his wife one day, the man got his gun and killed him, and there was no trial.

There were a boy's recurring sense impressions of a hovering violence, isolated acts that remained in my memory long afterward, as senseless and unpatterned later as they had been for me when they happened:

. . . Some white men came to see my father, when I was six or seven years old. I heard them talking at the front door. "We hear the niggers might cause trouble tonight," one of them said. My father went to town to buy some extra shotgun shells, and we locked all our doors and windows when the sun went down.

. . . A Negro shot and killed a white man at the honky-tonk near the town dump. When the time came for him to be executed, they brought the state's portable electric chair in a big truck from Jackson. We drove by and saw it parked in the back yard of the jail. The next day some older boys told me they had stayed up until midnight, with the lights on in their house, to watch all the lights dim when the nigger got killed.

. . . I was playing with some older boys behind the Church of Christ chapel. Three barefooted Negro children appeared in the alley and began rifling through the garbage can. One of them found a rotten apple core and started eating it. The other two stuck their heads inside the can looking for things. We stopped our game to look at them. One of the older boys I was playing with whispered, "Damn little bastards," then said in a loud voice, "What you boys *doin'*?" Before they could answer he ran at them and shouted, "Get outa here, you little coons!" and we all chased them away down the alley.

. . . One rainy night in September one of the Negro shacks in the river bottom near Mound Street toppled over. The shack belonged to a garrulous old Negro named Henry who worked on odd jobs for several white families. When my friends and I found out what had happened, we walked across town to take a look. One of the four stilts had broken, and the whole house had simply flopped down at an angle. Henry and his family had been listening to the radio in the front room, and had slid right into the kitchen. The family had moved out, but there was the house, tilted over at an impossible angle, its backside splintered and broken. A light drizzle was falling, and the more we looked through the rain at that crippled old house the less we could help laughing. The image of Henry, the radio, and the whole family sliding into the kitchen was too much. We laughed all the way home, and more the next day when we saw Henry and asked after his condition, and he said: "I picked up fifty splinters in my ass."

. . . I was walking up Grand Avenue to school. Just as I crossed the railroad track I heard a loud crash several hundred yards to the north. Looking in that direction I saw the early morning freight out of Memphis pushing the remnants of a car along the track on its cowguard. I ran up the track. The train had crashed into a Negro taxicab with a full load of passengers. Blood was everywhere; two people lay mangled and still inside the wrecked car. A third, a woman, straddled the car and the train. A carload of high school boys on their way to school screeched around the corner and the boys got out to look at the wreckage. The woman slowly regained consciousness, looked around her, and asked, "Where's the train?" One of the high school boys, the star tailback, replied: "Nigger, you sittin' right on it."

. . . One morning I awoke to hear that a neighbor had shot a Negro burglar. I ran down to his house, and a large crowd milled around on the porch and in the front room. Inside, the man was telling what had happened. He pointed to a bullet hole in the wall, and another in the leg of a table. He had awakened in the night and saw the nigger in the hallway. He pulled out his automatic and shot twice, and he heard a moan and saw the nigger running away. When he telephoned the police, all they had to do was follow the trail of blood to a house in niggertown. That morning we followed the blood ourselves, little drops and big ones in the dust of the alley and onto the concrete pavement. Then we came back and congratulated our neighbor on his aim. More people came in to hear the story, and he told them: "If that second shot had been two inches to the left, that woulda been one *good* nigger."

•

As we grew older, beyond puberty into an involvement with girls, it seemed as if our own acts took on a more specific edge of cruelty. On Canal Street, across from the old Greyhound station at the Bayou, there was a concrete bannister where the Negroes would sit waiting for the busses. On Saturday nights we would cruise down the street in a car, and the driver would open his door and drive close to the curb. We would watch while the Negroes, to avoid the car door, toppled backward off the bannister like dominoes. And the taunts and threats to the isolated Negroes we saw, on country roads and deserted white streets, were harder and more cruel than anything we had done as children.

Deeply involved with the unthinking sadism, and with the sudden curious affection, were the moments of pity and sorrow. One Fourth of July afternoon when we were in high school, we went in a large group to one of the lakes in the delta for swimming and a picnic. A Negro shack on the bank of the lake had burned to the ground the night before. The father had taken his wife and his several small children into a bare, floorless cabin nearby, alive with crawling things that came out of the rotten wood in the walls. All they had saved was the clothes on their backs. They sat around all day in front of their shack, watching us eat and swim; for hours, it seemed, they hardly moved. Finally my girlfriend and I walked over to them. We discovered that the children had eaten practically nothing in two days. The children sat there listlessly, not saying a word; the father said even the fish wouldn't bite for him. My girl started crying. We went back and told the others, and took up a collection that must have come to fifteen dollars, and gave them our hotdogs and cokes. The Negro family ate the food and continued to look at us down by the lake. Under their stolid gaze I felt uncomfortable; I wanted to head back to Grand Avenue again. We packed our things and went to the car, drove through the flat cotton country to town, and resumed our picnic on the back lawn of one of the big houses in our neighborhood.

7

THERE WAS a different violence among us, a violence that reached us from far away. During the early stage of the Korean War when the North Koreans and the Red Chinese began pushing south down the peninsula, many of the units in the Dixie Division of the National Guard, covering several Deep Southern states, were activated, including the one in town. The ranks of the local unit were filled mainly with country hard-noses, or boys from around Graball Hill, who had joined up in the late 1940s to draw their monthly pay and to impress the country girls when they came to Main Street wearing their army uniforms on Saturdays. They would strut down the street in a group, or lounge around the corner, showing their spit and polish, and the word was that you could make out with those country girls much better in full army dress than you ever could in mere Saturday go-to-town khakis.

The Guard meetings themselves did not amount to much. The boys in the ranks never cared for taking orders, and usually had to be persuaded to carry out a command, less by standard military discipline than with unique forms of cajolery. The nights they met for their weekly meetings, at the broken-down old armory that had been built by the WPA during the Depression, we would drive by and see them spread out on the grass, chewing clovers and telling stories, or lazily polishing their old rifles, or sometimes playing hide-and-seek in the dank interior of their headquarters. North Korea might just as well have been North Dakota for all they knew.

Then the word came from Washington that they were called up. Everyone knew this meant they would be shipped to Korea as soon as possible to fill up the breach. That afternoon I went out to the armory, and such a sight you never saw: army jeeps everywhere, and transport trucks, and wild shouts — "Let's get them Gooks!" Bob Edwards, the boy who had lived next door to me and then had gone off to the Second War, the one who sent me the German helmet and medals, was now a sergeant, and I saw him in the crowd trying to give orders and keep things under control. I had hardly seen him in two or three years; I walked over to where he was and said hello. "Boy, you've got big," he said to me. "How old are you?" "Going on fifteen," I replied. "Well, you might be gettin' in *this* one. It seems I'm always off to some war."

They shipped out to somewhere to learn the basic military tactics, and the next thing we heard they were in Korea. I began getting letters from a Graball boy named Joe Mathis, who had been in my grade, though he was three years older. He wanted someone to write to, he said, and he had always liked me better than most. The thing he had got into, he wrote, was the worst thing he ever saw; it was terrible just to wake up in the morning. He asked me to please write him, and get the other boys to. Boys who had been in the high school a grade or two up, boys both from the town and out in the country who could fight hard with their fists and match obscenities with anyone, but whose whole bearing and upbringing mocked the ways of the military, became heroes and won decorations. All this gave one some immediate sense of how the rag-tailed and downtrodden armies of the Confederacy had stayed in the field longer than some people had expected.

One day in the summer, an official in the local American

Legion telephoned me. He told me he had heard I could play the trumpet, and wanted to know who else could play. I told him Ralph Atkinson was the best of us at the trumpet, and Henjie Henick was almost as good, but both of them were on vacation out of town. "Well, we need a trumpet for a military funeral," he told me. "They're beginning to ship some of these boys back. We need you to play tomorrow." I got my old silver trumpet and shined it up, and practiced taps with the first valve down. The next day the Legion official and I waited at the open grave for the funeral procession to wind up the hill of the town cemetery, and after the guns had been fired I played that mournful tune, nervous as I could be and wobbling seriously on the high-F. We lacked an echo that day, but the Legionnaires told me after that first funeral had broken up that it was far from being my last one, and to find an echo as soon as possible.

As they began sending back the hometown soldiers who were being killed at the front lines in Korea, the three of us played for more funerals than we could keep count of. We took turns playing at the grave, and despite what the military protocol said we usually used not one, but two, echoes, one fairly close to the grave, the second as far away as possible. When school began that year we would be called out of class; one of the Legionnaires would come into our classroom and whisper to the teacher, and the moment we saw him we knew what was happening. Then we would get our trumpets and drive with the carload of Legionnaires, dressed up in suits and ties and wearing their blue caps with the braided yellow letters, "Roy Lammons Post 7, Yazoo City, Miss.," out to the town cemetery, or to one of the dusty little graveyards in the backwoods. The Legionnaires fired the shots over the grave; we got to know all of them, and heard their stories about the Argonne or Chateau Thierry, or about the goings-on at old First World War army camps long since vanished. One of them had fought alongside Alvin York, and talked about "Alvin" as if they had been bosom companions over there in France; then the stories about Alvin got more and more inconsistent, conflicting with one another so head-on that I ended up listening less for the facts than for the complications. After a funeral at Blackjack Baptist Church or one of the other country places, we would drive slowly back to town, listening to their driftless talk as they passed a pint bottle back and forth — for the "*re*laxation," they said. I grew to feel that they were not really storekeepers or clerks or used-car salesmen or farmers; they were honorably retired warriors.

The Legionnaires had a fine feel for drama. They would snap to attention just at the right moment and fire their guns with such a flourish that I often suspected they were secretly enjoying themselves. The ritual at the grave was enough to get anyone down: the pomp and display of the military service, the coffin resplendently covered in the Stars and Stripes, the moaning and wailing of the survivors sitting in the straight-backed funeral-home chairs. I remember especially one country family who came dressed up in cheap Sunday clothes for their dead boy's funeral. The father was tall and skinny; his hair was plastered down with sweet-smelling tonic, and his sunburned face and knuckles were a sure sign he was a dirt-farmer from up in the hills. Big tears kept rolling down his face, which otherwise was without expression, and his several small children cried as if it were doomsday itself, and his wife muttered throughout the preacher's recitation, "*Why, why, why, why?*" The boy had been killed by mortar-fire in some minor skirmish in some Korean town that everyone by now has completely forgotten, but when the guns had been fired and the taps played, the Legionnaires went up to the family with such dignity and sympathy, telling them how the son had died for his country and would always be remembered by everyone, and that they were there

representing President Truman who could not make it to the
funeral, that the father's tears stopped, and the whole family
quieted down and walked back to the funeral home's car with
a kind of doleful pride.

I always preferred playing echo. At the grave my hands would
get clammy with sweat and I would twitch every time the moaning reached a high octave; it was an ordeal just to get through
the notes. And you were also held responsible when anything
went wrong. One day when I was stationed at the grave, with
Henjie Henick the echo about 200 yards away in the woods, the
wind was blowing so hard from the wrong direction that Henjie
panicked. Since he was unable to hear much of anything from
the grave, he played the echo a full thirty seconds before I was
supposed to play. I had to make out as best I could, so when
Henjie finished I muted my trumpet with my left palm and
played echo to *his* echo.

Playing echo had other hazards. If you failed to watch your
step closely enough walking through the woods, your foot was
sure to end up ankle-deep in a fresh pile of cow shit. The cows
themselves could be troublesome. They would stand around
looking you over, and if they were the neurotic kind they might
start bellowing the moment you came out with the music. An
old red bull caught me on his home terrain on the hill one afternoon. He glowered at me and I glowered at him, not daring to
move a muscle. Down at the grave I noticed the service was
almost over. As casually as possible I moved over behind a briar
tree, but the bull began edging sideways in my direction. Then
the taps came from the cemetery, and when my turn arrived I
was backing up the hill away from that bull, looking at him
and blowing my horn all the while.

But being away from the grave was usually more peaceful and
quiet. Standing on a hill with my trumpet in hand, I would see
the funeral procession coming up the road, all mournful and

slow, the sun suddenly catching the colors of the hearse and the cars and the pick-up trucks, while down at the grave my Legionnaire friends poised smartly at attention. Then I would watch the service, which seemed like a pantomime from where I was, or a simple folk-drama with only the earth as the stage. The Legionnaires would fire their guns, and the sound would rumble out of the clearing far into the woods; then Ralph or Henjie would play his notes, slow as he could make them, and I would wait there three or four seconds for the notes to drift away, and that would be my cue.

During one such service I chanced to look down the opposite side of the hill on which I was posted; there was the town, laid out on its hills and flat places, and, closer by, the Brickyard section of niggertown, sending forth all its unpredictable sounds and smells. Then I saw four Negro children walking up the path toward me. They saw me propped up against a tree with my trumpet; a most unlikely spectacle I must have been to them in the middle of those woods. They came right up to me and examined the trumpet, asking me what the spit-valve and all the other gadgets on it were for, and they watched the solemn pantomime down in the cemetery with me; when the time came for me to play they stood there with such respect, quietly and attentively, that I felt a little like a god.

We only played for one Negro funeral that year. It was so far at the south end of the county that they had been unable to get any trumpets from Number Two. Even the white Legionnaires had been summoned to fire the shots. All of us stood at the grave in that woeful little graveyard, feeling edgy and out of place amidst the black faces. The mourning was louder and more animated than any I had yet seen, and when the time came for the flag to be folded and presented to the mother, I was in such a hopped-up state I was afraid I would be unable to get anything out; but the notes were surprisingly firm and true, and even the High-F sounded good to me. When it was over, the Legionnaires, as always, walked up to the family to present the gun shells and to say their boy had not died in vain, and on the way home in the car, when the pint bottle was being passed around, I talked them out of a swig.

One morning Ralph Atkinson and I were called out of school to play for a hero's funeral in the national cemetery at the Civil War battleground in Vicksburg. They put on a grand spectacle, with a troop of soldiers and Legionnaires, and a special army representative on hand. I was the echo that day, and I climbed up that green sloping hill to the top of the bluffs. I walked alone among the gravestones of the boys who had died there for Grant and Pemberton ninety years before; most of the stones were merely inscribed with numbers, and on higher ground I stood with my trumpet under my arm and read a plaque bearing the Gettysburg Address. *Four score and seven years ago, our fathers brought forth upon this continent. . . .* The words leapt out at me like living things, and filled me with an excitement and a sorrow I could not fully comprehend. There, stretched out before me, as far as I could see, was the old River, twisting and curving on itself out to the very horizon, brown and lonesome and seeming to move hardly at all in the glorious morning sunlight. Down below, among the hundreds of white crosses, the pageantry and color were the most beautiful I had ever seen; that was surely the best funeral of all.

•

In the autumn of that year they shipped home Thomas Putnam. He had joined the Air Force in his junior year in high school, and we had all known him well; we had played football together, and driven around the county in his pick-up. He was a short, bowlegged little boy with red hair worn in a crew cut, and his humor was wild and irrepressible. When the word came that he had been killed while trying to rescue a wounded friend from a plane that had crash-landed, his old girlfriend went hysterical in our classroom, and they had to send her home to bed.

The funeral was to be on a Saturday, and Thomas' coffin arrived on a Friday morning from the airport in Jackson, accompanied by an Air Force private from Kansas with a black patch over an eye. He was the one the dead boy had tried to save, and he came to our school that morning, to be introduced to our classes and recognized in the weekly assembly. He was a quiet, slow-talking boy with a slight stutter; even in his full-dress uniform he looked younger than seventeen or eighteen. We sat around on the lawn at lunchtime with him and talked about Thomas, and about Korea, and he said he was more than glad to be getting out of it and going home to Kansas.

That night was one of the big home football games, and the whole town was touched with a wonderful undercurrent of excitement, for on Fridays in the fall you could almost feel the tension in the atmosphere. It was Indian summer, and everything, the earth and the trees, touched by the airy sunshine, were the lazy golden-brown of that sad and lovely time; there was a faint presence of smoke everywhere, and the smell of leaves burning, and the sounds and their echoes carried a long, long way. It seemed not a good time to celebrate death, even heroic death, but rather a time to indulge one's self in the throbs and melancholies of the living. Wherever you looked there would be a truckload of raw cotton coming in for ginning; along the roads and even the paved avenues of town you could see the dirty white cotton bolls that had fallen to the ground. Leaves of a dozen different colors drifted down out of the trees, and whirled and rustled along the lonesome sidewalks and streets. The weeds and Johnson grass in the gullies and ditches on the delta side were already beginning to turn brown and seared, yet so rich was the land that they still grew, half-dead and half-alive. The county fair was on, and for the entire week we had taken in the 4-H exhibits — the vegetables and the bottled preserves of all the shades in the rainbow, and the pumpkins and the great slabs of meat. A Yazoo girl had won the county beauty contest, and in a big brown tent off at the far end of the fairgrounds we had paid a dime to see Flora, the belle of Memphis-town: "Watch her shimmy, watch her shake, like raspberry jelly on a birthday cake." The air was filled with band music from the football game at Number Two and the carnival tents at the fair. That afternoon the high school band marched down the streets, led by the sexy majorettes twirling their batons, and way out in the distance you could pick up the strains of "On Wisconsin," or "On Dear Old Army Team," or "Dixie," or the sounds and singing of the school fight-song, played to the tune of "Cheer, Cheer for Old Notre Dame," that a generation of small-town Southern boys and girls were brought up on:

> Beer, beer for old Yazoo High
> You bring the cocktails, I'll bring the rye,
> Send some freshmen out for gin,
> Don't let a soul but *seniors* in.
> We never stagger, we never fall,
> We sober up on wood alcohol,
> Watch that drunken Yazoo team
> Go staggerin' to victory.

That night 3000 people turned out at Crump Field for the game in the crisp, cool air. The cheerleaders whirled around in their tight skirts, cajoling the crowd to join the yells: "Y-A-Z-O-O. . . . That's the way to spell it, here's the way to yell it . . . *Yazoo!*" The victory over Belzoni was resounding, but I kept noticing the one-eyed airman from Kansas, sometimes sitting on the bench with the substitutes, or wandering among the crowds talking to the students and teachers, or hanging off to himself drinking a Coke. The girls would walk up to him and say, "Now you come to the dance after the game, you *heah?*"

The dance took place in a rambling country house on a hill right on the edge of the delta, and the whole landscape enclosing it was a rolling, dark-green golf course. Everyone arrived on time, exchanging those Friday night greetings which would later seem to me such a self-conscious amalgam of Old South and Modern Negro; then the dance music started — pop-tunes or jitterbugging the Memphis shuffle—and the couples swayed and rocked on the dance floor and out onto the porches.

Back in the men's locker room, where the older boys stashed their bootleg bourbon, the drinking was going strong by eleven. The airman got his pick of all the girls in the school to dance with. He made frequent trips to the locker room or to someone's car, and by midnight, when I saw him weaving back and forth on the dance floor, he was plainly quite drunk.

At one o'clock the party gradually began to break up. I walked out onto the porch to get some air, and beyond that to the golf green up the hill. In the moonlight I saw the airman leaning up against a tree, then walking alone and staggering around the sand trap.

"You all right?" I shouted, and walked up his way.

"Yeah, I'm okay," he said. "Just a little high."

"You got a ride home?"

"Yeah, thanks." Then he paused for an instant. I could tell he wanted me to stay a little longer.

"Thomas ain't in that casket," he stammered, all in a rush.

It took me a few seconds to let the words get in. "What do you mean he ain't in it?" I said.

"Just what I say. He's not in it, except maybe a finger or two."

"You mean . . ."

"*Yeah*," he snapped. "That's *exactly* what I mean. And his aunt wants to open it up, and I keep tellin' her she can't." He stopped for a second, and gazed down the sloping fairway out into the dark mists of the delta. "And besides, it's against the rules."

"Come on," I said. "Let's walk on back."

As we headed for the clubhouse, he chortled softly to himself. Then, turning on me, he said, "Don't tell anybody. I ain't told anybody but a couple of the other guys, and they're friends of his." I promised, and then a group of boys met up with him in the road and they drove away.

Next day a good part of the town came to the funeral. Someone had written a eulogy, patterned, I thought, after Ernie Pyle, in the school paper, and the preacher read it at church: "His old desk is empty, but with his spirit it will forever be filled." It rained at the cemetery, a hard cold Mississippi rain that meant the sudden end of Indian summer; at my post on the hill I got soaking wet, and my echo came out of a ghostly fog that shrouded the trees and the cows in the wood. On Sunday morning early, the one-eyed airman caught the Greyhound for Memphis. We never saw him again.

8

LIKE MARK TWAIN and his comrades growing up a century before in another village on the other side of the Mississippi, my friends and I had but one sustaining ambition in the 1940s. Theirs in Hannibal was to be steamboatmen, ours in Yazoo was to be major-league baseball players. In the summers, we thought and talked of little else. We memorized batting averages, fielding averages, slugging averages, we knew the roster of the Cardinals and the Red Sox better than their own managers must have known them, and to hear the broadcasts from all the big-city ballparks with their memorable names — the Polo Grounds, Wrigley Field, Fenway Park, the Yankee Stadium — was to set our imagination churning for the glory and riches those faraway places would one day bring us. One of our friends went to St. Louis on his vacation to see the Cards, and when he returned with the autographs of Stan Musial, Red Schoendienst, Country Slaughter, Marty Marion, Joe Garagiola, and a dozen others, we could hardly keep down our envy. I hated that boy for a month, and secretly wished him dead, not only because he took on new airs but because I wanted those scraps of paper with their magic characters. I wished also that my own family were wealthy enough to take me to a big-league town for two weeks, but to a bigger place even than St. Louis: Chicago, maybe, with not one but two teams, or best of all to New York, with three. I had bought a baseball cap in Jackson, a real one from the Brooklyn Dodgers, and a Jackie Robinson Louisville Slugger, and one day when I could not even locate any of the others for catch or for baseball talk, I sat on a curb on Grand Avenue with the most dreadful feelings of being caught forever by time — trapped there always in my scrawny and helpless condition. *I'm ready, I'm ready,* I kept thinking to myself, but that remote future when I would wear a cap like that and be a hero for a grandstand full of people seemed so far away I knew it would never come. I must have been the most dejected-looking child you ever saw, sitting hunched up on the curb and dreaming of glory in the mythical cities of the North. I felt worse when a carload of high school boys halted right in front of where I sat, and they started reciting what they always did when they saw me alone and day-dreaming: *Wee Willie Winkie walks through the town, upstairs and downstairs in his night-gown.* Then one of them said, "Winkie, you *gettin'* much?" "You bastards!" I shouted, and they drove off laughing like wild men.

Almost every afternoon when the heat was not unbearable my father and I would go out to the old baseball field behind the armory to hit flies. I would stand far out in center field, and he would station himself with a fungo at home plate, hitting me one high fly, or Texas Leaguer, or line drive after another, sometimes for an hour or more without stopping. My dog would get out there in the outfield with me, and retrieve the inconsequential dribblers or the ones that went too far. I was light and speedy, and could make the most fantastic catches, turning completely around and forgetting the ball sometimes to head for the spot where it would descend, or tumbling head-on for a diving catch. The smell of that new-cut grass was the finest of all smells, and I could run forever and never get tired. It was a dreamy, suspended state, those late afternoons, thinking of nothing but outfield flies as the world drifted lazily by on Jackson Avenue. I learned to judge what a ball would do by instinct, heading the way it went as if I owned it, and I knew in my heart I could make the big time. Then, after all that exertion, my father would shout, "I'm whupped!" and we would quit for the day.

When I was twelve I became a part-time sportswriter for the *Yazoo Herald,* whose courtly proprietors allowed me unusual independence. I wrote up an occasional high school or Legion game in a florid prose, filled with phrases like "two-ply blow" and "circuit-ringer." My mentor was the sports editor of the *Memphis Commercial Appeal,* whose name was Walter Stewart, a man who could invest the most humdrum athletic contest with the elements of Shakespearean tragedy. I learned whole paragraphs of his by heart, and used some of his expressions for my reports on games between Yazoo and Satartia, or the other teams. That summer when I was twelve, having never seen a baseball game higher than the Jackson Senators of Class B, my father finally relented and took me to Memphis to see the Chicks, who were Double-A. It was the farthest I had ever been from home, and the largest city I had ever seen; I walked around in a state of joyousness, admiring the crowds and the big park high above the River, and best of all, the grand old lobby of the Chisca Hotel.

Staying with us at the Chisca were the Nashville Vols, who were there for a big series with the Chicks. I stayed close to the lobby to get a glimpse of them; when I discovered they spent all day, up until the very moment they left for the ballpark, playing the pinball machine, I stationed myself there too. Their names were Tookie Gilbert, Smokey Burgess, Chuck Workman, and Bobo Hollomon, the latter being the one who got as far as the St. Louis Browns, pitched a no-hitter in his first major league game, and failed to win another before being shipped down forever to obscurity; one afternoon my father and I ran into them outside the hotel on the way to the game and gave them a ride in our taxi. I could have been fit for tying, especially when Smokey Burgess tousled my hair and asked me if I batted right or left, but when I listened to them as they grumbled about having to get out to the ballpark so early, and complained about the season having two more damned months to go and about how ramshackle their team bus was, I was too disillusioned even to tell my friends when I got home.

•

Because back home, even among the adults, baseball was all-meaning; it was the link with the outside. A place known around town simply as The Store, down near the train depot, was the principal center of this ferment. The Store had saw-dust on the floor and long shreds of flypaper hanging from the ceiling. Its most familiar staples were Rexall supplies, oysters on the half shell, legal beer, and illegal whiskey, the latter served up, Mississippi bootlegger style, by the bottle from a hidden shelf and costing not merely the price of the whiskey but the investment in gas required to go to Louisiana to fetch it. There was a long counter in the back. On one side of it, the white workingmen congregated after hours every afternoon to com-pare the day's scores and talk batting averages, and on the other side, also talking baseball, were the Negroes, juxtaposed in a face-to-face arrangement with the whites. The scores were chalked up on a blackboard hanging on a red and purple wall, and the conversations were carried on in fast, galloping shouts from one end of the room to the other. An intelligent white boy of twelve was even permitted, in that atmosphere of heady freedom before anyone knew the name of Justice Warren or had heard much of the United States Supreme Court, a quasi-pub-lic position favoring the Dodgers, who had Jackie Robinson, Roy Campanella, and Don Newcombe — not to mention, so it was rumored, God knows how many Chinese and mulattoes being groomed in the minor leagues. I remember my father turned to some friends at The Store one day and observed, "Well, you can say what you want to about that nigger Robinson, but he's got *guts*," and to a man the others nodded, a little reluctantly, but in agreement nonetheless. And one of them said he had read somewhere that Pee Wee Reese, a white Southern boy, was the best friend Robinson had on the team, which proved they had chosen the right one to watch after him.

There were two firehouses in town, and on hot afternoons the firemen at both establishments sat outdoors in their shirt-sleeves, with the baseball broadcast turned up as loud as it would go. On his day off work my father, who had left Cities

Service and was now a bookkeeper for the wholesale grocery, usually started with Firehouse No. 1 for the first few innings and then hit Number Two before ending up at The Store for the post-game conversations.

I decided not to try out for the American Legion Junior Baseball team that summer. Legion baseball was an important thing for country boys in those parts, but I was too young and skinny, and I had heard that the coach, a dirt farmer known as Gentleman Joe, made his protégés lie flat in the infield while he walked on their stomachs; he also forced them to take three-mile runs through the streets of town, talked them into going to church, and persuaded them to give up Coca-Colas. A couple of summers later, when I did go out for the team, I found out that Gentleman Joe did in fact insist on these soul-strengthening rituals; because of them, we won the Mississippi State Championship and the merchants in town took up a collection and sent us all the way to St. Louis to see the Cards play the Phillies. My main concern that earlier summer, however, lay in the more academic aspects of the game. I knew more about baseball, its technology and its ethos, than all the firemen and Store experts put together. Having read most of its literature, I could give a sizable lecture on the infield-fly rule alone, which only a thin minority of the townspeople knew existed. Gentleman Joe was held in some esteem for his strategical sense, yet he was the only man I ever knew who could call for a sacrifice bunt with two men out and not have a bad conscience about it. I remember one dismaying moment that came to me while I was watching a country semi-pro game. The home team had runners on first and third with one out, when the batter hit a ground ball to the first baseman, who stepped on first and then threw to second. The shortstop, covering second, stepped on the base but made no attempt to tag the runner. The man on third had crossed the plate, of course, but the umpire, who was not very familiar with the subtleties of the rules, signaled a double play. Sitting in the grandstand, I knew that it was not a double play at all and that the run had scored, but when I went down, out of my Christian duty, to tell the manager of the local team that he had just been done out of a run, he told me I was crazy. This was the kind of brainpower I was up against.

That summer the local radio station, the one where we broadcast our Methodist programs, started a baseball quiz program. A razor blade company offered free blades and the station chipped in a dollar, all of which went to the first listener to telephone with the right answer to the day's baseball question. If there was no winner, the next day's pot would go up a dollar. At the end of the month they had to close down the program because I was winning all the money. It got so easy, in fact, that I stopped phoning in the answers some afternoons so that the pot could build up and make my winnings more spectacular. I netted about $25 and a ten-year supply of double-edged, smooth-contact razor blades before they gave up. One day, when the jackpot was a mere two dollars, the announcer tried to confuse me. "Babe Ruth," he said, "hit sixty home runs in 1927 to set the major-league record. What man had the next-highest total?" I telephoned and said, "George Herman Ruth. He hit fifty-nine in another season." My adversary, who had developed an acute dislike of me, said that was not the correct answer. He said it should have been *Babe* Ruth. This incident angered me, and I won for the next four days, just for the hell of it.

On Sunday afternoons we sometimes drove out of town and along hot, dusty roads to baseball fields that were little more than parched red clearings, the outfield sloping out of the woods and ending in some tortuous gully full of yellowed paper, old socks, and vintage cow shit. One of the backwoods teams had a fastball pitcher named Eckert, who didn't have any teeth,

and a fifty-year-old left-handed catcher named Smith. Since
there were no catcher's mitts made for left-handers, Smith had
to wear a mitt on his throwing hand. In his simian posture he
would catch the ball and toss it lightly into the air and then
whip his mitt off and catch the ball in his bare left hand before throwing it back. It was a wonderfully lazy way to spend
those Sunday afternoons — my father and my friends and I sitting in the grass behind the chicken-wire backstop with eight
or ten dozen farmers, watching the wrong-handed catcher go
through his contorted gyrations, and listening at the same
time to our portable radio, which brought us the rising inflec-
tions of a baseball announcer called the Old Scotchman. The
sounds of the two games, our own and the one being broadcast
from Brooklyn or Chicago, merged and rolled across the bumpy
outfield and the gully into the woods; it was a combination that
seemed perfectly natural to everyone there.

•

I can see the town now on some hot, still weekday afternoon
in mid-summer: ten thousand souls and nothing doing. Even
the red water truck was a diversion, coming slowly up Grand
Avenue with its sprinklers on full force, the water making sizzling steam-clouds on the pavement while half-naked Negro
children followed the truck up the street and played in the
torrent until they got soaking wet. Over on Broadway, where
the old men sat drowsily in straw chairs on the pavement near
the Bon-Ton Café, whittling to make the time pass, you could
laze around on the sidewalks — barefoot, if your feet were
tough enough to stand the scalding concrete — watching the
big cars with out-of-state plates whip by, the driver hardly knowing and certainly not caring what place this was. Way up that
fantastic hill, Broadway seemed to end in a seething mist —
little heat mirages that shimmered off the asphalt; on the main

street itself there would be only a handful of cars parked here and there, and the merchants and the lawyers sat in the shade under their broad awnings, talking slowly, aimlessly, in the cryptic summer way. The one o'clock whistle at the sawmill would send out its loud bellow, reverberating up the streets to the bend in the Yazoo River, hardly making a ripple in the heavy somnolence.

But by two o'clock almost every radio in town was tuned in to the Old Scotchman. His rhetoric dominated the place. It hovered in the branches of the trees, bounced off the hills, and came out of the darkened stores; the merchants and the old men cocked their ears to him, and even from the big cars that sped by, their tires making lapping sounds in the softened highway, you could hear his voice, being carried past you out into the delta.

The Old Scotchman's real name was Gordon McLendon, and he described the big-league games for the Liberty Broadcasting System, which had outlets mainly in the South and the Southwest. He had a deep, rich voice, and I think he was the best rhetorician, outside of Bilbo and Nye Bevan, I have ever heard. Under his handling a baseball game took on a life of its own. As in the prose of the *Commercial Appeal*'s Walter Stewart, his games were rare and remarkable entities; casual pop flies had the flow of history behind them, double plays resembled the stark clashes of old armies, and home runs deserved acknowledgment on earthen urns. Later, when I came across Thomas Wolfe, I felt I had heard him before, from Shibe Park, Crosley Field, or the Yankee Stadium.

One afternoon I was sitting around my house listening to the Old Scotchman, admiring the vivacity of a man who said he was a contemporary of Connie Mack. (I learned later that he was twenty-nine.) That day he was doing the Dodgers and the Giants from the Polo Grounds. The game, as I recall, was in the fourth inning, and the Giants were ahead by about 4 to 1. It was a boring game, however, and I began experimenting with my father's short-wave radio, an impressive mechanism a couple of feet wide, which had an aerial that almost touched the ceiling and the name of every major city in the world on its dial. It was by far the best radio I had ever seen; there was not another one like it in town. I switched the dial to short-wave and began picking up African drum music, French jazz, Australian weather reports, and a lecture from the British Broadcasting Company on the people who wrote poems for Queen Elizabeth. Then a curious thing happened. I came across a baseball game — the Giants and the Dodgers, from the Polo Grounds. After a couple of minutes I discovered that the game was in the eighth inning. I turned back to the local station, but here the Giants and Dodgers were still in the fourth. I turned again to the short-wave broadcast and listened to the last inning, a humdrum affair that ended with Carl Furillo popping out to shortstop, Gil Hodges grounding out second to first, and Roy Campanella lining out to center. Then I went back to the Old Scotchman and listened to the rest of the game. In the top of the ninth, an hour or so later, a ghostly thing occurred; to my astonishment and titillation, the game ended with Furillo popping out to short, Hodges grounding out second to first, and Campanella lining out to center.

I kept this unusual discovery to myself, and the next day, an hour before the Old Scotchman began his play-by-play of the second game of the series, I dialed the short-wave frequency, and, sure enough, they were doing the Giants and the Dodgers again. I learned that I was listening to the Armed Forces Radio Service, which broadcast games played in New York. As the game progressed I began jotting down notes on the action. When the first four innings were over I turned to the local station just in time to get the Old Scotchman for the first batter.

The Old Scotchman's account of the game matched the short-wave's almost perfectly. The Scotchman's, in fact, struck me as being considerably more poetic than the one I had heard first. But I did not doubt him, since I could hear the roar of the crowd, the crack of the bat, and the Scotchman's precise description of foul balls that fell into the crowd, the gestures of the base coaches, and the expression on the face of a small boy who was eating a lemon popsicle in a box seat behind first base. I decided that the broadcast was being delayed somewhere along the line, maybe because we were so far from New York.

That was my first thought, but after a close comparison of the two broadcasts for the rest of the game, I sensed that something more sinister was taking place. For one thing, the Old Scotchman's description of the count on a batter, though it jibed 90 percent of the time, did not always match. For another, the Scotchman's crowd, compared with the other, kept up an ungodly noise. When Robinson stole second on short-wave, he did it without drawing a throw and without sliding, while for Mississippians the feat was performed in a cloud of angry, petulant dust. A foul ball that went over the grandstand and out of the park for short-wave listeners in Alaska, France, and the Argentine produced for the firemen, bootleggers, farmers, and myself a primitive scramble that ended with a feeble old lady catching the ball on the first bounce to the roar of an assembly that would have outnumbered Grant's at Old Cold Harbor. But the most revealing development came after the Scotchman's game was over. After the usual summaries, he mentioned that the game had been "recreated." I had never taken notice of that particular word before, because I lost interest once a game was over. I went to the dictionary, and under "recreate" I found, "To invest with fresh vigor and strength; to refresh, invigorate (nature, strength, a person or thing)." The

Old Scotchman most assuredly invested a game with fresh vigor and strength, but this told me nothing. My deepest suspicions were confirmed, however, when I found the second definition of the word — "To create anew."

So there it was. I was happy to have fathomed the mystery, as perhaps no one else in the whole town had done. The Old Scotchman, for all his wondrous expressions, was not only several innings behind every game he described but was no doubt sitting in some air-conditioned studio in the hinterland, where he got the happenings of the game by news ticker; sound effects accounted for the crack of the bat and the crowd noises. Instead of being disappointed in the Scotchman, I was all the more pleased by his genius, for he made pristine facts more actual than actuality, a valuable lesson when the day finally came that I started reading literature. I must add, however, that this appreciation did not obscure the realization that I had at my disposal a weapon of unimaginable dimensions.

Next day I was at the short-wave again, but I learned with much dissappointment that the game being broadcast on short-wave was not the one the Scotchman had chosen to describe. I tried every afternoon after that and discovered that I would have to wait until the Old Scotchman decided to do a game out of New York before I could match his game with the one described live on short-wave. Sometimes, I learned later, these coincidences did not occur for days; during an important Dodger or Yankee series, however, his game and that of the Armed Forces Radio Service often coincided for two or three days running. I was happy, therefore, to find, on an afternoon a few days later, that both the short-wave and the Scotchman were carrying the Yankees and the Indians.

I settled myself at the short-wave with notebook and pencil and took down every pitch. This I did for four full innings, and then I turned back to the town station, where the Old Scotchman was just beginning the first inning. I checked the first batter to make sure the accounts jibed. Then, armed with my notebook, I ran down the street to the corner grocery, a minor outpost of baseball intellection, presided over by my young Negro friend Bozo, a knowledgeable student of the game, the same one who kept my dog in bologna. I found Bozo behind the meat counter, with the Scotchman's account going full blast. I arrived at the interim between the top and bottom of the first inning.

"Who's pitchin' for the Yankees, Bozo?" I asked.

"They're pitchin' Allie Reynolds," Bozo said. "Old Scotchman says Reynolds really got the stuff today. He just set 'em down one, two, three."

The Scotchman, meanwhile, was describing the way the pennants were flapping in the breeze. Phil Rizzuto, he reported, was stepping to the plate.

"Bo," I said, trying to sound cut-and-dried, "you know what I think? I think Rizzuto's gonna take a couple of fast called strikes, then foul one down the left-field line, and then line out straight to Boudreau at short."

"Yeah?" Bozo said. He scratched his head and leaned lazily across the counter.

I went up front to buy something and then came back. The count worked to nothing and two on Rizzuto — a couple of fast called strikes and a foul down the left side. "This one," I said to Bozo, "he lines straight to Boudreau at short."

The Old Scotchman, pausing dramatically between words as was his custom, said, "Here's the windup on nothing and two. Here's the pitch on its way — There's a hard line drive! But Lou Boudreau's there at shortstop and he's got it. Phil hit that one on the nose, but Boudreau was right there."

Bozo looked over at me, his eyes bigger than they were. "How'd you know that?" he asked.

Ignoring this query, I made my second prediction. "Bozo," I said, "Tommy Henrich's gonna hit the first pitch up against the right-field wall and slide in with a double."

"How come you think so?"

"Because I can predict anything that's gonna happen in baseball in the next ten years," I said. "I can tell you anything."

The Old Scotchman was describing Henrich at the plate. "Here comes the first pitch. Henrich swings, there's a hard smash into right field! . . . This one may be out of here! It's going, going— No! It's off the wall in right center. Henrich's rounding first, on his way to second. Here's the relay from Doby . . . Henrich slides in safely with a double!" The Yankee crowd sent up an awesome roar in the background.

"Say, how'd you know that?" Bozo asked. "How'd you know he was gonna wind up at second?"

"I just can tell. I got extra-vision," I said. On the radio, far in the background, the public-address system announced Yogi Berra. "Like Berra right now. You know what? He's gonna hit a one-one pitch down the right-field line — "

"How come you know?" Bozo said. He was getting mad.

"Just a second," I said. "I'm gettin' static." I stood dead still, put my hands up against my temples and opened my eyes wide. "Now it's comin' through clear. Yeah, Yogi's gonna hit a one-one pitch down the right-field line, and it's gonna be fair by about three or four feet— I can't say exactly— and Henrich's gonna score from second, but the throw is gonna get Yogi at second by a mile."

This time Bozo was silent, listening to the Scotchman, who described the ball and the strike, then said: "Henrich takes the lead off second. Benton looks over, stretches, delivers. Yogi swings." (There was the bat crack.) "There's a line drive down the right side! It's barely inside the foul line. It may go for extra bases! Henrich's rounding third and coming in with a run. Berra's moving toward second. Here comes the throw! . . . And they *get* him! They get Yogi easily on the slide at second!"

Before Bozo could say anything else, I reached in my pocket for my notes. "I've just written down here what I think's gonna happen in the first four innings," I said. "Like DiMag. See, he's gonna pop up to Mickey Vernon at first on a one-nothing pitch in just a minute. But don't you worry. He's gonna hit a 380-foot homer in the fourth with nobody on base on a full count. You just follow these notes and you'll see I can predict anything that's gonna happen in the next ten years." I handed him the paper, turned around, and left the store just as DiMaggio, on a one-nothing pitch, popped up to Vernon at first.

Then I went back home and took more notes from the short-wave. The Yanks clobbered the Indians in the late innings and won easily. On the local station, however, the Old Scotchman was in the top of the fifth inning. At this juncture I went to the telephone and called Firehouse No. 1.

"Hello," a voice answered. It was the fire chief.

"Hello, Chief, can you tell me the score?" I said. Calling the firehouse for baseball information was a common practice.

"The Yanks are ahead, 5-2."

"This is the Phantom you're talkin' with," I said.

"Who?"

"The Phantom. Listen carefully, Chief. Reynolds is gonna open this next inning with a popup to Doby. Then Rizutto will single to left on a one-one count. Henrich's gonna force him at second on a two-and-one pitch but make it to first. Berra's gonna double to right on a nothing-and-one pitch, and Henrich's goin' to third. DiMaggio's gonna foul a couple off and then double down the left-field line, and both Henrich and Yogi are gonna score. Brown's gonna pop out to third to end the inning."

"Aw, go to hell," the chief said, and hung up.

This was precisely what happened, of course. I phoned No. 1 again after the inning.

"Hello."

"Hi. This is the Phantom again."

"Say, how'd you know that?"

"Stick with me," I said ominously, "and I'll feed you predictions. I can predict anything that's gonna happen anywhere in the next ten years." After a pause I added, "Beware of fire real soon," for good measure, and hung up.

I left my house and hurried back to the corner grocery. When I got there, the entire meat counter was surrounded by friends of Bozo's, about a dozen of them. They were gathered around my notes, talking passionately and shouting. Bozo saw me standing by the bread counter. "There he is! That's the one!" he declared. His colleagues turned and stared at me in undisguised awe. They parted respectfully as I strolled over to the meat counter and ordered a dime's worth of bologna for my dog.

A couple of questions were directed at me from the group, but I replied, "I'm sorry for what happened in the fourth. I predicted DiMag was gonna hit a full-count pitch for that homer. It came out he hit it on two-and-two. There was too much static in the air between here and New York."

"Too much *static?*" one of them asked.

"Yeah. Sometimes the static confuses my extra-vision. But I'll be back tomorrow if everything's okay, and I'll try not to make any more big mistakes."

"Big mistakes!" one of them shouted, and the crowd laughed admiringly, parting once more as I turned and left the store. I wouldn't have been at all surprised if they had tried to touch the hem of my shirt.

•

That day was only the beginning of my brief season of triumph. A schoolmate of mine offered me five dollars, for instance, to tell him how I had known that Johnny Mize was going to hit a two-run homer to break up one particularly close game for the Giants. One afternoon, on the basis of a lopsided first four innings, I had an older friend sneak into The Store and place a bet, which netted me $14.50. I felt so bad about it I tithed $1.45 in church the following Sunday. At Bozo's grocery store I was a full-scale oracle. To the firemen I remained the Phantom, and firefighting reached a peak of efficiency that month, simply because the firemen knew what was going to happen in the late innings and did not need to tarry when an alarm came.

One afternoon my father was at home listening to the Old Scotchman with a couple of out-of-town salesmen from Greenwood. They were sitting in the front room, and I had already managed to get the first three or four innings of the Cardinals and the Giants on paper before they arrived. The Old Scotchman was in the top of the first when I walked in and said hello. The men were talking business and listening to the game at the same time.

"I'm gonna make a prediction," I said. They stopped talking and looked at me. "I predict Musial's gonna take a ball and a strike and then hit a double to right field, scoring Schoendienst from second, but Marty Marion's gonna get tagged out at the plate."

"You're mighty smart," one of the men said. He suddenly sat up straight when the Old Scotchman reported, "Here's the windup and the pitch coming in. . . . Musial *swings!*" (Bat crack, crowd roar.) "He drives one into right field! This one's going up against the boards! . . . . Schoendienst rounds third. He's coming on in to score! Marion dashes around third, legs churning. His cap falls off, but here he *comes!* Here's the toss to the plate. He's nabbed at home. He is *out* at the plate! Musial holds at second with a run-producing double."

Before I could parry the inevitable questions, my father caught me by the elbow and hustled me into a back room. "How'd you know that?" he asked.

"I was just guessin'," I said. "It was nothin' but luck."

He stopped for a moment, and then a new expression showed on his face. "Have *you* been callin' the firehouse?" he asked.

"Yeah, I guess a few times."

"Now, you tell me how you found out about all that. I mean it."

When I told him about the short-wave, I was afraid he might be mad, but on the contrary he laughed uproariously. "Do you remember these next few innings?" he asked.

"I got it all written down," I said, and reached in my pocket for the notes. He took the notes and told me to go away. From the yard, a few minutes later, I heard him predicting the next inning to the salesmen.

A couple of days later, I phoned No. 1 again. "This is the Phantom," I said. "With two out, Branca's gonna hit Stinky Stanky with a fast ball, and then Alvin Dark's gonna send him home with a triple."

"Yeah, we know it," the fireman said in a bored voice. "We're listenin' to a short-wave too. You think you're somethin', don't you? You're Ray Morris' boy."

I knew everything was up. The next day, as a sort of final gesture, I took some more notes to the corner grocery in the third or fourth inning. Some of the old crowd was there, but the atmosphere was grim. They looked at me coldly. "Oh, man," Bozo said, "*we* know the Old Scotchman ain't at that game. He's four or five innings behind. He's makin' all that stuff up." The others grumbled and turned away. I slipped quietly out the door.

My period as a seer was over, but I went on listening to the short-wave broadcasts out of New York a few days more. Then, a little to my surprise, I went back to the Old Scotchman, and in time I found that the firemen, the bootleggers, and the few dirt farmers who had short-wave sets all did the same. From then on, accurate, up-to-the-minute baseball news was in disrepute there. I believe we all went back to the Scotchman not merely out of loyalty but because, in our great isolation, he touched our need for a great and unmitigated eloquence.

●

Joe's American Legion Junior team actually amounted to an all-star squad from all the country towns surrounding ours; it was easier to make the high school team first. On Tuesday and Friday afternoons we would ride in our red and black bus through the heavy green woods to the small crossroads towns to play the locals. The crowds would sometimes be in a foul frame of mind, especially if the farmers had got hold of the corn gourd early in the day. Since we were the "city boys," with our pictures in the *Yazoo Herald* every now and again, we were particularly ripe for all that boondocks venom. The farmers would stand around the field shouting obscenities at the "slickers," sometimes loosening up their lungs with a vicious organized whoop that sounded like a cross between a rebel yell and a redneck preacher exorcizing the Devil and all his family. More often than not, to compound the injury, we got beat. Yet far from being gracious in victory, those sons of dirt farmers rubbed our noses in our own catastrophes, taunting us with threats to whip us all over again in the outfield pasture, while their elders stood around in a group as our coach chased us into the bus and shouted, "You ain't such hot stuff, slickers!" or "Go on back to town now, boys, and get your *photos* took some more." One afternoon when I ruined the no-hitter the best pitcher in the county had going (he later made Double-A), with a broken-bat fluke into right field in the eighth inning, I thought those farmers might slice me in pieces and feed me to the boll weevils. "You proud of that little skinny hit?" one of them shouted at me, standing with his nose next to mine, and his companion picked up the broken bat that had done the evil deed and splintered it apart against a tree trunk. When we beat the same team two or three weeks later on our home field, I ran into their shortstop and catcher, two tough hardnoses, on Main Street the following Saturday. They sidled right up to me and waited there glowering, breathing in my face and not saying a word for a while. We stood nostril-to-nostril until one of them said, "You think you're somethin' don't you, bastid? Beat us at home with your crooked umpires. Next time you come see us we'll whup you 'til the shit turns green." And they did.

The next summer, when I made the Legion team, I finally came under the tutelage of Gentleman Joe, a hard taskmaster of the old school despite his unfamiliarity with "stragety," as he called it. Gentleman Joe would always have us pray before a game, and sometimes between innings when the going got rough. He was a big one for church, and began to remind me more and more of my old fourth-grade teacher. But his pep talks, back behind the shabby old grandstand of our playing field, drew on such pent-up emotions, being so full of Scriptures and things of God's earth, that I suspected we were being enlisted, not to play baseball, but to fight in the Army of the Lord.

That was the team which won the Mississippi champion-ship, beating almost everybody without much trouble. Before

the final game for the championship in Greenwood, with 4000
people waiting in the stands, Gentleman Joe delivered the best
speech of all. *"Gentlemen,"* he said, using that staple designa-
tion which earned him his nickname, "I'm just a simple farmer.
Fifteen acres is all I got, and two mules, a cow, and a lot of
mouths to feed." He paused between his words, and his eyes
watered over. "I've neglected my little crop because of this
team, and the weevils gave me trouble last year, and they're
doin' it again now. I ain't had enough rain, and I don't plan
to get much more. The corn looks so brown, if it got another
shade browner it'd flake right off. But almost every afternoon
you'd find me in my pickup on the way to town to teach you
gentlemen the game of baseball. You're fine Christian gentlemen who don't come no finer. But I saw you gettin' a little lazy
yestiddy, showin' off some to all them cute little delta girls
in the bleachers. We didn't come way up here to show off, we
come up here to *win!"* Then, his pale blue eyes flashing fire,
half whispering and half shouting, he said: "Gentlemen, I want
us to pray, and then . . . I want you to go out there on that
field and win this Miss'ippi championship! You'll be proud
of it for the rest of your lives. You'll remember it when you're
ole men. You'll think about it when you're dyin' and your
teeth are all gone. You'll be able to tell your grandchildren
about this day. Go out there, gentlemen, and *win this ball game
for your coach!"* After we prayed, and headed for that field like
a pack of wild animals, the third baseman and I shouted in unison, and we meant it: "Boys, let's get out and win for our
coach!" That fall they gave us shiny blue jackets, with "Miss.
State Champions" written on the back; I was so happy with that
jacket I almost wore it out. And when my old dog Skip died of
a heart-attack trying to outflank a flea that had plagued him
since the Roosevelt Administration, looking at me with his sad

black eyes and expiring in a sigh as old as death, that is what I wrapped him in before I took him in my arms and put him in the ground.

•

Two or three years later, when we were past the age for Legion competition, I had my last confrontation with baseball. The owner of the tire store organized a semi-pro team, made up of college and high school players from around the state. There was a popular tire that year called the "Screaming Eagle," and thus we were the Yazoo "Screaming Eagles," the pride of the delta. Out of a roster of fourteen, one made it to the major leagues, one to a Triple-A league, and two to Double-A. That team won the Deep South championship, and at the national tournament in Wichita beat the U.S. Navy and ended up close to the top.

The state league we played in, making $25 or $30 apiece a game, was composed of both delta and hill-country towns, and we played to big Saturday night crowds who had heard about the Screaming Eagles, under lights so faulty that it was difficult to see a ball coming at you in the outfield. Insects bigger than fifty-cent pieces caromed off the bulbs and zoomed around us in our isolated stations in the field, and the ground was full of holes, ruts, and countless other hazards. Playing center field one night in one of the hill towns, I went back to examine a sloping red mound of earth that served as the outfield fence; I discovered a strand of barbed wire eight or ten feet long, an old garbage can full of broken beer bottles, and a narrow hole, partially covered with Johnson grass, that looked as if it might be the home for the local rattlers. The most indigenous field of all was near a little delta town called Silver City. It was built right on a cottonfield and was owned by the two young heirs to the plantation on which it sat, one of whom later made it all the way to the New York Yankees. The grandstand would seat close to 2000 people, but the lights were so bad you had to exert all your finer perceptions to discriminate between the bugs and the balls; this took genius, and tested one's natural instincts. It was here, in the state finals, that a sinking line drive came toward me in right field, with the bases loaded and two out in the first inning; I lost track of that ball the moment it came out of the infield. A second later I felt a sharp blow on my kneecap, and then I saw the ball bouncing thirty feet away over by the bleachers. "*Get* it boy! Stomp on it! Piss on it!" the enemy bleacher section shouted gleefully, and by the time I could retrieve it three runs had scored. Between innings our pitcher, who soon would be pitching in the major leagues for the Pittsburgh Pirates, looked at me wordlessly, but with a vicious and despairing contempt. Right then, with the world before me, I promised myself that if I ever made it to those mythical cities of the North, the ones I had dreamed about in my Brooklyn cap, it would have to be with a different set of credentials.

9

I HAD GONE into high school with most of the same people who had started out with me nine years before. My best friends were the friends of my childhood, my teachers were women I had known or heard about for years — local myths with their own uinque suzerainties — and the standards of success —

good grades, versatility, joining as many organizations as
existed, and being, in the small-town Southern way, a "good old
boy" * — these were the same standards that had been set for me
ever since I first became aware that there were such things as
organized priorities. Being a "good old boy" was the hardest
priority of all. If you were intelligent and made straight A's,
got along fine with the teachers and occasionally studied your
books, it was necessary that all this be performed, among the
boys you "ran around" with, with a certain casualness that
verged on a kind of cynicism. So you would banter about
grades as if they were of no account, curse the teachers, and develop a pose of indifference to ambition in all its forms. And
you would speak the grammar of dirt-farmers and Negroes,
using *aint's* and reckless verb forms with such a natural instinct
that the right ones would have sounded high-blown and
phony, and pushing the country talk to such limits that making
it as flamboyant as possible became an end in itself.

My high school was a pleasant, settled place, a neat old brick
structure — just beginning to show the hard edges of wear,
but a little graceful and proud in its shabbiness, in the way honored old buildings in small Southern towns sometimes are. It
was at the end of the broad avenue, surrounded by tall trees
and sweet-smelling bushes and vines of a dozen varieties. The
inscription on the entrance said, "Education — Knowledge"
with a statue of Plato holding a book, and in the front lawn was
a large plaque bearing the Ten Commandments. A large section of the school has since burned down, but I cannot accept
its disappearance, so settled is the place in my memory — the
corridors with their tall ceilings, the big assembly room, the
graceful old study hall and library, the principal's office where

* See Ronnie Dugger's *Dark Star: Hiroshima Reconsidered in the Life of
Claude Eatherly of Lincoln Park, Texas*, for an amplification of this Southern
phrase.

you could often hear the muffled sounds of some country boy being paddled for missing school or writing on the walls in the boys' room. One afternoon when I was fourteen or fifteen, sitting in the study hall reading Booth Tarkington's *Seventeen*, I gazed out the window and lazily soaked in the soft spring afternoon, and all of a sudden I felt overcome for no reason at all by the likelihood of a great other world somewhere out there — of streamlined express trains and big cities, and boats sailing to other countries; the teacher snapped, "Willie, get back to that book!" Over in a corner of the big room I noticed Muttonhead Shepherd, sound asleep behind a pile of textbooks he had propped up in front of him, and Billy Rhodes writing out the words to popular songs, and Big Boy Wilkinson and Bob Pugh flipping for nickels under the table. Then that vast other world disappeared, and I turned back to Booth Tarkington, for I was content with my comfortable and easy surroundings, and would have seen no earthly reason to change them even if the opportunity had presented itself.

Like the earlier school, this one was also a seething small-town democracy. Being a "consolidated" school, it sought to educate boys and girls from out in the delta end of the county where there were no high schools; a handful of the Graball boys remained. The children of the town's middle class mingled casually with the sons of the tenant farmers, bankers' daughters dated boys from the other side of the Yazoo River, and the athletic teams — the unchallenged denominator of Yazoo High — were composed equally of the town and the country. Sports usually managed to soften the edge of violence that somehow hovered around us there, that crazy pent-up destructiveness that would sometimes erupt in fist-fights for no reason, or a frenzied and indiscriminate shoving, stomping, and kicking. Two boys in the school, over a period of two years, killed their mothers, and a third, several years younger, later killed his grandmother in an old plantation house, broke all the windows and mirrors, and then expired in a fit of well-deserved exhaustion. R——, who killed his mother during the spring floods, was a slow, inconspicuous boy who lived in the delta side of the county. He wore soiled khakis that smelled faintly of linseed oil, and Woolworth glasses so thick that his eyes inside them looked hazy — not reckless, just distorted. Fertilized and properly seeded, the dirt under his long fingernails might have yielded the equivalent of a bale to the acre, but the dirt went fallow; if the soil bank had been operating then, R—— could have brought $50 a season from the federal government simply by being around. One day he did not come to school; that afternoon they found his mother in their cabin, her head blown off by a shotgun blast. Later they found R—— hiding in the woods. V——, who lived on a small farm in the hills, played in the outfield with me on the baseball team. One afternoon after a game in Jackson I drove back to Yazoo in V——'s car; he spent the whole time describing his sexual technique with a girl from Sharkey County named Irma: "hot as the Fourth of July," he said. Like R—— before him, he failed to turn up at school for two days, and then the neighbors discovered that *his* mother was missing. The sheriff formed a posse and went to the farm to look for her. After a lengthy search they found her in the cistern, riddled with .22's. Soon after this discovery V—— came up to the front porch and sat down next to the sheriff. "Sheriff," he said, "I done it," for he had become upset with his mother when she did not let him use the car to pick up Irma. From Parchman, the state penitentiary farm, he sent a letter to one of his friends in the high school: "Don't never get sent up to *this* place," he said. That curious Mississippi apposition — of courtliness and extraordinary kindliness on the one hand, and sudden violence on the other — was a phenomenon which never occurred to me. We would laugh off the violence, engaging in it occasionally ourselves, while conducting ourselves according to the code as courteous and only slightly syrupy gentlemen, always ready with the proper word or the hospitable gesture. The apposition was merely a fact of our life, suggesting no irony. Among our elders, and in even the vaguest of "social" situations, the thing that mattered was *form*. In this schizophrenia we remained mindlessly content; and the young middle-class people of Yazoo were noted throughout the delta for their courtesies and their manners.

. •

For going to a small-town high school in the lower South in the early 1950s was a pleasant, driftless life; we dwelled on philosophical problems like "school spirit" and being "popular," and we expected a "good time" as if it were owing to us. Our superintendent was a wonderful old taskmaster, and he constantly exhorted us to settle down to work, but we failed to listen closely. We played the latest dance tunes as members of Muttonhead Shepherd's Barracuda, driving around in an open truck at night serenading the people of the town. As members of Coach Pop Thornton's forestry class we took trips out into the woods and the swamp-bottoms, classifying the trees and plants, fighting brush fires whenever we saw them and enjoying picnics on the lawns of delta plantation houses. The social life of the school, among the sons and daughters of the town people, was elaborate and highly organized, and on weekends there would be two or three parties and dances to go to, often in tuxedos and evening dresses. All the middle-sized towns of the delta were linked up in a ritualized social routine: the weekend dances in the delta country clubs or school gymnasiums, with a perambulating Negro band called the "Red-Tops" playing the music for the Memphis Shuffle, were suitable training for the feverish social life that would come later at Ole Miss or Mississippi State.

At the right times in the season we would travel from Belzoni to Greenville to Indianola to Clarksdale, wherever the Red-Tops would be on a given Saturday night; here we would learn all about the ranking delta belles, their eccentricities and their little preferences, and where they intended to go to college when the time came. Sometimes the college boys from Ole Miss or State would come down for a delta dance, lording it over the rest of us as if they owned half the delta, showing off their bejeweled fraternity pins — SAE or KA or PiKA — and drinking enough bootleg bourbon to impress anyone with their stamina and capacity. "Ya'll come back now, you *heah?*" the girls would say to us when a dance broke up. The Red-Tops would play the closing strains of "Good Night Ladies" and "Dixie," and we would be off again in the night down the straight flat road to home.

It was after one such occasion that I was witness to one of the great impromptu athletic events in delta history. It was midnight, and several of us had stopped at a run-down old roadhouse thirty miles from home for a beer. Across the room were nine or ten hardnoses, celebrating Saturday night away from their town in the red hills. We were dressed in tuxedos, and the country boys began taunting us for our gentlemanly attire; the shouts grew more vicious, and they began to question our origins, and then our manhood. They invited us, inevitably, to come over and play them in football, an enterprise in which they could beat us, they said, even if they used their cheerleaders and drum majorettes at tackle and guard. Then one of them yelled, *"Yazoo sissies!"* an incitation to violence clearer and more pernicious than a beer bottle over the head, or a glove-slap across the face. But we were outnumbered, and we contained our anger.

"See this big bastard here?" one of the hardnoses said, pointing to a tall, lean son of the earth drinking a Jax at their table.

"He's the best tailback in Miss'ippi. He can outrun all you bastards put together runnin' backerds." In our company was our
classmate, speedy halfback and sprinter, a deft little five-foot
five-incher whose father ran a car agency and who sported
around Yazoo in second-hand convertibles. Billy Bonner was
never much for schoolbooks, preferring to memorize the words
to all the latest popular songs, but only three weeks before he
had been clocked on the hundred in 9.9 with the wind against
him. Immediately one of our friends shouted back: "See this
little bastard right here? He can outrun that skinny tailback of
yours just hoppin' on one foot." As if to give substance to this
contention, Billy Bonner stood up, waving a beer bottle, and
yelled: "I challenge that skinny tailback to a *foot*-race."

Suddenly there was a turmoil of agitation. Bets were offered, and the pot went up to twenty dollars. Further insults
were exchanged as we departed for our car, followed by the hardnoses headed for their pickup truck. We drove south and
stopped at a dark and desolate stretch on Highway 49. Our
antagonists parked their trucks in the middle of the highway
and left the headlights on; we parked our car a hundred yards
down the road and left *our* lights on. Then we backtracked
down the road to the truck, which would serve as the starting
point, and helped Billy Bonner out of his shoes, his tuxedo coat,
and his suspenders. He finished the dregs of a beer and tossed
it into the cottonfield. The country tailback, meantime, shed
his jacket and took off his boots, while his friends slapped him
on the back and whispered encouragement. "Whip that little
worm," one of them said, "an' we'll have free beer up till
church." Then we and our opponents joined in separate groups
of two, one at the starting line, myself and several others at the
finish, under the headlights of our car down the highway.

From the hundred yards up the road I could see Billy Bonner
and the skinny tailback crouched down in the starting posi-

tion. The night was completely still; the stars shone stark and clear over the great delta, and the earth around us stretched away dark, vast, and impenetrable into endless stalks of dead cotton and thin rutted furrows. Not a car was in sight, and I squatted down at the finish line, feeling very small and negligible in the cold autumn silence. Then I heard the voices of several boys shouting *Go!* I heard the slap-slap of bare feet on the flat asphalt, and out of the delta mist I spotted Billy Bonner and his foe churning away in desperate vengeance. A dozen shouts of encouragement went up, and little Billy Bonner, swift as a bushy-tailed rabbit, moved several yards in front. Suddenly I heard a mighty moan from Billy Bonner, and in the reflection of the headlights I saw something that chilled my blood: Billy's trousers, bereft of suspenders, were slowly falling down! Billy moaned again, and as the tailback regained the lead, he tugged at his pants and caught them with his right hand. He had lost his balance, but now he had it again, and clutching his pants in his hand he moved on, a small streak of terror on Highway 49. He caught up with that tailback at what must have been 75 yards, then moved relentlessly ahead and crossed the finish line with a good five yards to spare. We congregated around our victorious friend and congratulated him. "It woulda been a 9.7," Billy Bonner said, "if it hadn'ta been for that damn *tux*." Over near the cottonfield the country boys gathered in a circle, bitching among themselves. Then their leader came over and gave us the $20. "That friggin' little bastard can *run*," he said, and we moved our vehicles to the side of the road, and we all had one more beer, in the sudden fraternity of well-earned victory in the face of adversity. Then, with reluctant handshakes, we went our separate ways, they east into the hills, we south into the delta.

Besides these accepted social indulgences, I was marked out for "versatility." At fourteen I was an editorial writer for the Yazoo High *Flashlight*, and on its pages in 1948 I wrote an article praising J. Strom Thurmond and Fielding L. Wright of the Dixiecrat Party for President and Vice-President, and urging all students to be sure their parents voted Dixiecrat to protect the Mississippi Way of Life. Later I worked my way up to the editorship, where my *Flashlight* prose resounded to strange, esoteric rhythms, supplemented with ambitious, unheard-of words.

I also worked part-time for the local radio station, a 500-watt affair beamed into the delta, where I became a disc-jockey, news analyst, and sports announcer. *"This is WAZF,"* I would say at the station breaks, *"1230 on your dial, with studios high above the Taylor and Roberts Feed and Seed Store, in downtown Yazoo City, the Gateway to the Delta."* The station occupied several tiny rooms on the second floor, and I learned to operate the elaborate control-board and the turntables. Three country boys worked full-time as announcers; sometimes they would give up during their newscasts when a big word came along in the wire copy and say, "Well, I just can't pronounce *this* one." They were eager, nonetheless, to put on a good show. Two or three of them would get in the broadcast room as one of their fellows read the news reports. They would make unusual faces, or give the "bird," or do anything to try to get their associate to break down while he read the news. Their colleague at the microphone, with his fingers on the control switch to turn it on and off, would say: "While in Washington today, Alger Hiss' attorney said . . . *fuck you, you bastards* . . . that the latest revelations . . . *go fart, Hancock* . . . of Mr. Chambers were . . . *worse than a turd in a snowstorm* . . . not to be taken seriously." On quiet Sunday mornings when I was the only announcer in the station, a quartet of Negro singers would casually drop in and ask if they could sing; I would bring them into the room and interview them, and mind the monitor while they did their spirituals. One afternoon, when everyone else was in Memphis for a radio convention, I warned our listeners there would be thirty seconds of silence, during which time I had to dash three stores up the street to broadcast the auctioning of the season's first cotton bale. When I returned to the studio, the phone rang, and a voice said, "Where you been, man? You been off the air thirty minutes!" I ran a disc-jockey program some nights, called "Darkness on the Delta," and one evening, for no logical reason in communications programming, I devoted the whole hour to classical music — Beethoven and Brahms and Bach — while the phone rang incessantly and the callers demanded I play some *real* music. In the middle of a Beethoven symphony, which I had dug out of the dusty end of the files, a hardnose phoned and said, "Play some Tennessee Ernie, you son-of-a-bitch, or we're gonna come down there and tear that place up. We're cruising up and down Main Street, and we're fed up." I played Tennessee Ernie until sign-off time.

In the spring and summer, between our own games, I would broadcast the country baseball games, sometimes wearing my own baseball uniform after an earlier game. On the day of a big semi-pro tournament, when the rain kept interrupting the play, I was on the air for fifteen straight hours. For want of anything to say, I took to drawing the dirt-farmers and the truck-drivers out of the grandstands into the press box, interviewing them about the baseball rule book, about individual players like the toothless pitcher Eckert and the southpaw catcher Smith, even about how their crops were doing. "Chewing Gum" Smith, who drove the laundry truck for the American Steam Laundry, and I talked for an hour about the various teams in the county, and Gentleman Joe came up and talked about *his* crops. By the end of the day I had interviewed half the people in the grandstand — including two policemen, a veterinarian, a cotton-duster, the mayor, and the county agent

— and had even brought up the men who sold hotdogs and beer to see how their business was coming. When I discovered there was a scout for the Philadelphia Phillies in the crowd, I summoned him for an interview:

"Tell me, Mr. Larson," I said, "what do you think of the brand of baseball we play down here in Mississippi?"

"Speaking with frankness," Larson replied, "I don't think much of it."

As part of these activities with the mass media, in the summer I served as "public relations director" to the town's recreation park, where I was chief assistant to "Coach" Buck, the high school football coach, and supervisor of a radio program each afternoon. The football coach and I would collect a carload of children every day at four and go to the radio station for our daily broadcast. We would interview them about softball games, ping-pong matches, shuffleboard and horseshoe throws, and list the various winners and their scores. The program was a hardship, however, on those days when no children at all turned up at the park; then the football coach and I would have to talk to each other on the air for half an hour, about anything we could think of that would fill up that time: once we talked for five minutes about a ping-pong table we had just nailed back together, and then about a bark blight a certain elm tree near the shuffleboard had caught, and another time we discussed at some length why the Nicholas children, who lived just across the street from the park, failed to show up on that day. The football coach surmised that they had probably gone out of town for a while; no, I speculated, I had seen them that morning eating popsicles in front of a colored grocery store. On one particular day when it had rained for several hours and no children came to the park, the football coach and I cruised all over town in his car looking for a child to interview; we had run out of talk ourselves, and anybody would do.

Ten minutes before our program was to go on the air, we sighted a little boy walking up the main street in the rain. It was Donnie Simpson, who spoke with a stutter. The coach drove the car up to the curb and shouted, "Donnie, come get in with us." The little boy dutifully got in the car, and the coach whispered to me, "Don't let him go now we've got him." We trundled him down to the station and interviewed him for twenty minutes. Such was my intellectual motion at age fourteen.

•

Our English teacher was the wife of the owner of the barber shop. She had grown up in a small town in Arkansas, and had even spent some time in New York City before settling down in Mississippi. In my first year in high school she lectured us for three weeks on Anglo-Saxon England, and on the Normans, and then on Chaucer. She made us take notes, because this was the way it was done in college, and she said she wanted her students to go to college someday. She had us read *The Canterbury Tales*, Shakespeare, George Eliot, Thackeray, and Dickens, and Byron, Shelley, Keats, Coleridge, Wordsworth, Tennyson, and Browning. Then she would have us give reports on the books and poems we had read; woe to the unfortunate student who tried to memorize the outlines of one of her novels by reading it in Classic Comics. She was unsparing in her criticism, and she got rougher as we moved into the higher grades. I must have parsed a hundred English sentences on the blackboard of that room, trying to come to reasonable terms with gerundives, split infinitives, verb objects, and my own dangling prepositions. It was the one course in that school where great quantities of homework were essential: novels, poems, themes, grammar, spelling. She would give the assignment at the end of every class, and a big groan would fill the room. She would say, "Well, you want to learn, don't you? Or maybe you *want*

to stay saps all your life." She had little patience with the slow
ones, or the ones who refused to work, but for those who tried,
or who performed with some natural intelligence, she was the
most loyal and generous of souls. She would talk about their
virtues to everyone in town who would listen, and sometimes
take them home to have dinner with her and her husband and
show them colored pictures of the Lake Country or New England or Greenwich Village.

Among many of the students she was a scorned woman. They
bad-talked her behind her back, tried to catch her in contradictions about her travels, and rumored that she worked people
that hard out of plain cruelty; I myself sometimes joined in this
talk, for it was fashionable. Although she had been teaching
there for many years, the students never would dedicate the
school yearbook to her, out of simple retaliation, until my senior year when a friend and I managed to get the dedication for
her. In the school assembly when the dedication was announced, her acceptance speech was a model of graciousness.
She talked about the honor that had been done her, and about
the generation of students she had taught in the school, and
about how she wanted to stay there in Yazoo the rest of her life.

There must be many another small town in America with
women like her — trying, for whatever reason, to teach small-
town children the hard basics of the language, and something of the literature it has produced — unyielding in their
standards, despairing of mediocrity, and incorruptible, and
perhaps for all these reasons, scorned and misunderstood. But
as for me, I had a long, painful way to go before the things she
tried to teach me could take hold. I read her books and parsed
her sentences to stay on her good side and to get A's. The books
themselves meant little to me, and made almost no impression
at all on the way I lived or how I saw experience. I memorized
the rules of the language, but my own prose style was like a

Mack truck churning up mud. I did not understand my own intelligence, and even if I had I would not have known what to do with it. Eliot, Chaucer, Keats — they were mere exercises for me, lacking in purpose or substance. I was extraordinarily dependent on the judgment of my elders and on my good standing with my own contemporaries. All the things I wrote and read in high school I relegated to the farther crevices of my mind. I was so deeply rooted in the attitudes and values of the small place where I was growing up that only the most severe physical and emotional removal could ever detach me from my own self-satisfactions.

In the summer before my final year in high school I was chosen as one of the school's two delegates to attend "Boys' State," a mock state government which would convene in Jackson, sponsored by the American Legion. I went to the town library to read up on Mississippi politics. One of the books I read was a plea for a new state constitution — "to bring Mississippi into the modern world," the author argued. When I visited the lawyer who sponsored us to discuss what my "project" at Boys' State would be, I said I thought I would "try to get a new constitution." I told him I had read that the present one was out of date. "It may be," the lawyer said, "but that's why we shouldn't change it. It's the best protection we have to our Mississippi Way of Life." I let the matter drop as a matter of course.

Elsewhere that year, in one of the national magazines, I read an interview with Linda Darnell, or one of the famous actresses, and she said that a man named Thomas Wolfe was her favorite writer, and wrote straight out of the South of an earlier generation. My curiosity was aroused, so I went again to the library and asked the librarian for *Look Homeward Angel*, which Linda Darnell had especially recommended. The librarian said, "I have

it, but you shouldn't read it. It's too bad a book." I let that
drop too.

•

There were other reasons I allowed Thomas Wolfe and the
Mississippi Constitution to take care of themselves, for I was
one of the few boys in school without a steady girl. This had
disastrous consequences during the round of parties which always accompanied the ending of an academic year, when the
host or hostess would put all the steady couples together and
then match the unpaired ones in the most un-Christian arrangement. Hence I found myself escorting the rejects. I grew to
dread those parties, and to silently promise myself something
better, for in a small Southern town of that day a permanent
sweetheart when you were sixteen was indispensable not just
for the glandular juices, which were central enough, but as a
working principle against being taken advantage of. For several celebrations at the end of that year I was paired off with
the ugliest girl in the class; it was hard just to look at her straight
in the face, and she talked such an endless prattle that I learned
to wind her up when the wind was with me and let her go so I
could think to myself about other things. That school, in the
Mississippi tradition, had some of the prettiest girls I have ever
seen, and when I showed up at the barbecues and the dances
with my partner and saw my friends with their girls, I wanted
to hide mine in the shrubbery and the pecan trees and keep her
there all night. I would deposit her for a while with the other
girls and walk over to talk with Bubba Barrier or Muttonhead
Shepherd, and one of them would say, "Well, she bit you yet
tonight?" or "When you gonna get her *inoculated?*" or "What
kind of bait you use, roaches or grub-worms?" One night I
kept putting off going to pick her up, driving around town by

myself. I ran into one of my friends, who leaned out the window of his car and said, "Say, ole Miz Pinson's *lookin'* for you." Sure enough, the girl's mother was going all over town trying to find me because I was late. So I went and collected her before her mother had time to get back home, and when we got to the party Bob Pugh whispered in my ear, "Did the vet charge much rent?"

But that summer brought a felicitous change, for I feel deeply in love, with a fifteen-year-old blond beauty from the upper end of the county. I gave her my senior class ring, and I was filled with pride when she marched in front of the forty-eight piece high school band as a majorette, twirling her baton and strutting in her tight satin uniform. She had light green eyes and an extraordinary body, and her taste in Nat "King" Cole records was the best in town.

Her father owned a monstrous slice of delta cotton land called Belle Prairie, so black and brooding that on a gray November day it looked more the far side of some forgotten planet than Walter Prescott Webb's kind of prairie. It was so far to the north end of Yazoo County that it remains even now isolated from the civilizing influences of the county seat, including the services of Southern Bell Telephone. I was constantly driving back and forth between there and town, taking the turn off U.S. 49 onto the rutted dirt road that wound crazily through the rich cotton fields, to the end of the road and the old antebellum house that sat right on the banks of the Yazoo.

At night, driving home from a dance or a movie at the Dixie Theater, that land rustled, moaned, and made apocalyptic noises; it was the *noisiest* land I ever knew. We would pull off the road into a clump of trees, and when the weather was cold our torrid, thwarted lovemaking would cause the windows to fog over with mist. One night we were lying there in a big tangle on the front seat, when all of a sudden we heard at close range such a God-awful blast that we sprang bolt upright in a crazy fright. Outside the window we saw Sonny Bonney and John Abner Reeves, doubled over with laughter. They had been out coon hunting and spotted my car, sneaked up to within six feet of it and fired both barrels of their shotguns into the air. Such were the hazards of "parking" in the delta.

We would "double-date" with others in our group, and every Saturday night that we were not off to some delta dance we went to the "midnight show" in town. Often, for big sports or band events in other towns, one of the coaches would drive us in the red-and-black bus, "The Chieftain," and let the steady couples sit together. Sometimes these trips would be up into the delta; and on the slow spring afternoons one could see, along the straight slab of highway, some Negro family walking toward somewhere — the man and woman far ahead, the children, barefoot and dusty, loitering behind. The children would catch sight of the big bus whipping toward them and they would stop in their tracks and stare — no waving or shouting, just a stolid look of intense curiosity. Other trips would be to hill towns: Canton, Kosciusko, Philadelphia, in the pine pockets and the red clay, or farther over into the dull foothills of the Appalachians. On the way home, late at night, there would be singing and kissing, and if it were spring you could watch out the front window of the big old bus as the bugs splattered softly on its windshield, tattooing the glass with delta things.

On football weekends, when some of the parents went away to Memphis or Oxford or Starkville or New Orleans, the steady couples would take over one of the empty houses in town. First all the lights would go out and the candles would be lit, then in would come a big washtub full of "schoolboy" — a mixture of gin, vodka, and beer, and orange, pineapple, and grapefruit juice, with whole oranges and tangerines added, laced at the end with three or four cups of pure alcohol. Then the dancing would start, and the rubbing up together; Tony Bennett singing "Tenderly," or Nat "King" Cole with "Unforgettable" would moan away on the phonograph, and there would be the light tinkling of ice in the tall glasses of "schoolboy." I was with the little plantation girl I loved, and old friends who had been friends for as long as I could remember, in a town as familiar and settled to me as anything I would ever know. I would never wander very far away.

10

ONE DAY that spring, two months before I was to graduate from high school, my father gave me some unexpected advice. He was reading the *Commercial Appeal* in our front room, and he turned to me and told me, quite simply, to get the hell out of Mississippi. I do not quite know why. Perhaps he knew something about doom, though his argument, he said, was based on a lack of *opportunity*.

At first I ignored this advice. I was obsessed with Belle Prairie and the blond belle who graced its gullies, swamps, and tenant shacks. I had my heart set, at the age of seventeen, on entering Mississippi's educated landed gentry — by taking a degree at Ole Miss, as all my friends planned to do, and by returning to that plantation with my majorette, to preside there on the banks of the Yazoo over boll weevils big enough to wear dog tags, pre-Earl Warren darkies, and the young squirearchy from the plantations abutting on Carter, Eden, Holly Bluff, Sidon and Tchula.

I saw no reason to leave. I was athlete, sports announcer, valedictorian, and, my greatest pride, editor of the *Flashlight*. I knew Mississippi and I loved what I saw. I had just been voted most likely to succeed. In Yazoo I knew every house and every tree in the white section of town. Each street and hill was like a map on my consciousness; I loved the contours of its land, and the slow changing of its seasons. I was full of the regional graces and was known as a perfect young gentleman. I was pleasant, enthusiastic, and happy. On any question pertaining to God or man I would have cast my morals on the results of a common plebiscite of the white voters of Yazoo County. "One shudders at the thought of the meaninglessness of life," I read years later in *Winesburg, Ohio*, in a moment when I was trying to remember these years, "while at the same instant, and if the people of the town are his people, one loves life so intensely that tears come into the eyes."

Yet more than being desperately in love, I was sorrowfully ignorant — ignorant of myself, ignorant of the world of moving objects I was about to enter. One hundred miles to the north of Yazoo, Faulkner was writing his great tales of violence and the destruction of honor. In the spring of my senior year, when I was at Oxford for a convention, I watched as they filmed the jail scenes for the movie *Intruder in the Dust*, yet this did not inspire me much one way or the other. Had I known that great books were for one's own private soul rather than mere instrumentalities for achieving those useless trinkets on which all American high schools, including small ones in Mississippi, base their existence, perhaps I would have found in Faulkner some dark chord, some suggestion of how this land had shaped me, how its isolation and its guilt-ridden past had already settled so deeply into my bones. Unfortunately this was to come later. Then I joined easily and thoughtlessly in the Mississippi middle-class consensus that Faulkner, the chronicler and moralist, was out for the Yankee dollar.

My first seventeen years had been lived rich in experience — in sensual textures, in unusual confrontations. I had moved easily among many kinds of people, I had seen something of cruelty and madness, and I had survived fundamentalist religion. My father had taught me the woods; from everyone I had had love. The town in which I had grown up had yet to be touched by the great television culture, or by the hardening emotions and the defensive hostilities unloosed by the Supreme Court in 1954. Something was left, if but an oblique recollection: a Southern driftlessness, a closeness to the earth, a sense of time standing still, a lingering isolation from America's relentless currents of change and homogeneity. Something else also remained, some innocent and exposed quality that made possible, in the heart of a young and vulnerable boy, an allegiance and a love for a small, inconsequential place. Only retrospect would tell me I was to take something of these things with me forever, through my maturing into my manhood. But then I could not connect them, because I had yet to go beyond the most fundamental awareness of myself.

What was it, then, that led me to leave, to go to a place where I did not know a soul, and eventually to make such a sharp break with my own past that I still suffer from the pain of that alienation? Was there some small grain of sand there, something abrasive and unrecognized in my perception of things, some hidden ambition and independence that finally led me away from everything I knew and honored? Was there something in me that needed some stark removal from my deepest loyalties?

In trying to recapture a turning point in one's life at such an age, it is almost impossible to ascribe tangible motives to some great change in one's direction, to isolate a thought, or a decision. But there are a handful of things that stand out so clearly that they become, after many years, almost symbol. They embody in retrospect the very substance of one's existence at a given moment. They may be fleeting recollections, chance encounters, the thread of an old thought, but they are revealing in themselves, and they become more than memory.

My father took out one day for Austin, Texas, to see the campus of what we had sometimes heard was the best and certainly the biggest state university in the South. Four or five days later, my friend Bubba Barrier and I, quite by chance, ran into him in the lobby of the Edwards House in Jackson. He had just returned. "That's one hell of a place they got out there," he said. They had a main building 30 stories high, a baseball field dug right out of stone, artificial moonlight for street lamps, the biggest state capitol in the Republic, and the goddamndest student newspaper you ever saw. "I think you ought to go to school out there," he said. "Can't nuthin' in *this* state match it."

I would wander off by myself to that place of my childhood, the town cemetery. Here I would walk among all those graves I knew that had given me such a sense of the town when I was a boy — of the reprobates and early settlers, the departed gospelists and bootleggers, and all the boys we had buried with the American Legionnaires. I cannot remember what my thoughts were on these excursions, except that I had the most dramatic conception of imminent departure. Something different was stirring around in my future, and I would brood over the place where I was and some place where I would end up, and for days I carried a map of the University of Texas in my shirt pocket. I was bathing in self-drama; perhaps it was my *imagination*, which had never failed me even as a child, that sought some unknown awakening.

I had been commissioned to write the prophecy of the Class of 1952 of Yazoo High School, and I delivered it on class day that spring in the school auditorium. Afterward one of the senior class teachers cornered me and said it was the most disgusting thing she had ever heard, that only the day before she had recommended me to two FBI agents as promising material for that agency, but that she was going to write a letter telling them I was unfit for their service. These were unusual words for me, the favorite of every teacher in school and the winner of the American Legion Citizenship Award, but on rereading this curious statement I saw what had aroused her. I had consigned each member of the fifty-two-member graduating class to destruction. Honest Ed Upton, the salutatorian, was to die an agonizing death in quicksand in a Mississippi swamp. Billy Bonner would be shot down by Italians in the streets of Brooklyn. All the others were to go the way of violence, treachery, corruption, and oblivion, except myself, their chronicler, who did not figure in the predictions. "You just as well get out of here to Texas," that teacher said, "because it's pretty clear you don't appreciate the people around you." On graduation night in the school gymnasium, on a wet spring night in June, my comrades who were doomed to destruction and I stood finally on the podium and sang the last lines of our alma mater: "Yazoo, Yazoo, in closing let us say . . . that forever and a day . . . we'll be thinking of you, Yazoo . . . Yazoo."

And one cold, dark morning in the early fall, sick with leaving for the first time the place where I grew up, and the blond majorette whom I had said goodbye to for the first and as it proved the last time in my old DeSoto car near the railroad tracks the night before, I caught a Southern Trailways bus in Vicksburg for Austin. My mother, as the story always goes, cried, and my father looked thin as death as the bus pulled out to cross the great bridge into Louisiana. I turned on the red portable radio the local radio station had given me as a farewell present, and I remember the song that came on over in Louisiana, a popular song of that time:

> Fly the ocean in a silver plane,
> See the jungle when it's wet with rain,
> Just remember 'til you're home again
> You belong to me.

PART TWO

Texas

1

WHAT STRIKES ME most in reading books like Alfred Kazin's haunting poetic reminiscences of boyhood in an immigrant Jewish neighborhood in the East, is the vast gulf which separates that kind of growing up and the childhood and adolescence of those of us who came out of the towns of the American South and Southwest a generation later. With the Eastern Jewish intellectuals who play such a substantial part in American cultural life, perhaps in the late 1960s a dominant part, the struggle as they grew up in the 1930s was for one set of ideas over others, for a fierce acceptance or rejection of one man's theories or another man's poetry — and with all this a driving determination to master the language which had not been their parents' and to find a place in a culture not quite theirs. For other Eastern intellectuals and writers whom I later was to know, going to the Ivy League schools involved, if not a finishing, then a deepening of perceptions, or of learning, or culture.

But for so many of us who converged on Austin, Texas, in the early 1950s, from places like Karnes City or Big Spring or Abilene or Rockdale or Yazoo City, the awakening we were to experience, or to have jolted into us, or to undergo by some more subtle chemistry, did not mean a mere finishing or deepening, and most emphatically did not imply the victory of one set of ideologies over another, one way of viewing literature or politics over another, but something more basic and simple. This was the acceptance of ideas themselves as something worth living by. It was a matter, at the age of eighteen or nineteen, not of discovering *certain* books, but the simple *presence* of books, not the nuances of idea and feeling, but idea and feeling on their own terms. It is this late coming to this kind of awareness that still gives the intellectuals from the small towns of our region a hungry, naïve quality, as opposed to the sharp-elbowed over-intellectuality of some Easterners, as if those from down there who made it were lucky, or chosen, out of all the disastrous alternatives of their isolated lower- or middle-class upbringings, to enjoy and benefit from the fruits of simply being educated and liberal-minded.

What we brought to the University of Texas in the 1950s, to an enormous, only partially formed state university, was a great awe before the splendid quotations on its buildings and the walls of its libraries, along with an absolutely prodigious insensitivity as to what they implied beyond decoration. Minds awakened slowly, painfully, and with pretentious and damaging inner searches. Where an Alfred Kazin at the age of nineteen might become aroused in the subway by reading a review by John Chamberlain in the *New York Times* and rush to his office to complain, we at eighteen or nineteen were only barely beginning to learn that there *were* ideas, much less ideas to arouse one from one's self. If places like City College or Columbia galvanized the young New York intellectuals already drenched in literature and polemics, the University of Texas had, in its halting, unsure, and often frivolous way, to teach those of us with good minds and small-town high school diplomas that we were intelligent human beings, with minds and hearts of our own that we might learn to call our own, that there were some things, many things — ideas, values, choices of action — worth committing one's self to and fighting for, that a man in some instances might become morally committed to honoring every manifestation of individual conscience and courage. Yet the hardest task at the University of Texas, as many of us were to learn, was to separate all the extraneous and empty things that can drown a young person there, as all big universities can drown its young people, from the few simple things that are worth living a life by. Without wishing to sound histrionic, I believe I am thinking of something approaching the Western cultural tradition; yet if someone had suggested that to me that September night in 1952, as I stepped off the bus in Austin to be greeted by three fraternity men anxious to look me over, I would have thought him either a fool or a con man.

I emerged from that bus frightened and tired, after having come 500 miles non-stop over the red hills of Louisiana and the pine forests of East Texas. The three men who met me — appalled, I was told later, by my green trousers and the National Honor Society medal on my gold-plated watch chain — were the kind that I briefly liked and admired, for their facility at small talk, their clothes, their manner, but whom I soon grew to deplore and finally to be bored by. They were the kind who made fraternities tick, the favorites of the Dean of Men at the time, respectable B or C-plus students, tolerable athletes, good with the Thetas or the Pi Phis; but one would find later, lurking there inside of them despite — or maybe because of — their good fun and jollity, the ideals of the insurance salesman and an aggressive distrust of anything approaching thought. One of them later told me, with the seriousness of an early disciple, that my table manners had become a source of acute embarrassment to all of them. That night they drove me around the campus, and they were impressed that I knew from my map-reading where the University library was, for two of them were not sure.

·

It was early fall, with that crispness in the air that awakened one's senses and seemed to make everything wondrously alive. My first days there I wandered about that enormous campus, mingling silently with its thousands of nameless students. I walked past the fraternity and sorority houses, which were like palaces to me with their broad porches and columns and patios, and down "The Drag" with its bookstores and restaurants, a perfectly contained little city of its own. On a slight rise dominating the place was a thirty-story skyscraper called the "Tower," topped with an edifice that was a mock Greek temple; the words carved on the white sandstone said, *Ye Shall Know the Truth and the Truth Shall Make You Free,*" causing me to catch my breath in wonder and bafflement. That first morning I took the elevator to the top, and looked out on those majestic purple hills to the west, changing to lighter shades of blue or a deeper purple as wisps of autumn clouds drifted around the sun; this, they would tell me, was the Great Balcones Divide, where the South ended and the West began, with its stark, severe landscape so different from any I had known before. I saw the state capitol, only a few blocks to the south, set on its sloping green acres, its pink granite catching the morning light, and away to the east the baseball field dug into the native rock, and the football stadium, the largest and most awesome I had ever seen. Then down again to the campus, where all the furious construction and demolition was going on, and where the swarms of students back for another year greeted each other with such shouts and screams of delight, war-whoops, and hoo-haws and wild embracing, and twangy "hello there's" with the "r's" exploited as nowhere else in the South, that I suddenly felt unbearably displaced and alone. Everything around me was brisk, burgeoning, *metropolitan*. It was bigger than Memphis when I was twelve.

I was a desperately homesick Mississippi boy of seventeen,

and the life I saw about me was richer and more flamboyant than anything I had known before. There was a kind of liberality of spirit there, an *expansiveness* which, as I was one day to learn, is one of the most distinctive qualities of Texans, even though it can be directed toward things that do not deserve being expansive about. There was something frenetic, almost driven, about the organized pursuits of these Texas students; even by the gregarious standards of my own high school there was not enough loneliness in them, not enough disaffection; they moved about in packs, and they would organize a committee — a service committee, a social committee, a committee on committees — on the merest excuse. Today this characteristic, which reaches far into adult life, seems most curious in a state which in most established quarters glorifies, perhaps more than any other region of America, some mystical individualism, with sources more contemporaneous with Goldwater and Buckley than Rousseau.

Yet I myself shared that compulsion to join, and join I did, everything from the Freshman Council to student government to the ROTC Band. This, I thought, was the mark of success, something one assumed without dispute. Versatility, gregariousness, the social graces, these were the important things, just as they had been in Yazoo; these were what the University of Texas could provide, only bigger and better. Yet as time passed I would grow progressively more lonely, more contemptuous of this organized anarchy, more despairing of the ritualized childishness and grasping narcissism of the fraternity life.

This taste of fraternities had a curious effect. The experience of seeing grown men twisting paper-mache into flowers for a float, or of social lions advising how best to impress the sorority girls, at least gave one some early insight into priorities. And in that day this fraternity was the best one there; the further one got down the scale, the more insufferable were the practices. The new members who had not been initiated were called out at all hours, for "exercise rallies," "walks," or "serenades," the latter custom consisting of group singing at midnight to some sorority; while the idiotic fraternity songs were sung, the girls on their balconies or porches would giggle or squeal their approval, with proper gradations of intensity depending on how close to the top those doing the serenading came on the social register. Some fraternities beat their new members with paddles and other instruments, or gave elaborate "pig" parties, in which each member was expected to bring the ugliest girl he could manage to get for the evening. Around the campus one got to know of the "perennial" fraternity boys; one in particular was over thirty years old, registered each semester for the minimum of courses and seldom if ever went to class, his purpose being to indulge as freely as possible in all aspects of the Greek Life. He escorted girls twelve years his junior, and gave bright little lectures on how to handle yourself in the best social circumstances. Once he turned on me for some minor trespass and said, "I wonder when you're going to grow up." Another "perennial" came to school each fall semester on what amounted to an athletic scholarship; he ran a service station in San Antonio, and because he was adept at throwing a football, his group paid his tuition so he could play on the intramural touch football team. Then he would drop out of school after the season and just before examinations.

I was unhappy and insecure with the fraternity men. I and another young country boy from a small South Texas town walked the six blocks from Brackenridge Hall for dinner with the brothers each evening, dreading what organized torments they might have in store for us next. Our talk was bitter, but mainly frightened. He had the courage of his fear to get out, but I did not, for it would have implied some failure in me, and I would not admit failure even when I felt it. I simply went less

and less and became more unhappy, until late in my junior year
when I was beginning to campaign for the editorship of the
student newspaper; with cynicism in my heart and the tally of
the fraternity and sorority vote in my secret ledger, I sought
their support. The difference was that in my first year I would
not have had the self-awareness to be cynical, because I did not
know that cynicism existed.

Some excellent men were involved in this debilitating preoccupation. Their names were Mohr, Little, Penn, Nagle,
Jacoby, Higgins, Eastland, Eckert, Williams, Dahlin, Finch,
Bailey, Ogden, Schmucker, Voekel, and a dozen others, most
with appropriately vivid and wildly Texan nicknames — they
were better by far as individuals than the organization to which
they gave allegiance. For the organization itself, within the
broader social framework of the fraternity and sorority system
on a big state university campus, was pernicious and destructive
— too encouraging of petty provincial snobbism, simple human
waste, and downright prejudice, too demanding on its immature
young people of social appurtenances and the trappings of respectability. At its worst this system could be cruel and despicably
smug; at its best it was merely an easy substitute for more intelligent and mature forms of energy.

Early in that year I was taken on my first "walk" by a campus
"service organization." It was late on a Saturday night in the
fall; the members blindfolded me and put me in their car. We
drove for miles, until the concrete gave out, and down some interminable gravel road until we stopped. They took all my
clothes, including my shoes, and tied me to a tree. After I heard
the car drive away, I worked the rope loose and started down the
road, walking in the middle of it to avoid the beer cans, broken
whiskey bottles, and other debris that always clutter the sides of
Texas roads. It was the last indignity: homesick, cold, alone,
naked, and lost, off on some meaningless adolescent charade.

That afternoon I had escorted to the football game a gat-toothed brunette they had picked out for me, from a "wealthy family in Dallas" the thirty-two-year-old perennial had said, and she had spent the whole time making fun of the way I drawled! Finally, at the top of a lonely hill, I got my bearings. Looking down from the hill I caught sight of Austin in the cold night air: the Tower, lit orange because of the day's football victory, and the state capitol, and the curved boulevards faintly outlined in the pale blue artificial moonlight from the old street lamps. There it all was, miles away, and I was bruised and tired, but that sky-line almost struck me over with its strange open beauty, the clear open beauty of the Southwest plains. Then, all of a sudden, I got mad, probably the maddest I had ever been in my whole life — at homesickness, at blond majorettes, at gat-toothed Dallas girls, at fraternities, at twangy accents, at my own help-less condition. *"I'm better than this sorry place,"* I said to my-self, several times, and be damned if I didn't believe it. Then I started walking again, having made a kind of toga of a greasy piece of canvas I had found by the side of the road. Two hours later I reached the concrete and flagged down the third car that came past, and got back to my dormitory just as the sun began to appear.

•

After an appropriate time for this kind of activity; there was a fraternity institution known as "hell week," a four-day ordeal of petty torture and sadism which preceded "initiation" as a full-fledged brother. As victims of this institution, we were made to go sleepless for most of the four days, and were forced to wear burlap under our usual clothes when we went to class during the daytime, causing a most agonizing itch that would have made any lecture intolerable. At night the established brothers amused themselves with a great variety of entertainment. One night we were herded into a large room, and for an hour or more our seniors, who had chosen as usual not to be in libraries or at lectures, poured molasses, castor oil, chicken feed, and sand on us. Then several hundred eggs were brought in, in large cardboard boxes, and from the far side of the room the brothers used us as moving targets. I was chosen as the special object for this diversion; a relentless stream of eggs smashed against me, and I was covered with the oozing yellow yolk, which stuck against the molasses and chicken feed and castor oil in a great soggy mess. Finally the brothers, having sated themselves, began drifting out of the room to watch television. The last to leave was an ex-Marine who chose to spend as much of his leisure time as possible on such scholarly pursuits. He was about to depart on what was colloquially known as a "fuck-date," and hence he was dressed immaculately in a navy-blue suit and bow tie. As we were being herded out of another door, I sighted an unbroken egg on the floor near me. I picked it up, took aim on the ex-Marine just as he was departing, let the egg fly, dashed through the back door, and heard the words: "*Hot* — damned!" The egg had smashed against the back of his neck, and the yolk had oozed under his shirt. This accomplishment proved to be the noblest of my first semester.

On the last night of "hell week" I was again blindfolded and taken on a drive by three of the senior members. Again we went up a gravel road, and I was led from the car and up a grassy, rolling hill. "Kneel right here," one of them said, in the tones of a Baptist preacher announcing a hymn. "Don't take the blindfold off for three minutes, and then when you see where you are, meditate for a while. Meditate *seriously*. This is your last responsibility as a pledge. Tomorrow you become one of us." I followed his instructions: when I heard the car leave I took off the blindfold. I was in the middle of a cemetery, kneeling on a grave; the gravestone identified the occupant as one of the founding members of the fraternity. "Well, hot shit," I said to myself, and went home to sleep for the first time in four days.

The next day the initiation was a traditional ceremony handed down by the generations. It was full of such garbled mumbo-jumboes and high-flown adolescent sputterings, all thrown together in some uneasy overlay of illiteracy, that I was reminded of the way Huck Finn and Tom Sawyer had negotiated their own private blood-oaths as pirates. It was so juvenile that the Ku Klux Klan, in contrast, might have resembled the American Association of University Professors. But when the new brothers were lined up and presented with fraternity pins, I noticed that several of my fellow novitiates were crying, apparently from the impressiveness of it all. I could not avoid admitting to myself that, even though I was fresh out of a small town in the Mississippi delta, I was either smarter than everyone else in the room or a damned sight less emotionally involved.

·

It was two things, and the bare suggestion of a third, that made my lonely and superficially gregarious freshman year tolerable, and helped shape my knowledge of that campus.

One was the mad, rudimentary life of the dormitory. Old Brackenridge Hall, a yellow-brick affair with Spanish stucco roofs, stood right at the edge of the long intramural field, only a quarter of a mile from the capitol, and just across a narrow street from a line of dingy shops and greasy cafés. We called it "The Slum Area," not only for its general dinginess but for its violence, both organized and sporadic, which erupted inevitably on the weekend nights after the beer houses across the street closed down. Brackenridge Hall was where life was, stripped of its pretenses, where one saw every day the lonely, the pathetic, the hopeless young men — often poor though sometimes not, often ignorant but not always, but never anything if not vari-

ous. Here a fairly sensitive boy could not avoid a confrontation
with his basic and bare-boned self, and see a big state university
in its true dimensions. My first roommate, who flunked out
soon enough with five F's and a D-plus, was an alcoholic from
Dallas who saw giant roaches in the middle of the night, though
the roaches may have been for my benefit. He would throw his
sliderule against the wall, or piss in the trashcan from a range of
six feet. As I sat in front of my typewriter composing my pieces
for the *Daily Texan*, he and his friends played poker and drank
rot-gut bourbon on the other side of the table, interrupting
themselves occasionally to make fun of my literary output
which, when they read it, to their eternal honor, they did not
appreciate.

I lived on the fourth floor, with a room overlooking the intramural field and the entire Slum Area, and down on the third
floor lived the baseball players. I became a sort of poet laure-
ate of that group, the resident egghead, it may have been, because I at least tried to study my books, and I actually did try
to write for the student paper, which they called "The Daily
Wipe."

Their floor was unquestionably the filthiest establishment
I have ever seen, and from it emanated the most savage and
grotesque, though until now unrecorded, happenings at the
University of Texas in the 1950s. It was the decade of
McCarthy, of Eisenhower and Dulles, the decade of students
that David Riesman would characterize for posterity as outer-
directed, the silent generation, I think it was called. These were
promising labels, but they missed the closer truth, for real life
at the University of Texas in the 1950s was like a circle with
many rings — the smallest ring in the middle consisting of
those students who were conscious of the labels and what they
meant, the other inner circles progressively less aware. At the
outside of that ring, the farthest out of all, was the third floor

of Brackenridge Hall. They came from small ranch towns and middle-sized cities on the plains, and it was their decade right along with Ike's. Old newspapers covered the floors, and two of their number slept on cots in the hall so that one room could be a combination TV room, bar, and pornography library. Every so often they had rummage sales there, and for bargain prices tried to get rid of old water-wings, empty bottles, stale socks, and waterlogged baseballs. Dust and dirt covered the newspapers and the walls. Held most in contempt there were leaders of student government, fraternities, and deans, and they could smell out a stuffed shirt fifty yards away.

They wandered around at night in the pipes under the campus, breaking into office buildings through the sewage system in search of examination papers. Somewhere under there they found the mechanism which controlled the big clock on top of the Tower, and whenever the chimes struck eighteen, twenty, or twenty-four, I knew they were down there again. One afternoon I went up to the top of the Tower with one of them and his girl; when we were on the observation deck he suddenly climbed over the barrier, balanced himself on a rainpipe, looked toward the ground thirty stories below, and shouted: "*He-haw: Sani Flush!*" They would spend hours on cheat notes, for they felt that an elaborate and successful set of cheat notes was a work of art, and in itself a kind of intellectual achievement. These were cunningly indexed with rubber bands for manual maneuvering, so that for a quick look at the Causes of the American Revolution one had only to flick the rubber band to C — and there, sure enough, were all seven causes, and in the right order. On a history identification test, one of them, his cheat notes not working, identified Daniel Webster as a colored Senator from Arkansas.

Once they caught several cadets from Texas A&M, the rival school out in the boondocks, marauding around the campus at night, and summoned aid from the whole dormitory; they shaved the Aggies' heads, painted them in orange and white enamel, paraded them at close drill around the intramural field, and in an unexpected burst of Christian charity sent them home in time for reveille. For fifty cents they would take anyone to see the cadavers in the Biology Building. They had a public address system which they would occasionally place in the window of the third floor and turn on at full blast. Once I was standing at rigid attention in the ranks of the ROTC on the intramural field while in total silence the troops were being reviewed by a general from San Antonio. Suddenly I heard a booming voice down the field, loud enough to be heard all the way to the capitol building: "Private Morris, Private Willie Morris, Company D, Squad C, take charge of your troops and dismiss them!" At another ROTC drill I noticed them up in the window again, fiddling with the loudspeaker, and I feared the worst, but the voice merely said: "The War is over, boys! General Lee just gave his sword to ol' Grant! Go home to your families and your crops!"

They spied on parked cars behind the baseball field, sneaking right up to the windows and looking inside, then startling the passionate couples by setting off firecrackers under the cars and shouting and circling around like Apache Indians. Some two dozen of them, myself included, hiding in the grass under the bleachers at the baseball field late one night, watched while the starting pitcher for next day's game performed the act of love on a waitress on the pitcher's mound. The only times I saw them attentive, or ruminative, was during "Dragnet," or "The Ed Sullivan Show," or when they were listening to telephone conversations with an elaborate device that tapped the dormitory switchboard. All this was far more representative of the American state university generation in the 1950s than deans would likely have admitted. Nihilism was more articulate than silence, and more colorful than respectability. In the souls of all of us is anarchy, and it can erupt on a whim — especially in the young. That is why college administrators, like politicians, would have us believe they have had a glimpse of the higher truth. They need every defense they can get.

•

The student newspaper, *The Daily Texan*, turned out to be one of the two or three best college dailies in America, with an old and honorable tradition. It was housed in a brand-new building in the middle of the campus, and its physical set-up was impressive; there were individual offices for the important editors, a "city room" with a big copy desk and two wire-service tickers, and a chute to drop the copy down to a modern composing room below. I felt good just walking into those offices, for it was obvious they were designed for professionals.

In its finest moments, and they had been often, *The Daily Texan* had defended the spirit of a free university even when the University of Texas itself was unable or unwilling to do so, and in these periods it had reached an eloquence and displayed a courage that would have challenged the mature profession. The tolerant seniors who ran it were bemused enough to give me a weekly column in my first semester, to report on the hundred or more college papers I was assigned to read every week. Here I began to read about strange ideas like integration, and issues of academic freedom, and observations that Dwight D. Eisenhower might be something of a bore. This was heady stuff indeed. On some nights I would stay up until three or four in the morning in my dormitory room, with the newspapers scattered on the tables and floors, trying to understand the incomprehensible goings-on in Berkeley or Ann Arbor or Colorado Springs or Chapel Hill. I gradually began to see the differences in all these papers; the ones from Harvard or Yale and a few big

state universities were almost daringly outspoken, and kept talking about "conformity" and "self-satisfaction" in a way that
both mystified and aroused me, but the great majority which
poured in from all over America spoke a tongueless idiom, im-
ploring students to turn over a new leaf at the start of each semester, give blood to a blood drive, collect wood for a bonfire, or
use their leisure time more wisely. Something was out of order
here, but I did not know quite what or why. I also wrote sports,
covering the minor stories that would be given to me, and came
under the blunt criticism of hard-headed types who may have
been turning out the best sentences on the campus in those
days. Once I wrote 2000 words on a baseball game; the six
veteran sports writers, gleeful, pejorative, and smelling of Lone
Star Beer, pointed out for me that the only thing I had neglected
to provide was the score.

It is my painful duty to describe myself one night, carrying
two dozen signs saying, "Be Sure to Vote Next Tuesday in the
Student Elections," trying to hammer them into the frozen
ground at strategic points on the campus, and finally, secretly
and in despair, throwing the whole batch of them into a sewer.
I returned to my dormitory one afternoon from a meeting of
the student government committee on public relations. One of
the catchers on the baseball team, who had been drunk since
just after breakfast, asked me where I had been, and I made the
mistake of telling him. He was enraged, went into a frenzy, and
tried to throw me out of the fourth-floor window. Some of the
poker players, not wishing tragedy or scandal to befall the dormitory, came to my assistance, and the fight for better public
relations at the University of Texas was allowed to survive.

•

Once I was invited to the apartment of a young graduate student and his wife. The walls of their apartment were lined with

books, more books than I had ever seen before in a private dwelling — books everywhere and on everything. I was astonished; I tried to talk with those people, but I was unaccountably shy, and I kept looking at their books out of the corner of my eye, and wondering if I should *say* something about them, or ask perhaps if they were for sale or if they formed some kind of special exhibit. It is a rare experience for certain young people to see great quantities of books in a private habitat for the first time, and to hear ideas talked about seriously in the off hours. Good God, they were doing it for pleasure, or so it seemed. The wife, who was also a graduate student, asked me what I wanted to do with myself when I graduated from college. "I want to be a writer," I said, but not even thinking about it until the words were out; my reply surprised me most of all, but it was much more appropriate in those surroundings to have said that instead of "sports announcer," which probably constituted my first choice. "What do you want to write about?" she persisted. "Just . . . *things*," I said, turning red. That night, stirred by the conversation and by all the books I had seen, I went to the library, promising myself to read every important book that had ever been written. I was at a loss, because I did not have the faintest notion where to start. I picked out the most imposing volumes I could find — Lord Bryce on the American Commonwealth, which put me to sleep for ten nights in a row. But once this fire is lit, to consume and to know, it can burn on and on. I kept going back to the library, taking out tall stacks of books and reading them in a great undigested fury: Hemingway, Faulkner, Wolfe, Dreiser, anything in the American literature and American history shelves that looked promising. I started buying Modern Library books with the money I made writing for the newspaper, and I pledged to myself, as Marilyn Monroe had, that I would read them all, and in alphabetical order.

I believe now that the University of Texas was somehow be-

ginning to give me an interest and a curiosity in something outside my own parochial ego. It was beginning to suggest the
power not merely of language, but the whole unfamiliar world
of experience and evocation which language served. That world
was new, and the recognition of its existence was slow, uncertain, and immature. Books and literature, I was beginning to
see, were not for getting a grade, not for the utilitarian purpose
of being considered a nice and versatile boy, not just for casual
pleasure, but subversive as Socrates and expressions of man's
soul. It took me years to understand that words are often as
important as experience, because words make experience last,
but here, in the spring of my freshman year, there were men who
were teaching me these things, perhaps with very little hope that
anyone in their classrooms remotely cared, and I think perhaps I may have been listening. Freshman English was the first
step; it was often the first and last time that many young people, headed in a state like Texas for insurance or business or the
Junior League, might have had for a kind of small internal salvation.

For freshman English there was Frank Lyell, a fellow Mississippian, and it was his high values, giving my outrageous
themes D's and C's when I had expected A's as something of a
birthright, which first suggested that the editorial texture I had
given the Yazoo High *Flashlight* would hardly serve in a world
where English was master tongue. This was not merely a matter
of syntax, discipline, and unheard-of-words. There came an
awareness that loose, insensitive, and poorly formed language
belie a loose, insensitive, and poorly formed mind. Lyell
assigned a 2000-word autobiography, which I began with a description of the fading lonely sunlight outside Brackenridge
Hall, went back through seventeen years of baseball, religion,
and small-town hopes, and ended up in a volley of rhetoric in
the same place six hours later. One sentence read: "My dog

Skip and I wandered the woods and swamplands of our Mississippi home shooting rabbits and squirrels." To which the professor appended the comment: "Who was the better shot, you
or the dog?" I was enraged. I can remember one morning the
teacher reading a passage from a novel and asking "Isn't that
marvelous?" The sorority girls sat there taking down everything
he said, while in the back of the room I could see three or four
ranch boys, who always sat there in a self-contained group,
nudging each other and snickering over the teacher's unusual
recommendations.

Yet there *was* loneliness in those fading Sunday afternoons,
and madness in the meaningless activities that served to make
one versatile and well rounded. The editors of the campus
humor magazine, a cynical and knowing lot, must have recognized this. In May one of them told me to be sure and read
the next issue; there was to be an article on me. It turned out to
be a burlesque of a young campus character named Willie X,
who had joined everything and wanted to know everything.
Late one night he was walking down the University "Drag"
reading a pamphlet, and as he crossed 24th Street something
fortunate occurred for the University of Texas. He was run
over by a two-ton truck.

That whole first year was also one peregrination after another between Texas and Mississippi and Mississippi and Texas.
At holidays there was the long bus ride through the lonely little
Texas towns — Round Rock and Carthage, Jacksonville and
Tyler and Kilgore, through the pine forests in the moonlight
into Shreveport — the layover in the station there for another
bus, then on through Ruston and Monroe to the big bridge
and Vicksburg. The two places, Mississippi and Texas, were
already beginning gradually to exist in separate realities for me,
one meaning one thing, one another, and I was as ambivalent as
my sense of place. Yet by the end of that first year I believe I al-

ready had had an unusual glimpse of this state university in the beginnings of the Eisenhower age: its ambiguity, its complexity, its promise.

•

In the early 1950s the University of Texas was trying desperately to come up in the world. The vast holdings the state had given it in the late nineteenth century, when it was mainly a collection of wooden shacks on a hill, had turned out to be rich in oil; its reputation had suffered from the egregious Texas myth. The school had never enjoyed the steady blessing of influential public support which had made the four or five great American state universities preeminent. It had had to struggle hard against the aggressive philistinism of its old agrarian culture, and time and again it had been hurt badly by ruddy nabobs and crossroads potentates who were suspicious of its very existence. As early as 1917, when Governor "Pa" Ferguson warned the people of the state that it was a nesting place for sinners and profligates, the University was having political troubles. The state legislature, quartered those few blocks down the street, had investigated the campus on several occasions, and once, when the University bought a $20,000 collection of Byron, Shelley, Tennyson, Browning, and Lamb, the lower house had protested that all these writers were "obscene or atheistic."

Some kind of turning point for the place occurred in the 1940s, when it suffered a series of blows that might have killed most struggling colleges. The firing of President Homer Rainey was something of a legend in American higher education. Rainey became president in 1939, and was confronted by a Board of Regents increasingly dominated by appointees of Governor "Pappy" O'Daniel, the flour salesman and radio entertainer who was himself a tool of some of the most uncivilized wealth known to man. The clash between O'Daniel's men and Rainey had been direct and brutal; professors were fired, books blacklisted, and a state which had contributed Martin Dies to national politics was clearly not ready to support a university with pretensions toward independence. When Rainey was fired, the American Association of University Professors after a three-year investigation censured the Regents' "systematic, persistent, and continuous attempts by a politically dominant group to impose its social and educational views on the University." The place was deeply damaged, and after that the only thing to do was forget.

The 1950s were a quiescent time at the University, just as they were not a very poetic time in America. There were no student protests, no sit-ins and stand-ins such as were to occur in the more activist 'sixties. There was as much, probably more to dissent from then, but I am convinced that the softening of disaffection on most campuses was an accurate reflection of the somnolence of our national life. The fire seemed to have gone out of many of the more rebellious old-timers, as if courage had been the victim of its own strength. The Rainey episode, which had split the campus in two, when 5000 students could march to the state capitol to dispute the latest barbarisms, carrying a black-draped coffin labeled "academic freedom," was still sensitive in many minds — and in none more so than the people who called the shots. The AAUP blacklist, if one mentioned it in the environs of the main building, provoked mild attacks of administrative epilepsy, and there were enough administrators over there to carry an epidemic a long way.

Texas itself, its chronic xenophobias fed by the passions of the McCarthy period, was not an entirely pleasant place in those years. There was a venom in its politics and a smugness in its attitude to outsiders and to itself. Democratic Party conservatism in the state was infinitely less sophisticated, cruder and more corrupting than its counterpart would be in the 1960s. Businessmen, Texas-style — promoters, a lot of Snopeses —

were firmly in power in the statehouse, just as they controlled the University. In my senior year every member of the Board of Regents was an appointee of Governor Allan Shivers, a strong follower of McCarthy. In the prevailing ethic, education was where it belonged: in the hands of oil and gas men, corporation lawyers, cattle ranchers, and experienced old wildcatters. Texas reformers in that day were much like the old American mugwumps of the last century, and their antagonists resembled the industrialists of the 1880s, who were similarly held to be — in Richard Hofstadter's words — "uneducated and uncultivated, irresponsible, rootless and corrupt, devoid of refinement or of any sense of noblesse." With rare exceptions among these people in Texas in the 1950s, there was not even yet the argument that higher education was good for attracting industry. The dominant attitude was that higher education attracted other, less desirable, elements and was to be handled warily, and, when the occasion demanded it, with all the old and tested dogmatisms. Varsity football stirred up the only undiluted enthusiasm among them. There was one student protest meeting in these years over McCarthy, where most of the speakers prefaced their remarks by tracing their loyal ancestry back to Sam Houston, Davy Crockett, or the Alamo, and if possible to Queen Elizabeth and King Alfred.

In this context it was not difficult to see the problems that Logan Wilson,* the president of the University, was up against. He was a highly capable if somewhat frosty administrator who added new dimensions to aloofness. If the mood were on him he would have thought nothing of condescending to the Virgin Mary during silent meditations. His aim was to heal the wounds of the calamitous Rainey era with analgesic balm and periodic injections of Novocain, and at the same time, in these years of spiritual drought, to build a better financial base

* Later president of the American Council on Education.

for the University of Texas while praying for rain. The challenge, politically and for the school's position in a conservative state, was to keep the lid on. For this reason Wilson's tenure may have been something of a bridge from more disastrous years to the 1960s, when the University of Texas would come alive again. But then it was a stolid and unimaginative time, and few were those to take a dare.

As for me, I slowly began to see many of these things, but mainly through a prism. It was only later that I directly faced these aspects of Texas society and found them tawdry and suffocating. What I mainly noticed then were the boorish remarks of Regents, who could make the most reflective and charitable monk in the most isolated cloister want to bite back, the mindless self-satisfactions of most of the students, and, politically, the general hardening of the arteries after the Supreme Court decision of 1954. It was also during this time, as a foretaste of later years, that a second-team halfback named Duke Washington broke away on a touchdown for Washington State against Texas. A large part of the Texas student section, myself included, stood up to applaud the first Negro ever to play in Texas Memorial Stadium.

I suppose it was the students, and the life they and their adult counsellors had devised for themselves, that I was noticing most, as always. Led by the organized structure of the fraternities and sororities, the great hotbed of philistinism in the 1950s, this campus, as others surely did, reached unprecedented heights of carefully planned frivolity — parades with homemade floats, sing-songs, carnivals — anything, in fact, to do something meaningless with all that energy. It was the era of the beauty queens, bless their souls and bodies, and they decorated the front pages of *The Daily Texan* and inspired their own mystique, like Hollywood starlets tied down unfairly by classes and lectures. They were Edna and Mary Lou and Lee, Sara Sue and

Jimmy and Debbie, and in Brackenridge Dormitory their relative virtues would be discussed philosophically, though always graphically. It was also the period of "retreats," when organizations, accompanied by deans, sub-deans, assistant deans, deans emeritus, and various other spiritual, marital, social, medical, and inspirational advisors, would isolate themselves at some dude ranch out in the hills. Here they would sit around in circles talking into the weary night about the virtues of greater campus "service" and all the nuances of human sincerity. My experience with one of them, with the deans leading the prayers at the beginning and end, brought back to me the religious youth meetings at the country churches in Yazoo County, except that these in Texas were much blander, devoid of exuberance, and somehow lacking *possibility*. If a new idea was ever unloosed by these strange semi-evangelical institutions it has yet to be reported, but may be hemmed in by the statute of limitations.

There was a core of serious, rather independent souls gathered around an institution called the "Christian Faith and Life Community," one of those robust experiments in community intellectual living that was in such stark contrast to the comfortable campus life of the 1950s. Despite the incomprehensible language they spoke, existential with a thin overlay of Calvin, which discouraged outsiders without training in structural linguistics or those who could not afford an interpreter, they kept their directions inside (sometimes, perhaps, *too* south-southwest of the inner light). The "Y" was a haven for other serious students, and as a forerunner to the flowering of the ecumenical movement encouraged controversial seminars and lectures on questions that usually mattered. These groups, and they were good people, were the repositories of whatever liberalism existed on a conscious level at the University of Texas at the time.

From all these things I had, by my junior year, become strangely removed, both intellectually and emotionally. I had ceased to be the torrid activist I had been before, and I was chiefly interested in the panorama. I knew so many different people — lonely twenty-year-old-failures who drank coffee and ate cheesecake at 1 A.M. in the Snak Shak, suave leaders of clubs and committees, janitors, sorority girls, campus cops, lady booksalesmen, ranch boys from West Texas, grubby graduate students, and an occasional beauty queen — one in particular, though she was a Phi Beta Kappa. They are now lawyers, politicians, manufacturers of toilet seats and garbage-can lids, Junior Leaguers, schoolteachers, members of the John Birch Society, doubles in Hollywood westerns, and wives of New York editors.

The beauty queen with the Phi Beta Kappa key was the one who would endure. Her name was Celia. She had come as an honor student from the most proper high school in Houston, a frenetically social institution on the fringes of that rich man's paradise called River Oaks, yet her own social instincts were decidedly on the wane. She lived in a palatial sorority house, but her elders berated her for carrying laundry out the front door, and she drank wine on the sly in her room and read Sartre and Tillich and Fromm and books on Renaissance art. She went to every "retreat" and spiritual seminar she could get her hands on, but finally they lost their steam for her; unlike many of the students of that day she spoke plain English, and took her existentialism with a healthy and detached curiosity. She began to shun all the beauty-queen elections with an honest, though complicated, disdain, but they still kept *electing* her. She was so beautiful, in the wholesome American way, that those elections were foregone conclusions. What could she do? she asked. She couldn't *resign*. With this contorted attitude she ended up being elected the official Sweetheart of the University of Texas, and five thousand people sang "The Eyes of

Texas" to her in the gymnasium, although Sartre, Tillich, and Fromm were not present. We would walk around the campus talking about Hemingway in the sunshine, or the Romantic poets, and we gave each other books with florid personal inscriptions from the Transcendentalists. We parked in borrowed cars out by one of Lyndon Johnson's lakes, or in front of the sorority house where couples loved and petted each night on public exhibit. When I turned twenty, one cold November night, we drank a quart of California wine, and for a birthday present she gave me a book of Victorian poetry, and with an unsteady hand and a big laugh she wrote on the flyleaf, "Grow old along with me, the best is yet to be, the last of life, for which the first was made." The laugh was to be on her.

•

I still lived in the same old dormitory, in a bigger and more officious room; I remember the place now on a late autumn afternoon of 1954. The sunlight streamed into the room from beyond the intramural field, and my roommate Collie, a genial West Texas ranch boy from Pecos, sat at the window chewing tobacco and watching the crowds drift by from the football game we had all been to in the afternoon. The football scores would start coming in on my old red portable radio that the radio station in Yazoo had given me — first from the little Eastern schools like Colby and Bowdoin and Amherst, or Niagara and Allegheny and Susquehanna, then the Ivy League scores which were just exercises, on to the big Midwestern or Southern ones that mattered, drifting slowly westward across the country like a great rollcall of America. Collie would sit there chewing and spitting into the trash can and complaining about his old hometown girlfriend, who had joined a fancy sorority called Zeta Tau Alpha and then promptly deserted him, and from downstairs we could hear the baseball players hooking up the dormitory firehose to wet down the Baylor band when they returned to their bus under the third-floor window. The lights on the beer joints of the Slum Area appeared, red-and-purple neons blinking on and off in the autumn dusk, and in the street near the gymnasium someone shouted, "Hook 'Em, Horns!" and the Texas band came by in their gaudy orange uniforms playing "Texas Fight." Then they halted and played "The Eyes," and from our window we could see all the Texas fans stop and come to attention and sing the words, for souls had been touched by the last-minute victory on that incomparable day. From the lower depths of the dormitory a voice could be heard shouting *"Chicken Farm!"* over and over again, the weekly call for the carload driving to the country whore house in La Grange. By this time the Greek temple on top of the Tower would be lit in orange, and the whole campus was sure to be a pendulum of activity — parties, dances, socials, beer-busts, barbecues, meetings of the old grads. Collie and I would go drink a beer in one of the Slum Area dives, already beginning to fill up with boys without dates or without cars to go anywhere; then I would leave him there, bitching about small-town women, and head straight for the sorority house where Celia lived. The Saturday night scene on the campus, as I walked across it to the "Drag," left nothing to the imagination — people in blue jeans and tuxedos, pedal-pushers and evening gowns, Stetson hats and orange string ties, and tiny clusters of foreign students from Saudi Arabia or India with nowhere to go and no football game to talk about.

•

For the truth is that the University of Texas in the mid-1950s was already hopelessly big, and the life of the place, as with most big institutions, was on its surfaces terribly public and over-exposed, yet at the same time, for those who demanded it, al-

most as private as one desired. There were the handful one ran
across who passionately believed, as William Arrowsmith was
to describe the best Texas students of the 1960s, that "human
greatness is both possible and necessary." That autumn Bill D.
Moyers was a quiet, earnest, journalism student making
A's, staying out of politics, and working for Lady Bird Johnson's TV station. Ronnie Dugger was just leaving the economics graduate school to begin *The Texas Observer*. James
Roach in his foreign affairs courses was teaching a generation of
Texas students that the rest of the world was something to be
rational about, and John Silber was about to start his brilliant
lectures in philosophy, where he would become the hero of the
best students and the bane of the more aloof administrators. Dr.
Bob Montgomery (we loved him and called him "Bushy
Bob" for his wild and improbable crop of gray hair) was still
captivating his classes in institutional economics, as he had for
years, with his tales of Mason and Menard counties. When my
girl Celia came into his classroom late to hear his most famous lecture on the A-bomb, Bushy Bob stopped in mid-sen-
tence and said: "It's the Queen herself! How many times have
you heard this lecture?" "Three," she replied, turning red, for
she had taken the course before, and kept returning to hear
Bushy Bob. And Bushy Bob, with a flourishing bow and a
courtly gesture of welcome, escorted her to an empty seat.

Finally, in the spring of that year, having worked for *The
Daily Texan* as sports editor, writer of my column called "The
Round-up," and editorialist, and having viewed the campus for
two and a half years as both a frenetic participant and a detached observer, I decided to file for the editorship. The race
was an elective one, and I began campaigning from one end of
the campus to the other. In the big student rally where all the
candidates were questioned, someone asked me about integration. I replied: "There's an inner turmoil in the United States;

there's an inner turmoil in me. The Supreme Court decision was inevitable, but I don't think any universal rule can be applied to the entire nation when the time for integration comes. I don't think Ole Miss is ready for integration. I think the University of Texas is."

•

Early in the summer, just before I became editor, I went back for a few days to Mississippi. I had an old car now, a ramshackle Plymouth with dual exhausts, and I took the southern route across Louisiana to Natchez. The road from Natchez to Vicksburg, over hills heavy in wisteria, vines, and unbelievably deep-green trees, parallels the River slightly to the west. There are few more lush or beautiful places than this stretch of Mississippi at the first of June; the very air was pervaded with an odor so fragrant as to make the senses reel with a wonderful anticipation and longing. I drove through Natchez, with its old homes set in their broad flowering lawns, north through the hills to Port Gibson, where the church with the hand on its steeple points to the sky, and where as a little girl my great-grandmother, over a century before, had testified in the old courthouse against the man she had seen kill her father; then on to Vicksburg and the broken hill-and-delta country beyond. I had the most overwhelming sense of coming *home*, to some place that belonged to me; I was not merely stunned by its beauty, for this was not new to me; I was surprised to feel so settled inside, as if nothing, no matter how cruel or despairing, could destroy my belonging. It was the last time I felt so strongly about a place.

I sat on the front steps of our house on Grand Avenue with my dog, too old now to climb trees or to do much of anything except lie with his nose in my hand and enjoy the warm sunshine. My father and I talked about baseball again, and friends came by in their cars to tell about college and what they would do when they finished; most of them would come back and go to work for their fathers. The blond majorette would be marrying soon and going to Memphis, and the other girls I once knew were already bearing children and settling into the easy social ritual of the Yazoo Country Club. A reporter from the local paper came by to interview me, about being chosen editor of a "real daily," she said, and when she finished she told me, "It's the same old place. It won't ever change much."

The third or fourth day I was there, people started talking about a "meeting." I heard about it everywhere I went. When my old schoolmate Bubba Barrier came by, I asked him what it was all about. The meeting was going to be that night, he said; I could go with him. Its purpose was to organize a local chapter of the White Citizens Council.

From several people I talked with, I began to piece together the story. The NAACP had selected the town as one of five targets in the state for putting the Supreme Court's school de-segregation decision into effect. The local NAACP submitted to the school board a petition signed by fifty-three Negro parents seeking an immediate end to segregation in the schools. The petition had shocked the whole town. Sixteen of the most prominent white men in town had called the meeting to deal with the situation.

Early that night we drove to the school auditorium; there were so many cars we had to park two blocks away. People walked toward the school in groups, and in the yard several policemen stood together, waving and shouting greetings. Inside the building, the auditorium was packed; some of the people were sitting in the aisles, others in the big open windows. It was a warm night, and the men in suits and ties had taken off their coats and rolled up their sleeves. Some were in blue jeans or overalls, and the women sat fanning themselves with the paper fans provided by the funeral home.

The moment we walked into that auditorium I sensed the tension. Many times later I would feel the pent-up hysteria of organized crowds angry and out on a mission, but this was my first confrontation with that experience, and from the beginning it made me clammy and uneasy. I could recognize a kind of claustrophobic terror in the place, accentuated by a low undertone of serious talk throughout the hall and sudden loud shouts as people waited for the meeting to begin: "Let's *go!*" and "Let's get them *niggers!*" Then the crowd began stomping their feet.

On the stage, sitting in straight-back chairs, were just over a dozen men. I knew them all; some of them were fathers of my best friends, men I had known and admired and could talk to on a first-name basis. In the audience were scores of men and women I had known as far back as my childhood. I saw my father there, sitting next to one of our neighbors. By this time the policemen we had seen outside were sitting in the windows, and I heard the police chief shout, "Come on, *let's get this thing started!*"

A handsome, graying man stood up on the stage and pounded a gavel. For a moment there was silence, and then everyone broke into applause and the yelling started up again. The chairman explained that this was the charter meeting of a new organization that would "protect our way of life." He talked about the NAACP petition and said the people who signed it did not know what they were doing. A stand had to be taken that night, he said. Give an inch and they would take a mile. If everyone stands together, he said, the niggers would regret the day they did what they did. Retaliation was a necessity. There was no other way.

The audience shouted their support while the chairman listed the steps to be taken. White employers would immediately fire any of the signers of the petition who worked for them.

Those petitioners who rented houses would immediately be evicted by their landlords. White grocers would refuse to sell food to any of them. Negro grocers who had signed would no longer get any groceries from the wholesale stores. "Let's just *stomp* 'em!" someone shouted from the back, but the chairman said, no, violence would be deplored; this was much the more effective method. Public opinion needed to be mobilized behind the plan right away. The new organization would not itself take these steps, but rather the whole white community would act spontaneously.

Out in the audience I noticed someone asking to be recognized. The chairman had finished his speech and three hundred different people were talking at once. Someone came out with a long rebel yell, and the chairman pounded with his gavel. The man waving his hand was a neighbor of ours, from the big house across the street, and the chairman asked for quiet so our neighbor could talk.

"I agree with everything that's been said and with everything we're trying to do," my neighbor shouted, his great bald head shining under the lights. "But, gentlemen, I work for a corporation, and all this is *unconstitutional*, it's against the Consti . . ." His words were abruptly drowned out by the roar from the crowd. "*Sit down, Ed!*" people yelled, and there was a collective groan, and boos and catcalls that might have wilted Judge Earl Warren himself. My neighbor smiled sheepishly, shrugged his shoulders, and sat down.

I sat there, quiet as could be. For a brief moment I was tempted to stand up and support my neighbor, but I lacked the elemental courage to go against that mob. For it *was* a mob, and I was not the same person I had been three years before. In the pit of my stomach, I felt a strange and terrible disgust. I looked back and saw my father, sitting still and gazing straight ahead; on the stage my friends' fathers nodded their heads and talked among themselves. I felt an urge to get out of there. *Who are these people?* I asked myself. What was I doing there? Was this the place I had grown up in and never wanted to leave? I knew in that instant, in the middle of a mob in our school auditorium, that a mere three years in Texas had taken me irrevocably, even without my recognizing it, from home.

I stayed around town a few days more, and that was long enough to see that the plans were working. Most of the signers were fired, and a number of them started leaving town. The last afternoon I was there I went to say goodbye to a girl I had known since we were children. She was on her front porch crying; I asked what was wrong. Her parents had just fired Henry, the man who had mowed their lawn for years. "It's *wrong*," she cried. "Henry didn't even know he was signing that ol' thing. And we up and *fired* him for it."

The next morning I packed my bag and went back to Austin.

2

IT WAS A viciously hot Texas afternoon in June when I moved my ten or fifteen favorite books, a toothbrush, an electric razor, an extra pair of shoes, and an emergency pint of Old Forester into the editor's office of *The Daily Texan*. Had I been able to predict the events of the next twelve months, I would have included the Book of Common Prayer.

We published the paper only twice a week in the summer, and the days drifted by in that heavy lethargy that anyone who has spent a summer in Texas would know so well. It was a time for lazy reading under the magnificent ancient trees of the campus, for swimming in the ice-cold waters of the natural springs at Barton's, for beer-drinking and political talk around the tables in the back of the old German beer hall. There was leisure enough to begin planning the editorial issues for the regular school year, when close to 20,000 students, a record number, would enroll, and to talk to anyone I wished to on the campus about the questions that would matter.

The most exciting administrator at the University of Texas in that day was Harry Ransom,* who as dean of arts and sciences had begun to give focus to the talents of the school's best students. Administrators almost as a matter of course were expected to be aloof and impersonal, but Ransom was different. Early that fall, with his encouragement and the backing of two of my professors, I applied for a Rhodes Scholarship.

I survived the campus and the state competition, and caught a plane to New Orleans for the Southern finals. The interviews were held in a big hotel in the French Quarter, and I got a room in a run-down flophouse just across the street. I stayed up a good part of the night before in that cold, bare room reading W. J. Cash, and went to sleep with the most terrible visions of imminent failure. Earlier that night, the old Rhodes Scholars who made up the interviewing committee had given a cocktail party for the twelve competitors. When I met the others, most of whom came from the best Eastern schools, in their carefully tailored suits and their button-down collars, I thought they were the smoothest people I had ever encountered, for they could talk with an easy grace about everything from the book publishing business to the stock market to all the nuances of the objective correlative. One of them was talking to me about the latest plays in New York, and in my discomfort I looked down

* Later to be President and Chancellor.

at the cuff of my trousers and noticed a big cigarette hole! The
rest of the evening I stood there with one leg crazily crossed on
the other, scratching at myself and wondering how I had ever
got into such a situation. In the midst of this torture I had a
long talk with the members of the committee from Oklahoma
and Texas, and they immediately put me at my ease. We had a
rambling conversation about state government and the college
generation and baseball; later, as I was standing off to myself,
half-listening to one of the Ivy Leaguers dropping the names
of a large portion of Europe's painters, poets, and playwrights
to the man from Oklahoma, I suddenly saw the Oklahoman look
over in my direction with a gesture of support, a kind of bemused and contorted grimace behind the Ivy Leaguer's back; I
went back to the flophouse to read W. J. Cash.

The next day I sat nervously with the other candidates while
the interviewing went on in a side room. Then my turn came,
and I took a chair in front of a long table where the committee
members sat. The interview moved on from American foreign
policy to Eisenhower's farm program to the modern novel. I
started talking about Faulkner, and somewhat to my surprise
discovered myself having to defend him against the criticisms
of the chairman, who owned a big lumber company in Alabama.
Then they asked about Texas politics and next about Mississippi, and I started talking about the Emmett Till trial. I
quoted Faulkner, "If we in America have reached that point in
our desperate culture when we must murder children, no matter for what reason or what color, we don't deserve to survive,
and probably won't." I began trying to discuss the various legal
complications of the trial itself, and got myself into a difficult
position over my interpretations of the law. One of the men was
giving me a hard time on these points, when all of a sudden the
Mississippi member, who served in the Mississippi legislature,

interrupted and said, "Mr. Morris is absolutely correct on his legal discussion. He knows the law and has presented a fair and accurate description of the trial." That ended the discussion. There were questions on a dozen other topics, and then I was through.

It was late that Saturday afternoon when all the interviews ended, and the twelve of us sat together while the committee deliberated for an hour. Finally they called us into their room and the chairman made a little talk about how only four of us could go to Oxford, although he wished all of us could. Then he read off the winners. "Did I hear right?" I asked Woods, the Mississippi candidate. "Did *I*?" he said. In a matter of seconds the whole group seemed to disappear, and the chairman of the committee on the way out caught me by the elbow and said, "Morris, I want you to know I admired the way you defended Faulkner. I liked your vigor and honesty. I even liked the way you pounded on the table. I couldn't disagree with you more, of course. If it were left up to me I'd have him tarred and feathered and shipped out of the South tonight." Then he too was gone. Alone in New Orleans that night, I wandered through the city in a happy state, down the streets George Washington Cable and Sherwood Anderson must have walked, up Canal Street with its extravagant stores and hotels, then to the flophouse again for a night of fitful thoughts about Oxford — "to the strands of the daughters of the sunset, the apple tree, the singing, and the gold."

When I got back to Austin, my professors were to tell me this was the first Rhodes Scholarship from the University of Texas in ten years. Yet there were to be no congratulations, personal or formal, from the office of the President, or his army of administrative deans, and certainly none from the Board of Regents, who were likely not aware of the existence of an Oxford

University. The main reason, however, is that during the early stages of my editorship of the paper, unusual things had been happening.

3

A GREAT IRONY occasionally besets an American state university, for it allows and at its best encourages one to develop his critical capacities, his imagination, his values; at the same time, in its institutional aspects, a university under pressure can become increasingly wary of the very intent and direction of the ideals it has helped spawn. It is too easy, too much a righteous judgment, to call this attitude hypocrisy, for actually it is a kind of schizophrenia. This involves more than a gap between preaching and practicing; it involves the splitting of a university's soul. There can be something brutal about a university's teaching its young people to be alive, aware, critical, independent, and free, and then, when a threatening turn is taken, to reject by its actual behavior the substance of everything it claims for itself. Then ideals and critical capacities exist in a vacuum. They are sometimes ignored, and in extreme instances victimized. And the greater society suffers as well.

For a year I had been reading heavily in politics, history, and the journalism of the great editors. I took to my heart the memorable statement in Joseph Pulitzer's will, now reprinted every day on the editorial pages of the St. Louis Post-Dispatch, and which I subsequently tacked to the wall in my office next to my typewriter, as I have in every office where I have worked: "that it will always fight for progress and reform, never tolerate injustice or corruption, always fight demagogues of all parties, never belong to any party, always oppose privileged classes and public plunderers, never lack sympathy for the poor, always remain devoted to the public welfare, never be satisfied merely with printing news, always be drastically independent, never be afraid to attack wrong, whether by predatory plutocracy or predatory poverty."

I read the journalism of H. L. Mencken, Lincoln Steffens, William Allen White, S. S. McClure, Bernard DeVoto, Hodding Carter, Ralph McGill, and Brann the Iconoclast. I read the files of *The Daily Texan* itself, learning of different and more alive times — the great editorials of Horace Busby, who brought sanity and courage to the campus during the Rainey disaster of the 1940s, D. B. Hardeman, Ronnie Dugger, and others. The political climate of the state had become more pointed to me, and in long and sometimes agonizing talks with the brightest and most perceptive student leaders I had thought out the huge responsibility of the largest and most prominent student newspaper in the South in a period when the integration issue was coming alive; my experience with my hometown Citizens Council had helped me judge the extent of my own personal change, and showed the sad barbarism of intransigence. I was suffused with the ideals of freedom of expression and the open marketplace. I had the most emphatic belief that this freedom should be used to positive purposes, that freedom is as freedom does, that the pages of this newspaper should reflect the great diversity of the place I had come to know, that the University of Texas was too much a part of its state and of the rest of the world to avoid editorials on significant questions beyond the campus, and that the campus itself — as so many others then — was bogged down in dullness, complacency, and the corporate mentality. My deficits, as I fully realized later, were a self-righteousness, a lack of subtlety in polemic, and an especially underdeveloped awareness of the diplomatic approach.

President Kennedy, Theodore Sorensen later wrote, liked to improvise on the passage from Ecclesiastes: "A time to weep and a time to laugh, a time to mourn and a time to dance, a time to fish and a time to cut bait." I did not know as much about bait-cutting then as I would later. But I wanted the paper which would briefly be mine to be a living thing, distinctive and meaningful, in both its own tradition and the tradition of hard-hitting, outspoken American journalism. The University of Texas itself had taught me to place a high value on these qualities; the necessity of the free marketplace of ideas was apparently high on its list of formal priorities. It was in the books in its libraries, the valedictions of its deans, administrators, commencement speakers, even on the buildings and statues around its campus. You cannot make gestures of support for all these things and expect them to have no context. They either apply to a particular setting or they do not apply at all. They are either watered down to appease the distrusts of a power faction or they are not. But uphold these ideas long enough, frequently enough, and with such inspiration, and some young people are not only going to believe in them, they are going to believe in them with the fervor of the young, and even arrange their lives and their sense of honor by them.

So it was that I came out fighting hard, and the reactions were no sooner than immediate. I erred, first of all, into editorializing occasionally about state politics, particularly its twin dieties, oil and gas. I suppose the authorities had not expected a gentle-natured Southern boy to overreach into areas ruled by hidden divinities; a student editor in Texas could blaspheme the Holy Spirit and the Apostle Paul, but irreverence stopped at the well-head. We were going against a set of scandals and money frauds that had rocked Governor Shivers' administration. We were seeking intelligence and good will on integration and lauding most Texans for their tolerant attitude. Occasionally we chided John Foster Dulles' view of the rest of the world. Against the reactions from the school administration we categorically defended student press freedom and our right to comment as we wished on controversial state and national issues. We were committing the crime of being vigorous and outspoken, naïvely idealistic and exuberantly but not radically liberal in a state that at that time had little patience with either, on a campus where exuberance was reserved for the minor furies, and in a decade which encouraged little essential ebullience in the young.

There began a series of summonses to President Logan Wilson's office, much like a grade-school student who had been caught throwing spitballs in class being called to the principal; I was immediately reminded of my tribulations with my fourth-grade teacher, the evangelical Miss Abbott. Wilson's personal secretary would telephone and say, "Mr. Morris, the President would like to confer with you. Could we see you at three?" Ushered into the offices of the principal, who ruled over an academic domain stretching from El Paso to Galveston, I would wait in the outer chamber for an appropriate five minutes and admire there the lush carpet six inches deep; then the President was ready to see me. I would be offered menthol cigarettes and dealt with soothingly, charmingly, and with the condescension befitting the occasion. These biting editorials had to stop, though for a while the issue was not presented quite that frontally. There were meetings with the corps of deans, especially the one who had been a captain in the Navy and who believed that when an order is given, people should hop-to; anyone to the political left of Eisenhower, he once told me, was stupid if not downright treacherous. At first he was baffled, but this gave way to rage; there was no bemusement in these quarters. The slight liquid film that glazed his eyes as I came into his office suggested that he was keeping himself under control with some difficulty; his apparent preference was to assign me to the brig. A good part of the time I was scared, and Logan Wilson must have been equally miserable; he was beginning to get caught in a vicious crossfire. The political appointees who ran the University were beginning to use the old and tested dogmatisms. And in the end more people than President Wilson and I were to be involved.

Finally the Regents erupted. At a meeting with several student leaders, including good friends of mine who were president and vice-president of the student body, they declared that the student paper should not discuss controversial state and national topics, and that college students were not interested in these things anyway. *The Daily Texan*, they said, had especially gone too far astray in commenting on a piece of natural gas legislature. There, now, was the rub! A little later they handed down a censorship edict. This was based, they said, not on principle but on legal considerations. They cited the rider on state appropriations bills, which stipulated that no state money "shall be used for influencing the outcome of any election or the passage or defeat of any legislative measure." Then they advanced one step further, a major step as it turned out, and announced that "editorial preoccupation with state and national political controversy" would be prohibited.

My friends and I on the *Texan* did some painful soul-searching after that announcement. Should we give in and avoid an agonizing fight? Was a fight worth it? The next morning, as I remember it, I drove out to Lyndon Johnson's lakes, to the one my beauty queen and I liked so much; I sat around under a scrub oak for a time reading some Thomas Jefferson. Then I came back to town and talked with Bergen, our managing editor, a shy, deceptive little man with an abundance of courage, and we decided in thirty minutes what Tom Jefferson likely would have recommended all along.

That began one of the greatest controversies in the history of American college journalism. Bergen and I stayed up all night in the editor's office, planning and writing editorials under the new censorship arrangement. We submitted critical editorials the next day, attacking the implications of the Regents' order, along with a guest editorial from *The New York Times* on the natural gas legislation* and several paragraphs from Thomas Jefferson on press freedom. All were rejected. The Jefferson quotes had been included in a personal column, and when he was censored there was thunder in the heavens, fire in the sky was reported over Monticello, and a thirty-minute moratorium on bourbon was declared in Charlottesville. But the student majority on the publications board outvoted the faculty representatives, and all the editorials were printed in toto in the next issue.

We kept right on going. We authorized a brilliant young law student, the "attorney general" for the student government, to examine the legal consequences of the Regents' order. He counselled with some of the state's most respected lawyers and legal scholars and refuted the applicability of the appropriations rider. The Regents' interpretation of this rider, he argued, had "terrifying implications" and could be used in the same way to stifle legitimate comment among students, faculty, and quasi-independent corporations housed on the campus like the alumni organization, the student government, and the law review.

In retrospect a number of things stand out clearly. One Regent saying, "The *Texan* has gone out of bounds in discussing issues pertaining to oil and gas because 66 percent of Texas tax money comes from oil and gas." And another adding, "We're

* This was the Fulbright-Harris bill that Eisenhower later vetoed for the exertion of "improper influences" on the Senate.

just trying to hold Willie to a college yell." ("There are our young barbarians, all at play!") . . . A journalism professor coming up to me the day after the controversy began and whispering, "I just want to shake your hand. I'm proud to know you." . . . My parents phoning long-distance from Mississippi and asking, "Son, you in trouble? They won't kick you out of school so close to graduation, will they?" . . . At one of the interminable meetings of the publications board, one faculty representative saying to me, "You know what you are? You're a *propagandist*," a gripping judgment coming from an associate professor of advertising . . . And I recall one afternoon soon after the Regents' action when I telephoned J. Frank Dobie, the indomitable and lovable old *pater familias* of Texas writers, who had lost his own teaching job at the University in the 1940s, and asked if he would consider writing to the letters column commenting on our troubles. "Hell," he said, "I been workin' on one all mornin'." The Board of Regents, Dobie's letter said, "are as much concerned with free intellectual enterprise as a razorback sow would be with Keats' 'Ode on a Grecian Urn' " — a well-known statement now despite the fact that this phrase, and many another colorful one, were deleted after I had gone home to sleep and the paper was going to press.

One day one of the few outspoken old souls on the faculty in that period, an English professor who had never ceased to fight the political appointees with scorn and satire even in the 1940s, stood up in a faculty meeting and asked what the student newspaper's troubles *meant* in terms of the entire university. "We should discuss this matter," he said, waving his walking cane at his colleagues, "and deplore a contemptuous, cynical attitude toward what the student body or what an elected student leader may say." He spoke of the "dignity of the student" as a "new citizen"; a university's funds, he said, "should

not be meant to *stifle* discussion but to encourage it." There
was no further discussion, however, from the faculty. I wrote a
lead-editorial on his speech and entitled it "Whispers in a Sleepy
Lagoon." The night of its publication, as I sat at my desk eating
a cold hamburger and drinking my fourth cup of black coffee,
one of the administrative deans telephoned. "You published
that editorial," he said, "but do you know that professor is
runnin' around on his wife?" I had barely slept in a week, and
at this point the fatigue had robbed me of any semblance of
cynicism or humor. "Why you old bastard!" was all I could say,
and hung up the telephone.

Looking back on it now, I had forgotten what a nasty time
it was, how it sapped the patience of all of us on both sides,
and the sad indignity with which many decent but weak men
had to try to enforce official demands that I think they would
have preferred in their hearts to ignore. One grew to be sympathetic, if not respectful, of some of these men, stripped as
they were of power and sometimes, I believe, ashamed.

Finally, after more troubles, after we ran blank spaces and
editorials entitled "Let's Water the Pansies," or "Don't Walk
on the Grass" and held to our prerogatives to publish what
we wished, there was a loosening up. There were no further official orders, and we remained free. But I was obsessed with the
fear that in winning the battle we had lost the war, and that
we had fought back wrongly and badly — and that the fight
had not been worth it.

Yet I do not believe it was coincidence that in May of that
year the Regents and the administration sought to impose in
the general faculty a sweeping set of restrictions on the involvement of University of Texas faculty members in politics and
political issues. One of the administration's spokesmen described these restrictions as the drawing of "a little circle"
around political responsibilities. "That little circle," one young

professor, the philosopher John Silber, said, "happens to com-
prise 90 percent of my political concerns." The issue was re-
soundingly defeated. For whom was the bell trying to toll? I
believed then there was a connection there; the contempt for an
independent student voice trying to engage itself in important
issues in that age of McCarthy and silence was reflected in an
effort to do lasting damage to a state university's most basic
civil liberties. Perhaps if the student newspaper had not chosen
to meet the whole question head-on and in public, the controlling political faction would have thought anything easy and
possible. Perhaps we won something more than a battle after
all.

People would tell me long afterward that this sort of thing
could never happen again in the later climate of the University of Texas, that everything became much better, that academic freedom, and freedom of expression, had been won, and
were old issues now. I am convinced this is true. The 1960s
were not the 1950s, and at our state universities these issues
would become, not more straightforward, but more complex,
involving considerations of the very quality of the mass society.
In 1956 the issue was a direct one, and it became bigger than
The Daily Texan, bigger than the Board of Regents, bigger
than the University itself — and it could never be old-fashioned.

•

I have often asked myself in the years that followed, would I do
all this again? I would be less than honest if I answered that
question simply.

At the time, as I understood later, the tone, style, and content
of public discourse meant much more to me than the practical
considerations of how one arranges complicated matters in
feasible, flexible terms. There could have been more subtle
and practical ways of dealing with the problem that confronted

us. For this kind of personal diplomacy I was too immature and too impressionable.

Yet I was twenty years old; the real antagonists were in the seats of power. To my credit I knew who the enemy was. It would be an unwarranted personal renunciation for me to say retrospectively that the indignation I felt in 1956 was unjustified. It is legitimate to assume that editors of student papers at any university have a right to arouse the authorities, and within the laws of libel to bring them down on him. It is right to be able to carry on an aggressive campaign against an ethic they consider sterile and contemptuous. The attempt to censor *The Daily Texan* in 1956 involved not a displacement of dissent, but the running roughshod over it by real power, and the more sophisticated kind of criticism that served as its forum — the kind of wealth which still encourages the idea in America that anything can be bought, including culture. A friend of mine in the state legislature would say to me a few years later, perhaps Texas can never become a truly civilized place until its great natural resources are gone.

For three years I had written my column, "The Round-Up," and in my "30" piece that spring, the last one I wrote, I said, with too many genuflections to Thomas Wolfe:

The University of Texas, I fear, has travelled all too swiftly toward beautiful buildings and sterling reputations. Its leaders, in submitting to those who relish the corporate purse, have too often, and even without reluctance, betrayed the corporation of ideas . . . It has existed at the whim of those forces which would readily crush its heart, its soul, and its mind.

The quick Texas rich, who apply the values of fast money to the values of higher education, have dealt foolishly and cruelly with the prerogatives of the spirit . . . As a result, our University condones the tyranny of the majority, and it encourages in its students sedate complacency to the national and regional arbiter.

It must lead, not follow . . . it must insist that society and the race can be made better. It must strive to show our people, our uneducated and our quick rich, that our civilization is doomed when the material can coerce the human spirit.

I believe that our University is lost, and that being lost has been silent and afraid, but that someday its destiny shall be fulfilled more courageously, more magnificently, and more humbly than we have ever imagined. It is in the bright promise of this vision that I close.

At graduation at the end of that year the air was heavy with the scents of the berry trees; most of the students were long since gone, and the campus was more lovely and still than I had ever seen it before. The chimes on the Tower rang with stirring processionals to the Class of 1956, and proud country parents stood in diffident little groups watching their children march past. I received my diploma, and before a packed audience walked out the wrong door of the auditorium. At the reception afterward a journalism professor said, "I told my wife, there goes Morris, lost again," and the mother of one of my classmates walked up to me and said, "Why, you look too *innocent* to have caused all that newspaper trouble." The next day I left the campus, my '47 Plymouth loaded with books and the paraphernalia of four years, and drove all night one final time to the place I had come from.

4

At Oxford I led, by the standards of the University of Texas, a quiet and detached four years. My first tutorial in 1956 had been on the Reform Act of 1832; I had stayed up straight through one fog-filled night applying the finishing touches. My next-to-last sentence said, "Just how close the people of England came to revolution in 1832 is a question that we shall leave with the historians." I read this to my tutor, and from his vantage point in an easy chair two feet north of the floor he interrupted: "But Morris, we *are* the historians."

So I, the young polemicist, became a part of history, and so enamoured of that haunting, beautiful place that I wondered if I could ever muster the strength to leave, for it suffuses you in a lethargic, dreamy isolation. Oxford is a place, as one of my American predecessors said, where there are always too many bells ringing in the rain. It was I who made the phrase, one cold and melancholy morning in late winter: "Oh to be in April, now that England's here." If Eugene Gant's professor (Merton, '14) at Pulpit Hill had been right, that Oxford does away with one's "useless enthusiasms," perhaps it might do away with the useful ones as well. I had wandered around that city at every opportunity, glorying in the old quads and the echoes of footsteps on wintry afternoons; the dining hall where I took meals in college was older than the discovery of my own country, and the concrete stairway leading to it was grooved by the paths of scores of generations. As the guest of one of the dons I had dined at the college high table, and in the flickering light of the candles I had overheard an august medievalist ask a companion, "Have you written his obituary for the *Academy?*" I was a long way, too long, from the Yazoo High cafeteria; too often that first year I had felt like Abimelech V. Oover, Beerbohm's Anabaptist from Pittsburgh.

I had taken a degree in "modern history," which went up to 1900, anything after that being considered journalism, and I had stayed on to do a period of graduate work. I had traveled all over Europe during vacations, so incorrigibly American that I kept being picked up in the late hours by American MP's. I had written for the Oxford magazines on American subjects, and I had introduced Adlai Stevenson to the American and Commonwealth students in Rhodes House shortly after his second defeat. Once I had escorted Robert Frost in a taxicab to Rhodes House for a talk. "Where are you from, boy?" he had asked. "Mississippi," I replied. "Hell, that's the worst state in the Union," he said. But, I argued, it had produced a lot of good writers. He said, "Can't anybody down there read them."

One day I got a transatlantic telephone call from my mother, telling me my father was dying; I borrowed money from the Warden of Rhodes House to get home, taking the first plane out of London, and sixteen hours later I was in Mississippi, dislocated to the point of schizophrenia. Later I had driven to Texas, and soon I was married to my college sweetheart. We returned to Oxford for one last year, and had a child who cost 82 cents; they let me watch him being born, and as he emerged I observed him out of the remotest corner of an eye: "What is it?" I asked, and the midwife said, "It's a big Texas man!" That night, when I placed a telephone call to Mississippi to tell the news, the English operator phoned back in half an hour and said, "I'm sorry to tell you this place Yazoo City does not exist."

We had lived that last year in a big dusty house on Norham Gardens, in a top-floor flat with frayed Victorian rugs and a hole in the bathroom window. Our landlady, a gnarled bent old woman of ninety, had been friends with Max Beerbohm; she had written a thin volume on George Meredith, and one of her companions had been Henry James' private secretary. Samuel Eliot Morison, she told us, had once lived in our flat, and every time we acted too much like uncouth colonials she reminded us that Mr. Morison had been "proper, very proper." She had been one of the first women to get an Oxford degree, and she signed everything, even her laundry tickets: "Mary Sturge Gretton, B.A., M.A., B.Lit., Oxon." She refused to concede that America existed, even in the mind of God, and hence it is somewhat ironical that I would stay up until three and four in the morning there reading nothing but American history: about the Civil War, Lincoln and his troublesome cabinet, the Mugwumps, the Progressives, the New Dealers, the Roosevelts, the La Follettes, the conventions with a hundred ballots: I lived with the clash and retreat of armies, the thunder of grand old causes, and always the lonely isolated voices. Finally it was this collective image of America out of its past from across the seas that moved me to dwell on our return, until one day a letter came from Ronnie Dugger, the editor of *The Texas Observer*. He had run out of gas, he wrote, and needed to go off in the woods for a long time to read some books and *speculate* on things. Would I come to Texas and take over the paper? The salary would be $110 a week. In that dark old house I myself had been speculating for too long; I accepted with alacrity, for I felt waterlogged with the past. I recognized then, with the same melodramatic seriousness as Jack Burdin, abandoning his PhD dissertation in *All the King's Men* to enter the employ of

Willie Stark, that I must "go out of the house and go into the convulsion of the world, out of history into history and the awful responsibility of time."

We took a snapshot of our son seeing America for the first time against the backdrop of the Statue of Liberty, and then we drove slowly home, stopping to see Hyde Park, Gettysburg, Harpers Ferry, Monticello, Charlottesville, and the Lee museum at Lexington, where a Yankee tourist was taking moving pictures of Traveller's bones; then on through the splendid battlefield country into the Deep South, and after that the same old route I knew so well into the Southwest.

5

By 1960 the effect of Dugger's *Texas Observer* had been profound.* Here was a journal whose readership had never got much higher than 6000, yet by the sheer force of its ardor and its talent, it was read by everyone in Texas whose opinions had authority. It was not merely that Dugger and the other *Observer* editors, William Brammer, Bob Bray, Lyman Jones, Larry Goodwyn (and a roster of contributors — including J. Frank Dobie and Walter Prescott Webb, from an older generation — who would do honor to any journal) began writing about what actually happened: the operations of the state legislature, the courage and disarray of a pathetically small political opposition in the state, the effect on Texas' culture of highly organ-

* *The Observer's* most illustrious forebear had been the old *Texas Spectator,* an unusual weekly edited by Hart Stilwell and the incomparable H. Mewhinney.

ized know-nothing groups working on civic clubs, school boards, and high school government classes. What had been more important was that provincial politics became the subject for serious thought and writing by young men concerned not just with reform at the state level, and it had been an unpropitious time for that, but with the broader reflection the Texas legislature and Texas politics and their terrible failures cast on social values in a democracy. The *Observer* was part muckraker; its antecedents were in the state laboratories of the Progressive era, and hence it had seemed curiously out of character in the decade of the 1950s.

Within the limits of weekly journalism, the *Observer* was also something of a literary undertaking, and many of its early essays would deserve a prominent place in an anthology of our best writing about American politics. When the state legislature was not in session, its writers had concentrated on Texas as a place: the silent tragedies of its small towns, the barren stretches of its Panhandle, the changing character of its cities. The *Observer* ran essays on the rural sharecroppers, the whores in Galveston, the Negroes in East Texas, the *Mexicanos* living in caves and shanties just across the border. It had brought a new element into Texas, because in a state which, unlike Mississippi, had not developed much of a creative literature, it had tried to tell about Texas as it really was; it caught the stresses and tensions of a frontier society becoming urban and American. The big dailies had not been interested in the activities of Tennessee Gas in the private clubs of the capital city, or in the last words of a seventeen-year-old Negro rapist on death row at Huntsville, or in what Norman Mailer said or did not say to the college students in Austin; the news value of Negro Cub Scouts sitting on the curb in front of a movie house in Dallas after having not been allowed to see *King of Kings* must have eluded their city editors.

When I had been in my third year at the University in 1955, the year the paper started, I recall Dugger, then twenty-four years old, sitting in a small dark office in the old frame building on West 24th Street in Austin, surrounded by newspapers and magazines. Brammer, his associate, was out getting drunk with the lieutenant-governor, and Dugger was writing the whole paper by himself in less than twenty-four hours. Once an issue was put to bed he would take out for somewhere in a woebegone 1948 Chevrolet, crowded with camping equipment, six-packs, notebooks, galley proofs, old loaves of bread, and sardine cans. Whenever the Chevrolet broke down, which was often, he would have it hauled to the nearest town and stay there, talking with the people in the town and taking notes on what was going on there. One afternoon Dugger telephoned me from a small town in East Texas. "Something radical's happened," he said. "The motor fell out." That car was an indispensable contribution to Dugger's understanding of Texas. His devotion to Texas as a *place*, as a state distinctive from other states — knowing its courthouse squares, its back roads, its people in cities as different as El Paso and Tyler, or Amarillo and Beaumont, its history, its dialects — was something that by the 1950s had all but vanished from America. "I love it here and belong here," Dugger once wrote, "an animal that feels best when he knows where he is. In a big place like Texas, you come and go with your friends, meet and stop meeting and still go on being friends across distances that often these days become physically insuperable for any casual purpose. If the stereotypers have done us no other favor, they have helped those of us who are friends hold on in an awareness of our common place, even across continents." Dugger is not only one of the great reporters of our time in America; more than that, he had imbued an entire group of young and inexperienced colleagues with a feel for Texas, for "commitment" in its most human sense, and for writing. Dugger will be judged not by what he wrote about corruption, or how to end corruption, but by the sense of fairness in the *way* he wrote about corruption. He taught those of us who passed through the *Observer* en route to our more personal work how to view public life as an ethical process, how to be fair. "He was a pariah in his own land," my friend and fellow *Observer* writer Larry Goodwyn once said — "a land of physical violence and rhetorical violence. He taught both his friends and his enemies the elementary lessons of civility."

The paper was backed in that day, and its deficit was inevitable, by a well-to-do woman from Houston, Mrs. R. D. Randolph — the Eleanor Roosevelt of Texas. She owned most of a county, a cotton and lumber county, in East Texas. "Some old ladies collect antiques," she told me when I first met her. "I want to try to help make the place we live in better." Then she added, "This is a free paper. You're the editor and the paper is yours."

We were to remain devoted on the *Observer*, as Roger Shattuck was to write, to "politics, its responsibility and thrall." It was not a very easy task to travel all over Texas and still get an issue out every week. For two men each to write some 20,000 words of presumably literate journalism a week under deadline, read all the copy and galley proofs and make up the pages, hobnob with politicians, and keep up a correspondence would mean staying up all night two or three nights in a row, and eventually setting up a desk by the linotype operator out at Futura Press on South Congress Avenue and handing him the final editorial page by page.* A finished issue would never be just an

* During one period there were special difficulties. Our night-shift linotype operator was a lovable old alcoholic named Gene. Quite often I would have to pick him up at two in the morning at the flophouse where he lived, sober him up on black coffee, and drive him to the print shop. One night I had been writing for about forty-five minutes in the room next to the linotype machine. Gene came in and said, "Willie, it ain't no use. I've done set the first five galleys in capital letters."

issue; it came out of the marrow of our bones. It was so much
our own it reflected not just our errors but our sins, from comma
blunders to the most critical shortcomings in judgment. (One
issue came fresh off the presses one Friday morning; to our
dismay we noticed that the main headline on the front page, in
bold 48-point, had a typographical error that we had missed:
Intergration. For three hours we worked feverishly pasting
the address labels by hand over the redundant "r" in Intergration. The task was too much, and finally we gave up, turning
over to our rickety address machine the job of placing the labels
wherever it chose on the faulty front page.) But it was good to
know that any week's issue would be read, and read closely, by
most members of the state legislature, the two U.S. Senators,
the governor, the Speaker of the U.S. House, and the Vice-President of the United States (who not only read it, I was to learn,
but underlined it with a ball-point pen). We would be inter-
mediaries in fights, some of them not specifically philosophical,
between the liberals. We had an unusual perspective on Texas,
because our shabby quarters in Austin would be the haven for a
good percentage of the displaced population: old Jewish so-
cialists with beards, far away from their native New York because they had come to a dry climate for their health, Negro
sit-ins on fasts, ex-Stalinists with nowhere to go, not even Russia. From Monday to Friday there would be a steady flow:
anarchists, beatniks, bums, *New York Times*-men, editors of
Eastern journals, FBI men, Michael Harrington, Goldwater
Republicans seeking some coalition, retired professors, and
Unitarians. Our phone was tapped and the office had roaches.
Sarah Payne, our secretary, the gentlest person I would ever
know, fought the roaches and tried to protect us from the more
casual intruders, but rarely was it possible to give thought there
to the disordered or despairing things we would see; that would
come later, when one was very much alone.

When I took over the *Observer* from Dugger, who promptly
went into the hills with everything Thoreau had ever written, I
had just turned twenty-five years old. I was not the same self-
righteous, moralistic boy I had been as editor of *The Daily
Texan*. I had the most earnest feelings that our little paper
was somehow involved, however modestly, in the great flow of
history on this continent, and that to understand a place like
Texas through its dissenters and its young rebels was to understand something of an older, vanished America; yet I also wished
to be rooted in my own anxious time, a time when a new generation of young Americans would, for a tragically brief and
poignant period, wield power. And somewhere along the way I
had developed what might be called a sense of humor, and perhaps even a sense of humility.

●

We lived in a house in a shady old section of town, just a few
blocks down the hill from the Texas state capitol. Every morning at ten o'clock, armed with two spiral notebooks and ready
with my best Mississippi handshake, I drove down to cover the
unusual human spectacle in what I later would call "The Big
Top."

A state legislature is a fertile source for a writer. Too many
crimes are committed there daily in an atmosphere of a service
club social, and the human flaws are so accessible. Sometimes it
is too much for one to bear, the more or less constant spectacle
of legislators backed by the sanction of powerful business lobbies frustrating the few good and intelligent men who are willing to labor in the maw of small-time politics. Until 1955, when
the *Observer* writers were set loose on it, the Texas legislature
had seldom expected to be taken seriously. It was a circus of
ordinary follies, a lane-end; stagnating in the backwaters of
provincial politics, it was rendered bloodless by the stereotyped

formulas of the big-city newspapers. The state had produced a
distinguished Speaker of the U.S. House and a Senate majority
leader who already had his sights on the Presidency, men with
towering national influence and the guarded instincts of superior professionals. At the state level they had charted a subtle
course somewhat between and above the conservative business
establishment on the one hand, and the growing post-war liberalism on the other; as far as the legislature of their home state
was concerned, it was less embarrassing for Speaker Rayburn and
Senator Johnson to avoid it than to do anything about it. The
place had had its heroic moments: the occasional populist calling for vengeance on Yankee bankers, the tiny group of reformers rallying against the giants of oil and gas for drawing the colony dry and leaving a pittance in return. A rigorous conservatism not only called the plays, it set the rules for debate. The
dramas and sorrows of this curious institution had been left
to the interpretations of tired newspapermen whose sensibilities had corroded from too much exposure to a diet of daily
deceit, mostly crippled cynics who were unable to tell an irony
from an obscene story. I was no novice to politics at the time;
my tenure on *The Daily Texan* had given me some early taste of
the extravagant world of Southwest politics, though I think I still
vaguely suspected there might be some *science* lurking in it, even
in a state capitol.

But the state legislature itself was something more directly
human, irrelevant to ivory tower polemics, and much like Mrs.
Lightfoot Lee's confrontation with Washington politics in
Henry Adams' *Democracy*, I was simply not prepared for it. It
is difficult to convey exactly the way I reacted those first days
there, but I remember it as a kind of physical sickness, the result
of a continuing outrage, for which even writing was no outlet. I
do not think this could be attributed to any moral righteousness, nor to an undue naïveté. I knew my Lincoln Steffens, and

I had more than a passing knowledge of the Whig House of Commons, which appealed to my decadent Mississippi instincts; I had always had a curious liking for politicians, and if the preference were between a sanctimonious old bastard with the right ideas and a politician with none at all, I would not have hesitated. Despite all this, I remained in a state of unusual anger. I would spend most of a working day wandering around the floor of both houses, eavesdropping on the big lobbyists, interviewing the strategists behind the legislative monstrosities which passed as conservatism, and drinking interminable beers with the representatives of what the *Dallas Morning News* called the "liberal-leftist axis." What I saw and heard, however, did less damage to my equilibrium than it did to Bob Sherrill's, my associate editor. Sherrill had been around. He was allegedly born in Frogtown, Georgia, a place which no longer exists, educated in California, and he had worked as a newspaper carrier, a janitor, a house painter, and a water analyst. He was a veteran reporter who had written, in the old tradition, for some twenty-five papers all over America. When he grew tired of one town, or began to hate an editor's guts too much for his own sense of balance, he would simply depart for another, usually in the dead of night. Sherrill was a painter and a poet, and had once worked briefly on a PhD at an Ivy League graduate school before concluding that the city room of any middle-sized daily was more civilized and usually more literate. He was also a cynic, but with a soft underspot he almost never showed, and he joined the *Texas Observer*, as he told me at the time, to see if idealism existed, and if so whether it was worth the effort. He had had almost no experience with politics, which he regarded as a form of athletics, but he had covered more rapes, muggings, frauds, murders, fornications, and mutilations than most men of comparable sensibility. Those first days in the legislature Sherrill would station himself in the most inaccessible corner of whatever room or chamber he happened to be in. I would often spot him across the House floor, lurking in the shadows of some statue, a sneer on his face. Sometimes he would sit on his haunches in a corner, the way farmers do outside the old general stores of crossroads towns, rolling his eyes straight up to the ceiling, cursing silently to himself. Gradually he would begin to move among the members on the floor, taking notes and shaking his great head. Our paths would occasionally cross in these peregrinations. Sherrill would whisper, "Jesus Christ," or "shi-*yeet*," and then recount to me something he had just watched or been told. I think he was ready to fight. Once he accosted me to talk about the activities of one particular big-city delegation which had five members, four of whom got around in wheelchairs. "I've been counting," Sherrill said, "and the ones from —— are all invalids, except D——, and that son-of-a-bitch is a *mental* invalid." Sherrill came to scoff, but I think he remained as long as he did because there was so much to scoff at.

•

I have gone back over the notes I took at the time to recall what most impressed me. In the first week there was an important committee hearing on appropriations. The chairman, a rural demagogue who liked to dress in the nattiest Ivy fashions — perhaps to help himself forget that in his constituency he represented more cows, centipedes, and horseflies than people — spent several minutes attacking a witness for what he called undue "lobbying." The witness's lobbying had consisted of pointing out that the State of Texas was appropriating several hundred thousand dollars for advertising the wildlife activities of its game and fish commission, $30,000 for financing a quail hatchery, and not a penny of a requested $10,000 for allowing a state council on migrant labor to remain in existence to make recommendations on vehicle safety, child labor laws, and minimum housing standards. That same afternoon I went to a committee hearing on the Senate side, where officials testified that the State of Texas did not have a single juvenile parole officer. The director of the Negro detention home said many of the children with no parents and nowhere to go when they got out would "often develop some problem to remain in reform school." A state Senator suggested, and his colleagues laughed in good fun, that perhaps they should put some of these delinquents under the animal wildlife board. The director of the state's youth services testified at another hearing the next day, "We simply don't have a single bed for neglected Negro children in this state." "Well," a Senator asked, "where do they go?" "Your guess is as good as mine, Senator," the director replied. The director later told me that these Negro orphans with no place to go had sometimes been sent to reform schools with hardened offenders, because these were the only state facilities which could take care of them.

Lobbyists for oil and gas, whom the old hands called "the Knights of Congress Avenue," usually outnumbered state senators at tax hearings. A joint session one morning heard a special address from one of those perambulating preachers in which the Southwest seems to abound; he was warmly applauded when he said the profit motive is the last good human instinct, Jesus upheld the profit motive, and "What's good for Kaiser Steel is good for the country." Fifty-thousand-a-year corporation lawyers flocked to committee hearings, especially on taxes and appropriations, to argue their favorite theme: "You can't tax a corporation; a corporation is *all* of us." For years a conservative governor had tried to get the legislature to pass an escheats bill — or abandoned property act — of the kind that had already been enacted by some thirty-six states, and in a debate which was a prelude to its being defeated again one man argued, in high seriousness: "Someone said this escheats bill was around a thousand years old. Let's think just a minute who it was that started it — the King of England.* Gentlemen, I don't believe in this law." In response to an appeal at a committee hearing for stronger school attendance laws for Mexican-American children, who then averaged only three and a half years of schooling, one especially outspoken female legislator, who reflected the majority sentiment on the committee, said, "If more children had to work younger today, they might *appreciate* luxuries." One morning a bill advocating a fifty-cent-an-hour minimum wage for Texas got 33 votes out of 150 in the lower house. Proposed tax increases on oil and gas were lucky to reach the floor. Occasionally they did, to be defeated.

The loss to Texas of its natural heritage, sold for pottage, had been one of the great shames of a state in which social services contrast so dramatically with basic economic wealth. If an enlightened tax program had been applied to oil and gas two decades ago, Texas in the 1960s might have had the best and most progressive state government in America. It was in this perspective that the constant destruction of decent appropriations took on deeper shades of meaning than in the legislatures of other, less endowed states. The reformers in the Texas legislature never missed an opportunity to argue that theirs was a state which ranked first in the nation in oil, with about half the nation's underground reserves; first in gas, with over 45 percent of the nation's underground reserves; first in cattle, first in cotton, first in everything from livestock and mohair to goats and pecans. Yet in basic social services the State of Texas ranked first in its caseload per state social worker; 41st in old-age pensions; 40th in public assistance programs in general, with almost three-quarters of these funds from the federal government; 40th in literacy; 42nd in aid to dependent chil-

* This may have been that arch-radical, King Edward III (1327–1377).

dren; 50th in vocational rehabilitation for injured workers; and close to the bottom in educational services. Despite its impressive natural beauty, its state parks were a travesty, and it could be judged nothing less than criminal in its negligence of the mentally ill.

Such arguments, made almost in desperation, were greeted, depending on the moment, with smugness, high hilarity, inattention, or a simple lack of intelligence. On the *Observer* we were sometimes overcome with futility and anger, the flaws seemed too great to be measured in terms of our own private contempt, and the sheer enormity of the task of reform from within the system made our occasional optimisms seem a waste of good energy. "If Texas won't," it was said bitterly, "then Washington will." The most intelligent of the reformers knew that the most crucial economic demand was to keep chipping away at the tax wall set up by oil and gas; the odds were overwhelming. It had become political legend, after a mere ten years, how a group of tax reformers patched together a coalition in 1951 for a "gas-gathering" tax. Friends of the oil and gas interests forced an extra session in the hope that the five-dollar per diem pay would force the "tax-eaters," as the papers called them, to disband and go home. But the gashouse gang, as they became known, pooled their money and rented an old house on Nueces Street in Austin. They kept going on free food from their sympathizers, and sometimes on bourbon from the liquor lobbyists, the best and kindest of their breed, who mainly appreciated the show they were putting on. Eventually the gashouse gang got their tax, but they had legislated on a shaky principle, and it was not the work of an influential anthropomorphic God who has doubts about Standard of New Jersey that their tax was struck down as unconstitutional.

Bob Eckhardt, a legislator from Houston, once remarked to me that the state capitol in Austin was "built for giants and inhabited by pygmies." The legislature was starkly out of character with its surroundings: the big, distinctive old building on a rise overlooking Congress Avenue, the broad lawn with the gnarled oaks, the portraits of the Alamo, of Mirabeau Lamar, Sam Houston, Stephen F. Austin, Jim Bowie, Davy Crockett, Jim Hogg, Sam Rayburn, Lyndon Johnson. Both houses, as elsewhere, were gerrymandered beyond coherence. The lower one had 150 members, the state Senate, 31; they were from El Paso on the west to Texarkana on the east, from Mexico on the south almost to Kansas on the north. Of these 181, there were no Negroes. There were about eight *Mexicanos*, young men educated in the night schools or sometimes not at all, angry and intelligent and willing to take on the best legal talent the corporations could offer.

The great majority of the legislators were white, Anglo-Saxon, and Protestant, yet one would have had to go to the national Congress, of all other American parliamentry bodies, to find a legislature which encompassed so many differing regions and values. There were a bare handful of Republicans, new arrivals who usually dressed better, disowned Lincoln, and were prone to caucus in phone boths. Their idol was Senator Goldwater, and ideologically they occupied the low ground somewhere to the right of Ethelred the Unready, though by no means without company from the ranks of their Democratic colleagues. The provincial political manner, a back-slapping exuberance coated with an uneasy literacy, dominated the place. An East Texas racist could attack a man in the morning as an enemy of the commonweath, and ask his advice in the afternoon on whether his son should go to "one of them Ivy League schools." There were men with meanness written on every feature, heavy, red-faced meanness, men you would not want to cross if you could avoid it, and there were decent, friendly, and well-educated men who sought one's respect and attention; it took time to recognize that the votes of the decent and friendly ones against social legislation, against Negroes, and against any meaningful taxes counted as much and usually more than the votes of the straightforward reprobates.

There we were, existing theoretically within the old institutions: majority vote, most of the time, free speech, and the dictates of an informal country courtesy. It was good to be a gentleman, even when it was not consistently possible. Sometimes, as in *Lord of the Flies*, someone threw away the conch shell. One night, in a bitter floor debate in the lower house, one legislator pulled the cord out of the amplifier system, another hit him from the blindside with a tackle; there was mass pushing, hitting, clawing, and exchanges about one another's wives, mistresses, and forebears. Sweethearts and wives, who were allowed on the floor with friends and secretaries, cowered near the desks. In the middle of the brawl, a barbershop quartet of legislators quickly formed at the front of the chamber and, like a dance band during a saloon fight, sang "I Had a Dream, Dear." This was an exceptional occurrence, but I recall it took place during an interim in which the parliamentarian was looking up a complex point in parliamentary procedure.

Sex in the lower house was an electric and wonderful presence. The secretaries, with their chairs right next to the legislators on the floor, were less secretaries than co-workers, colleagues, soulmates, and, as such things go, partners in extracurricular engagements. In a state as big as Texas, politicians during a legislative session could be a long way from home, as far from home as the buxom girls who swarmed to the capitol for the extravagant festivities of opening day. But in regard to the more blatant sexual activities, there was between the liberals and the conservatives an unwritten rule more sacrosanct than

Roberts Rules of Order, or the common law. This was that no one would blow the whistle on anyone else, and although it had never been committed to parchment or to any other kind of paper, as a corollary of daily existence it was inviolable and unchallengeable. Had either camp violated this doctrine, the democratic experiment in Texas might have been destroyed forever. There was something in the atmosphere of the beginning of a new session that was distinctly *sensual:* the garlands of flowers and the popping of flashbulbs, the ritualistic pomp and display of power inherited in its somewhat bastardized form from Mother Parliament, the pretty girls looking for the jobs and sinecures. The wild parties with free liquor from the lobby lubricated the politician's inevitable quest for sympathy and admiration, and the uninhibited flow of natural juices. On the closing night of a session, when the legislators and their female companions might wear Hawaiian leis in anticipation of the all-night celebration at some posh watering-spot, the floor of the Texas House of Representatives looked less like an institution of polity than a small-town nightclub.

The state Senate, on the other hand, was more like a mortuary parlor, which befitted an institution whose greatest contribution had been the sure death of any faintly progressive piece of legislation. It was a plush green chamber, just large enough to accommodate thirty-one senators — so small that in its earlier days the business lobby could control the entire state government by more or less owning thirteen senators.* Three

* In this regard, the techniques of the big lobbies had changed considerably. It had not been too long before in Texas that the lobbyists mainly resorted to the "three B's" — bourbon, beef, and blondes. The methodology became more sophisticated. On important issues the business lobby began to go outside the legislature to cultivate grassroots public-relations campaigns among a legislator's constituents, especially the more wealthy and influential. In this way it had learned to pressure the individual legislator where he hurt the most: his fear of defeat in the next election. In the Texas legislature in 1961, a state sales tax was finally passed after extensive work of this kind in the constituencies. The oil and gas lobby was the strongest force behind the sales tax, organizing something of a front group called "Citizens for a Sales Tax" which actually asked for

or four senators would laugh and banter for hours about
whether non-resident brewers should pay state fees, or discuss
the jurisdiction of notaries public, or how corpses could best
be diverted for medical science, all this while loan shark bills
rotted for lack of a hearing, air pollution bills for lack of a sponsor, and while the two or three first-team leaders worked effi-
ciently behind the scenes to make sure no pipelines taxes ever
reached the floor.

The first time I went into the state Senate for a floor debate,
I wrote down my reactions: "A young reporter turned to me
and asked, 'How can I tell the truth about what it's *really* like
over here in a news story?' Under the format of a daily newspaper it is impossible. A good journalist with a mind of his
own can see right through the deceits. He knows the man is lying, and he knows the *man* knows he is lying. It is like a game.
Indignant outbursts are accompanied by sly grins; laughter
creeps into the most heartfelt speeches. Nothing whatever has
the ring of truth." One night while the Senate was considering
a gas tax bill, I was in a private club in Austin with a well-
known county judge from El Paso noted chiefly for his capacity
for whiskey sours. He began exploring the place and came back
and told me, "I've just uncovered a covey of old birds." He led
me to a back room and pulled the curtains. Seated at the table
were the chairman and five members of the tax committee of
the state Senate and the four biggest oil and gas lobbyists in
Texas. "Senator Regan," the judge shouted, sticking his head
through the curtain, "y'awl decidin' on that gas tax?" The Senator turned and said, "Judge, it's got us all up in the air."

•

small contributions from average citizens. The change to more sophisticated
lobbying techniques was probably taking place along much the same lines in other
states, just as it had in Washington. In Texas the custom of the three B's simply
lasted longer. There was still considerable skullduggery in the early 1960's; it was
just more civilized.

A man could not have edited a newspaper with the acute degree of contempt one felt in those first days. As often happens to people deeply involved in everyday politics in America, I think I relaxed, or perhaps weakened, as a means of survival. In the Texas legislature at the time, even when one saw every human decency violated, and many of the violations actually put into law, one learned that there was little future in indulging outrage and anger at the personal level. Otherwise one's daily existence among politicians would have consisted of more or less uninterrupted physical violence. The experience of calling a man a turncoat or a scoundrel in an editorial and then shaking his hand and exchanging banal pleasantries on the House floor the next day was not a comfortable one at first, but it somehow kept a balance between anarchy and the parliamentary forms. It also helped when an editor built up his private intelligence network to a perfection such that the opposition began ratting on each other, a practice which was indispensable on a journal like ours. There is a myth, and it dies hard, which says that politicians who vote alike are natural friends, but in a roomful of like-minded country representatives there are jealousies of an intensity that in contrast would make the court of the Sun King seem like Our Town.

But the country politician has a remarkable resilience. I once subjected an important lobbyist to a half-hour of detailed questioning concerning a certain malpractice on which I had been reliably informed (in this case by the Governor of Texas), and afterward the man cordially asked me to have a drink with him at his club. Ronnie Dugger had once called a politician a crook in an editorial, and two days later the man crashed a dinner party at Dugger's house. I expected my shots to have greater effect; I hoped to see my victims rage in vengeance or in guilt, to come at me with a coal-black .45 the way they do in the Northern journalism prize citations, but they never did. When

I ran a list of the forty-five ranking diehards in the Texas legislature, based on a voting analysis which cited votes against everything from free toilets for school children to industrial safety bills, one legislator — later promoted to Speaker of the Texas House — came to me and demanded a correction: he had voted against all these measures and his name, "Goddamn you" (as he patted me on the back) had not been included. A Texas politician with a tenth-grade education had hidden springs of sophistication in such matters. I found him less violent about politics, both in the physical and psychic sense, than the average young matron with a college diploma and an executive husband who thought, in the year 1964, that Barry Goldwater could salvage our honor.

After a time one began to see such politicians, quite simply, as a reflection of the broader system. The quality of human matter in most state legislatures in America had never been epic, and an apportionment based on acreage rather than people had tended to tolerate similar vast and empty expanses in representative epicrania. This legislature was no worse than many, considerably more entertaining than most, and in its young men, like myself, it encouraged a true sense of being close to the source. They were human beings, Texas people, and fairly typical products of Baptist Waco, racist East Texas, or the more disturbingly reactionary sections of the Panhandle. They were lesser men, most of them, than the men who organized the game, and although they moved about like barnyard fowls in their glory, there was something rather pathetic in their performance. It was difficult if not impossible for many of the country boys to resist the courting they got in the city: the plush hotels and parties, official attentions, little courtesies from important people, the first-name talk with the bankers and oilmen up from home. One of them had once delivered a lengthy diatribe against a tax bill on the floor of the lower house, an oration riddled with distortions and strange simplicities. I went over to talk with him about his exercise in logic, which would doubtless be on the front pages of most of the dailies the next day, and which had obviously been successful in helping marshal an impressive majority. After several minutes of conversation I made an unexpected discovery: he had the brain of a small bird. He had almost no grasp of the issue or its consequences, or even of the implications of the speech he had just made. He really did not care one way or the other, he had spoken his piece and voted, and he preferred to forget the whole business and be a jocular companion.

On another occasion, the lower house had just voted down a bill requiring that trucks hauling migrant laborers be inspected to make sure the windshield wipers were working, and the headlights, and the tail reflectors, and other such things. I cornered one of the more amiable conservatives who had helped defeat it. "Joe," I asked, "now why did you vote against that bill?" A great wave of intensity bathed his features, and he said: "Ol' buddy, I ain't against the migrants, and I ain't against their kids. I had it rough myself. But if you get this kind of legislation started, there ain't no tellin' where it'll stop."

After a time, in fact, I grew to like a number of the country conservatives. They enjoyed putting on a good show for us, and often one or more of them would come to me, just out of amiability, with the low-down on something secret that had happened. We would eat Mexican food or drink beer with them, and taunt them unmercifully about their voting record or their performance on the floor. "Well, you boys are *smart*," one of them said to me. "Our fellows don't never read books." They went through the hectic round of the city's political parties in a genial and aimless inebriation, and bear-hugged their liberal foes as if politics were a happy sport among friends. The "kamikaze" liberals outside the legislature, as I liked to call them, hated these boys with a righteous passion, and thought them the personification of all evil. "Newsmongering calls for action, not reflection," Lincoln Steffens wrote in his *Autobiography*, "and Tammany, hungry and irritated, was providing us with a world of public enemies to expose. The only obstacle that troubled us was that we did not hate, we rather loved, our enemies, who rather liked us."

In this environment it took me a few weeks to learn that the heavy hand was not only ineffective, it was usually irrelevant. Humor was essentially a way of surviving, and it was no coincidence that every good man I knew in the political life of the state had a deep and abiding sense of the absurd. Humor also was an offensive weapon, the best way of expressing one's contempt. An editorial could go on for 5000 words against a charlatan or a liar, one could quote every authority from St. Thomas Aquinas to Murray Kempton, but the barb or the burlesque was the better way to stalk an enemy. The country legislator is filled high with his own importance, he esteems his own peculiar boondocks cynicism, but he seems deathly afraid of humor when it is employed against himself. For this reason the annual Oscars awarded by the *Texas Observer* included: Oil and Gas Man of the Year, Oil and Gas Rookie of the Year, Pipelines' Utility Man, The Standard of New Jersey Good Conduct Medal, Most Likely to Secede, the Wall Street Combat Ribbon with Oakleaf Clusters, DAR Revolutionary of the Year, the Most Outstanding Swinger of Birchers, the Frates Seeligson Purple Heart (named after one of their associates who had unexpectedly fallen in combat the previous election), Neanderthal of the Year, and Most Disappointing Neanderthal of the Year (for moving back and forth too indecisively between the Neanderthal and Cro-Magnon periods).

·

The preponderance of mediocrities in the capitol could only deepen one's appreciation of the good men. They came from likely places — Houston, San Antonio, and El Paso — as well as from the most unlikely ones: Roby, Jacksonville, Denison, Refugio, Tulia, Alvin, Trinity, Goliad, Liberty. I think first of Bob Eckhardt,* a gentle and learned man, undoubtedly one of the outstanding men in state politics in America. The role of the anecdote, the story, is a powerful one in Southern politics, and Eckhardt was a genius in the milieu; his humor was usually sad and quiet, like Lincoln's. He wore a big hat and had a thick Southern drawl. Once I asked him, "Eckhardt, why do you wear that dirty old hat?" and he said, "A man with a hat like that and a drawl like this *couldn't* be a liberal." He told the story about how a voter in Houston walked up to his mother, who was helping him campaign, and said, "Mrs. Eckhardt, we're favorably inclined toward your son, but we're worried about his views on the race issue." She replied, "Oh, I'm afraid that's my fault. I raised him to be a Christian." Once, at the end of a floor debate in which the conservatives, taking their cue from the Goldwater primer, were trying to cut state aid money to illegitimate children, Eckhardt went to the microphone and said, quietly, "I'm not so much concerned with the natural bastards as I am with the self-made ones." The only time I saw Eckhardt angry, under the most trying conditions, was after the opposition had butchered his oil and gas tax by adding several unconstitutional amendments. He marched up to Judge "Twinkletoes" Foster, the biggest oil lobbyist in town, shook his fist, and, in a voice trembling with child-like rage, said, "You ruined my tax, Judge. You made it unconstitutional, and you *know* it." Otherwise, Eckhardt kept his balance, even when he was one of only two men in the Texas legislature who refused to vote for a resolution praising the House Un-American Activi-

* Later elected to the United States Congress.

ties Committee. His weapons were a relentless logic, a towering dignity, and the power of humor. He knew more oil and gas
law than all the lobbyists in Austin; one afternoon I saw him
take on every major lobbyist and lawyer the pipelines could
muster in a committee hearing and plainly best them all. Fancy
lawyers who specialized in testimony before the important
finance committees regarded him uneasily. The one-night stand
corporation defenders who would fly in from the East or the
Midwest to make buffoons of the backwoods reformers on particularly dangerous tax legislation had been forewarned about
him. I heard on good authority that these perambulating lobbyists, masters of ridicule, condescension, and the complexities
of the law, were tipped off about Eckhardt by their bosses in
approximately this manner: "Now when you go down to Austin
to testify against this franchise tax, there'll be a fellow on that
tax committee named Eckhardt, with a drawl like a dirt farmer,
but when he starts asking questions, you'd better stop and think
about the answers. He knows more than we do." When one
of these lobbyists for a large paper corporation warned a tax
committee one day that tax reformers had wrecked many another state, that his company contributed a lot more to Texas
than Texas contributed to it, and that a tax revision would drive
his corporation to ruin, Eckhardt asked:

"Mr. Combs, can you tell the committee why your company
decided to come to Texas?"

"What do you mean, Mr. Eckhardt?"

"Well, can you tell us why you decided to locate in Texas
rather than, say Albuquerque, or Wichita, Kansas, or Oklahoma
City?"

"I don't quite see what you're driving at, sir."

"I wonder," Eckhardt said, "if it had anything to do with
water and trees" (pronounced *whaa-tu* and *treeehs*). He then
proceeded, in the most brilliant statement I have ever heard on

the subject, to attack big corporations which "come down here and take our natural resources out of the earth, and take our water and our trees, and drive their big trucks on our roads, and send their children to our schools, and send you lobbyists down here to our legislature, and don't even begin to give us a proper social payment in return." On another occasion there was a hearing on an industrial safety law. Texas was the only industrial state in America with no regulation; the sponsors of a safety bill tried to point out that some one thousand workers were killed on the job every year, and thousands injured. Witnesses from the corporations argued that it is impossible to "legislate safety." One of them said, "It's the workers, not the machinery or management, that's always at fault." To this Eckhardt replied, "Well, you know in the lumber mills, those big hooks that come down and grab a log and pull it into the saw, sometimes they grab a worker and pull *him* into the saw. But I guess you'd call that worker failure, because the machinery was workin' just right, and it sawed up that worker just like he was a log."

•

There was Mullen, the most sensitive one of all. He represented a Mexican-American constituency near the border, where his father owned a town. He would sit off in a corner, at times on his haunches next to Sherrill under the portrait of Sam Houston, sipping gin from a Seven-Up bottle. He was a member of one committee that had an especially long history of razing professors, non-fundamentalist preachers, and intellectuals. It was probably the most racist and xenophobic of all the legislative committees, and Mullen would stand off on the peripheries, drinking always from his Seven-Up bottle. The only time he ever spoke seemed to be out of some final desperation. Once

the rural conservatives, to put the city liberals on the spot, had
introduced a bill that would require all professors and teachers
in state-supported schools "to acknowledge the existence of a
Supreme Being." At the hearing on the bill, the sponsor was
testifying on its behalf. One of Mullen's friends on the committee interrupted to read Jefferson's Act Establishing Religious
Freedom in Virginia.

"Well, that's just fine," the sponsor, a loquacious gargoyle
named W. T. Oliver, replied.

"Well, W. T., it looks like we'll either have to be for you or
for Tom Jefferson," Mullen said.

"Yessir," W. T. said, "that seems to be the choice."

"W. T.," Mullen said, "you're makin' it awful hard on us."

There were those with memorable eccentricities, like
Huggins, who was still relatively young in a seedy way but had
spent enough years in those environs on the losing side to deserve being shell-shocked. He was a fighting reformer from the
old school, and his idols were Maury Maverick, Sr., George Nor-
ris, and the elder La Follette. When I had been a student at the
University, Huggins was already serving in the legislature as a
law student. Many an afternoon I would run into him lounging
around in front of the student union, quoting Adlai Stevenson
to anyone who would listen, berating pretty co-eds to learn
about politics and read Arthur Schlesinger, Jr., the way their coun-
terparts did at Smith, Wellesley, Radcliffe, and Vassar, and engaging in heated argument with campus politicoes. He had
been the pattern for a genial but somewhat unattractive character in William Brammer's political novel, *The Gay Place*,
and I suggested to him he ought to be angry. "But I'm not," he
said. "Why, to be in the pages of a book, so that people can
read about you fifty or a hundred years from now, that's gettin'
a little *immortality*." Huggins campaigned for re-election from
a sidewalk café in Paris against a blind female justice of the

peace; his platform was "one-hundred-per-cent Americanism."
He was the only politician in Texas who read the *New York
Times* every day, the *Nation*, the *New Republic*, the *Progressive*,
the *Washington Post*, and the *Hudson Review*. He scored his
highest triumph one day when a visiting Eastern intellectual,
out from New York to ascertain if the rest of the country
were, as rumor had it, inhabited, glanced at the newspapers
and journals on his desk and whispered, "My God! A civilized
man in the Texas House of Representatives!" Huggins and
Mullen once rented a house where the liberals could meet,
and named it "the Russian Embassy." Huggins confided to
me at the Russian Embassy one night, "You know, a politician's
got to sell out to somebody, it's just a matter of pickin' the
right people to sell out to. I've sold out to the truckers and
to liquor. I may be their property, but I've never yet cast
a vote against the people. The truckers aren't a bad group,
and the good thing about the liquor boys is that when you vote
for the truckers when you really don't want to, you can go off
and get drunk about it free of charge."

There was McGregor, an intellectual elected at the age of
twenty-one by business interests, and who in three sessions became the smartest and most articulate of the minority.* There
was Henry Gonzalez† who broke the national filibuster record
in the state Senate on a racist bill, and who used to describe
a Latin-American as "a Mexican with a poll tax." There were
B—— and B——, both of whom had been in the state legislature for ten years beginning when they were twenty-one. Once
they got so angry after being defeated by a particular lobby on
an important vote one afternoon, they broke into the lobbyist's house that night and stole three dozen sirloin steaks from
the deep freeze. And, finally, there was Spears, the toughest

---

* For a later glimpse of McGregor among the New York literati, see page 355.
† Later a United States Congressman.

fighter of them all and the one who would probably go the farthest, who told me he won on a piece of legislation "because
I got mad and I stayed mad." Once, after a bad defeat, he
pointed to the lobbyists in the gallery and shouted, "Today was
the Alamo, but San Jacinto is yet to come."

But San Jacinto seldom came. One measured victory, not in
terms of winning, but in the few additional votes picked up in
defeat. In the lower house there was a big electric voting board,
green lights for aye, red for nay, and we got used to seeing the
same lights, the angry flashing nays, beginning with Alaniz and
ending with Zbranek, always scattered and outnumbered.

It sometimes seemed like a charade, gathering in the gloomy
old house where the liberals met to dissect their most recent
defeat. What went wrong? Why did somebody desert? Who
would handle the fight against the racists' newest bill the next
morning? Empty beer cans and cigarette butts littered the
floor. Tempers would flare; there seemed little or no leadership,
no focus. Some conservative would telephone and ask them
to join a celebration party at the Driskill Hotel: "You boys take
yourselves too goddamned serious." But after a while even
Johnny Alaniz from the San Antonio West Side could forget
politics and devote himself to dedicated, uninterrupted beer-
drinking, the way beer is taken in Texas.

•

Yet this was not all. Sometimes, by surprise, on some lazy
afternoon the chamber would suddenly break into eloquent,
angry exchanges, going straight to the dilemmas of our politics.
The bill under debate might be nothing, but Eckhardt would
begin with a sad lament for something gone wrong, then shift
imperceptibly into a brilliant exposition of all the things that
had contributed to the failure of state government in Texas
and elsewhere. This would move Spears, who would follow with

a defiant diatribe full of emotion and fight; then would come Mullen, with a terse set of questions aimed at the opposition, challenging their credentials and their future efficacy; and then Huggins, with a memorable story illustrating the follies of inaction. By this time they would all be on the floor shouting for recognition; someone would have told B——, who was in the rotunda smoking a cigar and trying to arrange something with a sexpot of a secretary, that his friends had the floor and were fighting mad. He would rush to the Speaker's apartments to get Kennard, sitting at the window drinking bourbon and staring into space; the two would go the floor and engage in mock questions and answers mimicking a lobbyist. McGregor might get up and, to illustrate a point about the race issue, exclaim, from Styron, "The ground, gentlemen, is bloody and full of guilt where we were born," a poetic outburst as comprehensible to most of the assembly as the later plays of Bertolt Brecht or the cantos of Ezra Pound. Caldwell would talk about, of all things, the common law and the Constitution of the United States, and Whitfield would quote King John at Runnymede or the Emancipation Proclamation.

At this point, as one got some brief foretaste of what a radically reapportioned legislature might promise, the conservatives would have given up, for they were outclassed if not outnumbered. The press table would be deserted; the specialists for the dailies would see little consequence in the libs talking into the thin air; but under the portrait of Sam Houston, Sherrill would be taking notes.

6

IN OUR DAY Lyndon Johnson, more than any other American politician, symbolized *power*, represented it, gloried in it, knew all its hidden levers. His shrewd understanding of the shifting power structures in Texas had given him a base for a national prominence unmatched by any Southern-rooted political figure since the Civil War.

As elsewhere in the one-party South, the Democratic Party in Texas had been a loose and rather purposeless brotherhood, broad enough to include the corporation lawyer and the Negro tenant farmer, the oilman and the labor organizer, the young executive on the make and the restless liberal egghead. But after a time a financial community undergirded by tremendous natural wealth was bound to clash with the workers, the small farmers, the small businessmen, and the dispossessed minorities, with direct repercussions on the one existing political institution — the Democratic Party. In the New Deal years the entire party hierarchy was almost entirely pro-Roosevelt. Texas in the mid-thirties was still an agrarian society, giving frequent vent to the old Populist-type rhetoric against Wall Street and the Yankee profiteers. But by the end of the Second War the state had undergone a major transition. Oil was booming, the utilities and the banks and the insurance giants were becoming a focus of power, cities like Dallas and Houston were steadily growing, and the new-rich began looking to politics. Labor and the federal government became living issues. The Democrats splintered into interest groupings, with differing goals and philosophies. The liberal wing, largely oriented to the modern national Democrat Party and advocating sweeping reforms at home, grew stronger and tougher, despite the usual propensity for fratricide within its own ranks. The conservative wing of the party became, if anything, more states-rightist, suspicious of all reform, increasingly critical of a national Northern leadership which it criticized for deserting the pristine traditions of Jefferson and the Founders.

In the middle of the party were the amorphous and often unpredictable moderates, ill-defined in either numbers or political convictions, swinging slightly left or right under guidance.* Either these moderates in combination with the conservatives, or the conservatives alone, had ruled the Texas Democratic Party since the war. There had never been an effective liberal-moderate coalition, and the liberals alone had been far from wielding real power. And for all its internal friction, the Democratic Party had never been far removed from the state's financial and industrial nexus: the corporations, oil and gas, banks, construction, and the utilities.

These internecine party battles were more than mere factionalism. They were bitter fights to the finish for outright control. Lyndon Johnson understood this better than any other man.

In Texas during the 1950s, Johnson had managed to play both the Dixiecrat-type conservatives and the Democratic liberals against one another to secure his own power base, and the savage party in-fighting of that decade left enough scars to cause a permanent, irrational hatred of Johnson, not only among staunch conservatives but also among many liberals. This ha-

* The terms liberal, moderate, and conservative may sound high-flown when used so frequently in a somewhat provincial setting, but they were necessary. This was a largely one-party state that was nonetheless drifting steadily away from the old sectionalism and toward a more well-defined class and group-interest politics.

tred would persist into the 1960s. Intelligent people became
victims of the political past, which is easy in a region where statewide politics lacking in real two-party organization stirs passions and animosities of an unusual intensity. In the stale-
mated Eisenhower years Johnson's Congressional leadership
grew stronger; he could, and did, deal ruthlessly and effectively
with any homegrown political opposition threatening his hold
on his constituency. Liberal Democrats would perhaps remember too much of those years when, totally isolated and subject
to all the McCarthy-like denunciations, they advocated not
only civil rights and reform in Texas but national programs
Johnson himself would foster a decade later. In 1952, when
Ralph Yarborough,* a liberal with populist leanings, began his
first of three unsuccessful bids for Governor against the Mc-
Carthyite incumbent, he traveled to a middle-sized city in East
Texas and was greeted by only three townspeople. One of
them said, "Ralph, we came less to offer political support than
physical defense." Johnson himself had worked both through
and around the Texas "establishment," the oil and business and
financial leaders who pulled the strings and controlled the
party. Privately he called the liberals "the Red Hots," and negotiated their defeat at important state conventions.† Johnson's
foremost agent in Austin, "Big Daddy" Ed Clark, later to be
ambassador to Australia, was the ranking business lobbyist in
the state; I would see him in the capitol building whenever a
big tax issue was up for consideration, but he almost never came
over for the minor causes. The man who got the money for
Johnson's campaigns and moved around for him among that
"establishment" was another poor boy from the country, John
Connally. Although I never doubted that his heart lay with his
New Deal origins, Johnson's closest friends and associates in

* Later a United States Senator.
† For a splendid account of Johnson's maneuvering in his home state, I recommend "My Hero LBJ" by Larry L. King, *Harper's Magazine*, October 1966.

Texas were conservatives; two or three of the conservative organizers we saw walking the corridors of the state capitol in 1961 and '62 would one day be working in responsible positions in the White House.

A young man engaged in the workings of Texas politics in the 1950s and early 1960s inevitably, in one form or another, felt the pull of Johnson's rise to power. The Johnson "stories" were many and graphic, and filled even the most casual conversations in Austin. We would see him around town, his tall figure leaning over upon some hapless soul in a hotel lobby jabbing away with a finger, or we would catch a glimpse of his big car speeding around the streets at night. The first time I saw him was at a reception for former governor "Ma" Ferguson at a downtown hotel in 1955; when I walked up to him and requested an interview he said, "Boy, my Mama's in the next room and I'm gonna go talk to my Mama." The power which he generated touched a whole cross-section of intelligent young Texans of that day; it brushed them in different ways, and in different ways it would irrevocably change their lives.

•

I was always struck by the incredibly wide range of these young men who in such different ways were drawn to him, as well as by the extraordinary loyalty he demanded and — despite his personal abuses, his unforgivingness, a certain vein of destructiveness — he so often got. This alone would suggest that Johnson was one of the most complicated and resourceful men ever to enter the White House, despite the simple stereotype many Easterners would hold to. Horace Busby was the brilliant editor of *The Daily Texan* in 1945, and he entered the old New Dealer Johnson's orbit two years later. A fiery liberal intellectual at the age of twenty-one, he moved steadily toward that shifting political center which Johnson, reflecting the predom-

inant Texas conservatism of the 1950s, began to occupy in both
Washington and Texas; Johnson's essential pragmatism and his
success in dealing with Texas' big money had its appeal, and
Busby became editor of a weekly newsletter informing Texas
businessmen about political and economic trends. At the
same time he wrote some of Johnson's best speeches and later
supervised his foreign travels as Vice-President; he and Johnson walked the streets of Brussels, alone and unrecognized, one
month to the day before Kennedy was assassinated. William
Brammer, Dugger's associate on the *Texas Observer* in its early
days, would go to work for Johnson the Majority Leader, writing letters and speeches. Brammer, unlike many of the others,
was basically apolitical, unattracted by suaveness or finesse in
political methods, but he was fascinated by Johnson's raw energy, his crude and vigorous Southwestern style. He was in such
awe of Johnson's exercises of power, if not of the human being,
that he began his political novel on a typewriter on Alben Bark-
ley's old desk in the Senate Office Building; when the novel finally
appeared, with a flamboyant character many took to be his former chief, Brammer was totally ostracized by the Johnsons, and
lived a life of fluctuating isolation in Washington, Spain, New
York, and Austin. Lloyd Hand, a debonair student president
at the University of Texas in the 1950s, became a Johnson lieu-
tenant; he liked the glamour of power and enjoyed a difficult political fight. The stories of how Johnson berated him before others for casual oversights became legend among us, but later he
was chief of diplomatic protocol in Washington, posing for
pictures with the Pope and other luminaries ("I don't know
who the old gentleman in the robes and holding the scepter is,"
a mutual friend from Texas wrote in sending me a clipping of
one of these photographs, "but the fellow next to him is
Hand."); later he entered the maelstrom of statewide California politics. Harry McPherson, a young East Texan, also en-

tered the orbit in the 1950s as chief counsel to one of Johnson's
Senate committees; he was probably the most thoroughgoing
intellectual in the Johnson entourage, and he was drawn to public service in its broadest sense and went on to the White House
as a valued advisor.

The most curious and fascinating example of all was Bill D.
Moyers, a classmate of mine at the state university in 1956. At
one point he supported the U.S. Senate candidacy of "Dollar
Bill" Blakley,* a wealthy Dixiecrat from Dallas, the choice of the
party powers. Later I saw him, during the Kennedy-Johnson
campaign tour of Texas, quietly on the fringes of the crowd at
the airports, usually a few steps away from Johnson. Moyers
seemed more like a Kennedy appointee than a Johnson man, but
ironically he became the one who functioned best in that context — a talented idealist and public servant, driven by ambition
and harboring a certain necessary ruthlessness that his Baptist
parson's social rhetoric largely disguised — who recognized a
broader social good that might ensue from being close to the
fulcrum of national power. (Bobby Baker, the young South
Carolinian, would be a different case altogether. His methods
were necessary to the tight control Johnson exerted on the
Senate as its leader; but Baker, the cynic, eventually used the

---

* Blakley, also called "Cowboy Bill" because he campaigned in cowboy suits
and cufflinks, at least deserves a footnote, though nothing more. He was twice
appointed to the U.S. Senate by conservative Texas governors to fill interim
vacancies, the second time coming after Yarborough had roundly trounced him
in 1958. As temporary Senator in 1961, he earned considerable publicity with
his belligerent questioning of Robert Weaver during the committee hearings on
his appointment as Administrator of the Federal Housing and Home Finance
Agency. A small excerpt from the transcript illustrates the kind of Senator two
Texas governors appointed:
  BLAKLEY: I understand the August 1948 issue of *Masses and Mainstream*,
  the successor to *New Masses*, a Communist magazine, appears to review
  your book, *The Negro Ghetto* . . .
  WEAVER: Do you know who wrote it? I might be able to identify it better.
  BLAKLEY: Yes. This seems to be by J. Crow, realtor.
  WEAVER: Who?
  BLAKLEY: J. Crow, realtor. Dc you know J. Crow?
  WEAVER: I did not know he ' rote book reviews.

power to which he was attached for his own materialistic ends. In private Baker called his boss "The Big Pumpkin.")

Ronnie Dugger was touched in a reverse way. Like Moyers he was an idealist, heavily influenced by his reading of the Transcendentalists; he distrusted the compromises of political power and saw his own role in Texas as that of the social critic, the journalistic conscience, the polemicist. "Let those flatter who fear, it is not an American art," was the phrase from Jefferson he placed at the top of his editorial page. As editor of the *Observer* during the political wars of the 1950s, he was one of Johnson's main public antagonists. Once in 1955 Johnson invited Dugger to his ranch for a bout of persuasion, and when Dugger went back and wrote up the episode in his paper, that ended any possibility of a working relationship between the high-minded young Texas liberal spokesman and the pragmatic leader of the U. S. Senate. I quote Dugger's column on that occasion as an intriguing document of the time, and for what it says about such differing roles in politics:

The good Lyndon Johnson has a mind like a pistol with an automatic loading mechanism. The mechanism has rows of cartridge clips — .22s, .45s, blanks, dum-dums — one of which it feeds into the gun as soon as the Senator has taken the shape of his target. Then he begins firing.

You might say: but that is a lousy simile. How can one gun fire so many kinds of bullets? If you say that, my friend, I will reply that you obviously know more about similes than you do about Lyndon Johnson.

I do not know just how I got into this work on the *Observer* — it is a long story — but be that as it may, or had to be, I have come to be known among a few of those who categorize people by their political views as a liberal liberal. (In Texas, we have liberals, and we have liberals.) The Senator had become aware of this propensity on my part, and I believe the clip was in place before I arrived.

It became clear at once that Senator Johnson has done more

for liberalism in America than any of the cryers-out-in-the-Texas-night. Since the Senator has, indeed, done exactly that, score one.

It became clear soon thereafter that the appointment of Ben Ramsey as national Democratic committeeman is a trivial thing compared to the over-riding need for a Democracy united and strong. Since, when you put it that way, the national committee-manship *is* pretty trivial, score two.

It became clear forthwith that a politician can't do anything for the people who elect him if they don't elect him. Since a politician was the point at the juncture of that forthwith, score three.

I confess that even after a long and convivial evening, I had to persist in the position that the new committeeman is a political reactionary, that his double-kiss from Senator Johnson and Speaker Rayburn . . . placed him in an excellent position to run for governor next summer, and that Texas needs liberals in the state capitol quite as much as Texas needs leaders in Washington.

But my rebuttals were respectful, not to say cryptic. The debate style of the Pedernales School was a new experience for this observer. When you differ with someone else's beliefs, Johnson says *he* doesn't "hate" anybody. It is a question whether he thinks of politics more as the rights and wrongs of policy or as the debts and enmities of people.

I don't suppose I ever met a man with such wondrous ability to concentrate — it is a total *focusing* — on his controversial partner. His staccato arguments, his pungent, homely examples, the *personalness* of his contention, and his thumps on your chest and slaps on your knee at once establish a tense rapport and an irresistible trend in the talk.

It is more apparent when one is not under the kleig light. We went over to see how the work on the guest house was proceeding, and a friendly country kind of man, who is an expert carpenter, was there rueing some bad work that had been done. Senator Johnson set about to persuade him to come early the next morning (he was on another job) to straighten it out. As we left the guest house, I walked up beside the car, leaving them in the headlights. The senator talked, the senator wheedled, and

the senator listened; the senator put a hand in a pocket and a
hand in the air; the senator tapped the carpenter on the chest
and stared him in the eye; the senator swayed from the hip and
leaned his face into his man's. Imperceptibly, the carpenter fell
back. Though he held fast to his dignity throughout, refusing to
hurry his words, casual to the last, it was no contest, and he knew
it . . .

He is an experience, a man you like, a will you awe, a man you
indebt to. You are a Lyndon Johnson man, or you're not.*

My own contact with Johnson was never so direct. In 1956,
on my way to England, I stopped off in Washington. Brammer
had arranged for me to see Walter Jenkins, Johnson's administrative assistant. We talked about my going to work on the
Johnson staff; Jenkins said I might be welcome to work during
the summer vacations. Almost as a matter of course, as it
turned out, I chose to see Europe and to read my history books.
When I returned to the *Texas Observer* Johnson was already so
hostile to it, and it to him, and so many of his political friends
were our political enemies, that anyone associated with it was
automatically deemed a foe.

•

Soon after I returned to Texas, just after the Los Angeles convention of 1960, the Hill Country people had a big barbecue
for Johnson in the little town of Blanco. Late that afternoon
my wife and I drove out there. The town itself is west of Austin
and across the Balcones Fault, where the land suddenly rolls
and tumbles, with scraggly mesquite and rich young cedars,
blue hills, and occasional patches of hard rock enclosed in green
fields; this is neither west nor south — it is almost neutral
country. In the courthouse square, across a main street shared

* *Texas Observer*, Nov. 30, 1955. For another fascinating personal glimpse of
Johnson in the national context during this period, see Arthur Schlesinger, Jr.'s
A Thousand Days, pages 10 and 11.

with the highway, a banner said: "A Leader to Lead the Nation."
Beyond town the celebration had already started. A smell of
barbecue drifted down from the hillside, along with the sound
of some loud western rhythms. Down near the banks of the
Blanco River, people in shirt sleeves, blue jeans, and western
hats stood in line for the barbecue. Negro cooks dipped into
the pits and forked out the meat that had been laid on the fires
the day before, and the Geezenslaw Brothers sang some tunes.

Then Johnson and his wife appeared, and everyone started
shouting "Lyndon!" and "Bird!" The mayor of Blanco, who
made the introductions from the speaker's platform, called the
Kennedy-Johnson ticket a "kangaroo ticket, one with all its
strength in the hind legs," and Price Daniel, the Governor of
Texas, said, "I agree we have a good ticket — in reverse," and
added, "If I had no other reason to support it than that a Texan
was on it, why I'd be workin' for it all the way." Then Johnson
stood up to the shouts and clapping. This was the first time
I had seen him working at close quarters, and it was an indicative glimpse of him among his own people; I was impressed
by his extraordinary range of rhetorical moods, from mock-sol-
emn to satirical to blustering to fighting-mad, punctuated occasionally by serious soliloquies that could border on the maud-
lin. Later his oratorical style, his whole public bearing, changed
so radically as to be almost unrecognizable from this; the country talk, the easy colloquialisms, the waving of arms and sway-
ing of head, gave way to the restrictive national norm. That
night, as he spoke without notes, I got some first-hand insight
into the man and his sources.

"My grandfather practiced law here from 1887 into the
1900s," he said, stepping out toward the crowd. "My mother
spent her girlhood days in this town — she was always the greatest influence on my life. Every time I make a decision affecting
millions of people I think, 'Would Mama agree with this?'

or 'Would Daddy think this wise?' They were good people, they never sought power, but were just friends of human beings."

He went on for some time in this vein, and then turned to the serious part of his talk. One-third of the world, he said, are fanatic atheists, one-third Christians, and one-third hard-working people "like you." Waving a hand at the small children playing in the crowd, he shouted, "The children in these uncommitted lands are a lot the same, the only difference is they have tapeworm, and leprosy, and eczema, and their daddies make only about $200 a year. Let's take some of that wheat stacked two miles high and put some food in those hungry stomachs. Put some fiber on their bodies, food in their stomachs. That'll do more than all the worn-out tanks we're sendin'. I want a fellow who can sit there and when they tell about a mother and her hungry child, I'll be able to see a little tear comin' down his cheek." Then he offered to compare poverty with Richard Nixon, whom he called "the barefoot boy from Whittier. The Cabots and Lodges," he added, "haven't exactly been on relief up there."

He explained why he took second place on the ticket. "I didn't run for the Vice-Presidency. But I never ran away from anything in my life." It was a fair convention, he said, he finished second, and he felt in his heart that his decision was in the best interests of the nation; the world situation had also played a part in his decision. About Kennedy he said, "I knew he was an informed man who knew every state in the nation — of course, he's spent enough time travellin' around in 'em — and he's a courageous, able, diligent man." He praised the war record of the Kennedy boys, and said that throughout the world "all religions are outnumbered 18 to 1. I've looked in John Kennedy's eye more than any of you. I can tell you this: no human being in the world will dictate what *he* does."

He said he could have "taken my baseball bat and gone home" after the convention. But the Vice-Presidency was too crucial a post; he would be sitting on the National Security Council with the chiefs-of-staff. Cactus Jack Garner, he added, did not sit on a security council.

"It's not easy to try for first place and get second, and ride around in back cars and everything," he said, in a phrase that would return to haunt me a few years later. But he had started thinking about the responsibilities of the job, and the importance it now has. And in his conclusion he declared, in his suddenly almost melancholy tones:

> I started out right here 51 years ago. The only thing I want out of government is to secure the wealth, happiness, and freedom you people are entitled to. I just want it said of me, I'll leave people better than I found 'em.

I was impressed with this performance before his home people, particularly with the way he had tried to describe the responsibilities of the national government to them, but my wife, who was not much accustomed to politics at that point, remarked, "Boy, what an ego!" A few moments later she was taken aback when a woman of our acquaintance who had worked three years for Johnson said to her, "Lyndon sure was mild tonight."

The next time I saw him at such close range was three months later, early in the afternoon after the 1960 election. I had stayed up all night waiting on the result, and when Illinois was finally announced I drove down to the Johnson television station. Gone were the swirling crowds of the night before. Johnson was already there, with only four or five reporters and a handful of friends; he was roundly criticizing the chief of the UPI bureau for some error he had just made in a story. We milled around the studio waiting for the Johnsons to go on national television. Johnson looked drawn and tired as he glanced occasionally toward a TV set several feet away at the image of Kennedy weaving his way through the crowd at the armory in Hyannis Port. Then the networks switched into our studio; Johnson read a brief statement and then answered some questions. His activities as Vice-President, he said at the end, would "largely depend on the President himself."

That afternoon I went back to my office to write a column praising Johnson for his vigorous role on the ticket and arguing that without him Kennedy could not have won,* a contention that was to anger a large number of Texas liberals, who felt Johnson's nomination a moral and strategic disaster. I ended the column:

> . . . on the pages of our children and grandchildren's histories, Johnson's place in the story of our times will rest on this consideration: Liberated now from his Texas constituency, will he have the vision to rise above the provincial interests which have so often seemed to enclose him and become, with Kennedy, a genuine national leader and spokesman? . . .
>
> Johnson is no ordinary man from the provinces. He is a man of great abilities. He has wielded enormous power, perhaps more than any legislator in our history. But he has often wielded that power without purpose or vigor, as if in a vacuum. How much he rises now to genuine statesmanship will depend partly on the manner in which his own presidential ambitions feel out the

---

* Johnson's "Dixie Special" train during the campaign, in which he used all his powers of persuasion among the Southern politicians to keep enough Southern electoral votes in line, soon became legend. The first stop was in Culpepper, Virginia, where Johnson made his famous remark: "What has Dick Nixon ever done for Culpepper?" Later I had a talk with a friend of mine, the son of a prominent Mississippi politician; he had seen Johnson operating at first-hand during the Dixie tour. "Don't even *mention* that goddamned train!" he moaned. I myself had spent a few days in Mississippi during the campaign, and was struck by the raw, unyielding hatred expressed for Johnson as a "turncoat." I agree with Arthur Schlesinger, Jr., as I wrote at the time, that without Johnson, Kennedy would have lost Texas, and probably South Carolina and Louisiana — without these three, the election would have rested on the unpledged electors in Alabama and Mississippi.

shifting terrain. But most of all, as with all politicians . . . Johnson's evolution into something more than he has been will rest on that subtle chemistry of decision and change, of belief and human feeling and courage within the strange depths of his own baffling self, where a man's essential character lies.

•

A few days after the election, Kennedy decided to pay Johnson a visit at his ranch. The day he was to arrive, all the other newspaper people in the area were to fly out on a plane from Austin; I drove the seventy miles in my car and got there before anyone else. The skies in the late November afternoon were deep purple, threatening rain. Across the Pedernales about two hundred yards from the ranch house a small crowd was waiting to catch a glimpse of the plane that would bring the next President of the United States into the airstrip. Three flags — the American, the Texas, and the LBJ — unfurled in the nipping breeze, and highway patrolmen and secret servicemen guarded every entrance and gateway.

Behind the house, near the hangar and the runway, ranchhands and a few local people in the welcoming delegation stood aimlessly about, peering into the dark skies to the east. Johnson was standing casually in front of the hangar, wearing a big hat and cowboy boots. "Art, I believe we're gonna get it in before it rains," he said to one of the men nearby. The crowd milled in front of the runway. "Bobby, you killed a deer yet?" a man asked. "I killed one two years ago," Bobby replied. Finally, one by one, the planes started coming in. A Convair landed, taxied to a stop, and unloaded its cargo of national and Texas reporters.

If you have ever seen a large group of American reporters covering an event of this kind, perhaps you have noticed their similarity with a roving pack of particularly energetic dogs who trot around each other on instinct when some potent springtime

smell rides the air; the dogs dance on their toes and sniff at the
breeze, snapping each other behind the ears and bristling, or
sometimes barking nervously just out of exuberance, a great
whirling mob of animal flesh going in circles and tangents. Occasionally, when dogs run in packs like this, one of their number will fall down and tumble on his back, and the others will
walk right over him, giving a nervous bite or two en route.
The reporters pounced out of their plane in a similar rush, snarl-
ing at one another to get out of the way, and headed over to
Johnson to shake his hand and congratulate him on the election. He shouted familiar greetings to them, and Johnson's
wife came over and shook hands and embraced two or three of
them. Then another plane full of reporters landed, and the
strong wind from it whipped Johnson's hat off his head onto
the top of the hangar. Someone retrieved it forthwith.

The third plane, a small twin-engine Lodestar, slowly circled the field, its red lights flashing in the semi-darkness. I
glanced around and noticed that every eye there was on it; it
landed and taxied over within fifty yards of the hangar. Johnson and his wife, followed by the great mob of reporters and
photographers, headed toward the plane; a reporter from Washington knocked me sideways into a burly photographer, who
said "Move, you son-of-a-bitch," and by the time I got to the
plane the two hosts had already gone inside it.

In a few minutes Johnson and Kennedy emerged. The local
welcoming delegation sent up whoops and applause, and the
chairman presented Kennedy with a ten-gallon hat. He tried
to get Kennedy to put it on, but Kennedy was not about to,
perhaps because the photographs might make him appear someone else's temporary property. Johnson took Kennedy by the
arm and led him to a white Lincoln convertible nearby; despite
the darkness and the rain, which began to fall in big dampening
drops, they were going to take a tour of the ranch. The report-

ers and photographers, who by now numbered about fifty, clawed their way into a Greyhound bus just behind the Lincoln convertible to take the same tour. The engine cranked up and the bus driver did his best to follow the car in front. When the convertible stopped, and Kennedy got out quickly to shake hands with some cowboys, a few of the reporters broke through the doors of the bus to try to listen. They got back in, wet but successful. "Jack said to Lyndon, 'You have a better layout here than Joe B. Kennedy,'" one of the reporters shouted to the others, and they all scribbled into their notebooks.

George Reedy, Johnson's assistant, stood at the front of the bus and, in his deep, clear voice gave a running account of the tour through a public address system. It was an academic gesture; the reporters peered through the windows, but it was too dark to see more than three feet out. The bus bumped and groaned along the narrow, winding road, provoking curses and moans from the motley cargo inside. Tree branches scraped against the top, and someone uncorked a bottle on the back seat.

The ranch itself, Reedy was saying, is around 300 acres. "The Senator has a herd of white-faced Hereford cattle of which he is very proud. That's h-e-r-e-f-o-r-d, *hereford*." Some of the men wrote this into their notebooks.

"The Senator's grandfather Sam Eli Johnson and his brother settled here in 1848," Reedy said. "At that time there was nothing much around here except Comanche Indians." This is the Texas Hill Country, he continued. "It's very rugged country."

"It's certainly *bumpy*," one of the reporters shouted.

The bus reached the family cemetery, where the white convertible had apparently stopped briefly. Mrs. Johnson boarded the bus and the reporters shouted their greetings. "I just want George to tell about the graveyard and the house where Lyndon was born and so forth," she said, and returned to the car. Reedy explained some of these.

"The Senator has two live oak trees in the front yard," he said. "Live oak — *l-i-v-e-o-a-k*."

"How big is his herd, George?" a reporter shouted.

"Around seventy-five."

"Seventy-five what?"

"White-faced Hereford. That's *h-e-r-e-f-o-r-d*."

The bus arrived at the old schoolhouse. "This is where the Senator went to school as a very small boy," Reedy explained, although no one could see it. He started to school at a younger age than usual, as the story goes, "to keep him out of trouble and to keep him from falling in the Pedernales while he roamed around the ranch." The big bus splashed as it hit water. "This is what you call a low-water bridge," Reedy said.

"George, why are we so vague about who's coming tomorrow?" a reporter asked. That set off a low undercurrent of dissatisfaction throughout the bus, and biting mumbled assents. Reedy explained that the visit had been for Kennedy to relax and do what he wanted to, and there was no definite agenda.

The bus slowed down. "We missed the birthplace," Reedy said. "It's too dark anyway." He described the house in some detail — a simple little frame structure where the Senator had been born fifty-one years ago.

"Say, George," an Eastern reporter in the back shouted, "is that the one with the manger in it?"

In the headlights the white convertible was turning around now, and the bus followed. Highway patrolmen with flashlights helped the driver to head back toward the house. "You're going over a cattleguard. Anybody want to know what a cattleguard is?" Reedy asked. When someone said yes, Reedy explained its functions. The bus drove past the front of the ranch house, and in the rain the swimming pool was a deep, eerie green. Reedy described the house, and said Kennedy would sleep there that night.

"When we gonna get some news out here, George?" someone shouted, and again there were wide rumbles of disapproval. But by this time the tour was over, and the bus turned and moved back toward the hangar near the runway. The Kennedy and Johnson party had gone into the house, and in the hangar, as the rain fell more heavily than before, the reporters drank beer from a large keg and compared notes. They looked toward the lights of the house; they wanted inside there so badly they could feel it. Then, one by one, the press planes took off again, through the dark clouds back to Austin, and a secret serviceman told me the party was over and would I please leave.

●

Six months into Johnson's Vice-Presidency, my friend Maury Maverick, Jr., of San Antonio and I decided to make some concrete gesture toward getting Johnson and the hardcore Texas liberals on speaking terms. It was the least that could be done. Johnson was proving to be a loyal and vigorous supporter of Kennedy's programs; a historian we knew had heard him speak to a closed session of civil rights activists and said his talk had been more impressive, more human and full of fervor for Negro rights, than the Kennedys themselves had been. It was foolish for the old antagonisms to persist under new circumstances.

Maverick had just returned from Washington, where he spent some time with Johnson, and I wrote a column quoting Maverick and praising the Vice-President. Subsequently, it was picked up by some of the big dailies, including the *Post-Dispatch*; Johnson himself was sure to see it.

Johnson had taken Maverick to the White House to see Kennedy. On the way over there, as Maury described it, "Some guy in the front seat kept briefin' Lyndon on outer space. People were always briefin' him. Everywhere we went we were runnin' and people were always briefin' him as he dog-trotted." All over Washington, Maverick said, people's reactions to Johnson's Vice-Presidency were "very, very favorable. Watchin' Lyndon in Washington is like watchin' Toscanini. He handles his office superbly. You know, you have different pressures on different jobs. While he was Senator from Texas, he had the pressures of Texas provincialism workin' on him. Now it's different. In my opinion, he's realizin' the great need for liberalism." The piece went on in this vein.

"He discussed the race problem with me. He said several times he wants to make a success of the President's committee on equal employment opportunities. I talked to the staff members of that committee, including Soapy Williams' boys from Michigan. Everyone said Lyndon was being forceful and cooperative. The Negroes on the staff told me the same thing." Maverick talked with reporters who had followed Johnson in Africa. "They told me Johnson worked the crowds like a Texas barbeque. He'd head straight to the slums to shake hands. He was even shakin' hands with some lepers when the doctors warned him not to." And when he went to a baseball game at Griffith Stadium "the Negroes in the bleachers whooped and hollered and shouted.

"You know, Johnson's broken my heart a thousand times. I needed his help in the McCarthy days when I was in the legislature and I couldn't find him. His Ed Clarks aren't my cup of tea. But he may be goin' back to the Lyndon Johnson of his youth. I don't know.

"He's really one of the most magnificent politicians in Washington today, whatever you think of him. And everyone in Washington tells me he's all for the Kennedy administration. Jimmy Roosevelt told me the other day, 'My old man really loved

Johnson.' I wanted to go out and drink a lot of whiskey and cry like hell when I heard that."

Johnson undoubtedly was feeling the frustrations of his secondary role in this period, and it was probably natural that his immense sensitivity was working overtime. A few days after the column appeared Maverick and I learned that someone asked Johnson in a group of friends, "What do you think of the way the *Texas Observer* praised you so much?" And Johnson replied testily that we should have known better: he had always opposed McCarthy.

7

By 1960 industrialization and urbanization had given Texas a much closer affinity with states like Michigan or California than with Mississippi or Arkansas. There were few traces of the Deep South, in which most Texans would probably have wished to be counted, along the great industrial axis of Houston and the Gulf Coast, or in the Latin culture of South Texas and the Rio Grande Valley. The South was markedly alien to a rigorously capitalistic West Texas, just as it was to Dallas, that self-satisfied city of bank vaults and choirs. Only East Texas, with its oil and plantation economy, was genuine Southern country. But so rapidly had the state changed, and with such dislocation, that beneath its modern frenzies its old layers intruded everywhere, and these gave it a patchwork kind of complexity, an unexpectedness, that made it a rich and fertile ground for the young reporter with an eye out for irony. Rigid fundamentalism flourished in modern, skyscraper cities, old Negro women carried laundry on their heads past the low-cut houses of the new suburbias, oil derricks rose high above swamps and cotton fields, television aerials decorated the roofs of sharecroppers' shacks, Republicans organized clubs in lazy courthouse-square towns that had never heard of two-party politics, and politicians of a previous generation tried to make comebacks in an age in which their old methods seemed ludicrous and even pathetic. There is a Russell Lee photograph, one of his most memorable, of a scene at the Texas Relays in Austin, the first year an all-Negro team was allowed to compete — two little white boys are getting the autograph of a Negro track star. Once, in the *Observer*, we published an account of a fist-fight which took place in a Protestant church in East Texas during the Sunday service; the leading deacon and his son tangled with the preacher, and the fight was over politics. I traveled all over Texas, from one end to another, and my memory of it as a physical place is like a montage, with brilliant lights and furious machinery in the background, and in the foreground a country café with old men in front, watching big cars speed by.

•

One day Larry Goodwyn and I took off to drive 500 miles into West Texas, my first trip into that bare and severe country: somewhere beyond Austin the trees give out and the cactus begins. As we drove through Lampasas, a little town fifty miles northwest of Austin and the Balcones, Goodwyn said, "Take a good look at the Confederate statue in front of the courthouse. It's the last one you'll see." Beyond that was the West for me, and the discomfort I felt on that first trip was a sure sign of agoraphobia — fear of that awesome, uninterrupted space. "It's not much like the Mississippi delta, is it?" Good-

wyn asked, for he was a Texan and he was having fun with my
bleak reactions. Farther on we saw an enormous road sign saying, *Jesus Saves!* in large block letters, sponsored by the local
Chevrolet dealer, and far out in the distance a gaunt and solitary brick building, an old courthouse in some forgotten town
that had been abandoned years before when the railroad went
the wrong way. We went through places that had been founded
as late as 1910 or 1915, and thriving yet strangely desolate cities
which had been tent and lean-to boom towns twenty years before.* In one little town, after interviewing a newspaper editor
whom a county sheriff had taken a pot-shot at with a shotgun,
we stopped off for coffee in a half-deserted café. Out there high
school football was a religion, a way of coping, and it produced
one of the most violent offshoots of the game in America; we
started a conversation with a man at the counter about the local
team. "Say, you *integrated* out here?" Goodwyn asked. "Well,"
the man said, "we only had a coupla colored families, and the
kids went to a one-room school and one of the boys weighed
210, did the 100 in 10.1, kicked 50 yards barefoot, so we integrated."

El Paso, 595 miles from Austin, was like an oasis for me. I
came to give a lecture on "The Liberal's Case against Communism," and the 300 middle-class people in the Presbyterian
church listened politely, though I sensed with skepticism. It
was Christmastime, and at night the lights in the city's tallest
building were arranged in the form of a huge cross, big enough
to be seen across the border in Juárez. People in the suburbias

* ". . . men would spray asphalt over the long, prairie-straight wagon trails
and throw up brick siding against the stabbing sand. But the effect on the people would be the same. The wind, endless, unengageable, would still haunt the
women and leave the men feeling strangely diminished. The plains wind would
intimidate, as in the earlier time, and restless people would feel a need to pro-
claim their own identities . . ." See the chapter "Land, the Enduring Value,"
from Larry Goodwyn's excellent book *South Central States* (Time-Life Series on
America, 1967).

were talking about Communist leaflets blown by the wind
from Mexico into the front of their houses, where Mexican
maids worked at $10 a week and meals, and in the biggest bar
in Juárez, County Judge Woodrow Wilson Bean (to whom Lyndon Johnson had once said after some political double-cross,
"I'm gonna give you a three-minute lecture in virtue, then I'm
gonna *ruin* you") held forth on Texas politics to all who would
listen. At a basketball game at Texas Western four of the five
starting players were Negroes, and the fifth was Italian; and a
young lady I had known in the fanciest sorority at the state university was married to a lawyer whose idealism had led him to
practice among poor Mexicans. As a boy, the artist Tom Lea
told me, he had watched the battles of the Mexican Revolution from the hills of El Paso. From the second floor of Malcolm McGregor's house in the best part of El Paso was a view
one would find nowhere else in America: across into another
country, a hill covered with shanties and marked with hundreds
of caves where people lived.

Always there were the stories to cover, little unexpected
events to describe, political clashes and small tragic happenings that no one would write about but us. I spent a week in
a little town in Southwest Texas that had been split into war-
ring halves on a referendum that would decide whether the town
would do away with a one-room school for its two Negro children and "integrate" the white school. The referendum was defeated; on the day of the vote the local editor told me, "Red-
birds and blackbirds don't mix, God didn't want it that way.
Abe Lincoln educated himself by candlelight with borrowed
books. Why do these little niggers expect so much?" Later I
drove to South Texas, to a different part of the border, to write
about a beautiful lady with a Phi Beta Kappa key who worked
among the Mexican children and had been called a Communist
in public by a high school principal; and then on through the

little towns of the Valley approaching Mexico. In each little
town I would see the *latino* political leader, who would sum-
mon his friends ("El jefe del *Observer* está aqui," one of them
phoned a compadre) and in ten minutes we would have a full-
fledged beer-bust going, and the talk would be about state politics, or "Lyndon and Ralph," or the goings-on "up in Austin."
At the border itself the plane from the customs bureau flew
low over the dried-up Rio Grande on the lookout for wetbacks
sneaking across into American soil. The Episcopal preacher at
the proper dinner party in McAllen was amazed I was going
into Mexico the next day. "There's nothing over there for you
but *trouble*," he warned, and I sensed something of the border
fear, the middle-class dread at the fringes of Texas of something dark, brooding, latin, Catholic on the other side — unpredictable, alien, to be avoided. In the little bars on the Mexican side the next day, drinking cuba libres with Tom Sutherland
and Jack Butler, the Mexican bartenders treated us to red-hot
dishes of Cervando's rice, tortillas, enchiladas, and heavy brass
songs, and flamboyant toasts were exchanged: *Viva Mexico,
Viva Los Estados Unidos, Viva Benito Juárez, Viva Kennedy,
Viva Tio Lyndon!* At the dance hall the bandleader gave me
his trumpet, and I played Dixieland, ending up for good measure with my old rendition of taps; the Mexicans stood raptly at
attention, feeling something ceremonial. Across the way in
the night the lights of Texas seemed austere and protective.

•

Farther up was Houston, a phantasmagoric place, grown almost from nothing in a generation. A college acquaintance of
mine, returning home after six months' absence, reported that
someone had built a new church in his back yard. A Rhodes
Scholar friend at Oxford, named Hofheinz, had been from here.
He spoke four languages and was learning Chinese, and his fa-

ther was talking about building an air-conditioned stadium with a roof on top; we didn't believe him. People talked about the next skyscraper, which would be the tallest west of the Mississippi, and at Frankie Randolph's liberals of all races met and discussed the minimum wage, racial prejudice, the evils of the oil depletion allowance, and the John Birchers. Here River Oaks was a graceful enclave of millionaires' houses, and from another part of town they would one day be sending someone to the moon. Broad, unending boulevards, some of them brand new, and maddening expressways on the city's peripheries seemed somewhat like Los Angeles; the whole area was raw and seething like Southern California. Its main street on Saturday night was like Upper Broadway in Manhattan — big cars speeding past, the whole spectrum of human colors; Negroes walked jauntily by Neiman Marcus or the Rice Hotel, where I sat in the middle of the Protestant preachers, exhibiting my most pious Mississippi countenance, and heard Kennedy tell why being a Catholic should not disqualify him from the Presidency.

I sat over cocktails here one afternoon in the plushest private club in the city, high atop a new building, talking politics with a young liberal who had just come within 25,000 votes of being Governor of Texas. There we were, talking about Negroes and liberal coalitions and industrial safety laws, while oil millionaires sat at the next table, eavesdropping perhaps on our curious dialogue. "I saw you on television, suh," a Negro waiter whispered to my companion. "I done all I could." The candidate talked about the tactics of the election. "If I'd just had $50,000 more," he said to me, "that's all I woulda asked for — two more TV appearances and I'd been over the top"; we agreed that most of the men in the lounge with us could sign a check for that amount right then without calling a bank. "Any man who can get the money necessary to be elected Governor of Texas," my companion said, "doesn't deserve to be Governor of Texas." A business lobbyist I knew from the legislature waved from across the room, and strolled over with a bourbon in his hand to our table. "What you boys plottin'?" he asked. "Whatever it is, I bet you ain't up to no good." All three of us laughed uproariously, and then the lobbyist put on a serious face and said, "You ran a good race, Don; had us shook up for a while at the end," and before retiring again to his companions grasped us both on the shoulders with each hand — a gesture of understanding in disagreement, a hint from him that democracy works after all among good fellows. Read some political *history* and Robert Penn Warren's *All the King's Men*, I advised my friend, who said he would, while outside those broad plate-glass windows the city was laid out on all that flat land, a city that seemed so new as to be irrelevant to any past.

.

And then there was Dallas, always a cavernous city for me, claustrophobic, full of thundering certitudes and obsessed with its image. From the first I was admittedly prejudiced about the place; I would detour fifty miles to avoid it. Later events would only reinforce my strange Dallas phobia. There was no other city remotely its size in America, except in the Deep South on the one issue of race, where, in Silone's phrase about a somewhat more coherent phenomenon, it was so nearly impossible to be an "adversary in good faith," where intolerance and the closed mind were so inclusive, and where violence could be so manifestly political. Three decades before, Dallas had not been distinguished for any notable lack of diversity — for physical assaults on Vice-Presidential candidates and their wives,* or

* Lyndon and Lady Bird Johnson were attacked by a vicious mob of middle-class patriots in the lobby of the Adolphus Hotel a few days before the 1960 election. "I never *saw* a Republican till I was fifteen," one of Johnson's staff-members told me, "and I never saw a mob like that of any kind. The obscenities some of those ladies shouted were astounding." The incident was widely publicized and was a factor in Kennedy and Johnson's thin margin of victory for Texas' crucial twenty-four electoral votes.

for the divinity of its own intentions. Even *The Dallas Morning News*, which later became the most venomous of big American dailies and the very symbol of the city's grim xenophobias, was constructive and moderate. People in neighboring Fort Worth, I am told, looked to Dallas as an enlightened example. Sarah Hughes, the distinguished judge, would recall that as a liberal political candidate from Dallas in the thirties she could play one business interest against another and actually get elected. The city may not have been a paragon of virtue, but neither was it a citadel for the self-righteous.

But Dallas was growing, like many American cities, much too rapidly. Its economic character was becoming too uniformly financial: banks, insurance, the utilities, marketing. In 1936 its leading businessman, who succeeded after much effort in raising several million dollars to bring the Texas Centennial to a city which had played a smaller role in the state's history than a dozen dying hamlets, had learned an important lesson. Dallas' most influential leader said at the time: "We had to have men who could underwrite . . . We didn't have time for no proxy people. Then I saw the idea. Why not organize the 'yes' and 'no' people?" In the late 1930s, without an election or a local concensus, the city's most powerful businessmen decided to run Dallas. The government of the city was a group called The Citizens Council, consisting of the men who on their own could commit their companies to whatever policies they choose. The consequences of this monolith had not been trivial. Civic dissent had been successfully excluded by furious appeals to community "loyalty"; there had been no partisan rivalries because the leaders, in making their decisions, did not recognize parties.

By 1960 a strikingly high proportion of Dallas' citizens were in managerial, professional, and white-collar work. In a city like this, almost wholly white-collar in character, standards were set by the employer. Political and social conformity worked downward, to the middling manager and below; conservatism became synonymous with social acceptibility, and as status became more vulnerable, the salaried worker often became even more immoderate than his superior.

Much of this could have been said of other cities, but no other American community of this size had so mutely acquiesced in the sacrifice of diversity. As Dallas expanded in the war years and its financial structure solidified, its very spirit was being shaped by self-made businessmen whose success derived from their talent for controlling large numbers of employees. There was little manufacturing, and not much organized labor. In older cities dominated by business there had at least been countervailing forces to challenge the prevailing power, or merely to nag and prod. In Houston, only 250 miles to the southeast, business conservatism had never exactly been impotent, and the radicalism of its rightists had often exceeded Dallas'. Yet Houston was no monolith; it was, as one of its writers would say, a whiskey and trombone town, openly in conflict with itself, and its very disorder had encouraged a rough and open democracy. Dallas, in contrast, had grown sick from its very *order*, from the organized caution and self-interest of an ethos which demanded undeviating conformity.*

•

In 1960, Ronnie Dugger and I followed John Kennedy around the state. We ended up in Dallas, riding in a cattle truck with the photographers just in front of the convertible that carried Kennedy and Johnson. The caravan came in from the south,

---

* I am not arguing that the city would always conform to this description. Later events in 1963 may have changed something of the city's spirit. Its afternoon newspaper, the *Times-Herald*, was for a brief time to become more outspoken and vigorous. But the fact remains that by the 1960s many Texas intellectuals were viewing Dallas as an enclave. Two revealing books were later published on the city: *Dallas Public and Private* by Warren Leslie and *The Decision-Makers, The Power Structure of Dallas* by Carol Estes Thometz.

through the underpass and past the Texas School Book Deposi-
tory, on through the narrow, constricted business section. Dugger would write of the trip: "Anywhere along the route from
Fort Worth to Dallas the candidates could have been shot;
there was nothing to stop it but one motorcycle patrolman on
each side of their car." And I observed something Theodore
White noted in *The Making of the President, 1960*. On the
streets the crowds, the office-workers and secretaries, applauded
the candidates, politely if not exuberantly; but looking up, into
the windows of the tall buildings bordering the streets, you
could see the executives in suits and ties, looking down quietly, suspiciously, on the turbulent scene below.

After the Kennedy and Johnson tour had departed, Dugger
and I walked down through the business district, where I invariably would get the shakes; I simply did not like the *looks* of
the place. Dugger, out of spite, loosened up his lungs with an
awesome rebel yell, and a policeman on the other side of the
street gave us a cold look, staring in our direction for another
fifty yards. "This is the only city in America," Dugger observed,
"where jay-walking is a capital crime," as we cut across the middle of the street.

We had decided to go and interview the preacher at the largest Baptist church in the world. He had been saying some harsh
things to his congregation of 12,000 about Catholics who wanted
to be President, and, having grown up around Baptists of various sizes and shells, I wanted to hear his views first-hand. We
had little trouble finding the church; it covered almost a whole
city block and sprawled into several nearby buildings. Inside,
after a long search through endless halls and meeting rooms, we
found the pastor's office. A secretary looked us over warily,
then walked in to tell the preacher, "Two boys from a newspaper want to see you." After a few minutes' wait we were ushered inside, and were immediately given a warm reception by

a big, friendly man. One glance told me this was the kind of preacher from my childhood who would tell a funny story or two to get you in the mood for redemption. When we started asking about politics and the Pope, however, a grim, earnest expression came over his face, and I knew there would be no jokes.

I asked him what he thought of Senator Kennedy's appearance before the Protestant ministers in Houston earlier that week. The pastor had not seen the event on television, but a friend had told him about it. "He told me that it was the biggest farce he ever saw in his life," the pastor said. "On the right side was the press, and on the left side a bunch of labor toughs and priests in ordinary clothes — any way to get him elected." Well, Dugger asked, what did he think of the sermons the Reverend Smith, at the University Baptist Church in Austin, was preaching about how there should be no religious restrictions on the Presidency? "He has an inferiority complex," the pastor snapped, swiveling around in his chair — "an inferiority complex to me, to my church, and my congregation."

"Your church sure is *bigger*," I said, and the pastor agreed. "But, sir, how do you view Kennedy's promises to resist all pressure from his Church?"

"One, he's either a sorry Catholic, in which case he oughta get out of the church," the preacher replied. "Two, if he's a good Catholic, he shouldn't be President."

"But Kennedy has said no threat of punishment would make him change his mind. How do you take that?"

"He's lyin'. You just don't know the terrible fear of excommunication a Catholic has."

"Doctor," Dugger said, "how did you vote in 1956?"

"For Eisenhower."

"How about fifty-two?"

"Eisenhower."

"Forty-eight?"

"Well, I didn't like Truman."

"Have you ever voted for someone other than a Republican?" At this point the conversation trailed off, and the pastor started talking again about Catholics. He went on to say that Catholics should be barred from public office.

"You mean," I asked, "you'd disqualify Catholics from running for any public office in America?"

"Yessir."

We talked on in a desultory way for a few more minutes, and then got up to leave. We shook hands, and the preacher said as we departed, "now you boys come back and see us any time."

We walked out into the streets of Dallas again, and Dugger said, in a conspiratorial whisper, "Maybe we should inform Pope John about this."

•

Riding all over Texas in my Plymouth with the dual exhausts, I gave in, as everyone else I knew, to the euphoria of the Texas road, to that curious, liberating exhilaration that comes with taking a car along a flat and empty highway to some place hundreds of miles into the distance. I would keep the speedometer right at 70, wheel-straddle the dead dogs, cats, buzzards, snakes, armadillos, and tarantulas, and aim for the scalding heat mirage rising up from the concrete a mile to the front. Driving back from Dallas that day, after a detour to another town for another story, Taylor fell behind, and Thrall, Rockdale, Hearne, Franklin, Buffalo, and Jewett, each with the same wide street it shared with the main road. When night came I switched the radio to Del Rio for the gospel-singing and the religious advertisements (portraits of Jesus that glowed in the dark, the smallest Bible in the world) to fight that empty loneliness. The most convincing testimony to isolation is inarticulate, felt: the simple vista of Main Street in a small Texas town, wrinkled men in khakis under an awning shade, waitresses with their terrible fixed boredom, signposts pointing to towns hours away — of being lost in a vastness too big, and for the natives of being forgotten or mocked or ignored by people on wheels who stop only to scratch, or to drink coffee, or to empty their bowels.

One day, having been stranded in Houston without a car, the owner of the hotel where I was staying, a friendly subscriber to my paper, said he would "set me up to a free trip home." On the street in front of the hotel a double-length Cadillac limousine waited, with two uniformed Negro chauffeurs and a bar in back. The back seat, approximately twenty feet from the driver, was made of soft cushion, and I sank into it and combed my hair. We took off for Austin down the main highway, and I sipped Lone Star Beer while watching the passengers in other cars peer inside at me. I lit up a big cigar from a box at the bar, and I had the chauffeurs stop at two or three small towns along the way, to allow the citizens a glimpse of me as I got out to stretch. In one of these towns I adopted a dignified pose near the limousine, while the drivers wiped the bugs off its hood. Several old men standing around on the street corner came over to admire the car, and then backtracked to whisper among themselves about who I might be. People in the cars driving down the street slowed up to look; one man was so enthralled he smashed into the back of another car. Then we took off down the highway again, and in a driving Texas rainstorm made it to Austin.

·

For coming home to Austin was the best part of it all. From the highway to the north I would catch sight of its faint purple hills, and then the University Tower and the Capitol, like picture postcards against the night sky, as breathtaking as they had been when I went on my first "walk" as a college freshman. Austin was where the excitement was. The University of Texas, as so many American campuses during the Kennedy years, had exploded with vitality: protest meetings, sit-ins, stand-ins, debates; outstanding young professors were being imported from all over the nation, and everyone who mattered was stopping there to lecture or to talk with the bright young people engaged in the "liberal movement." In Austin you could always see Texas with something approaching a perspective; in late afternoons you could sit under the trees at the old German beer hall and drink frosty glasses of draft beer with philosophy professors, Republican organizers, labor lawyers, ranchers from the Hill Country, or state senators in blue jeans. Friends of the John Birchers sat arguing with country-boy populists about the Kennedys, Republicans and liberals plotted the joint overthrow of the Texas "establishment," aspiring writers debated on the early Malraux, legislators who had just assailed one another on the floor of the House chug-a-lugged Lone Star together and talked about women. Here the talk was always spirited and occasionally vicious, the spectrum of opinion went 180 degrees, but there was never violence. The great mugs of cold beer were the common bonds keeping us together, the waitresses were our parliamentarians, and we argued the fate of the Republic with a patient, disciplined civility. This was our common room, our Oxford union, our forum.

One night we were sitting here, talking about the legislature's tax struggles, when the waitress told me I had a telephone call. I went inside to take it.

"Hello."

"Hello, this is the Governor. What're you boys doin'?"

"Just sitting out here at Scholz', Governor."

"Who with?"

"Korioth and Dugger and a few others."

"Get Korioth and Dugger and come on down to the Mansion. I'd like to have a talk."

"Right now?"

"Yeah. And come around the back."

Korioth was a liberal in the legislature, and he was eager to go. We drove to the back of the Governor's Mansion, and a highway patrolman whisked us inside; I had the distinct feeling this was not a public visit. We waited in the sitting room, admiring the portraits and feeling the cushions in the easy chairs, and in a moment the Governor came down the stairs, shook our hands, and sat cross-legged chewing on a small cigar. A waiter came in. "Who wants some orange juice?" the Governor asked.

"Governor," Korioth said, "is that all you're offerin'?"

"I thought you'd say that," the Governor said. "It's orange juice or nothin'."

As we sipped orange juice the Governor, a wry, shrewd little man who had once served an undistinguished term in the U.S. Senate before coming home for "my life" ambition," to be Governor of Texas, said, "I brought you boys down here to talk about this sales tax. If the libs don't get behind the compromise we're gonna get something worse." So we sat there talking about sales taxes, and sales tax compromises, and voting blocs, and half a loaf as compared with a whole loaf. He chewed on his cigar, never once lighting it because he was against smoking, and asked us if we would use our influence, or ponder the problem and try to get something going. He listed the names of the rich people behind the sales tax, and said this was what he was up against. He tipped me on a good source for an exposé. After a while he got up, and we shook hands again, and the highway patrolman led us out the back door. I got a good exposé, the libs fought the sales tax, and in the end we not only did not get half a loaf, we didn't even get a slice.

•

Some moments were out of the past, as when I saw an old politician trying to relive it. W. Lee "Pappy" O'Daniel was one of those purely American demagogues whose career, in retrospect, seemed mythical. At the state university I had "studied" him in a political science course. In 1938 when he was a flour salesman, and he and his hillbilly band, the Doughboys, led by a guitar player named Leon, sold flour on the Texas Quality Radio Network. On Palm Sunday, 1938, "Pappy" O'Daniel told his radio audience he was thinking about running for Governor; what did his listeners think about the idea? Within the next few days he received 54,499 messages asking him to run, and only four telling him not to. His platform was the Ten Commandments, opposition to a sales tax, abolition of the poll tax, and pensions for old people; his motto was The Golden Rule. He was elected over a large field without even needing a second primary. As Governor he was a rank reactionary, despite the way he could talk to "the plain folks." It was his appointees to the Board of Regents who almost wrecked the University of Texas. In 1941, he was elected to the United States Senate in a close race with Lyndon Johnson, where he served until 1948. Then he more or less vanished into obscurity.

When I was writing for the *Observer* O'Daniel decided to make a comeback; he was running again for Governor. I made a couple of phone calls to the right people and arranged to meet him in West Texas; the three of us — Pappy, his campaign manager, and I — rode around for three days campaigning in an air-conditioned white Cadillac; I liked the old bastard enormously, and he made me understand more than my textbooks had told me about the substance of American demagogy.

Going through West Texas with him, he was like a ghost riding the range. He looked old, he was old, he walked with an old man's shuffle; it took me only three or four hours to recognize that, far from being someone's villain this time, he was a lonely old man wanting to retrieve the past. I sat in the back seat of the Cadillac, and he would lean his red oval face over in my direction and tell me stories. Once he handed me his campaign card; on the back of it were the words to "Beautiful, Beautiful Texas"; "Boy," he said, "I wrote that song." As we drove through San Angelo he pointed to the courthouse. "See that?" he said to me. "Back one night in '38 there were 13,000 people there at a rally for me. I was a little late gettin' there and I walked up to some people in the back and said what's goin' on, and some fellah said, we're here to see W. Lee O'Daniel. Once in '38 about 7000 people showed up for one of our rallies at the Midland courthouse, and we were twelve hours late, and they were still there waitin' when we finally showed up."

He would get out of the car and do some campaigning, but the crowds were small at his scheduled speeches. "So many people have moved into the city," he said to me, after he had been silently sitting in the car during one of the long stretches on the road. "There aren't nearly so many people in the country now."

We were driving along at about ninety-five on the road between Pyote and Pecos, and a man was stranded in that barren, desolate area with a flat tire. We flashed past him; O'Daniel looked over at his campaign manager for a second or two, then said, "I reckon we better go back and help that fellah." We turned around, and Pappy, the campaign manager, and I helped the man fix his flat. He turned out to be a German from Schulenberg, and not much of an idealogue. When the tire was finished the campaign manager said to the German:

"You know who this man is?"

"What man?" the German asked.

"This man here. This here's W. Lee O'Daniel."

"That so?"

"Yeah, and he's runnin' for Governor, and we want you to vote for him and get all your neighbors to."

"We —— eel," the man said, "I ain't much interested in pol . . ."

"I used to have a *number* of friends in Schulenberg," Pappy said. "A whole lot of friends."

The man stood there, vaguely uneasy; he wasn't quite sure of himself. Then the campaign manager gave him a fistful of cards, which he carefully put in the pocket of his overalls, and we were off again. "There's a vote," Pappy said in the car, three or four hundred yards down the road, "and maybe a few more. He'll tell his friends. Politicians don't fix tires no more." This set him on another train of thought, and he turned again to talk to me. "Back in '38, you may not remember him, you were just a boy," he said, "I was runnin' against Bill McCraw, and Bill stopped to help a woman fix a tire, just like we did back there, and he fixed that flat for her without tellin' her who he was, and he got ready to go and she said, will you do just one more thing for me, and he said sure. Then she said, vote for W. Lee O'Daniel."

We stopped in a courthouse town for a campaign lunch; only twenty-five people were there, and only about half the places set at the long table were occupied. Pappy stood up, and said in his deep, drawling voice, "It's been good to go into the homes, to see those old friends who supported me that first time. Some are invalids now. Some have children who were little back when I started, and now they've taken their place. Others have passed on. I go see my old friends now and they pull out old pictures and I enjoy lookin' at them." He told about a barbershop he had been into; there was an old picture of "the boys," the hillbilly band, on the wall — faded now, he said, but still there.

Later that day, in another town, Pappy made a radio talk. I

sat in the tiny studio next to him; he seemed suddenly to come alive. He loosened his tie and stood before the microphone; the people in the station offered him a chair, but he refused to sit down. "You listen to this, son," he said to me, just before he went on the air. Shouting and waving his limbs, with a new spirit in his voice, he said, "The millionaires are leaving skimmed milk for the masses!" The conditions are the same now as they were in 1938, he shouted. "The Governor is thinkin' up new taxes right now. An income tax will just make things worse!" He went on in this vein for ten minutes, and almost lifted the roof with an exclamation about "lobbyists and their contributions."

"That was a damned good talk, Governor," I said to him in the car, knowing now how he had achieved power. Then compulsively, he started talking to me about the Texas Quality Network, and how people no longer listened to the same thing on radio the way they used to. "Back when we were broadcastin'," he said, "we'd cross the river and go down to Piedras Negras to use that powerful station. Mexicans came in droves to hear us and to listen to the music. Once we got a request from some prisoners in a penitentiary way over in Alabama, and pretty soon convicts from everywhere were writin' to get us to play songs for their girl friends."

The next day we drove deeper into West Texas, over the same routes O'Daniel once followed when he was selling flour. He sat on the edge of his seat; he was excited, and he pointed out old landmarks. This is the country where the wind whistles when you drive through it and the old people sit around big old tables in the parched little railroad towns playing dominoes in the afternoons. Pappy understood this country.

He would walk into a grocery store in some weather-beaten crossroads town. There would be the same wrinkled faces, the stained teeth common to this region, the soiled khakis, the smells of drying bacon and pork. He would introduce himself simply, with a slightly exaggerated touch of humility, "I'm W. Lee O'Daniel, and I'm runnin' for Governor." All the faces in the store would magically come to life, and the old people would get up slowly and shake his hand.

Many of them had met him and shaken his hand years before. The man who sold groceries in Barnhart had met him at Taylor in 1938. The women who waited tables in Ozona had met him in Midland. The son of the used parts man in Mertzon once went to one of his rallies, four years old and bawling all the way through the speech, so his father said. Sometimes they would not say a word, but just stand there and stare at him, a little stymied about what to do next. For a time there would be a silence, disturbed by the whine of a fly or the sound of a car whipping along the highway outside. "Well, pass them biscuits, Pappy!" someone would finally shout, and this would set them off. "Why, *I'll swan*, Pappy," an old woman would say, "What you doin' way out here?" or "Where's your boys, Pappy?" or "Still sellin' flour, Pappy?" O'Daniel would look at the floor a moment, his broad neck thrust out of his loosened collar, and then he would say: "Yeah, I'm runnin' again, I'm out to clean up that mess in Austin, just like '38, when I was through here first time I ran."

In Mertzon there was an old inconsequential wisp of a woman working behind the meat counter of a store, dressed in a greasy white apron. O'Daniel had been shaking hands with some men in front; he saw her and went back to the counter. "I just want to shake your hand," he said to her. "It's sure great to be among my old friends again." She looked down at her hand, and up at the ceiling, and then said, solemnly as could be: "We used to listen to you all the time. My husband and I used to listen to you every day. Every time you run for somethin' I voted for you, and I'm goin' to now." Then, having said this, surprised perhaps by having come out and said it, she gazed down at the floor, and retreated again behind the counter.

Later, in Monahans, a toothless, unshaven old man in the furniture store walked up to O'Daniel. "Pappy," he said, shaking his hand like a well pump, "I never will forget back then. I saw ol' Jim over at the drug store an' I said Jim, I said, I bet you twenty-five dollars to a hundred Pappy wins, and Jim says that's a bet, and I went around day 'fore the 'lection and I says Jim I bet another twenty-five ol' Pappy don't even need no run-off, and surenuf, long about 'lection day Jim calls me up and he says, come on over you sonufabitch and get your money." There was a group of old people in the dry goods store in Ozona. One of them said, "W. Lee, where's Leon? You bring Leon this time, like you usta?" A wave of tenderness swept over that big, red face. "Leon didn't come this time," Pappy said. "Leon's in heaven." In Wickett he stopped off at a small garage, where there were several men working on cars; the men were covered with grease. O'Daniel came up to shake hands. One of them said, "We're awful dirty." "I don't care," Pappy said. "Why, I'm out to see the people."

"I met an old colored man on the street somewhere over in East Texas," O'Daniel told me farther up the street. "I offered him my hand and he said, you mean you're goin' to shake hands with me? Sure, I said, I'm runnin' for Governor, ain't I, and I mean to serve all the people." The next day, campaigning through another small town, I went with him to see a Baptist preacher who had asked him to do something about clamping down on liquor. "Well, what do you think about this segregation business?" Pappy asked. The preacher said, "You know how I feel. It's in the Book, ain't it? It's right there in the Book."

"Yeah, it's in the Constitution too," Pappy said. "The Lord didn't want us mixin' when he made us."

We drove into Fort Stockton, and Pappy wanted to stop for a Coke. We found a café and parked the car. Inside, Pappy saw a group of cowboys drinking coffee. He chose one and stretched out his hand.

"Hello there. I'm W. Lee O'Daniel and I'm runnin' for Governor."

"Pappy O'Daniel?" the cowboy said. "I thought he was dead." The other cowboys doubled up and laughed.

"Not yet," Pappy said. "I've got plenty of service in me yet."

But he did not finish his Coke; he sat at the table for a while, not talking much, and then he said he would meet us in the car. A few minutes later I walked out of the café. I saw him on the edge of the highway, alone. He was standing still, his hands were limply at his sides, and he was looking at something out beyond the railroad cars in that still and deserted place, out beyond the plains to the sky. It was that hour just before dark, and he looked old and pathetically alone. Watching him then, I wondered what his thoughts must have been. Leon playing his git-fiddle? Old rallies on courthouse lawns? The uses he had made of his power? Then he turned to get into the car; he saw me standing there behind him. "Come on, boy," he said, waving his arm. "We got an appointment in Pecos."

8

THE RADICAL RIGHT in the 1960s would probably provide the historians with a great deal of mystery. In Texas we were sitting on it. The time was also propitious; Kennedy's election, promising reform, had stirred the rightists from the lethargy that had gripped us all in the fifties. I had written an article in *Harper's* about the John Birchers in Houston; Kennedy himself, I learned, had read it and was disturbed. Reporters from the East invariably came by to interview us about their activities. They thought we were on the front lines and falling by the minute. Some of them seemed to think Barry Goldwater was fomenting a revolution.

Soon after the word had been circulated in the early 1960s that President Eisenhower was in the employ of the Kremlin, Senator Goldwater said that all the people he knew who were members of the John Birch Society were fine, decent people. Later the Senator asked us to consider the proposition that the agitated temper in pursuit of a certain form of liberty would postpone — and God willing even halt — the great Republic's decline. I would like to consider this proposition not abstractly but in its own terms, through an incident that took place in 1961 in Austin. Symbolically, Austin was the capital of the state which Senator Goldwater had exploited as his national base during his short-lived heyday. Without Texas we would not have had a Johnson, and I seriously doubt if we would have had a Goldwater, at least not the same one: Goldwater spent so much time in Texas in this period that some people believed the state had had three U.S. Senators.

At the time, the John Birch Society was flourishing nationally. It was under persistent attack by the Establishment press, sensation-seeking columnists and interpreters, and hence it was gaining daily in adherents. This was some time before the pristine views of the Society would be muddled by Eisenhower's denying that he had been on the payroll of the NKVD, with a monthly salary and a substantial, if not spectacular, share in the profits. It was also three years before Ike himself would cause doubts in the minds of his detractors by unleashing the angry delegates to the Republican convention in San Francisco against the deception of Eastern journalists. And three years would pass, too, before the Presidential nominee of a major party would give the Society unexpected respectability by recommending extremism as a virtue or, to put it another way, exposing moderation as a vice.

•

One night my wife and I were eating dinner at home in Austin when my phone rang. The caller, speaking in whispers, gave his name as Bunch and briefly described his mission. He said he needed to see me as soon as possible. We arranged a safe rendezvous in an out-of-the-way roadhouse.

Bunch was a curious young man of about twenty, with a predilection for speaking in cryptic whispers, even when no one was about, for punctuating key sentences with sighs, and for never sitting with his back to a door. He was one of the most solemn people I have ever dealt with. I admit that from the beginning I suspected his intentions. For three days I was wary that he might have been using me in some elaborate campus hoax, perhaps a fraternity plot to make a fool of my newspaper, which, circulating as it was at just a shade over 6000, could ill afford to lose its honor, much less its head. He pulled out a John Birch Society official membership card, which I examined carefully. He had even brought a sheaf of notes with him, and with an earnestness that would have subuded the doubts and tribulations of a Mark Lane, he began telling me his story. He said that he had joined the Birch Society out of curiosity. His past was clean enough, and in due time, after serving quietly and diligently, he became a member of a select and dedicated cell, No. 772. This cell had been organized earlier in the year by Jack Bigby — one of the John Birch Society's most trusted and experienced coordinators, a man of firm determination and great physical strength — for the purpose of bringing about a full-fledged investigation of the University of Texas. The members, young patriots chosen for their courage and resourcefulness (they were, one might say, a Texas version of a small nineteenth-century Balkan spy ring), were charged with the job of spying on their professors so that subversion at the University might be ferreted out.

Bunch gave me a list he had made of the other eight student members of Cell 772. He described Miss Ledbetter, an aggressive and wily piano instructor who provided the secret meeting place. Cell 772, he emphasized, was not merely secret, it was *super*-secret. He intimated that even the highest authorities up North might not know its every move.

Cell 772 had been working in close cooperation with a business firm downtown, Enterprisers, Inc., a front for the Birch Society. Here a corps of people had been amassing information on supposed subversion and subversive activities at the University of Texas. Here elaborate files were kept on private citizens. Here lists of supposed Communists, crypto-Communists, Communist dupes, and liberal Democrats in all the colleges and universities of Texas were kept up to date. But chiefly they had their eyes on the state university itself, which had a library, and whose teaching ranks included many home-grown dissenters and Yankee intellectuals.

Jack Bigby had advised the members of Cell 772 to use pocket-sized tape recorders in lectures at the University. The president of 772, a young man named Judson Chapell, had also informed his associates that they would be aided in their work by two members of the investigative arm of the Department of Public Safety, a sort of boondocks FBI, though with a less efficacious technology. State Representative Clarence "Stonehenge" Bailey of Houston, whom President Chapell had identified several times as an active John Bircher, would, in the meantime, push for an investigation of the university by a special legislative committee composed of the "right people." Textbooks used at the university were being checked by another special unit within 772, the Group for Book Review, against a master list (supplied by Enterprisers, Inc.) of alleged subversive works.

Bunch had more to say about Jack Bigby, whom he liked to call "the Big Man." At one of the meetings, Bigby had suggested that the cell (or, as they preferred, chapter) members write anonymous letters to parents of fellow students who had been involved in "liberal activities." He had also told them that the Birch Society and Robert Welch were the only answer to the Communist problem and that the front-group tactic used by Communists was most effective. And he had warned the young conspirators several times that no one could be trusted, "not even ourselves." Bigby apparently was also a judo expert, and he had lectured at length at a cell meeting about judo, remarking that he would like to use his judo on some of the sit-in demonstrators who had been picketing movie houses near the campus. When a cell member complained in exasperation one night that perhaps the best way to treat the enemies of the John Birch Society would be to kill them off, Bigby said that might not be a bad idea, but that there were too many.

Cell 772, Bunch further informed me, had been addressed one evening by Dr. Felix J. DeSpain, a leading Birch Society intellectual who in professional life was a veterinarian specializing in cow skin diseases, with a free-lance constituency at a nearby zoo. The cell members had brought Dr. DeSpain up to date on its activities, and he had agreed wholeheartedly with their objectives. DeSpain had just been to Southwest Texas State College at San Marcos, Lyndon Johnson's alma mater, to get a cell going. There had been a little difficulty. One young man who had already joined the Society turned out to be an atheist. DeSpain finally settled the problem by deciding that the student could still be effective against Godless Communism at Southwest Texas State College, even though Godless himself.

Bunch later met with another important figure, Mrs. Clara Saxon, at Enterprises, Inc. Since she had received good reports on his work from other cell members and the adult leaders, she took him into her confidence. She showed him a copy of *Sex and Love in the Bible*, which she said was being pushed by Communist-front groups at the University, such as the YMCA and the Wesley Foundation. At this meeting, for the first time, Bunch was shown the list of subversive educators.

Bunch, together with two other cell members, also met with two special investigators, Burns and Hare, at the Texas Department of Public Safety. The meeting had been arranged by State Representative "Stonehenge" Bailey. The cell members identified themselves to Burns and Hare as members of the John Birch Society. They presented the investigators with certain evidence on subversion at the University. Burns and Hare warned that they could not be implicated in any way, because they were not supposed to mix in politics. They told the cell members that they would provide them with two pocket-sized tape recorders, if, beforehand, they could bring the investigators one "juicy" lecture on their own. Then Burns and Hare took the names of Bunch and the two others and said they would check their reliability.

•

Young Bunch had told me a tale of enigmatic proportions, elaborately documented by the notes he had taken at home after every meeting. What was I to do with this information? It was quite possible that he was a counterspy, a sort of double agent, sent out by Bigby.* I therefore determined to proceed with

* A later speculation about Bunch proved to be the right one: He was starved for drama, and being also an enemy to what the Birchers stood for, he felt he would get in a few good blows for the Western ethic by being a kind of reverse subversive, satisfying at the same time his sense of the fanciful and remote.

caution. There were two factors working in my favor. One, members of the John Birch Society had persistently insisted that their organization was not secret. Two, one had the word of Texas' third Senator, Senator Goldwater, that all the Birchers he knew were decent and affectionate souls. I had little doubt that I could check out my informant's allegations with such an above-the-table group.

I began with the State Representative. One afternoon, during a floor debate in the House of Representatives, I walked over to "Stonehenge" Bailey's desk and sat down. I had met him before on several occasions, and as I have suggested previously about the political manner in Texas, our ideological disagreements, which in stormier times might have been the basis for a holy war, were softened by an amiable first-name relationship. "Stonehenge," I asked, "have you heard anything about an investigation of the University?"

"I've heard rumors," Bailey said, "that they're gonna investigate everything from playpens to the UN."

Had he played a role in an imminent investigation? "It's none of my affair, actually in a sense," he said. Well, did he know young Chapell, the president of Cell 772? He said he did not. Was Bailey himself a member of the Birch Society? "No," he replied, with much ardor. "I'm not a member, never have been, and never will be." Well, what was his opinion of the Society? "I am frankly presently trying to form an opinion," he said. "I'm reading the pro's and con's."

Next on my list were the two investigators at the Department of Public Safety. I phoned Hare for an appointment, and drove out to the large modern building on the Dallas highway. The atmosphere inside was one of muted efficiency, and I wondered how many friends of mine they had on file, what they or their cybernated facilities might know of their politics, their habits, their behind-the-scenes sexuality.

I climbed up the stairs and found the door marked "Burns and Hare." They were sitting behind separate desks in a small-ish, cluttered room. Both were big and beefy country boys, I could sense — perhaps from Killeen or Dripping Springs or Pflu-gerville. Later I would see quite a lot of both of them, back on the fringes of the crowd at campus meetings. I once spotted Hare looking over a gathering that turned out to hear Dwight Macdonald on anarchism; I would not have been astonished to see him walk up to the curious goateed figure and clamp on a pair of silver handcuffs. On another occasion I saw Burns in a crowd of students listening to Norman Mailer, and I wondered what he reported on *that*.

Hare motioned me to a chair, and as I bent over to sit down, I was surprised to see, next to each other on top of a large pile of printed matter, two publications: *The Texas Observer* and *The Worker*. I had never really considered this juxtaposition. It was a strange feeling, seeing one's own byline next to that of Elizabeth Gurley Flynn.

"I see you have good reading matter here," I said to Hare.

"We read everything out here," Hare said. "In this job we have to keep up with what's going on." Behind his desk in the corner, Burns was doing some paperwork, but I could tell he was simulating it. He was very much aware of me, the back of his neck was taut; he was chewing gum, and occasionally he would glance up and look me over. I was rummaging around in forbidden terrain. Here were two Texas country boys accus-tomed to judging quickly, and not used to changing their minds.

I began by asking if they had conferred with members of the John Birch Society in gathering information for an investiga-tion.

"We have informants, sources of information, and sometimes these sources are in a position of controversy," Hare said briskly. "Because we use an informant doesn't mean we're in sympathy

with him." Had they offered the group the pocket-size tape recorders? "Definitely not," he said. "It would be out of order for
any state equipment to be loaned to any individual or organization." Wasn't there a question of propriety involved, I asked,
when public officials worked with members of a group like the
John Birch Society? "As for the propriety of our association
with anyone," Hare snapped, and Burns rustled in the corner, "I
can't answer that. If we are to do a service to the state, it is necessary to have informants in all walks of life." With that, slap-
ping his hands on the desk, knocking *The Texas Observer* and
The Worker off their pile into a disarranged ideological jumble, he closed the interview.

•

Judson Chapell, who, according to Bunch, was the president of
Cell 772, had a room in a streamlined air-conditioned dormitory near the university campus. When I identified myself, he
was quite cordial, but nervous. He offered me a chair and asked
what I wanted.

"How long have you known State Representative 'Stonehenge'
Bailey?" I asked.

"Not long, actually," Chapell said. "I ran into him at the
Capitol. He's a very nice guy. Do you know him?"

"What did you talk about?" I persisted.

"Just all kinds of things. We talked about some investigating
committee, some standing committee, but I don't think it went
through."

"Is 'Stonehenge' a member of the John Birch Society?" I
asked.

"I don't know that he is," Chapell said. "From what I understand, they don't tell who they are. He's the one to talk to about
that."

"How long have you been a member?" I asked.

"As a matter of fact, I'm not," he said. "I don't know any more probably about it than what I read in the papers."

I asked if he knew Jack Bigby. "I don't believe I do," he said. I asked if he knew the piano teacher, Miss Ledbetter, who owned the house where the secret meetings were held. "I don't think so."

"I have information that you're president of Cell 772 of the Birch Society. Is that true?" I asked.

"I'm flattered," he replied. "Go on. I didn't even know chapters had presidents." He turned his head and contrived a laugh.

Had he heard about a secret campaign to gather material on "subversives" at the University? "No," he said, "I don't know what that would be. More power to 'em if they can." Had he been to see Hare and Burns at the Department of Public Safety? "No."

What did he think of the John Birch Society? "Actually, I don't know much about it," he said. Did he believe there was any subversion at the University? "Well, The Daily Texan, you know, the student paper. But it's not subversive, I guess, it's Democratic, it pushes the Negro, but I don't know if that's subversive."

I left Chapell's dormitory, found a phone booth on the campus, and phoned Bunch. He was angered by my report of the interview with the president. "He's lying through his hat," Bunch said.

That night, I got another call from Bunch. "I have something that will make you sit up and listen," he whispered. We arranged a meeting at the apartment of a reliable friend.

A large tape recorder was on the table in the room. Bunch, considerably calmer than in our previous meetings, sat in an armchair and explained what had taken place. Sometime after I had left Chapell, Bunch decided to phone him on the pretext that "some reporter" had been around looking for him. On his own initiative, and with his own tape recorder, Bunch had taped the ensuing telephone conversation.

He started the tape recorder. I reclined in my chair to hear this unusual piece of evidence.

Chapell, after a moment of apparent suspicion, told Bunch that, alas, the reporter had talked with him only a short while before.

"He knows everything," Chapell's voice said. "I mean everything, with all the letters capitalized."

The voice of Bunch interrupted: "You mean he knows you're . . . ?"

"He knows *everything*," Chapell repeated. "I mean, everything."

"How did he find out?"

"We're working on that now," Chapell said. He then advised Bunch not to tell a single member of Cell 772 that the news was out. He also warned Bunch to prepare for the reporter, to remain calm when confronted with his startling information, and to feign ignorance.

"Have you talked with Bigby?" Bunch asked.

"Yes," Chapell said after a pause, and then added in a dramatic flourish, that no matter what happened, "the work of the chapter will go on. He knows I was lying. He'll know you're lying, but lie anyway. He'll publish our names, but the work will go on. One other thing," the president warned. "When you want to talk with me, come over here personally. Don't talk on this phone. We have reason to believe it's, you know. . . ."

There was a momentary silence on the tape.

"*Tapped?*" Bunch whispered, incredulously.

"Yes," the president said.

Bunch turned off the recorder. He sat down in his chair,

glancing my way with a bemused expression. "Now what do you think?" he asked.

But that was not all. He had more evidence. He had spent part of the afternoon downtown at Enterprisers, Inc. The people down there, he said, had told him that the pending investigation was just a matter of time. He also reported that the workers at Enterprisers, Inc. had just sent to the House Un-American Activities Committee for information on three University professors; one in economics, one in government, one in philosophy. He then reached into a folder and withdrew a copy of a list of eleven "subversives" in Texas colleges, which he had helped type out that afternoon. A well-known writer whom I knew was included. Under each name was a detailed list of the man's activities.

Then he produced another document, an information blank which members of Cell 772 were using in tabulating subversion at the University. Here it is:

Faculty
A. Sources of Documentation
B. Test of Socialist-Communist sympathizers
C. Listed Citations

Courses
A. Emphasis on Keynes-Socialist Principles & Philosophy
B. Lack of Courses on Americanism
C. Student Comments on Course Contents
D. Ridicule of Christian Doctrine

Textbooks
A. List of textbooks each item to set out
    1. Author, title, publisher, date
        a. Author's known activities

Student Organizations
A. Official
B. Unofficial thru YMCA, Unitarian Church, Christian Faith and Life Community

Daily Texan
  A. Clippings
  B. Irresponsibility
      1. Staff
      2. Faculty Advisors
      3. Illustration of JBS letter complete falsification

It was now midnight. I resolved that the following day I
would talk with Mrs. Clara Saxon at Enterprisers, Inc., Dr. Felix
DeSpain, and ultimately Jack Bigby, the Big Man himself. It
would be a significant day. Wrapping my black cloak about me,
I carried my speculations home, and foregoing Seymour Martin
Lipset, I put myself to sleep reading Conan Doyle's *The Red-
Headed League.*

•

Early the next afternoon, after the morning session of the legislature, I got in my car, doing three loops around the Capitol to
make sure I was not being tailed, and drove to Enterprisers, Inc.,
which occupied a ground-floor office on South Congress Avenue.
From the outside it seemed eminently respectable, a prototype
of a solid bourgeois undertaking.

I walked inside and was greeted by a the noise of several type-
writers. I asked a young lady behind the front desk if I could see
Mrs. Clara Saxon.

As I was ushered into her private office, Mrs. Saxon gave me
a warm welcome. She was a large, lively lady who seemed about
my size, though when I reflected on her in hindsight, I concluded that she must have outweighed me by roughly one
stone. I weighed approximately 175 at the time, and was not in
bad condition, but I think on a careful weighing she would have
tipped the scales, with the heavy dangling earrings not included,
at approximately 190. She had an animated manner, seemed
well coordinated, and was altogether cordial. I was not certain
I had the proper lady.

She invited me to sit down. "Mrs. Saxon," I asked, "what kind of business is Enterprisers, Inc.?"

"Well," she replied, "the list on the window outside describes it. We're a bookkeeping service."

I wrote her remark in my notebook. "What do you want this for?" she suddenly asked.

I explained that it was merely a routine inquiry; then I tried to take her with her guard down. "Mrs. Saxon, how long have you been a member of the John Birch Society?"

She was absolutely furious. "I haven't such information," she replied, growing red in her face, the earrings tinkling faintly against her earlobes. Yet for some reason she managed a contorted smile, which only served to emphasize her rising anger.

"You're not a member, then?"

"No."

"Do you know a young man named Judson Chapell, the president of Cell 772?"

"No!" she shouted. "What is all this about? This is no business of yours!"

"I have reliable information," I said, "that your business is a front for the John Birch Society. Is that true?"

"Well, isn't this something!" she exclaimed. "This is a bookkeeping business." She was in a state of extreme agitation, but I gave her credit for trying to control herself. She obviously did not want to mug a reporter on her home grounds. "Look," she said, "I am very busy. I have a job I have to finish today. I'll have to ask you to leave." She stood up.

"Can I see you later this afternoon, then?" I asked. No. "Tonight?" No. "Tomorrow?" No. "Day after tomorrow?" No. The lady never wanted to see me again.

Glancing at a table to my right, I noticed at that moment about a dozen copies of a book entitled *The Life of John Birch* by Robert Welch. "What is this?" I asked. At this point, Mrs.

Saxon, the kindly matron of a few moments before, began pushing me toward the door. She came at me from the left flank.
"Let me have those notes you took," she shouted, and grabbed
for my notebook, tearing a page. Retaining a manly grasp on it,
I retreated toward the entrance. The girls in the office, intrigued
by these impromptu gymnastics, stopped typing, and in the silence Mrs. Saxon glowered at me from her doorway. She could
have been a Russian female discus-thrower. I left.

•

The next person on my list was the veterinarian, Dr. Felix J.
DeSpain. I had had some dealings with DeSpain a few months
before, soon after the Birch Society had burst forth on the national scene. The trouble with DeSpain was not that he did not
talk, but that it was impossible to get him to stop once he had
started. He not only admitted that he was a member of the Society, he discoursed unendingly about why he was. One could
not get within close range when he was heated up and going
strong; a fine misty rainfall of saliva reinforced his ideological
contortions, and one worried about radioactivity. At the time
he had praised Senator Goldwater as a great man, but he believed Robert Welch, the Birch Society's leader, was greater.
He had called the editors of *Time* "a bunch of pinks" and apolo-
gists for socialism. "Like the *New York Times*," he had said.
"Would *anyone* say they're not soft on Communism? Wouldn't
you say they're soft on Communism?" he asked me.

"I think there might be some question," I had answered, arguing that most of its reporters were our fellow Southerners, and
that its managing editor, like myself, was a Mississippian. No
Mississippian, I said, had ever been caught in the act of subversion.

"Oh my God! We have clippings and clippings where they
definitely agree with the *Daily Worker!*" What had disturbed

him the most, however, was the extent to which the Fabians
had taken over the country. "Fabianism is going to the same
goal as Marxism. They're all going to Chicago, except on different routes — one on Route 15, the other on Route 12."

I reached DeSpain's office, and he was available. We retired
to a back room, full of scalpels and hypodermics. "Doctor," I
asked, "is the Birch Society a secret organization?"

"There's nothing secret about it at all," he answered enthusiastically. "The only thing secret about it is this — the United
States has gone so far to the left in Socialism and Communism,
and the newspapers are always ready to treat us unfairly, the
minute the news gets out that you belong to the John Birch
Society, the papers will write it up." The only secret aspect, he
said, was not to disclose the names of other members — "to prevent any member from being harassed through reprisal."

Was the local Birch Society doing anything secret these days,
I asked? The doctor said they were writing letters to Congress-
men, that sort of thing. "Some lunkhead in Washington called
it a fascist organization. But we don't want totalitarianism of
any kind — Communist or fascist. We just want good conservative Jeffersonian democracy."

How long had the local Birch Society been secretly gathering
material on "subversion" at the University? "I didn't know it
was going on," he said, a little apprehensive now, looking across
at me with squinted eyes. "You see, we have several chapters
here — twenty-six in all. One chapter never knows what another's doing."

How long had Bigby been a Bircher? "Oh, he was a charter
member. We were in the first chapter together." How long has
Mrs. Saxon over at Enterprisers, Inc. been a member? "Oh, she
was one of my chapter members," he replied. "We were in the
original chapter in Austin." Had he been to a meeting of Cell
772 at the piano teacher's? "No, we don't attend other meet-

ings," he said. Had he attended any other meetings? "Yes," he said. Where? "I can't tell you where. I could, but I won't." Did he know about the plan to tape-record University lectures? He said no. "Even if they are, I don't see anything wrong with it. The Communists make a great to-do about the citizen going out and bringing in information on other citizens working against the state. Do you see anything wrong with it?" By this time we had walked to the front door and were standing on the porch in the sunlight. "Well, Doctor," I said, "do you think secret recordings would be, you know, hitting below the belt?"

"I certainly don't," he said, jabbing my shoulder blade with his hand. "Look, my son is going to be at the University next year, and I think it would be a good thing for him to do something like that. If they *are* brainwashing these young people like that, I think a parent has a right to know."

●

Bigby was next. Bunch had told me that the youth leader was hosting another Birch cell meeting that night; I could imagine the concern which must have seized the local brotherhood. I found Bigby's house, a large two-story place down a dark side street. It was a gloomy night, and there was lightning in the skies off to the west. I parked in the shadow of a pecan tree and waited several minutes, until one by one all the cars had driven away. As I approached the house, rain began to fall softly. A bright yellow light shone on the porch. I knocked four times on the door. Did one need some special password, some designated knock, before he would come? I knocked again. There were heavy footsteps from inside. The door opened, and a tall, very dark, and heavily built man, perhaps in his forties, looked out. I was sure he had been expecting me, because almost before I could identify myself he motioned me out to a roofed patio in the yard.

I patted Bigby's dog, a grizzly terrier. It was a wasted gesture. Bigby was less communicative than the terrier. He grew more and more belligerent with each question I asked. He would not talk with me, now or ever. He did not want me around, and he invited me to leave the premises immediately. He proved to be the most profound disappointment of the entire venture. It was difficult to see how he could have reached a position of such eminence.

•

At our final rendezvous, Bunch was disillusioned by the equivocation of his former colleagues. There was no one else to see, nowhere else to go. The investigation was complete, except for the secret files of Cell 772, which had been entrusted to my informant. Bunch escorted me to his dormitory room, and handed me the files. At any moment the other members of the cell, perhaps Bigby himself, might come to retrieve them, but the world had to know. Safe in my study at home, I looked through this staggering collection of evidence. Here are the most important documents:

On April 20, 1961, Thursday, during Speech 803 class, during which members of the class were giving speeches, a girl from Longview, Texas, (I believe) gave a speech regarding the subject that the modern male is less useful than in the past. The subject was a critical analysis of the modern male. The girl concluded by saying that even if the modern male was useless, she was glad he was around. At that time, Mr. Foster, the class instructor, asked her if she was glad the male was around because of the reproduction act. Shortly later in the discussion of her speech by members of the class, the instructor asked her if the male was useless how did she plan on continuing the race (humans)? He went on to say that she could use artificial insemination.

Throughout the semester Mr. Foster has taken many opportunities to make obscene remarks in the presence of two female members of the class.

I intend to obtain the name of the girl involved and include her name on this sheet . . .

(signed) Lee Luscomb

Another document:

On April 20, 1961, an English instructor, Mr. Shawn, said to his English 601 class: "The New Testament has some basic inconsistencies. I hope you won't report me to the Board of Regents, but . . . it (the New Testament) is hard to reconcile."

These statements were made to show that the Bible should not be considered in making decisions regarding morality. The subject arose out of discussion of the lead characters of Huckleberry Finn.

I would like to complain about this attempted discrediting of the Bible.

(signed) James L. Moore

Another document contained a list of fourteen "subversives" on the faculty, including one department head, noted across the campus for his conciliatory roles and his Christian activities, who had not uttered a controversial statement in a quarter of a century. A cryptic note was attached to the list: "Check committee who are selecting president of University."

Another document noted:

In the summer session of 1959, Professor Laird said the following in essence at the beginning of the semester . . . "Does anybody in here really believe that the main reason we're here on earth is connected with the hereafter? I don't think so." (Show of hands, about four or five raised hands.) "The assumption of this course will be that the hereafter is not the question of importance, but to establish a world that is best for man's life here."

This Professor Laird made fun of belief in God, and said he doubted the existence of God, and that it was stupid to consider him in organizing the world.

P.S. this upset me enough at the time to write a letter to the American Mercury Magazine — which I may have a copy of at home.

The secret file also contained diverse reports on other lectures: "Trial by jury is feudal"; "federal aid to education is nothing new"; "segregation is not local custom but was forced by legislation"; and more.

That very night Cell 772 found its spy. When he returned to his room, Bunch told me the next day, four cell members were waiting. They demanded the secret files. He said he did not have them. They invited him outside. The president reached into his pocket and slowly pulled out two dollars, the monthly dues. Handing him the money, Bunch said, the president told him, "We ought to smash your face in." Then they left.

•

For quite some time after this incident, I watched many other romantic activists at work in the Southwest: retired generals, evangelists, insurance salesmen, ex-FBI-men, renegade leftists from the country club set. At first I was entertained, but finally I grew a little tired of the whole charade, and became increasingly disturbed by its vigilante effect at the local level, where such activity usually hurts the most. Yet I never ceased to be intrigued by the resourceful view they had of the world. I once heard a self-proclaimed expert on Marxism, asked when *Das Kapital* was written, reply, studiously, "Before Marx died." At a formal convention of a group, known as the Constitution Party, out there on that misty terrain where even Karl Hess, Bozell, and Shadegg feared to tread, or would do so at their risk, I was solicited to help adopt the pansy as the national flower, and to replace the Eagle with the Mother Hen. I talked with Mr. Bunker Hill Castle about loose and strict constructionalism. One speaker, whom I heard on a later occasion publicly challenge Lyndon Johnson to a fistfight, remarked that the 1960 Democratic Convention reminded him of "a bunch of drunk Mexicans in a house of prostitution with a credit card," and another commented that "the only person who could be elected President today is a Catholic nigger from Tennessee named Cohen." To my recollection these were the only two attempts at humor I ever heard from a zealous rightist.

Traveling about the region, I was subjected to diverse arguments. There were appeals suggesting a state department in every state to counteract America's centralized conduct of foreign affairs; I would not have been surprised by a plea for local control of outer space. I heard it explained, in so many words, that when Christ expressed the sentiment, "Lord, forgive them, for they know not what they do," it was a private remark to the carpenters, was off-the-record, and was not meant for general consumption. I followed the trail of that most flamboyant of Goldwaterites, a perspicacious old brickbat named J. Evetts Haley (whose book, A Texan Looks at Lyndon, was a runaway bestseller during the 1964 Presidential campaign) and his organization, "Texans for America," as they traveled about like the old justices of assize, winnowing the subversive and the obscene from school textbooks. These middle-class patriots intimidated public school officials, successfully promoted major revisions in a number of textbooks, and by proxy recruited a majority of the state House of Representatives to their cause before the intellectuals and professors began to fight back, typically, at the last moment.* Haley and his followers opposed any favorable mention in schoolbooks of the income tax, social security, TVA, federal subsidies to farmers and schools, and had harsh words for any mention of John Dewey, the UN, the League of Nations, UNESCO, disarmament, integration, and the Supreme Court. They further demanded that publishers

* One lady testified on an economics textbook that it included a picture of the UN building very close to a paragraph on free enterprise. "This layout," she said, "gives the student a mental picture that the UN is the proper vehicle for the defense of free enterprise. The UN is a socialist organization, an equalizer." Another said, "If you think we're a bunch of scared crackpots, you're right — but we're scared of Americans, not Russians."

remove from their books the names of Sinclair Lewis, Theodore
Dreiser, Jack London, Pearl Buck, William Faulkner, Ernest
Hemingway, Louis Untermeyer, Charles Beard, Henry Steele
Commager, Allan Nevins, and J. Frank Dobie. When Dobie
led a delegation of Texas writers to protest against the censorship
movement, J. Evetts Haley called the delegation a group of
"fatheads," "supersophisticates," and "leftwingers." When a
professor quoted from John Milton's *Areopagitica*, one lady in
his group whispered to another, "Who's John Milton?"

This was a mentality that flourished on its own private evidence, carried to dire extremes: films, books, pamphlets, and
tape recordings. In any of the "patriotic bookstores" in the
Southwest, alongside *Conscience of a Conservative* and *Why
Not Victory?* one would find, among others, *A Youth's Primer
to the Confederacy — What the Historians Left Out*; *How
to Plan an Anti-Subversive Seminar*; *The Income Tax — Root
of All Evil*; *Why Do Millionaires, Ministers of Religion, and
College Professors Become Communists*; or *Essays on Segregation*, billed as "a collection of writings by six Episcopalian
clergymen, one of them a bishop, exploring the Christian foundations for the racial settlement in the South called segregation, and exposing 'integration' as an attack on mankind's
greatest treasure, faith in Jesus Christ." I read more even about
subversion in high places than I had read about Whittaker-
Chambers' bad teeth. After a generous sampling of this and
similar lore, one could begin to understand how the brooding
and uncomplicated mind, with proper encouragement, might
detect subversion not only behind the UN and the TVA, but
also the French and Indian War, the Pure Food and Drug Act,
compulsory vaccination for smallpox, the abolition of entail
and primogeniture, the bank holiday of 1933, the British Reform Acts, Red Cross blood banks, the Congress of Vienna, the

election of Grover Cleveland, Teapot Dome, and public venereal
clinics.

•

I do not wish to be unfair to the third Senator from Texas, who
had known nothing about Cell 772, and who I am sure would
have been hesitant at any time to solicit pleasantries on a ham-
radio line from Bigby, DeSpain, Mrs. Clara Saxon, or, for that
matter, Bunker Hill Castle and J. Evetts Haley. Yet the fact
remains that under his leadership a major American political
party, in the year 1964, not only refused, but refused with ardor
and militancy, to adopt a resolution denouncing such people.
To understand what this refusal implied, one needed some prior
insight into the nature of the Goldwater mystique. During
his ceaseless peregrinations in the late 1950s and the '60s, after
a typically well-attended speech in the Southwest, Goldwater
would usually depart on the next plane out, leaving us fixed
residents to live with the curious voltage with which he had
imbued our atmosphere. For the truly imaginative of the Elect,
he was regarded as the advance man of the Apocalypse; it is difficult to convey the religiosity with which he was embraced.
Within hours after his departure the local ideologues would
engage themselves and their neighbors in spirited mumbo-jum-
bos against the United Nations, the unexecuted Hiss, the socialist schemers in the next subdivision, Dean Acheson's striped
trousers, American diplomacy in Europe, and, for that matter,
diplomacy in general. General Marshall's ghost stalked a thousand suburbias, and hausfraus who had never heard of Harlan,
Hughes, or *Marbury v. Madison* cursed the mere mention of
Justice Warren.

Richard H. Rovere, in his book *The Goldwater Caper*, had
been impressed by the difference between the "two Goldwaters,"

between "the agreeable man with the easy Aw Shucks manner who speaks in rightist platitudes but has only a loose grip on ideology," and "the dour authoritarian polemicist" who dominated his books and many of his collected speeches. What Rovere did not discuss in this penetrating study was the fearsome influence that the *combination* of these two qualities had on the hard-shell far-rightists among the Goldwater partisans — those people, and they numbered in the thousands, to whom the faintest suggestion of comedy, fallibility, or dissent was threatening. Goldwater's direst warnings about the growing power of the national bureaucracy or the insufficiency of our gunpowder supply were the greatest single stimulus to the basically simple folk who preferred the primer to the history text, and the quick-action revolver to both.

I am not referring here to that vast respectable middle-class community, yearning for the lost days of the Articles of Confederation, which James Reston in 1964 believed had to be understood for a rounded view of the Goldwater mystique. Respectable they may have been, even with many of my old classmates among them; and their numbers would have indicated something gone badly wrong with America then. But what I found even more intriguing at the time was the interplay between Goldwater and the professional Goldwater organizer on the one hand, and rigid political fundamentalists like DeSpain and Bigby on the other. It was a relationship of magnetic affection, and only in the late stages of the 1964 campaign of a most reluctant and tentative qualification. The general aura which surrounded the man was a prime source of the invaluable sustenance he gave this absolutist mentality: his simplistic view of "good" and "evil," his indifference to the meaning or importance of words, his lack of concern with the real world. Much more effectively than McCarthy, he encouraged a whole demonology, a veritable Yoknapatawpha of ghouls and adversar-

ies. He was both symbol to the most ingrown local patriotism
and the hero to that quality of mind which Richard Hofstadter,
in examining the "paranoid style" in our politics, saw as one of
"heated exaggeration, suspiciousness, and conspiratorial fantasy."
Hero and symbol, he was revered in a way that Lyndon Johnson
— political practitioner, neutralizer of the factionalist and forever to be suspect for it — never could be.

As editor of the political-literary journal which Hare and
Burns read each week, I discovered that one could get along
tolerably well with the Goldwater organizers, the pros of the
trade, for there is a curious everyday dialogue in the cynical
workings of politics. But it was something else with the rank-
and-file, for which political discourse seemed less a way to
argue rationally than a mode for registering unchallengeable
prophecies and undeniable accusations. One never developed
an argument with a typical Goldwater matron, for instance, for
the simple reason that to confront her with a perfectly reasonable contention would lead her afield to fancies so irrelevant
that one might as well have been talking to an entire backfield,
or to the local chorus of the DAR. As for making any contact
with the full-fledged mystics, this was impossible; you were sub-
verting them by your presence.

The three elements — the professional politician and organizer, the middle-class partisan, and the nervous activist of the
Bigby and DeSpain school — made an interesting *mélange*.
The professionals sometimes knew that their activists, when in
a state of extreme titillation, could be an embarrassment, but to
disavow them would not have been politically wise: they served
as a kind of panzer corps, making forays into enemy ground, involved in an endless diatribe that carried Goldwater's own messages to thunderous conclusions, often by merely taking them
verbatim and adding their own footnotes. All this could only
encourage the vague restlessness to be found among the less

frenetic partisans. These respectables, in turn, sometimes being community pillars, by their mild and tacit approval or by their unwillingness to disapprove, inspired a gentler community regard of the battle tactics of the shock troops. In many cities of the Southwest and West, in fact, large numbers of these respectables would turn out for the cold war seminars or the anti-subversive forums in 1961 and 1962 and 1963 to listen from curiosity, and they would often remain to participate actively in the genuflections and blood oaths which were substitutes for tea and coffee. Goldwater himself, with his careless talk of plots and thievery, had cast a broad umbrella over the *mélange*.

•

Living later in New York, removed from the wellsprings of such strenuous disaffection, I would occasionally brood on how the nation stays together. The differences in the land sometimes seem too deep for pacific co-existence; we are a great paste-up job. Where, I have asked myself, would I take DeSpain if he dropped in unexpectedly for a visit? A coffee-house in Greenwich Village? A publishing conference at Harper & Row? Columbia? The tapestry room of the Cloisters? The Little Church Around the Corner? *My Fair Lady*? Each in its way would be off-limits: only the Bronx Zoo might serve as common ground. In the early 1960s in America, the politics of fantasy and the real world faced one another across a chasm too vast for any human act to bridge.

9

OF ALL THE PEOPLE I knew in Texas politics, Maury Maverick, Jr., was probably the most colorful and certainly the most complicated; he knew that we Americans are a paste-up job, and he pondered our complications endlessly. He was a worrier, a brooder, and he would wrap himself around some political problem with such a pessimistic tenacity that one sometimes wondered if he would ever let go. When he was working on a speech he would growl and moan, slumping into a chair and glowering wordlessly down at the floor, cursing himself in the vivid San Antonio idiom considerably more than he cursed the opposition. The next day he would go out and give a speech so full of fight and flourishing with such an old-time optimism that a friendly audience would cheer and applaud with tears in their eyes. At the same time he was one of the most unusual storytellers I ever knew. Some uproarious political tale would come out of that sad, hang-dog countenance and would almost always take you unawares, for in truth Maverick is one of God's last angry men with a sense of humor.

It would have been difficult, if not impossible, to appreciate Texas without appreciating the Mavericks, one of the great and distinctive families of the Southwest. Maury Jr.'s great-grandfather in refusing to brand his cattle contributed the noun *maverick* to the language, and it was an appropriate one, for the Mavericks have never been the property of any man. An early

Maverick had met the British at the Boston Massacre. Samuel Maverick had been one of the signers of the Texas Declaration of Independence from Mexico, and had been dispatched from the Alamo to Washington-on-the-Brazos sometime before the Alamo fell to Santa Anna. And in the New Deal years, Maury Maverick, Sr., was one of the most flamboyant and outspoken politicians on the national scene.

The legend of Maury Sr. was alive and growing when I was covering Texas politics in the early 1960s. He had been the leader of that colorful band of radicals elected to the U.S. House of Representatives in 1934, and his radicalism was intensely, fervidly American, unmoved by the European ideologies he thought alien. He coined the word "gobbledygook" and scorned the high-flown Marxian language of the Eastern radicals. He bitterly criticized what he called the "Manhattan mind," which he believed was corrupting native American reform with meaningless rhetoric and empty ritual, and all through the 1930s he attacked the Communists with his own memorable mixture of bombast and ridicule. "He looked on San Antonio with the same proprietary devotion that La Guardia lavished on Manhattan," Arthur Schlesinger, Jr., once wrote, "and his solicitude for the Mexicans of Texas was akin to that of La Guardia for the immigrants of New York. And like La Guardia, Maverick was a radical but not a socialist; in essence, he was a pragmatic American politician who wanted the oppressed to get a better break."

I have yet to meet a family with such an exuberant sense of pride — pride in its own American roots, in a place, in a past. They are cut from the old grain; they grow tougher and prouder with age. Several times I drove around San Antonio with Maury Jr., who will take you on a tour of the place on the smallest excuse, ending up inevitably with frosty beer and enchiladas in some Mexican restaurant on the West Side. He loves that city

as few American cities are loved these days, or deserve to be
loved, and he could give a half-hour lecture on every landmark
there. The Maverick property is on a hill with a glorious view
of San Antonio. My wife Celia asked Maury one day, "Maury,
where did you get this property?" Maury replied, "Sweetheart,
nobody's owned this land but the Mavericks and the King of
Spain." This does not imply that Maverick Jr. lacked a certain
perspective. During the 1960 Presidential campaign, he was in
charge of the arrangements for Senator John Kennedy's visit.
Kennedy gave a speech before 10,000 people in front of the
Alamo; when he had finished, Maverick and the other local
Democratic leaders took him and his party on a tour inside. One
of Kennedy's men said, "Maury, let's get Jack out the back
door to avoid the crowd." Maury replied, "Hell, there's not a
back door to the Alamo. That's why we had so many dead
heroes." Unfortunately a reporter from a San Antonio newspaper overheard this remark, and the next day the headline read:
"Maverick Says No Back Door." This kind of wit can be expensive, especially with a reporter around, and Maury wrote an
abashed apology to the Daughters of the Republic of Texas.

•

Being such a firebrand, and a friend of the hopeless and downtrodden, Maury Maverick, Sr., had inspired an acute hatred
among the respectable classes of the city, particularly when he
returned from Congress, having failed at reelection in 1938, to
become mayor of San Antonio. His son would tell the story of
the time Maury Sr. unexpectedly went to church one Sunday
morning. After the service, as he was leaving, a lady from one of
San Antonio's most upstanding families accosted him. "Why,
Maury Maverick!" she exclaimed. "It's so good to see you down
here at the Episcopal Church. Some of my friends are going
'round saying Maury Maverick is a *Communist*, a big friend

with all these Reds. But I know any man who comes to the
Episcopal Church on Sunday morning *couldn't* be a Communist." Without so much as a pause Maury Sr. replied, "Why,
Alice, it's awfully good to see *you* in church this mornin', because some of my friends down at city hall are goin' around
sayin' Alice —— has been doin' a little whorin' on the side, in
the afternoon now and then, but I say to 'em, why Alice couldn't
be a whore because she comes to this Episcopal Church every
Sunday mornin' of the year." This story in years hence had acquired certain flourishes, but this was its essence.*

In the early 1950s, when his father was still alive, Maury
Jr. was the spiritual leader of the tiny group of liberals in the
Texas legislature. At their caucuses over bourbon and pretzels,
when everyone else was in despair, Maury Jr. would say, "Tomorrow we will fight." One afternoon the majority put up for
a floor vote a resolution praising Senator Joe McCarthy and
inviting him to come and deliver a speech to the Texas House of
Representatives. Maverick offered a floor amendment substi-
tuting Mickey Mouse for McCarthy, and made a speech suggesting that if the Texas legislature wanted to invite a rat, it ought
to invite a good rat.

On a less propitious occasion, however, the conservatives presented another resolution demanding that a particularly outspoken liberal professor, Clarence Ayres, be fired from the economics department at the University of Texas. In these years,
even among fighters, this called for tactical withdrawal. The

* Maury Sr. had been a good friend of La Guardia; they shared many of the
same characteristics. During the War, Nazi aviators were dropping leaflets behind
American lines; a picture of La Guardia was juxtaposed with a picture of a
baboon, and the caption said: "Which is the baboon?" La Guardia sent Maverick a copy of the leaflet to San Antonio; in a letter he said that "my old friend
Maury" had often complained about how his political enemies in Texas fought
dirty, and to take a look at what he, La Guardia, had to live with. Maverick
replied by telegram to La Guardia: "Which *is* the baboon?" at which point,
as Maury Jr. told it, La Guardia telephoned his father long-distance and cursed
him out in three languages.

liberals, including Maury Jr., quietly got up and retired to the men's room, the place where Texas legislators always have hidden to avoid casting a vote. Some of them hid in the toilet cubicles, putting their legs up on the toilets so the pages could not see their shoes under the doors when they came with the quorum call. The resolution passed with only one dissenting vote. In a day or two Maury Maverick, Sr., found out what had happened, and in a phrase that was still in currency in 1962 he branded his son and his friends in the state legislature as "shit-house liberals."

Such an unusual life deserved a characteristic and brilliant departure, and got it. In the summer of 1954 Maury Sr. was dying in a hospital in San Antonio. Maury Jr. went to see him; they both knew it was the last time. Maury Jr., as he told it to me later, sat around talking with his father and then, on the verge of tears, got up and left the room. He was a few steps down the corridor when he heard a rasping growl, *"Maury Jr., come back in here!"* Maury Jr. walked back inside the room, and his father said to him, "Well, at least you didn't turn out to be as much of a horse's ass as that Elliot Roosevelt."

•

Maury Jr. retired from the state legislature before he had turned forty, and in 1961 he became a candidate to fill Lyndon Johnson's seat in the U.S. Senate. It was a typically fractured Texas political situation; in the same race with Maverick was another well-known Texas liberal, the *latino* leader Henry Gonzalez. It was a sad and ironic campaign — a Maverick, member of a family who loved and was loved by the Mexicans, pitted in the same race against a man with the surname Gonzalez. Both fought hard, and both lost badly.

At the height of the Senate campaign I drove to Houston to spend the day watching Maury at the hustings. I had arranged to meet up with his party at the Houston airport, and when I got there the people at the control tower were in a state of considerable panic. They had lost radio contact with the small airplane Maverick was traveling in; the last word they had was that the landing mechanism was not functioning. Finally someone spotted the plane approaching the farthest edge of that vast concourse, and I got in a jeep with a mechanic and sped to a hangar near a cotton field. The plane managed to land at the end of the runway and came to a skidding halt near the hangar. I went out to greet the passengers; Maverick was the first to emerge.

"How are you, Maury?" I asked.

Maury glowered at me for a few seconds and said, "I just switched from a low Episcopalian to a high Episcopalian."

That afternoon Frankie Randolph, the patron of the *Texas Observer*, had arranged for Maury to address a large group of Negro preachers who were having a meeting in a Negro Baptist church in the middle of the Houston slums. The three of us walked into the church, where the preachers were engaged in a spirited prayer meeting. I whispered to Maury: "I hope you'll try to catch the mood of this gathering." Mrs. Randolph was respected by the Negroes of Houston only as a scion of an old Southern family who becomes militantly and uncondescendingly engaged in the cause of civil rights can be; she made a brief, dignified introduction. Then Maverick began speaking, flourishing his head and jabbing at the air with a clenched fist as was his custom. Suddenly he asked, in a kind of rumbling shout: "Can any of you gentlemen tell me the name of the Negro who was shot down at the Boston Massacre?" Two or three of the preachers shouted, *"Crispus Attucks!"* "Crispus Attucks is right!" Maverick exclaimed. "Crispus Attucks was a great American. And do you know *Crispus Attucks died in the arms of my cousin Samuel Maverick?"* The shouts from the congregation were loud and animated: "Amen, Brother Maverick," and he then proceeded to speak about Negro rights in Texas in a Biblical rhetoric that would have done justice to John L. Lewis.

Out of politics, he would continue to be active in hard, and sometimes lost causes: civil rights, civil liberties, the cause of the poor and oppressed of the Southwest. As local counsel for the ACLU, he handled the case of Madalyn Murray, the woman who had started the litigation that resulted in the Supreme Court's prayer decision. She had been picked up in Mexico, thrown out of the country, and turned over to the authorities in San Antonio to be extradited to Maryland. The press asked Maverick where he was when he got word that she was in jail. "I was on the banks of the Llano River," Maverick said, "having a drink of sherry like a good Episcopalian should on a Saturday in solemn contemplation of the Sabbath. 'Thank God you are here, Mr. Maverick,' she said when I went to her cell. A woman like that can't be all bad."

Earlier he had defended a bookseller in San Antonio who was considered to be a Communist. The man's books were seized by the police as subversive, including Lenin, Erich Fromm, *Pacem in Terris*, Pope John XXIII's encyclical, and a copy of a dissenting opinion of Hugo Black. The case went all the way to the U.S. Supreme Court, and this exchange is on the record:

Justice Stewart: "Did they [the Texas law enforcement officers] return the dissenting opinion of Mr. Justice Black?"
Maverick: "No, sir. I have high hopes they will read that opinion and grow in stature."

The same defendant was tried in the District Court not long after Kennedy was killed; feelings were tense. Plainclothesmen and detectives were planted about in the courtroom to keep Maverick and his client from being hurt. In the middle of the trial a somewhat sinister man walked in wearing large black eyeglasses. At the moment Maverick was at the bench, directly in front of the judge, whose name was Solomon Casseb. The judge told Maverick, "Mr. Maverick, please move to the left or right a few feet. If you get shot now I will get it right between the eyes." "This so unnerved me," Maverick said, "I had a paralysis of my vocal cords and had to go in a conference room and lie down to recover my voice."

I would remember Maury best of all at a hearing of the text-book committee of the state legislature before several hundred right-wingers in San Antonio in 1962. These were the groups that were trying to censor schoolbooks; they had learned that Maverick was going to testify, and they had circulated a leaflet condemning "two generations of Mavericks for serving the cause of Communism." In the crowded auditorium where the hear-ing took place, Maury stood up and invoked the memory of his father; the audience immediately hissed and jeered, and Maury turned a deep, petulant purple. He waited for the boos to sub-side, and then he addressed the legislative committee and the audience. Throughout his speech the crowd continued to jeer and laugh, but he kept going, his voice getting louder and more spirited over the organized turmoil. I quote a small part of that speech for what it tells about the ringing, old-fashioned human-ity and the courage which the Mavericks have always inspired:

I present testimony before you in behalf of the book *Our Widening World* by Dr. Ethel Ewing. What is the book really about? For one thing, it is not about any one nation or its heroes and wasn't intended to be. This book is about the family of man, something that we Americans should appreciate most of all with our melting-pot culture. We have a great nation not for the reason that we are all alike but because we are trying to live together in friendship despite our differences and diversity.

San Antonio is an appropriate place to talk about our widen-ing world. Here the Franciscans came and built their missions. Here to what was then called the New Philippines came the

Canary Islanders, and before them the Apaches and Comanches watered their horses at San Pedro Springs not far from here. To San Antonio the Anglo-Saxon began to migrate — pushing his way through East Texas not so long after George Washington left the office of president.

Here a young West Point graduate, Lt. A. W. Magee, joined together with Bernardo Gutierres in a joint Anglo-Mexican effort against the Spanish Crown. Gutierres was one of Father Hidalgo's men and on the streets and plazas of San Antonio men talked about liberty and died for it.

Go to the Irish flats while you are here and you will learn about a people who came to Bexar County suffering from economic poverty. Go down to what we call with some humor and much affection Sauerkraut Bend and you will learn something about people with names like Herff, Steves, Oppenheimer, and Altgelt, who fled a despotic Germany in search of liberty.

And while you are weighing the evidence presented by this hearing, go by the Alamo, Texas' greatest shrine, and understand that to a substantial degree it was defended by foreigners from our widening world. Where did the defenders come from? 15 men from England — 10 from Ireland — 4 from Scotland — 2 from Wales — 1 from Denmark, his name was Zanco — 2 from Prussia — 8 were native born Texans with names like Guerrero and Fuentes — 32 were from Tennessee — and the rest from the other American states, although even some of these also emigrated from Europe . . .

Don't you agree that we cannot adopt the censorship tactics of a fascist Spain or a communist Russia? Don't you agree that he who would intelligently cope with any totalitarianism must first love democracy most of all?

Gentlemen, let me conclude with a Texas saying which my old professor, Pancho Dobie, taught me. It describes a man who won't run out on you or on an ideal. It goes like this: "He'll do to ride the river with." I know you committee members will do to ride the river with. Ride it for liberty, ride it for academic freedom, ride it for good school teachers to keep them from being bullied around, ride the river for the glory of Texas and these United States of America!

When Maverick had finished, there was a crescendo of boos and catcalls, punctuated by scattered applause here and there. Maury strode off the stage, and already he was glowering again at the floor.

•

Maury Maverick, Jr., was of the younger generation, but I got to know the best of the older Texans as well — old men who made one proud to be discovering the state's most human traditions. Pancho Dobie was one, and Walter P. Webb, and Block Smith, the man who had led the "Y" at the University of Texas, pronounced "God" as a rich and anthropomorphic "Gawd," and taught three generations of Texas students that Christianity was no idle nor self-satisfied creed. Another was Judge Oscar Dancy, who had been a county judge longer than any man in the history of the state.

When Sam Rayburn died in 1962, James Reston described his political generation, in words that would also describe Judge Dancy: "The Old Frontiersmen were from the land, usually, born in poverty, matured slowly like good mountain whiskey, educated in the little colleges and night schools or not at all, and full of common sense and the rhythms of the Bible." Dancy was an old-time politician in the best sense. The people knew the Judge, and the Judge knew the people.

I walked in on him one autumn afternoon in 1961 with my friend Tom Sutherland, one of those many Texans I knew who would take off whenever they felt like it and drive all over the state, just dropping in on friends. The Judge's office was in the county courthouse in Brownsville, not far from the Mexican border. The shelves were crowded with old lawbooks, and on the wall was a picture of Franklin Roosevelt.

Dancy is a gentle, fine figure of a man, with a warmth and a humor that made the day we spent with him one of my most memorable in Texas. Almost every morning since 1922 he had stopped for a cup of coffee and a biscuit at the Texas Café, and got to his office by 5:30 A.M. His door was always open and he was accessible to anybody, from 5:30 A.M. to dusk. The county judgeship is one of the last remnants of freewheeling personal politics in Texas. Its duties are amorphous; the man makes the job. In four decades Dancy had used the position to help and encourage the *latinos*, to oversee the construction of one of the finest road systems in the state, and to stress the conservation of the land in a region which reached prosperity only after a long and sometimes losing battle with the rugged brush.

We talked in a rambling South Texas way, the three of us, about the Valley and politics and religion and a sense of belonging in America. One subject would get the Judge started on another, and sometimes he would interrupt himself with a new thought altogether; as the shadows lengthened in that musty old office he spoke almost in whispers to us, until at the end it was a remarkably human eighty-two-year-old man reminiscing, and us listening. He had been born in Wilkes County, North Carolina, in a staunch religious environment named, as Carolina irony would have it, after the vivid helion and ardent democrat, John Wilkes of London. "I first saw the light of day in a Primitive Baptist home," he said, "and I was never outside the Blue Ridge Mountains 'til I ran away from home to become a high private number three in the Spanish War. If you've never heard of a high private number three, I can tell you it was the lowest in the ranks. My military record wasn't brilliant, but at least it was clean."

When he was seventeen he started teaching in the little schools of the Blue Ridge backcountry at $20 a month. "I got very little education but *McGuffey's Reader* and the *Blue Back Speller*. McGuffey's has some of the best of the old-time wisdom you ever read — some of the old-time masterpieces. I don't think they've improved 'em. They should never've discarded 'em." He got a law degree at Southern Normal University in Huntington, Tennessee, in 1900, and came to Texas — he remembered the date — on January 9, 1909. The first time he voted for a President was in 1904; he voted for Alton B. Parker over Teddy Roosevelt.

"I raised three boys and two girls. All the boys are in the grave. Within a period of a little over three years I lost my wife and my three boys." He gazed out the window for a brief moment, and then he began talking about his political philosophy.

"I'm a Democrat" (he pronounced it *Demicrat*) "because it's the party of the *people* — it's for a fair deal for the common, everyday man. That Homeowners' Loan Corporation, for instance — the Republicans say it cost the country one billion dollars. You know, they took loans the banks wouldn't take, they took loans business wouldn't take, and they *made* $21 million. Franklin Del-i-no Roosevelt was the greatest American leader of this century because he did more for the common man and for humanity."

Talking in his soft Southern drawl, he would interrupt his chain of thought with a chuckle and a mischievous movement of the brows, as he did when he brought up the Primitive Baptists. "The Primitive Baptists believe in the final perseverance of the saints. They believe that what *is* to be, *will* be — even if it never happens. They wash each other's feet, they pay their debts, and they vote the Dem-i-cratic ticket — and if you can't get into heaven on that ticket, there just ain't no heaven at all.

"They wash each other's feet, like Christ and the disciples at the Last Supper. If you've never seen it performed, you might make fun of it, but I can tell you it's a ceremony of great reverence. Remember, 'they came to scoff, but they remained to pray'? They tell me Sam Rayburn was baptized three years ago in the Primitive Baptist Church. His father and mother were Primitive Baptists, just like mine.

"You know, I think Sam Rayburn is just about the greatest man in the world. Ralph Yarborough and I shook hands on that the other day. He's a man of unquestioned integrity — and *any* public man ought to be that. But I think that little Kennedy fellow is gonna be a wonder."

He had supported his friend Lyndon Johnson's nomination for President the year before. "When Kennedy got it I sent Lyndon a telegram: 'Stoop to Conquer by Accepting Second Place.' "

"I guess maybe I got into a rut as county judge and don't want out," he said, whimsically. "But it's an opportunity for constructive work. There's no greater opportunity in the country — workin' with people, hearin' their problems. You know, this poor devil of a Mexican really needs help, and nobody in the world appreciates fairness and common everyday courtesy more than a Latin. He hasn't had too much of it in the past. But, my, haven't they gone forward. You go to these high school graduations these days. There's more Latins in the graduatin' classes than Anglos.

"When I first came to the Valley, it was a jungle almost. It's the greatest country under the flag, as beautiful as those North Carolina mountains are. And as much as I love goin' back to my rel-i-tives, my brothers and nephews in the mountains, I just can't be there forty-eight hours without missin' it so much. I think the Valley's got possibilities that you can hardly imagine. We've just scratched the beginnin'. Why, Texas has the broadest boundary of any state with Latin America, and we're the county that penetrates Latin America like no other county."

"Judge," our friend Sutherland said, "I want to ask a very silly question. If you had the chance to talk with any five people who ever lived, an afternoon like this each, I wonder who you'd choose?" The Judge thought a few seconds. "That's not a foolish question at all," he finally said.

"First would be the Humble Master. Then I think my second choice would be the Apostle Paul, then Robert E. Lee, then George Washington — and you may laugh at this, but I'd almost say George Washington Carver, that Negro over there."

He paused for a moment to consider the consequences of this last choice: "Now there was a great man. There wasn't a selfish bone in his body. They offered him $100,000 to be a chemist and he turned it down. And what great things he did for the South. And he found more things in the peanut than what was in the peanut before he started.

"You take that fellow Paul, now wasn't he a spellbinder? They turned the beasts on him, the snakes bit him all over, he got tossed into the Mediterranean Sea, and he just kept right on goin'. And Robert E. Lee — do you know he turned down a job as president of a big insurance company to go back to a small college for $125 a month?"

Characteristically he started talking about books. "I think we should push adult education to the extent there's not a single person in Texas or Latin America who doesn't know the three R's — readin', writin', 'rithmetic. One of the greatest ways to fight communism is to educate the masses.

"That John Birch Society, ain't that one hell of a society? Communism is the greatest menace that's ever been in the world, and I think societies like that help make communists. You know, it's the way these people've been *treated* that makes communism. Look at the way the czars treated those poor people in Russia. Not so much the last czar as the ones before. I think they killed the wrong czar."

The Judge would lace his talk with quotes from Burns and Goldsmith and Sam Johnson. He said he liked Shakespeare best of all. "He touches — it's just full of human nature, human nature in the raw, full of *truth*, that's what it is. Why, how could one man know what he did, and he died in his 'fifties."

Later, Tom drove the car on the way to the Judge's house, and
the Judge pointed to the old houses and the landmarks of the
city, and some of the new ones as well. He lived in a simple frame
house on the outskirts of Brownsville. Dusk was falling, and
there was the sound of children across the street and down the
block, shouting at each other in two languages.

"I think it's good a young man like this is interested in politics," the Judge said to Tom, gesturing in my direction. "Politics
is the same as it always was, son, just more complicated. But it
still has to do with people, with *people*, that's the important
thing. And some folks lose sight of that."

We stood briefly there on his front porch, looking out into the
fading afternoon. "We moved into this ol' house in 19 and 14,"
he said. "My wife and I raised five children here. I miss the
sound of their voices. Now I'm alone and I tell you, brother,
I'm pretty sad."

He opened the screen door and started to wave goodbye.
"Judge," Tom Sutherland said, a lover of the Valley and its people, "you're in excellent company even when you're by yourself."

•

Finally, in addition to the legislative liberals, the conservatives,
the John Birchers, the Republican organizers, and the old-timers
like Judge Dancy, there were a number of individuals whom I
eventually began to call the "Kamikazes." They were aggressive,
belligerent liberals, and they were knowledgeable about politics.
They were also inflexible, dogmatic, contemptuous of those in
disagreement, full of spleen and a contorted, intemperate hate.
Frequently they would accuse people like Bob Eckhardt, Maury
Maverick, Jr., or even Ronnie Dugger of "selling out," which
was their favorite and most categorical invective. They never
forgot the smallest slight, they distrusted power, and they did

not believe in the political process; sometimes I suspected they held their greatest scorn for the people on the same side.

One of them in particular, I will call him Henderson, was in his early thirties; he had lived through the savage Texas political fighting of the 1950s. He was widely read in politics and was unyielding in political debate. He could talk about nothing else but politics. The world of the enemy was inhabited with ghouls and demons, and was dominated by the most sinister villain of all — Lyndon. Friends were constantly backsliding into the camp of the enemy. The man could not even drink a glass of beer with you; he was too mad.

I had known him when we were students at the University of Texas. Once a friend of mine asked him, "Have you read *The Sun Also Rises*?" and he replied, "Hell no, but I saw *Sunrise at Campobello*." One night when I was editor of *The Daily Texan*, he and I were standing around in the composing room talking to the shop foreman. A cub reporter rushed in and said, "The chief of the campus police has just died of a heart attack!" Without a second's pause Henderson said, "Was he a Democrat?"

For a brief period Henderson held a patronage job in Washington; one of the Texas politicians in Congress got him a position as a policeman at the Capitol, where he wore a uniform and carried a gun. One afternoon he was patrolling the corridors on the Senate side when a door to a committee room opened and out came a large group of Senators. "Just think," he said about the incident, "I had four bullets. I could've used one on Lyndon, one on Dirksen, and still had two left over for Hickenlooper and Long before they got me."

Late in my tenure on the *Observer* I wrote a long editorial on a political race, taking a stand I knew was going to anger many of the liberals. I asked the composing room foreman to make only one galley proof and to give it to me. It was mid-afternoon, six or seven hours before we finally went to press; I saw Henderson, sneaking in through the back door of the press room snooping around among the old copy; he had sniffed something in the air. Two hours later a strange thing happened. I began getting long-distance telephone calls from liberals all over Texas, quoting my editorial and calling me a fool and, occasionally, a "sell-out." Henderson had located the galley of type, secretly made a galley proof for himself, and telephoned all over the state to warn of the treachery that was afoot. He even wrote a column, accusing me of "selling out to Lyndon and the big monopoly interests," which a sympathetic kamikaze editor in East Texas ran under his own byline.

10

"THE COUNTRY is most barbarously large and final," William Brammer wrote in *The Gay Place*. "It is too much country, boondocks country, alternately drab and dazzling, spectral and remote. It is so wrongfully muddled and various that it is difficult to conceive of it as all of a piece." With this large, fractured facade, the only thing that could be said with any consistency about Texas in the 1960s is that it was *American*, American in an almost driven way, sometimes a parody or a burlesque of America, but sharing in its extravagant standards and its hungry values. Unlike more settled places, Texas was still moving — toward what I was never quite sure. But the drab commercialism of Dallas, the hectic industrialism of Houston, the makeshift suburbias of a dozen cities, were not provincial phenomena, they were American realities. Its small towns may have seemed lonelier, dustier, more pathetic, but the only quality distinguishing most of the cities of Texas from others elsewhere was their curious *looseness*, as if they were straining for remote distances.

The most distinctive quality of the place, I came to believe, was an extenuated sense of its own existence, a desperate sense of identity. Texas intellectuals, I saw, *knew* Texas, and felt the pull of it. Compared with other regions of America which had something of this feeling of self-identity — the Deep South, some stretches of California, New England in its older yearnings — its myth was kept somehow alive by the vast and desolate terrain which remained, and by the peculiar way its differentness came to its young. In Mississippi, as one grew up, the myth was heavy, almost stacked against you; in Texas the young felt they were sharing in something expansive and volatile. The career of Lyndon Johnson would be symbolic, for it had bridged the older, simplistic Texas and the new, that turbulent period which saw the evolution from agrarian provincialism to a contemporary place out at the edge of modern America. Johnson, Murray Kempton would write in a perceptive commentary, "had to engage and survive a time when the regional speech was dying and when, more and more, Texas was coming to be different from the rest of America only as a wide color screen is different from an ordinary black and white one." It was this exaggerated quality, and the old provincialism straining far away from itself, that made it unique for me.

Texas, I came to feel, would never engage my whole emotional being the way Mississippi had, for to live childhood and adolescence in a brooding, isolated place shapes one forever in its image, but Texas would never cease to have a hold on my imagination; it had given me a deep and liberating confirmation of values. Mississippi would lurk forever in the heart; Texas was where I reached maturity.

There it was politics, the ambivalent and exposed world of the politician, that taught me about the complexity of human affairs, about the irrelevance of most dogmatic formulas, about loyalty and courage and devotion to human causes—and about "the fragility of the membranes of civilization, stretched so thin over a nation so disparate in its composition, so tense in its interior relationships, so cunningly enmeshed in under- ground fears and antagonisms." * It was impossible there, as anywhere in America, to make a rigid distinction between personality and ideology, for ideology merged subtly into the personality, but in Texas the personality of the public man, the complicated nature of personal positions, were more intense, more meaningful, than any abstract ideological formulations. One's faith and trust came to reside in the integrity and respon- sibility of a group of people, people with shared assumptions about reform and liberality, rather than in the superiority of certain coherent groupings of ideas about society. Hence the emphasis in these Texas memoirs on storytelling — storytell- ing as it embraced the deeper political qualities. The best fighters for justice and humanity in Texas were the best human beings, dealing compassionately with the enemy even in the heat of the fight. The problems with which we tried to deal were so diverse, the divisions between the haves and have-nots so broad, the undercurrents of violent alienation so explosive, that a co- herent ideology, even when we sought after one ourselves, would have been incapable to indicate, much less to comprehend or encompass, the complexity of the failings of the place we shared. We were activists in Texas in Kennedy's 1960s; we were not in the East in the 1930s. A cohesive pattern, a clear set of reform-

* Arthur Schlesinger Jr., A Thousand Days, p. 725.

ist goals, were simply irrelevant to our situation; this was not so much our own failing as an expression of the reality of our context and our age. The bitter clash of interests, the impetuosity of disagreements, the old tormenting hatreds at the surface of things, were the sources of my experience as an editor in Texas. I gradually perceived that they, likewise, were only intensified there, that they also existed throughout the America of that time; not so much our common nationality, I concluded, as our common humanity would be our greatest hope against our own destructiveness.

•

I had run out of gas, as Dugger before me. He was ready to come back, and I was ready to leave, and I yielded once more to that catastrophic wanderlust of my generation of Americans. Roger Shattuck, who wrote *The Banquet Years*, organized a banquet on the eve of my departure, patterned, as he suggested, after the famous banquet for Henri Rousseau in Paris in the 1890s. We rented a graceful old house in the hills near Austin; thirty of my friends were there. We may not have borne any direct resemblance to the avant-garde of the Left Bank at the turn of the century, although we *were* in some ways the dissidents — politicians, professors, writers, a perambulating bum or two. This was scant preventative to enjoying the alien Gallic luxury. Like the banquets in Shattuck's book, we stood and made toasts: to Texas, to events from the past, to each other. Maury Maverick, Jr., presented me with a silver medal, the last of fifty which his father had coined to memorialize the cooperative colony he had founded in the 1930s; on it were the symbols of the workers, of the globe turned on its axis to the Americas, of the Alamo inset in the great Lone Star of Texas. And finally, at the end of that evening, there were the Texas stories, extravagant, reflective, ironic, boisterous — but always *relevant*, and exuberantly alive.

PART THREE

New York

1

ALL THE IMPORTANT junctures in my life seem to have involved buses. This time it was a double-decker Greyhound to the East. In an important Greyhound station in a big American city you saw the desperate transience of our life — the young soldiers with pimply faces and clerk's ratings moving from one assignment to another, the families going on the economy ticket — listless and stoic and heading toward God knows what — the lonely adventurers in tight blue jeans and grubby sideburns sipping from pint bottles of cheap whiskey in the men's rooms, the country girls with their cardboard suitcases off to some $50-a-week job in whatever passed as the nearest city. The Greyhound express bus whipping across the great middle-belts of America toward the cities of the East, speeding at night through the dark inconsequential towns that all seemed the same, was a least common denominator of the affluent society. Under the surfaces of our deceptive middle-class wealth one had a glimpse of Harrington's other America — poor, shabby, rootless, on the move.

We had lived for a brief spell in California, to "see another part of America," in a suburban nightmare called Palo Alto, taking graduate courses at Stanford until the money ran out. The campus itself, set down in that sprawling suburbia, always reminded me of a high-class prison with its grim architecture — "Late Southern Pacific" — its broad gray quandrangles, its bedraggled tower named after the school's most illustrious alumnus, Herbert Hoover, the Leland Stanford, Jr., Chapel with its redundant inscription carved in the stone: *"Hope, Faith, Love, and Charity."* Nearby ran a road, from San Jose to San Francisco, less a road to me than a reminder of what we had reached in this country in the 1960s; its name was El Camino Real, mile after mile of chrome and asphalt horror, slicing through the debris of this American age: the used-car lots, the hot-dog stands, the drive-in movies, the jumbled-up shopping centers, the motels owned by movie stars and lesser entrepreneurs — streamlined abominations that looked as if they would be lucky to last twenty years. Ten miles to the west the land ran out; at the shores of the Pacific the game was up. Among the few compensations for these surroundings, and for the pinched, in-grown life of the graduate students, were the lectures of the critic and teacher, Irving Howe. In those classes filled with fraternity boys, automobile heiresses, and a handful of tense and deadly earnest PhD candidates, he spoke brilliantly of the nineteenth century, which deserved no place in Palo Alto, of Mark Twain and Howells and James, of those sleepy unencumbered mornings on Huck and Jim's raft on the Mississippi, of Manhattan replacing Boston as the cultural center three-quarters of a century ago. At lunch at some outdoor roadside hamburger stand, squeezed in between a motel and a used-car lot, we talked with Howe about New York, where he belonged; one sensed it by the way he glanced out at El Camino Real, a tentative glance, suggesting some private obliteration.

I had left my family behind in all this; armed with several job references, $75 in traveler's checks, the battered old suitcase I had bought when I first left Mississippi for Texas, and a dozen paperback novels, I left San Francisco on the Greyhound transcontinental express for Manhattan — for Thomas Wolfe's Fabulous Rock, for, as I would soon call it, "The Big Cave."

The journey took five days, via Reno, Salt Lake, Cheyenne, Omaha, Des Moines, and Chicago. This was seeing America in an unlikely purple haze, through bone weariness and fitful dreams, a fatigue so deep and tenacious that even the great landmarks of the West came and went in a restless unreality. An Indian family — a father and mother and six small children — crowded themselves together on the back seat; they had one knapsack, a paper bag filled with flip-top cans of beer, and a box of crackers. The children galloped up and down the aisle at three in the morning in that stagecoach country, playing out a Greyhound ambush; the father drank beer and ate crackers and snored. In the seat behind me a soldier just returned from Korea strummed on a guitar and talked with his companion, a skinny old Air Force corporal, about going home to the used-car business in Laramie. At 5 A.M. on a superhighway in Wyoming, two days out of San Francisco, I tried to read Bernard Malamud, and when Malamud did not work, to indulge in glamorous fantasies about the literary life of New York; everything, sense impressions, thoughts, anticipations, were gray and disembodied. I tried to read the first half of *Roughing It*, to associate Mark Twain with my reverse journey over that same terrain a century later, but the spit-spat of the Greyhound's tires and the "rest stops" in the greasy little cafés made Mark Twain's wild perceptions remote and irrelevant. One dawn I stood in front of a café in the West, in Wahoo, Nebraska (surely the first man from Yazoo to come to Wahoo), and watched the sun come up on the plains; I with my obsessive sense of place was not even sure what state I was in, and I did not care. In a bar across from the teeming Greyhound station in Omaha, I tried from loneliness to telephone an old friend from University of Texas days, a gargantuan first-baseman who barely missed the major leagues and who now ran a laundry in Scottsbluff, Nebraska, but no one answered. Outside, on a street corner, I stood in a crowd that smelled blood, and watched two young Negroes circle around one another with knives, gesturing and making fake angular motions like boxers in the ring, exchanging curses and mad laughs, sweating faintly in the sunshine. I looked at my watch and had to race again for the bus. From across the broad street I glanced back one final time; they were still in their melancholy dance.

The Chicago terminal was the dividing point, the crossroads of all the double-decker expresses, a mass of tired ashen-faced humanity in the dim morning. One bus from the South, just arrived, unloaded a stream of black passengers, some in bright sports clothes, others — whole families — wearing ragged shoes and clothing, keeping together for protection and simple animal warmth. Where, I wondered, would they go next? What promise would await them here? I remembered the texture of Ralph Ellison's words: "In relation to their Southern background, the cultural history of Negroes in the North reads like the legend of some tragic people out of mythology, a people which aspired to escape from its own unhappy homeland to the apparent peace of a distant mountain; but which, in migrating, made some fatal error of judgment and fell into a great chasm of maze-like passages that promise ever to lead to the mountain but end ever against a wall." Not that he is worse off in the North, but that he has left "a relatively static social order" and having experienced and been formed by its brutality "he has developed those techniques of survival to which Faulkner refers as 'endurance' and an ease of movement within explosive situations which makes Hemingway's definition of courage, 'grace under pressure,' appear mere swagger." But now they neither swaggered nor moved with grace — they emerged into the huge warehouse of a waiting room with a tired, open-eyed caution, as if waiting for something but not expecting anything.

Beyond Chicago the double-decker hit the Ohio Turnpike,

heading north-northeast, four days out, one more sunset and eighteen hours to go. That magnificent turnpike, laid out across the flat land, took you where you wanted to go, but one paid its price: the unrelenting sameness, the "rest stops" at Howard Johnson's, each the precise replica of the one before, as if they had hauled the one you had just left by rapid transit and put it down a hundred miles ahead, for one's comfort and *déja vu*. Each had postcards of itself inside, displayed near the twenty-eight different flavors; I began sending postcards to my family from each one: "roughing it" in Howard Johnson's Brady's Leap, or Glacier Hills, and the last one went out from Mahoning Valley.

When you come toward it in a super-Greyhound from the west, the skyline of Manhattan greets you, not suddenly, but slowly and teasingly, by perceptible degrees; at first it is but a solitary speck way out on the eastern sky. Now you are in the industrial wastes of New Jersey, a gaseous and grotesquely functional piece of earth where even the sunsets seem venereal. From this grim landscape the great skyline comes closer and closer, until from just across the Hudson there it all is, as it has always been in the mind's eye, shimmering a little in a smog's glow, so immense and spectacular as to stir one's passionate dreams. On this soft spring evening in 1963, after five days on a bus out of San Francisco, the vista of the great city from midway between Elizabeth and Newark, with the beginnings of a half moon out over the Atlantic, was a sensual achievement.

2

OUR LITERATURE is filled with young people like myself who came from the provinces to the Big Cave, seeking involvement in what one always thought from the outside was a world of incomparable wonder, hoping for some vague kind of literary "fulfillment." In the 1960s, as always since New York became our literary and journalistic marketplace, there would be thousands of them clustered around the great axis of publishing, newspapering, and broadcasting, starting out at minuscule salaries, living in unfamiliar, claustrophobic walk-ups, fighting the dread and alien subways twice a day, coming to terms with the incredible noise and crowdedness. Most of them would not "make it"; the more resourceful and talented might.

Why did we come? Not because the materials for our work did not exist in those places we knew best. Not merely for fame and money and success, for these also some of us could have had, and perhaps in more civilized ways, in places far removed from New York. Not even because we wanted to try ourselves in the big time, and out of curiosity to see how good the competition was. We had always come, the most ambitious of us, because we *had* to, because the ineluctable pull of the cultural capital when the wanderlust was high was too compelling to resist.

Yet there were always secret dangers for these young people from the provinces in the city. It became dangerously easy to turn one's back on his own past, on the isolated places that nurtured and shaped him into maturity, for the sake of some convenient or fashionable "sophistication." There were temptations to be not merely careless, but dishonest, with the most distinctive things about one's self. The literary and publishing worlds of the city were perilous vantage points from which to understand the rest of America. There was a marked sense of superiority, amounting to a kind of distrust, toward other American places. This had always been true, and it was likely to become more so, as the older regionalism died in America and as the cities of the East became more and more the center of an engaged and argumentative intellection. Coming to New York for the first time, the sensitive outlander might soon find himself in a subtle interior struggle with himself, over the most fundamental sense and meaning of his own origins. It was this struggle, if fully comprehended, which finally could give New York its own peculiar and wonderful value as a place, for it tested who you are, in the deepest and most contorted way.

I spent that night with an old friend from Mississippi, in a cramped apartment high above Washington Square. He was teaching now at the New York University Law School. The last time I had seen him had been the previous summer, at the Ole Miss law school, to which he had returned from Oxford, England, to finish three courses; outside class that summer, he had spent his whole time getting drunk in front of an electric fan, either that or indulging himself in wild, uncontrollable outbursts against the young middle-class racists who were his fellow students. He was a "liberated Mississippian" who had just joined New York's burgeoning and implacable Southern expatriot community; he was the first of many Mississippi "exiles" I would see in the Big Cave — for, in truth, as I would come to understand, Mississippi may have been the only state in the Union (or certainly one of a half dozen in the South) which had produced a genuine set of exiles, almost in the European sense:

alienated from home yet forever drawn back to it, seeking some form of personal liberty elsewhere yet obsessed with the texture and the complexity of the place from which they had departed as few Americans from other states could ever be. We sat talking until midnight about people we had known, about old forgotten high school football games in the delta, about Ross Barnett and James Meredith, Paul Johnson and Hodding Carter, about unusual weekend celebrations at country clubs in the hills. Then, groggy from the transcontinental Greyhound, I went off to bed.

The next morning I arose early to set out to find a job. On the recommendation of a mutual acquaintance I had made an appointment with a well-known editor — he was described to me as "tough-minded," a glowing description for anyone in those days — in a distinguished publishing firm. I strolled through Washington Square, walking past those sepulchral warehouses of NYU, the magnificent old townhouses on the north side which had yet to give in to the wrecker's hammer, the red brick apartment towers to the west. Then I sat on a bench to while away an hour, watching the old men playing chess on the concrete tables, and the bums and the beats who congregated in agitated little circles making activity out of nothing. Two young men with sandals and long hair appeared from nowhere and accosted me on my bench. "Could I have fifteen cents for a cup of coffee?" one of them asked. I forked over fifteen cents. Then the other said, "Could I have fifty cents for a *Partisan Review*?" When I declined, he shrugged his shoulders, whispered *square*, and he and his running-mate ambled off.

I sat there counting out my private responsibilities. Besides having to get a job to support a family, I needed to find an apartment, one with enough room for a three-year-old boy to roam around in, next to a big park perhaps, and preferably overlooking some body of water: a place with a study, and dark-oak paneling, and within walking distance of my office. I started feeling again, as I had not since my sophomore year in Austin, as Thomas Wolfe had felt, coming north to this Rock. *Only the dead know Brooklyn*, he said, and he got a book published, and he went to literary cocktail parties in Park Avenue penthouses; he stood on their terraces and heard the tinkling of the ice in the glasses of those critics and editors and authors, and watched the lights of Manhattan come on. At that point he always felt he would never die.

All of a sudden, in the middle of these harmless recollections, I saw a slightly familiar figure from the corner of my eye, from the arch at the north side of Washington Square. Be damned if it wasn't Mr. DeMent Warren, who ran the men's clothing store at the corner of Jefferson and Main in Yazoo City during my boyhood. I stood up to go and greet him, but I saw it wasn't Mr. DeMent at all — only a big balding man in a topcoat uncommonly heavy for that time of year. A few minutes later the same thing happened. Over near the fountain I saw, of all people, Earlene Whitt, a fine well-constructed beauty queen from the University of Texas in 1955. But it wasn't Earlene: only a big blond Village girl taking her beagle on a morning's walk. Within the next fifteen minutes I spotted four people I had once known: "Jap," the old yellow-skinned Negro man who had cut our yard for us when I was in grammar school; A. J. "Buddy" Reeves, an American Legionnaire from Yazoo County, who used to go out with us when we played taps for the military funerals; Bibb Falk, the baseball coach at Texas; and Wallace Miller, a rotund conservative in the Texas legislature — all apparitions! They were my first experience, all of them, of what would become my own peculiar New York eyesight. With my mind on the past, only haphazardly thinking of long-ago things, just basking lazily in old events as is my wont (even something as ephemeral as a touch football game in Lintonia Park twenty years ago, or the funeral of a friend's father in 1948) people all around me — on the sidewalks of Broadway or in a subway — would take on known shapes, tangible recognitions. All they had to do, when these moods were upon me, was to bear some vague resemblance to someone who once had had a meaning for me, in a period of my past I was thinking about, and my dastardly subconscious would toss up for me a real person! I believe the crowds did it, and the awful and unfamiliar isolation of the city when thousands of human beings are around you and none knows you nor cares. I later grew accustomed to this phenomenon that the city worked on me, and even to enjoy it, but on that day it struck me as passing strange; it made me fear the extent to which my rambling imaginings of past places that had intimately shaped me could, in this unknown and uncaring city, produce forms so tangible as to make the present itself incongruous and ghostlike. I had returned, among the smog pelts and pollution indices, to my childhood's land of seething mirages.

.

Every time I had gone into a new and unknown place, those times I knew I might be around for a while, I had made it a point to take in as many first impressions as possible. At the University of Texas, on my first day there eleven years before, I had gone immediately to the top of the Tower, to look out on that catastrophic fault which divided the South from the West; this was part of my responsibility, the way a new ambassador presents his credentials to a head of state. On this first day in New York I would take a leisurely ride up Fifth Avenue, the boundary between the east side and the west, and present my credentials to an august American publishing house.

I had been in the bus no more than two or three blocks when an unexpected thing happened. There was not much traffic this far down on the Avenue, and the driver swerved the bus

toward the curb. I looked out the window and saw he was block-
ing a taxicab. The bus driver opened the front door and shouted
down at the cabbie.

"Hah, ya bum, ya sorry good-for-nuthin' bum. Where ya think
ya goin', ya no good punk!"

The driver of the cab opened *his* door and yelled back, "Who
ya think ya are, red-nose bastard? Can't ya drive the thing,
hah?"

"Stan' still and I'll drive it over that yella cab, ya sorry punk!"

I was ready for a good Fifth Avenue fight. The cab driver,
by now out of his car and leaning on the side of the bus, yelled:
"See da game last night, a good game, a close one, punk!"

"Nah," the bus driver said, "nevah go on weeknights, I hafta
work, more than *you* do, *skinny*."

As this strange dialogue unfolded, a few more sentences exchanged, it became apparent to me that these men were *friends*,
that they had seen each other just by chance and stopped to
offer affectionate early-morning greetings. Even the crude violence was extended in affection, ending in the mutual gestures
of farewell — not waves, but motions of the hands downward, in
mock disgust, the way people show contempt over an object,
or a thought. Then we were off again northward.

Below 34th Street, Fifth Avenue looked like most any American city, cavernous, dingy, the sidewalks and curbs slightly
dirtier perhaps, with little dust-devils of grit swirling on the concrete, except for two things: the height of even the average buildings, and the exotic gold letterings on the upstairs windows.
These latter in themselves were worth the ride: "A. Silverstein,
Furriers"; "Loonberg and Sons, Oriental Tapestry"; "Miron
Brothers, Imported Quilts," a range of merchandise in those
somber buildings that would have embarrassed a large-sized
state fair. But north of 34th, at the big Altman's store, the city
opened up. The shops and stores were stunning in their riches,

displaying the glittering wares of 1963; the giant American flags
gave the Avenue a holiday air, and the crowds on the sidewalk
were brisk and lively, each person self-contained and oblivious
to his fellows. This, I surmised, was the New York the popular
songs told about — *Manhattan, Autumn in New York* — all
those mindless little ditties that country people were groomed
on. When we passed Scribner's, its dignified black front setting
it off from the neighboring places, I thought of Hemingway,
and Fitzgerald, Ring Lardner and Tom Wolfe, and Maxwell
Perkins himself, bless his memory. And I wondered how many
latterday Perkinses there were scattered around in the big plush
houses that put their imprints on books.

Up in the high forties I got out, and walked over to Madison
to my appointment. I had no trouble finding the address; the
building itself was splendid, the way a publishing house *should*
look. It was a big nineteenth-century structure, its stone dark
and weathered in contrast to the new buildings in the surrounding blocks. It was solid, musty, assuring, the way Victorian novels in old bindings are. It had character. It was also
the most famous publishing firm in New York, not so much because it published many of American's best novelists as that its
director, a man noted for his jokes and puns, appeared regularly on the television networks, where he was expert at guess-
ing people's occupations and identities. Once he had come to
the University of Texas, during my editorship of the student
paper, and the people who met him at the airport told me his
first words on getting off the plane were: "I want to meet that
kid who's giving the administration hell." I had met him and
liked him; he said, "If you're in New York, give me a call." It
was not he I was calling upon, however, but a younger man,
identified to me as the best and most intelligent editor in New
York, an editor who published *the important things*, and who
in that very year had helped start, by raising the necessary

funds, an ambitious book review that would revolutionize and give ideological coherence to the reviewing business, which had fallen on flaccid and, as some would tell me, corrupt days. It was this project, having captured my admiration in its early numbers with its courage and outspokenness, that interested me the most. Why not start with the most ambitious?

Inside a broad corridor with high ceilings I gave my name to the receptionist and sat down. The minutes passed. I stood up and paced the hall, and looked into a large set of rooms not far from my chair. A big sign on the wall inside said, "Fuck Communism!" This was more my style. Perhaps I should ask *that* editor for a position. From down the corridor a man pushed a sizable wagon, which contained what looked at first glance to be about three thousand books. Up on the wall, on display for solicitors like myself, were the book jackets of three or four Faulkner novels. They were like old friends, familiar and comforting. I supposed Faulkner himself had been in this building, though I suspect he did not have to wait so long for an appointment, at least not after his speech in Stockholm.

The receptionist motioned to me. "Would you go up now, please?" I walked up a marble stairway and was directed by another secretary into the editor's office.

As he leaned over from his telephone I could sense he was a brisk and hard-working man. Books and manuscripts were piled everywhere, seemingly without any coherent design, on the big desk, the windowsill, the bookcases, even the floor. The conversation with the party on the telephone was esoteric, about orders and schedules.

When he had finished he leaned over and gave me a limp handshake. "What can I do for you, Mr ——," he looked down at his desk calendar, "Morris?"

I identified myself as the friend of mutual acquaintances and explained I was job-hunting.

"What makes you think you want to work in New York?"

"I've got some experience, editing and writing, and I guess everybody wants to come to New York for a while."

"It's a horrible place," he said.

The telephone rang. The editor picked up the receiver. It was obviously his wife. He talked again in a faraway, esoteric tongue; the only words I was able to recognize were "Dwight Macdonald." After a pause he said, "I've had an awful day. The phone ringing every two minutes. People coming in. Let's go to a flick tonight. What's worth seeing?"

As he mentioned these words I was suddenly overcome, for the second time that morning, with the most urgent drama. Though he seemed less likable than a boondocks Texas reactionary after a successful vote, here was an important figure in the New York literary world, his office stacked with important manuscripts waiting to be sent to the presses and out to every state in the Union and to Canada, the demands on his time ferocious, talking with his wife about *going to a flick*. I had an image of the woman, tall, slender, exotic, perhaps a figure of some significance in this world herself; perhaps they would skip a literary party to go to this flick. Perhaps they would invite me. I was no bumbling innocent, but I would be less than honest if I denied I was excited by this wondrous world within my reach.

In a few seconds he put down the phone, looking down at his watch. "What kind of job are you after?" he asked.

I mentioned the new book review and how much I liked it. I said I could write tolerably, was excellent on headlines and make-up, and had been around the country.

"Not a chance, I'm afraid," he said. "We barely have enough money for the next number."

"Well . . ."

"What other jobs do you have in mind in New York?"

I mentioned two institutions, one a magazine, the other a

large daily newspaper. Both had indicated they were interested in me.

"Those are two of the most boring publications I know of," he said.

I mentioned two executives from other publishing firms that I might see.

"They're not very intelligent people," he said.

"Well, you know, a job's a job."

"I guess so," he said, looking again at his watch.

At this point I was beginning to get mad. A slow Mississippi boil was rising north from my guts, a physical presence that had always warned me to go easy, to beware of my heritage of violence, bloodshed, and spur-of-the-moment mayhem. Confederate colonels on horseback flashed in my mind, and Jeb Stuart and his men, and the siege of Vicksburg; I would not have wished to begin my new life in the city by throwing this little man out of a second-story window into a courtyard.

At this point, however, the editor had to terminate the conversation. We shook hands again, and he expressed a faint *good luck*. I walked down the marble stairs to the entrance, and out again onto the street. The whole session had lasted five minutes. I would see the editor several times in the course of the following year, professionally and otherwise. I would still think of him as one of the important editors in the whole of the Cave. But I resolved to myself that day, a little naïvely and sententiously perhaps, that if I were ever in a similar position, and someone came in fresh off the Greyhound, I would not make him feel the pluperfect hick.

That afternoon I had an appointment at the *New York Times*, with Harrison Salisbury, the Russian expert who had become chief of national correspondents. I got to the big warehouse of a building on West 43rd Street a little early, and decided to look up my friend Homer Bigart. I announced myself at the reception desk and, for the second time that day, sat down to wait.

I had met Homer Bigart, the greatest reporter of our time, in Texas the year before. The man who had won two Pulitzer Prizes for his reporting during World War II and Korea, who had written in his sparse clipped style about more than his share of this earth's skirmishes, wars, and revolutions, had come to Austin after a stint in South Vietnam to do a series of pieces for the *Times* on Texas politics. Saigon, he told me, had been peaceful by comparison. He had a big open face and a contagious kind of cynicism — not crabbed at all as is the case with many reporters who have been around a long time, but a kind of organizing principle for viewing large amounts of bullshit. We had sat at a table behind the old German beer hall in Austin, talking to the blue-jeaned state legislators. When I bitched about the ungodly work involved in editing the *Texas Observer*, Homer said, "Well, you'll probably look back on this as the happiest period of your life." At the Texas-Oregon football game later, when Oregon's great Negro halfback Mel Renfroe was having a field day, Homer had gotten a laugh out of two Texas fans sitting next to him. As Texas was kicking off one of them shouted, "Don't kick it to that nigger!" and the other added, "Hell no, kick it to that white boy!"

Homer emerged from around a bend in the hall and escorted me to the main *Times* room. The sight that greeted me was an unexpected one: a little like the Chicago Greyhound station, though more chaotic. The room was roughly the size of a large gymnasium floor, and the reporters were packed into little individual spaces at desks just large enough to turn full circle in. "You can see space is at a premium in New York," Homer said. A loudspeaker kept booming on and off, paging the reporters for urgent errands. What would happen in that room, I wondered, in case of fire.

Homer took me over to meet Salisbury in a kind of fenced-in area on the main floor, where the brass sat in somewhat less tempestuous surroundings. We sat and had a quiet talk about politics. He was a nice fellow, a far call from my previous interview, but he was obviously looking me over. The phone rang; it was Senator Mike Monroney, who had a complaint about some story, and Salisbury proceeded to soothe his anger. Then, turning again to me, he said, "We're probably going to be opening a bureau in the Southwest. Would you be interested in running it?" Where would the bureau be? I asked. Well, it couldn't be in Austin, Salisbury said, because the plane connections from there weren't good enough. Houston maybe, but Dallas best of all because of the airport; one had to be in a position to get away fast, on a moment's notice. *Dallas!* the city I had always hated with a blind, incoherent passion. Besides, I said, I was here in New York and thought I ought to stay awhile. Then we went farther over into the fenced-in area to meet Clifton Daniel, who in turn wanted me to meet my fellow Mississippian Turner Catledge, but Catledge that very day was away on urgent business. I exchanged pleasant handshakes with Salisbury and Daniel, told them I would consider their offer, and departed again into the wild afternoon scenes of Times Square.

The next day at noon, after two or three other desultory interviews, I had a lunch engagement with John Fischer, the editor of *Harper's Magazine.* The red brick building which housed Harper & Row as well as the magazine sat unprepossessingly on East 33rd Street, just behind the Vanderbilt Hotel on Park Avenue; not as imperial as the publishing firm I had visited on the previous day, but graceful in its way, a little crowded it seemed, but not without a quiet dignity. Here was one of the oldest publishing houses in America, with the oldest magazine. Here William Dean Howells had eventually come, leaving the contained and righteous world of Boston; it was a symbolic gesture,

signifying that New York had become the cultural center of
America and New England had lapsed into the stagnant back-
waters, with the *Atlantic Monthly* to remind it of past glories.
This was Mark Twain's publisher, in his later years, and Tom
Wolfe had come here after his obsession with the rumors that
Maxwell Perkins at Scribner's was writing his novels for him. Senator John Kennedy had written an outline of an essay, on Senator
Ross of Kansas, and sent it here asking if he should stick the finished manuscript into the magazine or write something more
ambitious at book length. The editors suggested that the Senator
might do more profiles like this one.

I waited in the small reception room on the sixth floor, admiring the dark paneling and the old bookshelves filled with
"house" books: Sherwood's *Roosevelt and Hopkins*, Gunther's
Inside USA, and Cheever's *The Wapshot Chronicle* caught my
eye in passing. The comfortable old room had an aroma of age
to it, in just the right doses, an air of facility, a little too proper
perhaps. Before I could get settled in and sense the atmosphere
further, a side door opened and out came Fischer. "I'm sorry
I'm a little late," he said, in a curious neutral accent, hurrying
me into the elevator, introducing me to everyone who got on:
the elevator operator, a couple of editors, a man named Can-
field with a ratty overcoat, a secretary. Then he hailed a cab to
go to "The Century."

Fischer and I had corresponded frequently ever since my newspaper troubles at the University of Texas. He was a regular reader
of the *Texas Observer* and had particularly enjoyed our attempts
at humor, and more than anything else the miniature stone-
axes which had been our awards to Neanderthal and Runner-Up
Neanderthal of the Year in the state legislature. Subsequently
I had written three or four long pieces for his magazine. He
was a Texan himself, either that or an Oklahoman, for he had
allegedly been born on a farm which straddled the state line

and was not sure which side he was on at the time of his birth. To meet him personally, one would never have guessed he authored his prickly and abrasive Easy Chair columns, which had made almost everyone in America angry at one time or another. From these writings in America's oldest journalistic column, one might have expected a villainous cynic. Sitting next to me in the cab going up Park Avenue, however, he was the epitome of shy gentleness and humanity, though tense around the edges, as he pummeled me with questions about topics ranging from cattle-farming to the NASA program to Ronnie Dugger.

We got out at "The Century," which turned out to be an immense private club of some kind on West 43rd Street, dank and secret on the inside, very dour. The frayed edges in the carpet looked as if they had been carefully put there and protected, with a couple of servants, no doubt, in charge of keeping the frays properly clipped and seared. Fischer took me over and introduced me to three gentlemen who seemed to go with the furnishings: Richard Rovere, John Kenneth Galbraith, and Walter Lippmann. They talked quietly and amiably for a few moments. I told Lippmann I had met him at Creekmore Fath's in Austin a couple of years ago, had sat next to him on the sofa until the Vice-President unexpectedly sent a car for him. "Ah, yes," he said, trying, I could tell, to work me into what must have been his endless store of names and faces, and a slight smile wrinkled the edges of his mouth, and then he chuckled. I was sure he remembered.

Upstairs, after being introduced to General Gruenther, a couple of admirals, three publishers, and one lone writer, we took a small table in a corner. All this time Fischer continued to barrage me with questions. Then, abruptly, he asked:

"How would you like to come to work at *Harper's*?"

"To do what?"

"To be an editor. You've had some sturdy editorial experience, you've been around the country, your writing is adequate and sometimes better than adequate. We can't pay much,
but if you're fool enough to want to live in New York, it'll get
you by."

How much? I asked.

"$115 a week to start, and more if you work out."

$115 a week! I had been making more than that on the *Texas
Observer*, and New York was rumored to be the most expensive
city in Christendom. I said this, diplomatically, adding that I
had a wife, and a young son who ate enough to keep three dober-
man-pinchers in good health.

Fischer relented, went up to $125, and said he would give
me a thousand dollars to help get me settled in the city. "And if
you don't like it," he said, "try it a month or so, and you can
leave with no hard feelings."

"When do I start?" I asked.

"As soon as you want. Find an apartment first if you wish."
He paused, waving goodbye to a publisher. "There's only one
other problem, and that's space. I don't know where the hell
we're going to put you. Every inch of space is taken up in the
office. We'll just have to move you around until there's a permanent place." For some reason I thought he might be joking,
until I started to work several days later. I worked in a hallway,
in an alcove, and one week in a kind of large linen closet, carrying my manuscripts from place to place. But even the linen
closet turned out to have better acreage than the reporters had
at the *New York Times*.

•

The apartment I found was in the east twenties, between Madison and Park. The other places that I had seen and liked, airy
places with parks nearby, never rented for less than $250 or
$300 a month, for rents in the city were criminal. This one

rented at $125, and it occupied the third floor of a narrow gray building next to a parking lot. The exposed side was pocked with holes and ridges, and someone had written on it in white enamel: "The Dukes." Looking at this unusual structure from a block down the street, one was struck by its lean-to quality; it seemed to have no business existing at all. It rose from the west side of the parking lot, gaunt and improvised. Someone walking down the street with the address almost always walked right past it, thinking that the place might not be inhabited. One reason may have been that there was a red canopy over the sidewalk at the front door advertising the short-order take-home service which shared the entrance off to the left.

One walked up the three flights through several padlocked doors, often past the garbage which the landlords had neglected to remove for two or three days. Once inside our place, things were not bad at all. There was a big front room with an old floor, a little alcove for a study, and to the back a short corridor opening up into a tiny bedroom for my son and a larger bedroom in the back. The kitchen was in the back bedroom. I had not been able to find a view of an extensive body of water at popular prices, but from the back window, about forty yards out, there *was* a vista of a big tank, part of some manufacturing installation in the building under it, and the tank constantly bubbled with some unidentified greenish substance. From this window one could also see the tarred rooftops of the surrounding buildings, and off to the right a quiet stretch of God's earth, this being the parking lot next door.

From the front room the view of the street was more animated. Across the street there was a large bar which seemed to remain open twenty-four hours a day, and in front of this, on the corner, one could look down at any hour and see the little circles of people, just standing, watching the mad traffic on lower Madison. We were without sunlight, which was unable to penetrate down from the tall office building across the street; and when it rained, which was often that first year, I remembered the hard cold rainfalls in the Mississippi delta of my childhood, and how they encompassed the green earth and fields and trees in such a torrent that one seemed at the mercy of nature itself; here, from the front window, the rain merely kicked up little pools of dirt and debris on East 26th, and sent people under the canopy of the bar. One oppressive Saturday afternoon, our old Texas friends Ronnie Dugger and Larry Goodwyn sat here in our front room with us; our separate work had all brought us briefly together in New York City. We sat here talking of old times and places; then, out of a gray sky, there came a blizzard. We watched the big flakes come down for a while, a little depressed and intimidated. Suddenly Goodwyn opened the window, stuck his head out, and gazed down at the scene on East 26th. Then he put his head back in, turned around, and said, "Well, boys, they got us all up here together . . . and then they *snowed* on us." The subway was also difficult to get used to. There was a station twenty yards from the building; every five minutes the building rocked and groaned at its very foundations.

I was only seven blocks from my office at *Harper's*, and in the mornings I could walk up Madison to work. On a fine day, carrying my black briefcase with poems from housewives in the Midwest, or stream-of-consciousness prose from the graduate schools, I enjoyed making my way up the avenue through the bustling crowds on the sidewalks, feeling very much the cosmopolite. But on some grim foggy morning, when the steam came out of the sewers in the streets as if the earth beneath were on fire, the city had a dreadful claustrophobic quality, like death itself: closed-in, blind, and airless, compressed by the endless concrete and asphalt exteriors. The horns from the cabs, the cursing of the drivers, the harsh violence of the streetworkers

dodging the already clogged traffic, caused a new arrival to feel
that humanity here was always at war with its machines and
with itself. In the course of a year, walking seven blocks to work
and back over the same route, I saw three people killed by cars
and four others badly hurt. The most likely place for this
mayhem was the curious intersection of Park and 33rd. Here
there was a tunnel which came suddenly out of nowhere. Cars
whipped out of it at terrific speeds, catching pedestrians crossing against the red light on Park. There was no sign suggesting
the existence of this tunnel, which added somewhat to the spirit
of adventure. At first it would be disrupting to see the white
sheet covering an unfortunate pedestrian caught by surprise by
some taxicab coming out of the tunnel, the crowds milling
around with that sullen big-city curiosity looking at the blood,
the cop or two waiting perfunctorily for the ambulance to arrive. After a time I grew used to the spectacle, however, and
would walk gingerly past the broken body and its spectators as
if it were all in the morning's walk.

Many times, walking home from work, I would see some un-
knowing soul venture across that intersection against the light
and then freeze in horror when he saw the cars ripping out of
the tunnel toward him. For a brief instant the immobile human would stand there, transfixed by the vehicle bearing down
upon him, the contrast of desperate vulnerable flesh and hard
chrome never failing to send a horrible tremor through an on-
looker's being. Then, suddenly, the human reflex would take
over, and the pedestrian would jackknife first one way, then another, arms flaying the empty air, and often the car would literally *skim* the man, brushing by him so close it would touch his
coat or his tie. If another car coming behind did not nail
him then, much the way a linebacker moves in for the kill after
the tackle or end merely slows down a ball-carrier, the pedestrian would stand there briefly, all the blood drained from his

face, oblivious to the curses from the driver of the car which had just missed him. If there was a cop on the corner he would wait while the man staggered in his shock to the sidewalk beyond, there to accost him: "Ya crazy, hah? Ya stupid? Walkin' against the light! Hah! Ya almost got killed, ya know it? Ya *know* it?" I saw this ritual several times; on one occasion, feeling sorry for the person who had brushed against the speeding car, I hurried across the intersection after him to cheer him up a little. Catching up with him down by 32nd I said, "That was good legwork, sir. Excellent moves for a big man!" but the man looked at me with an empty expression in his eyes, and then moved away mechanically and trancelike, heading for the nearest bar.

On a number of occasions on my peregrinations from 33rd to 26th there would be some bum sprawled out on the sidewalk, and the people would walk right past him, or sometimes step over him, glancing back a little nervously, usually saying to their companions, "Somebody should call a cop." The first time I saw a man lying prone on the concrete, blood trickling slightly from his nose, I bent over and asked him if he was all right, and he moaned a little, and I went into a restaurant and phoned the police to report his distress. But after a while, like the others when confronted with such a sight, I would keep going too, though always a little guiltily, wishing a cop would come by soon. Why should people in such a city be *expected* to stop and do something about their fallen wounded, not knowing them nor caring? The existence involved in moving daily to and from work in the immense and faceless crowds inevitably hardens one's senses to violence and despair. I came to feel it perfectly natural, this isolated callousness of the city-dweller. Anyone who expected valor or compassion in everyday acts in a monstrous American city in these times expected too much of human nature, and would sooner or later be disap-

pointed. The cops became the guardians of benevolence; they
were our salaried Samaritans.

Along the sidewalks in our neighborhood roamed two old
walkers who made their mark on the area. One was a bent-over
old man who wore pince-nez; he carried an American flag, a
Bible, and a megaphone. At almost any hour of the day you
could hear him, standing on some street corner nearby, deliv-
ering a feverish sermon on sin, redemption, and patriotism, or
moving along the sidewalk with his dragging gait shouting
vengeance on every moving object in the vicinity, animal or vegetable. He was just as content trying to convert a Chevrolet
pick-up truck as he was in shouting his evangelical threats to
the little Italian boys who congregated at the fruit stand on Lexington. There was a horror to this old man, to the echo of his
grating voice coming down the narrow streets between the big
buildings. Thin trickles of saliva would form on his mouth and
drip to the pavement; his moist insane proselytizing seemed as
inexorable and illogical as the city itself, as its insane flow of
vehicles and people. One Christmas morning, as my son played
with his toys in the front room of our apartment, I heard him
from down the block, and through a drab December mist I saw
him shuffling along on 26th street, solitary and mad; suddenly
I felt sorry for him, alone on this Christmas day. I picked up a
couple of cans of fancy sardines and rushed down the stairs,
catching up with him on the sidewalk. "Merry Christmas," I
said, the first words I had ever spoken to him, and handed him
the sardines. A puffed-up smile creased his face. He took the
gift and said, "What is your religion, young man?" "I'm an
old Mississippi Methodist," I replied. "Ah . . . Methodist,"
he said. "Then you don't believe in Jesus. Pity on you, young
man." And he walked away, gingerly putting the sardines in his
coat pocket.

The other neighborhood apparition was a woman of about

sixty, a gaunt old specter who worked regularly as clockwork. She was a junkie, and every afternoon from three to five she roamed the streets shouting some demented gibberish, a considerable tumult for such a scrawny old woman. Once I saw the evangelist and the drug addict meet by chance in front of a shabby building on Lexington with a plaque explaining that Chester A. Arthur had been sworn in here as President of the USA after Garfield was assassinated, and they shouted at one another as if mortal enemies, and the old man walked away, whispering through his megaphone, "*Doomed. Doomed!*" The woman's shouts were even more disrupting than the man's, however, because they were self-inflicted, and because she worked on a schedule, coming out of God knows what place every day to exercise her private perspectives. Both were always alone and always ignored. Except when taunted by the neighborhood kids they seemed quite self-sufficient.

In our apartment my son walked and crawled around the front room, exploring the edges of his new existence. There was nowhere to take him to run. Running him down the sidewalks of Madison or Park or Lexington in early evening was like taking a nighttime trot in the Carlsbad Caverns. Once the traffic had thinned out at night, traffic lights for the taxis were as physically efficacious as a resolution of the UN General Assembly; I had never seen red lights ignored with such disdain. Madison Park, the closest piece of earth in the vicinity, was a good place to watch the drunks and the old men sleeping under shrubs, but no likely retreat for a three-year-old child. Finally I took to playing with him in the parking lot next door, throwing a tennis ball against our apartment house and letting him retrieve it, until the man who owned the lot came by one bright fall evening and said, "Cancha see that *sign*: it says *private property*. If ya can't read, mistuh, go back to trainin' school."

We missed the easy, open life of Texas, the impromptu beer

parties in our house on Bridle Path, the casual way people had of dropping by on friends, the old German beer hall and the tables under the trees in back. The only person we knew in the neighborhood was Nick, who sold newspapers at a little stand on Madison. I could leave my son with him for half an hour or so while I went off on an errand, and come back and find the child behind the counter, helping sell the *Journal-American* and the *World-Telegram*. Returning to the newsstand one night, I sidled up to the papers and saw my son selling a *Post* to a cabdriver, who gave him a nickel tip; the Harpers of Mississippi seemed far, far away.

We decided our third month there to give a cocktail party for some of the people I had dealt with on *Harper's Magazine*: a few editors, a writer or two, some reporters. The day of the party I noticed that the garbage had not been collected from the hall outside our door. There was three or four days' of it, tomato peels and eggshells trickled out on the floor, and coffee grinds poured out of a hole in a sack. I phoned the landlord.

"We're having an important social occasion in apartment three tonight," I said, "and there's garbage in the hall."

"What's that? What?"

"There's garbage in the hall outside apartment three. Please send the janitor to get it right away. We're entertaining tonight."

"The janitor's off. He'll be back tomorrow. Wait till tomorrow."

"We can't do that. Important people are coming. Some of the most important people who ever came to this apartment. And the stuff stinks. It's fetid."

"It's what?" the voice said.

"It's *fetid*."

"I tell ya we can't get it till tomorrow. The janitor's *off*."

"Look," I said, "we've got some unusual people coming."

"Fellah, I'll try to get one of the boys up there, but I can't promise, see? We're busy, *understand?* Okay?"

"Okay," I said. "Then just send somebody up before six." By six o'clock, however, no one had come. I went to the dime store on Lexington Avenue and got two big cardboard boxes, filled them up with the garbage, and when no one was looking put them under a Chrysler in the parking lot.

The narrow old building which housed our walk-up apartment was attached not only to the short-order take-out shop, but to a hardware store and to a huge cafeteria which stayed open until 4 A.M. every morning of the year. All these, including our building, were owned by a man and his two sons, whose offices were in the building. They were Jewish people, from the Lower East Side, but now they owned most of the entire block.

The cafeteria had large plate-glass windows, and displayed there under the cellophane were the specialties of the day: a shank of ham, perhaps, or some greasy fried chicken, or an apple pie. Inside the place was brilliantly lit, a sharp glaring light that gave to the tables and the floor and the great rows of food behind the counter a sterile, antiseptic look, much like the cafeterias one sees in hospitals. It was always crowded, even in the early hours of the morning, with cabbies, truckdrivers, newspaper vendors, drunks who wandered in for coffee — the night people. It was a harsh, driven place, lacking in even the smallest courtesies: a ragged, hard place, filled with muted violence and petty cruelties. Behind the counters the men in their starched white uniforms shouted to the line of people waiting to be served: "Move it, move it! Whatta ya *want?* Ya think we got all night? Come on, come on, make up your damned mind, *will ya?*" Every so often someone would be tossed out on the sidewalk, for not having enough money to pay or for being a little too drunk. Two of the men behind the counter would rush out to the floor and take some pathetic old reprobate by the elbows, dragging him through the front door and giving him a little push, shouting "Outta here, ya bum!" Once my wife and I were getting lunch at the counter; as she hesitated between the meat loaf and the lamb the man serving up the meats shouted, "Come on sister, get a move on. Whatta ya want, hah? *Hah?*" Standing across the counter from this angular, glint-eyed son of the city I shouted back at him: "Don't you know how to treat a *lady*, friend? This is a Southern belle from Texas. Or did you grow up without any *manners*. You got any *decency?* Hah?" I felt the Mississippi boil rising again; the people around us were staring hard, eager for an incident; customers never shouted back like that in this place. The man behind the counter looked at me; he was taken by surprise. Then he laughed, apparently a form of apology: "Mister, I ain't *seen* no lady. What makes ya think I know a *lady?*" And he dished out the meat loaf, shaking his head in mock bewilderment.

The owner, who was our landlord, was a big pot-bellied man with a great shock of gray hair; he spoke in a croaking bullfrog's voice. He wandered in and out of the cafeteria and the hardware store, dressed in his starched white intern's suit, even wearing white shoes and socks. His two sons, both in their thirties, wore the same uniforms, policing the place from time to time to supervise the treatment of the bums and derelicts. They shouted orders to the employees from across the big room, or stood off in a corner, their arms crossed, looking out expressionlessly at the customers gobbling down their food at the long aluminum tables.

Several times a month I came into the cafeteria, to bring a check for the monthly rent or to complain about the service in the building on 26th Street. The old man had a small office with a big padded door in the hardware store adjoining the cafeteria. There was a buzzer next to the door, and when I pushed it I would hear the voice from inside, "Who the hell is it?" I would identify myself, and he would push a buzzer inside automatically opening the door. "Here's the check for apartment three," I would say, handing it to him. He would take it, hardly looking up, saying "Yah, okay, okay," in a kind of grumble, never once exchanging pleasantries, no hellos or goodbyes, and then go back to his paperwork. My complaints, however, began to mount. His workers continued to go for three or four days without taking away the garbage in the hallways. The heating system in our apartment was controlled from the furnace in the cafeteria, and when the cold season began there was sometimes no heat at all. The other tenants in the building, a German girl who dated an editor of *The National Inquirer* and a Japanese artist who barely spoke English, were too frightened to complain; having lived there for some time, they were intimidated by the landlord and his sons. I took to phoning the landlord more persistently, or going to see him. Often it would take three or four calls before they would turn on the heat. The landlord and his two off-spring treated every complaint with a hurried, exasperated crudity. I had known Mississippi red-necks, mother-killers, grandmother-killers, sixth-year graduate students, and spitballers who threw at your head; I had never run up against people so lacking in the human graces.

One Sunday in the winter the thermometer in our apartment registered forty-two. I began calling down to the cafeteria at ten in the morning. Four calls proved fruitless. Finally I burst down to the cafeteria and asked for the landlord or his boys. They were all away. I found the assistant manager and button-holed him in a corner. "I want that furnace turned on!" I shouted. He shouted back: "We can't get to da furnace!" I returned to my apartment and phoned the landlord at his home on the Upper East Side. "I'm tired of your bitchin', ya *punk*," he said, and hung up. The next day I advertised in the *Times* for someone to take over the lease. We had a taker within three hours of the first day, and I went off and found a place on the Upper West Side.

The next-to-the-last day in our apartment, the telephone was still ringing from the ad in the *Times*: $125 a month rent got takers in New York City. I had turned down the offer of three bribes. I had rejected callers who pleaded for preferential treatment. Shortly before the telephone was disconnected, there was another call.

"I've seen your ad about the apartment," a man's voice said. "I understand it's only $125."

"That's right," I said.

"Has it been taken?"

"Well, yes and no. It has been, but I'm open to discussion."

There was a pause at the other end. "I see," the man finally said, for New Yorkers understood these things. "Can you tell me about the apartment?"

"It has four large rooms, a modern kitchen, air-conditioning, and a nice system for heat. Very comfortable in all seasons."

"What floor is it on?"

"Well, you see, it's in the subway."

"In the *subway!*"

"That's right. It's about ten yards or so from the track, right in the station."

I could hear the man mumbling to someone else, his wife perhaps. "It's in a *subway* station," he was whispering. "Yeah, right in it." Then he addressed me again. "That sounds pretty inconvenient to me. I never heard of an apartment right in the *subway*."

"It's not inconvenient at all. It's very convenient to the subway. And the noise isn't the least bit bad, except during rush hours."

"Is it built into the concrete, or what?"

"Well actually, the kitchen goes out over the tracks a few feet."

"Over the *tracks!* I never heard of such a thing."

"It's part of the agreement, you see. You don't expect a nice apartment for $125 for nothing, do you? During rush hours my wife or I have to open the kitchen door to let the express through."

"What?"

"Yes, but not on weekends. It's actually quite colorful, being a part of the transit system. It's only three minutes from Grand Central. It's not nearly so bad as it sounds."

The caller paused. "Well, it's certainly unusual. When can I come to look at it?"

"Let me call you," I said.

"Fine, I'll be here all tomorrow." He gave me his number. "How do I get there?"

"Take the Lexington avenue express," I said, "and get off when you see a red kitchen overhanging the tracks," and hung up. The next day I moved my family to the Upper West Side.

3

THE BIG CAVE in the 1960s lived frenetically in the present, bereft of the tangible reminders of its own history. The ubiquitous drills — "New York music" — relentlessly destroyed even many of the settled places. A crowded and noisy city almost totally lacking in landscape, full of fumes and smog, without open spaces and growing things, encouraged a certain desolation of the senses; after a time a man who was not born to this environment accepted the rattled edges of daily existence in the same way he might grow to live with pain, hunger, or unhappiness. One wondered most of all about the children, growing up with no local *belonging*, no feel for place or of generations gone. The massive office buildings where people worked, the jostling for position in the elevators taking them up to their work, the windows opening out onto other office buildings equally massive and impersonal — all this was part of a way of living unknown to me, uprooted from the earth and its sources. On some gray and rainy day in the winter solstice, when the sun began to set in late morning, with the wind rattling at the panes of the window, one's office seemed less a place to work than a cell, without the relief of something more *open* a few minutes away from it. Leaving work each late afternoon, having spent a day reading sober or responsible, or wild and imaginative, prose by writers who seemed to matter to America, one went down into the claustrophobic crowds, and jostled against people who had never heard of your writers, and cared less. Occasionally, on the night of a heavy snow, before the filth of a workday turned the snow into a sooty mush, the city was slow and quiet under the winter stars, out of character in its strange loveliness. The night all the lights went out in 1965, after the first panic, one could actually see the moon; the whole city was enveloped in an elemental blackness, and nine months later the births were more numerous than usual.

I would take the subway to work every morning — the Seventh Avenue IRT from the Upper West Side. I bought the *New York Times* in the newsstand on Broadway and 96th, and headed downstairs to get the express to Penn Station. As soon as I got to the platform in that stale, airless place I folded the *Times* to the news index section, then I started my preliminary jousts for position near the track in order to be closer to the door of the train when it arrived. In three years of waiting on this platform I had yet to hear one "good morning" exchanged among any of my fellow passengers, for human communication was normally restricted to atavistic grumbles and more direct early-morning obscenities. Far down the track, in an eerie dark, the light of the express glared and winked, and then in a terrible roar and screech of brakes it was upon us. The crowds at the platform waited for the people to emerge from the car; then there would be one solid mass of flesh pushing forward through the doors, somewhat like the scrum-heap in English rugby football, though larger, more motley, and less sporting. There was a loudspeaker in the station, and the voice would say: "Step lightly, folks, step lightly." And after a pause, "Get that arm out of the door, buddy!" or "Pull in that leg, sister!" Once this mass was crammed into the subway car, two or three hardy souls, holding back the doors when they were closing, would literally squeeze themselves in, which served to push the mass even closer upon itself.

At this moment, if I had three or four inches of elbow room and a reasonably secure position, I would bring out the paper and read the news-index section three or four times during the fifteen-minute trip south. If this elbow room was not available, however, I read the advertisements on the wall of the train, about quick cash loans, employment agencies, Miss Subway contests, and Preparation H for shrinking hemorrhoids without surgery. Then I would stare sullenly at the other passengers, who sullenly stared back, seeking diversion as much as I. Once I spent the full fifteen minutes examining a peculiar wart under the nose of a neighbor three or four inches away — a strange yellow wart that might have benefited considerably from Preparation H. At other times I would close my eyes and think about such items as green fields in the springtime, or the vast desolate terrain of West Texas, or Five Mile Lake during a summer thunderstorm. There was a certain identifiable expression on the faces of New Yorkers in these moments. It was "subway glaze"; their eyes might be open but they were not looking; they were *obliterating*, which required great practice and an extraordinary will. The train rocked and moaned, sometimes knocking a few passengers against one another in a sudden multi-racial jumble. The juxtaposition of human matter was so intimate, one feared that a sneeze, or an obnoxious cough, might set off an urban epidemic like the black plague. I wish John Donne could have taken the Seventh Avenue IRT during the morning rush hour, before sitting down to write about islands, clods, promontories, and bells.

I discovered most of all in these trips to work each morning that they brought out in one his old, latent, controlled hostility toward people of other races — an inevitable battle, if one speaks honestly, that requires the total application of a man's civilized acquisitions.

One morning on the IRT the passengers at 96th Street were crammed into the subway car even more closely than usual. I was unable to get a grip on the holding-pole or on one of the dangling handles; I stood there at the mercy of motion. Halfway between 96th and 72nd the train suddenly lurched, and I felt myself flying helplessly into the other passengers. Instinctively I grabbed for something, and it turned out to be the arm of a Negro next to me; he was about my age. When the train steadied again, reverting to my old Mississippi accent as I always do under stress, I told him I was sorry. He gave me a cold stare, and then he sneered.

"I'm sorry," I said. "I didn't have anything to hold on to. This is a hell of a way to live."

"It beats them hills, don't it?" the man said, in a strong Negro Southern accent.

"What hills?" I asked.

"Them hills you come from with that cracker accent."

"If I wasn't a liberal I'd hit you for that," I said.

At this point the other human matter standing face-to-face with us started looking away and grinning.

"Hell, ain't *nobody* liberal," the man said. "Who's liberal?"

"Well, I'm not from the hills, I'm from Mississippi."

"The *mud* then. Don't this beat the mud?"

"The mud's dried."

"Wait till spring," he said. "Then it'll be mud again."

We stared wordlessly at each other, two sons of the South on the IRT. Finally, at the next stop, ashamed and a little guilty, I clawed my way out, into the dusty glare of the subway platform.

•

Hospitality and the old Southern instinct to help a new arrival or a mere visitor feel at home might offset one's introduction to the city's mode of interior travel. When Michael Harrington had come to Texas during my *Observer* tenure gathering material for a book, he remarked that Texas liberals were the most hospitable breed he ever saw. "Every time I turned around," he said, "someone was offering me either a drink or lifelong friendship or both." Perhaps political outsiders anywhere, like the old frontier scouts, were lonely for mutual reaffirmation. Therefore, soon after I came to the Cave, both as a genuflection to my days on the Texas front lines and seeking new friendships in this unfamiliar place, I took to dabbling in political circles in Greenwich Village. This came chiefly through the good offices of a young man named Norman Dorsen, a brilliant lawyer who headed the civil liberties program at the New York University Law School, a man of wide-ranging intelligence and sympathy who, with his particular vivacious Jewish hospitality,

welcomed an unsettled Southerner in the city. Dorsen had
been a reader of the *Texas Observer*; he liked to swap exotic political stories. A few years before, when he worked for Thomas
Dewey's proper and affluent law firm on Wall Street, he was sent
with a senior member of the firm to Oklahoma to defend a client in an oil suit. After three drinks he began attacking the
client for the inequities of the oil depletion allowance; this
was like bringing combustible coal to Newcastle. One night
Dorsen and I sat in a bar on Sixth Avenue with Congressman
John Lindsay. Dorsen spoke to Lindsay for half an hour, about
why and how he should run for Mayor. He spoke brilliantly of
the prevailing political conditions, of the chaos of life in the
city, of the strategy necessary to a successful election. Lindsay
listened solemnly, and when Dorsen had finished stating his
case the Congressman said, "I agree with everything you've
said. But what would I do if I got elected?" Later that evening Dorsen invited me to attend a meeting of the Village Independent Democrats, a group I had admired from a distance for
their efforts in unseating the Tammany Tiger, Carmine De Sapio.
The meeting, Dorsen said, would give me a chance to compare
reform methods in New York and Texas; I could sit in as a visitor.

We walked down the narrow winding streets of the Village
and arrived at the address, a walk-up apartment in one of those
unexpectedly plush Village houses standing in the middle of
warehouses and fruit stands. On the third floor we could hear
the noises from the meeting; we rang the doorbell and were
ushered inside. We sat down on the floor to listen to the
speaker, a bald fellow named Koch. He stopped talking and
looked over our way. Then he and two or three advisors whispered to one another. Heads turned to look me over, sitting
blandly there on the floor. Dorsen was motioned to the front,
and I could hear him saying, "But he was editor of the *Texas*

Observer. He's just visiting with me." They talked some more. Finally Dorsen shouted to me, in an angry voice, "Let's get the hell out of here. They don't *trust* you." At the door he accosted one of the troops. "This is disgusting," he said. "Inhospital." "Come on, Dorsen," I said, "I don't mind." As I opened the door to leave I noticed that the Village Independent Democrats, in convention assembled, were still watching us suspiciously; I might just as well have been De Sapio's favorite nephew in purple-tinted horn-rimmed shades.

•

In the Village I did meet, with considerable more hospitality, a remarkable old Eastern Yankee, Roger Baldwin. He reminded me of Judge Oscar Dancy down in Brownsville, though he had gone to Harvard rather than Southern Normal, and had never considered joining up with the Primitive Baptists. He was the first of that breed of respectable Easterners I would meet who devoted themselves to reform and unpopular causes, and we got along so well, talking about politics and the South and civil liberties, that I kept going back to see him on the merest excuse.

One night when I visited him at his townhouse on West 11th, Baldwin had just put in a working day at three places: the American Civil Liberties Union, the UN, and the International League for the Rights of Man. He had aged like an old waterfall; at eighty he was the only man in America who had professionally covered the entire modern era of civil liberties. For three decades he *was* the ACLU, which he had founded in 1920. Though technically retired in 1950, he had remained active in its hierarchy, devoting most of his time to the International League, an organization accredited by the UN which aimed to spread civil liberties around the world.

Although one did not suspect it talking with him over coffee or a beer, he was a monument and an eminence, honored at

fancy dinners, awarded the Japanese Government's highest ci-
vilian decoration. All this was a long way from the days he defended Wobblies, anarchists, pacifists, and his old friend Norman Thomas, fought a repressive government, and spent nine
months of a year's sentence in federal jails for refusing to serve
in World War I. He had bridged a period in our history which
had seen civil liberties change from a cause for radicals and
wealthy eccentrics to one which the most respectable Wall
Street lawyer might embrace with equanimity and without
embarrassing either his social standing or the moderate wing
of the Grand Old Party. This, of course, was a long way from
the Texas I had known; contexts have a way of shifting in America. In its own unique way, his career had also paralleled that
of many of his generation who began by protecting the native
radicals as the idealistic crusaders many of them were, praised
the Russia of the 1920s as the colossus moving slowly in the
right direction, participated in the United Fronts, were disillusioned by the Nazi-Soviet pact, distrusted the post-war reds even
while defending their right to exist, joined anti-Communist
fronts, and then, in the 1960s, sought some *modus vivendi*
with the Russians, as John Kennedy had tried to do after the
Cuban missile crisis, as the first faltering hope for survival.
Through it all Baldwin had led, unlike a good many of his contemporaries, an intensely public existence, with few traces of
introspection, self-pity, or intellectual anguish.

He was a highly likable man, lean and a little rumpled. At
our unusual quarters on East 26th one night, at a small dinner
party, Baldwin found himself among a handful of young Southern intellectuals several decades his junior. He remained the
center of attention from the first with his talk about the UN,
the Fifth Amendment, Clarence Darrow, Maury Maverick,
Norman Thomas, and the La Follettes; he ended up by clearing the dishes off the table and helping my wife wash them.

"Don't these boys know how to *help?*" he asked. When he left, presumably for bed, it was at a fast saunter.

I once asked him what he was most proud of in his years in civil liberties. Characteristically he said, "Pride's not one of my attributes. Either pride or disappointment or failure doesn't enter my calculations. I don't do something just because I think I'll win. It's the reformer's instinct, I suppose. It has nothing to do with doing people good. I just try to put things to rights. I tackle the things that arouse me — injustice, cruelty, unfairness." On another occasion, remarking on how the polls usually show a majority of Americans hostile to civil liberties, he said, "Sometimes you come out of it feeling that civil liberties hasn't got much of a chance. Yet I believe these feelings aren't representative of behavior so much, but of what people think they ought to think. People are generally against anything dissenting or upsetting. The majority has rights, but they can take care of themselves. It's the new ideas, the new forces that come out of minorities, which make social progress."

He was a product of the old Progressive era, when young gentlemen of proper breeding turned to reform. Both his parents descended from Mayflower immigrants, and though the Boston tradition may have been in its twilight, there was enough of the residue of free-thinking and abolition to have given a young man at the turn of the century an awareness of something other than banks and finance. At Harvard, where he studied under Ralph Barton Perry and Charles Townsend Copeland, he considered himself a conservative, refusing at one time to attend the lectures of Jack London, and in 1906 he was still weighing a career in business. But when he was offered a job in social work in St. Louis, he took it. For some time he headed the probation work of the Juvenile Court and helped to organize the National Probation Association, the kind of work which did not especially recommend him later as a typical federal prisoner. In an atmosphere where the civic reform of the day was thriving, he moved on to head a citizens' organization for good government. His first two civil liberties cases involved defending Margaret Sanger's right to make public speeches on birth control and the demonstrations of unemployed workers during the depression of 1907 and 1908 against police prohibitions.

When the war came, he left St. Louis for New York and joined the American Union Against Militarism, which included people like Lillian Wald, Jane Addams, Norman Thomas, Max Eastman, and Oswald Garrison Villard. He was soon running the Civil Liberties Bureau of that organization. "Up to then," as he recalled for me, "there had been only scattered civil liberties movements: the abolitionists, the suffragettes, the Free Speech League. This was the first time the wholesale attack on civil liberties forced a non-partisan defense of the Bill of Rights of a country-wide character." In 1918 Baldwin was convicted and sentenced to a year in prison for refusing to be drafted. He told the court: "The compelling motive for refusing to comply with the draft act is my uncompromising opposition to the principle of conscription of life by the State for any purpose whatever, in time of war or peace. I not only refuse to obey the present conscription law, but I would in the future refuse to obey any similar statute which attempts to direct my choice of service and ideals. I regard the principle of conscription of life as a flat contradiction of all our cherished ideals of individual freedom, democratic liberty, and Christian teaching." A few of Baldwin's friends visited him one day in prison and found him planting tomatoes outside the walls. When the whistle blew he shook hands hurriedly and started back. "I almost got locked out the other day," he said.

It was his energy and courage which kept the ACLU going throughout the 1920s. He defended Upton Sinclair and striking longshoremen in California, he took obscenity cases, and he was responsible for the Scopes evolution trial. In 1922 he started the International Committee for Political Prisoners, an organization which tried gamely and usually unsuccessfully to convert the bureaucracies in Russia, Italy, and Germany to a more libertarian policy. During the thirties, while defending labor pickets, Jehovah's Witnesses, and the rights of fascists, he was an active member of several United Fronts; then came the Nazi-Soviet pact — the most shocking experience of his life. What followed, in 1940, after considerable debate on the ACLU board and national committee, was an ousting of all anti-anti-Communists from the governing boards and staff of the organization, which prompted some 200 protest resignations, and not all of them fellow travelers.

Over the years the ACLU had offended just about everybody. It had supported civil liberties for Communists, brown-shirts, racists, nudists, Senator Taft, Henry Ford, Gerald L. K. Smith, and Ross Barnett. It had defended *The Merchant of Venice*, *Uncle Tom's Cabin*, and *Ulysses*. It had angered friends by supporting more democracy within unions and by defending non-union workers; it had a few things to say about segregation in unions. "I always felt," Baldwin once told me, "that you had to defend people you disliked and feared as well as those you admired."

Knowing Roger Baldwin put one in touch with the issues of an older America, but it was interesting how the older questions would, in my generation, raise themselves again, in different forms. "There was a time," he told me, "when the Bill of Rights was applicable only to *local* citizenship. The cities and the states, the state legislatures, the local police prevailed. The federal government didn't intervene. The significant thing that has happened since the New Deal era is that the protection of civil liberties and rights has become a national concern." Yet one had to go out into the provinces, from which I had newly arrived, to see just how beleaguered the ideal remained. "In the East people can afford to be a little more courageous," Baldwin said to me. "But I know there are some very lonely people throughout this country."

•

After three months in the city we were invited to our first full-fledged literary cocktail party, at a large apartment on the Upper West Side. The host, a fellow editor in a publishing house, warned me everyone was going to be there. I looked forward to the event with apprehension and curiosity, for I had heard from good authority that big literary gatherings in New York depended not merely on the wet goods available but on some subtle electric quality in the atmosphere. If this electric quality were present, the normally mean people would be nice, and the normally nice people would be mean, giving the evening the right touch of exasperation. I had met literary people before, two or three famous writers on lecture tour at the front lines, an editor or two, but I had never seen the legendary New York literary world *en masse*. During the week I re-read *The Web and the Rock*, about the literary evenings Esther Jack planned for Tom Wolfe of Asheville, and descriptions of Sherwood Anderson of Clyde, Ohio, in New York, and how Sinclair Lewis of Sauk Centre behaved in his first days on the scene, and what Faulkner did on his visits from Lafayette County to the Cave. At such confrontations, I again noted, these four were — respectively — innocent, belligerent, drunk, and aloof.

On the morning of the party Malcolm McGregor, my old political friend from Texas, telephoned that he was unexpectedly in the city. I immediately got the host for the night's party to invite him. McGregor lived in El Paso and had gone to college at Texas Agriculture and Mechanical, where he had majored in animal husbandry. Somewhere during poultry sci-

ence, however, he discovered books. This event came late in his
career at Texas A&M, and he began reading history and literature with a passion that relegated the chickens and horses along
those banks of the Brazos to a subsidiary academic role; he gave
up the animals for the humanities. While a student in the University of Texas Law School, McGregor had been elected to the
state legislature by his hometown banks and big businessmen; the more books he read, however, the more he moved to
the left. When he lost his temper in the legislature he would
move like a big bear to the front microphone, yelling "point
of order" so suddenly and frequently that the parliamentarian
actually suffered a heart attack, and in the hospital under seda-
tion kept mumbling: "McGregor, point of order, McGregor,
point of order." McGregor was one of the three or four intellectuals in Texas politics; he was a student of El Paso and its environs in much the way Maury Maverick, Jr., was a student of San
Antonio. He had attained his knowledge of books and art, his
love of ideas, with much difficulty — after an earlier commitment to other, more accessible values. He did not take the intellectual life for granted; he looked upon its various forms
open-eyed and with a kind of naïve wonder, with a touch of sad-
ness and of the absurd. When he read a work of fiction, *Invisible Man*, say, or *The Bear*, he read it for its human qualities,
to illuminate the passions and the contradictions of his own
unpretentious existence. He would talk about some especially
marvelous passage with an innocent enthusiasm that would
have made the novelist prouder by far of this response than he
might have been of the brilliant analytical dissections of a dozen
critics. McGregor realized that creativity and intellection went
only so far in this country, and that beyond these were the old
rock-ribbed philistinism, the go-getting and the know-nothing-
ism, the embittered boondocks self-righteousness that in the
end could always ensnare by their sheer tenacity and pervasive-

ness the good, the beautiful, and the daring. Hence, he was a realist, a working politician who pursued his own idealism with an everyday wisdom and a very human knowledge of our limitations and his own. I was sure the literati of New York would find him not merely interesting, but a kind of soulmate in the trade.

It was a fine autumn evening, the air crisp and clean, the Cave at its best. We drove up Park Avenue in a taxi, looking out at the rich — all furred and tuxedoed — as they emerged from the hotels and the high-rent apartments to begin their Friday evenings, waiting under the broad canopys while the doormen in their purple drum majors' suits blew whistles to attract the cabs and limousines. The leaves from the small trees in the middle of the avenue blew across the pavement, modest swirls and eddies, but nice, nonetheless, for the cultural capital on such an evening. "Hot-*damned*," McGregor said. "This is class." This was his second trip to New York, and the normal lights and window displays on Park Avenue, he said, were better than Juárez on Pancho Villa's birthday. "You think I'm going to embarrass you?" he asked. "Just don't throw your shoe at anyone," I said, for we had once been to a party in Texas where a politician had thrown his shoe at a political scientist and then, for good measure, dragged the host's refrigerator into the back yard.

The taxi stopped in front of the apartment house, one of those austere blockbuster buildings with brassy lobbies and sleepy doormen in frayed jackets — a Riverside Drive house. On the tenth floor we were warmly greeted by our host and escorted inside. It was a huge room, about three-quarters filled with people. Two bars were doing a brisk nine o'clock business. We were introduced in short order to two distinguished literary critics, a well-known editor, and an avant-garde playwright. We stared at each other uncomfortably. Should I try to talk to one of the critics about his *work?* About the great seminal study of his that I had read in 1954, at three in the morning in Brackenridge Hall at the University of Texas, before I knew what *criticism* was? I tried to talk with them, and so did my wife and McGregor, but they did not seem to hold much immediate value in our worth. The four of them talked among themselves, in an agitated fleeting manner, and after a while turned into a semicircle and ignored us altogether. We retreated to a corner, a little sheepishly, not looking at one another, and gazed out on the party.

After a few seconds I had the distinct impression that everyone was looking at everyone else. A few ideological discussions were taking place, but beyond these I noticed that people were brazenly looking over other people's shoulders to see which groups were where and doing what. Across the room Norman Mailer, frizzly-haired and pugnacious, had launched into a filibuster against which no cloture could have been invoked; he was plainly the top attraction of the evening and was holding forth to an assembly of about a dozen people down from Columbia. An *enfant terrible* of New York letters, a beautiful young lady of about thirty who had suddenly become the subject of many conversations in the Cave, wore a brilliant Chinese dress and conversed with a lean and tired-looking novelist, the winner of the National Book Award three years before. Sitting on the floor in front of a sofa, surrounded by several young admirers, a noted man of letters was speaking in a rapid monotone about the criticism of T. S. Eliot. I moved over next to the couch to eavesdrop on the seminar, and to look at the man's great mane of hair; I noticed that the tie that he wore with his button-down shirt had not been tucked in, so that it came out over his collar rather than inside it; I would not tell him of this, however. The host, seeing our isolation, led us over to a famous art critic and a young editor of one of the literary quarterlies, a distinguished journal which had gone through more ideological contortions than Uncle Earl Long sipping whiskey from a Coca-Cola bottle while speaking to the joint session of the Louisiana legislature. We were introduced as new arrivals from Texas, but much as we tried there were no courtesies, merely frosty politeness. The art critic and the brilliant young editor, after a decent silence, went back to their conversation, recalling for me the time an American Rhodes Scholar on his first day in New College had walked up to an aristocratic English undergraduate and said, "I'm Dick Burtis from America," the Englishman saying, "Really?" There was a brief moment of common jubilation, when Jules Feiffer attempted to walk out onto the terrace, not realizing there was a glass door separating him from his destination. Then the gathering settled down again into its slightly drunken intensities.

I decided to go it alone. I wandered about the room listening in on the talk, occasionally recognizing some writer or professor or critic from photographs on book jackets or from the educational television channel. A bomb in the center of the room, I knew, would wipe out the cream of Eastern letters. Occasionally I spotted some editor I had met previously in the city, in the line of work; they would nod, rather vaguely I thought. Our indefatigable host again gathered my wife and me together, and took us by the arm to a well-known lady writer, one of the more caustic of the critics for one of the famous reviews just then getting started. I had "lunched" with her a couple of months before, and I noticed she was talking heatedly with an American historian, one of my true heroes. "Ah, yes," she said, looking away for a moment, "*Mississippi* . . . *Texas* . . . am I right?" I complimented her memory. "*Harper's*, isn't it? And how do you like it *there*?" with a curt edge on the word *there*. And when she and the historian started up again, once more my wife and I found ourselves moving toward a neutral

corner. I waved across the room at the editor who had interviewed me my first day in New York; he looked me over closely
and returned a faint gesture of the right hand, wiggling his little finger before turning away. "Let's go home," my wife said.

Suddenly, out of the cigarette mist, McGregor loomed, leaning against the wall by himself, drinking bourbon from a beer
glass. We went over to him. "How're you doing, McGregor?"
I asked.

"This is the first team," he said. "I feel like a stalk of green
corn wavin' in the breeze."

"What do you mean?"

"I try to talk politics, and I've told two or three stories, but
nothing happens. This man over here," he said, pointing to a
figure in the middle of a scrimmage, "said to me, 'El Paso. My
God!' We've been here forty-five minutes and I've pulled three
faux pas. I even told Norman Mailer how much I liked *From
Here to Eternity*."

"What did he say?"

"He said, 'so does James Jones.' "

"Let's go home," my wife said. We sneaked down the hall,
out the door, and into the elevator.

"Well, what did you *expect*?" I asked, when we were outside
on Riverside Drive, more to myself than to the others. Mc-
Gregor said, hell, he didn't know what to expect, and so expected nothing. My wife said she expected a little more common *civility*. We had come from different backgrounds, from
other and different places, but we did not exist except on their
own terms. Such was their milieu, they were willing to have no
surprises and to countenance none. She was getting angry. "It
was the first team, all right," McGregor repeated. Then we were
silent. The taxi sped down the long hill of upper Riverside
Drive in a smoggish evening's fog. From the Hudson there was
the echo of a boat's horn, from far away down the river. In our

apartment we talked about people and places we knew and cared for and tried to dismiss the evening, but we were all, I knew, a little hurt. Then we ended up direct-dialing seven different people in Texas, Louisiana, and North Carolina.

•

It was in a similar, but considerably less pointed, mood of homesickness for friends and places that I sat in my office on East 33rd one Friday morning in November. I went out to lunch alone. Then I returned to the office and sat for a few moments staring out the window, at the sight of three or four dozen office-workers in a big drafting room across the street as they fetched their personal mugs and lined up, grammar school style, for coffee. The telephone rang.

The caller identified himself. He was a philosophy professor who used the language extravagantly. I had been working with him on an article, largely as his translator.

"Have you heard the news?" he asked.

"What news?" I replied.

"Kennedy and Johnson have just been killed in Dallas."

"Oh God, no!"

"I don't want to be the person who broke the news to you," he said. "But I'm calling to see if this will have any effect on the article."

I barely heard him; my immediate thoughts were about Dallas itself, about the day Dugger and I had walked down its streets to the big Baptist church to interview the pastor. Most of all in this moment it was the downtown streets that I thought of — so lacking for me in the humanity and color that one saw on the streets of other Texas cities, so serious, grim, and prohibitive.

"Will this affect the article?" the professor repeated. "There were some references to Kennedy, you know."

I was overcome with revulsion for the man and his question. "I'll let you know," I said, and hung up.

Across the street in the other office building the workers were still lined up to get their coffee. There was a fire siren in the distance on Park Avenue; the sound of the drills below drifted up to my window. I stirred myself and walked around the office, still deserted at lunchtime.

Finally the secretaries returned. We got a radio and listened to the reports. "Those goddamned right-wingers," I said; I recalled the route Dugger and I had taken in Dallas three years before, following Kennedy and Johnson in the cattle truck with the photographers. Then Evan Thomas, from the publishing house, came in and said we were Kennedy's publishers and the office was closing immediately.

Out on the streets people laughed and shouted, but an occasional stroller came past with a transistor, spreading the somberness everywhere. On one of these I heard that Johnson had been sworn in as President. In such moments of despair one's memory can deal only with inconsequential things; there was the sight of six or seven little Puerto Rican boys gathered together on bicycles at the corner of Madison and 35th, talking loudly: One of them shouted, "*Kennedy está muerte!*" — and then they took off again, pedaling furiously up the avenue. That night a New York television station telephoned me to come and explain as a Texan my views of the new President. For fifteen minutes I tried to explain his contradictions, his immense failings and virtues, his various and shifting roles in the politics of the state I had known so well.

It was an ill and desolate weekend. One writer, with a somber fatalism, said the most likely places in America where this could have happened were Mississippi and Texas. There, he said, the violence and disaffection from what America had become were, of all the states, the most obvious and manifest. In my grief I shrugged this off as righteous sociological talk, but still his words kept recurring to me, as if in some large and inchoate dream: *Mississippi* and *Texas*. On Monday morning, the day of Kennedy's funeral, I went to my office to try to write for a while; later, as I stood in front of the old red building one of the book editors whom I did not know stopped to talk with me. After a few moments he asked, "Where do you come from?" Some unusual impulse seized me. I replied: "Northern California."

4

SOON AFTER the assassination, at the behest of my employers, who did not know any of the men close to the new President, I arranged to have lunch with Bill Moyers in the White House. Moyers and I had been classmates at the University of Texas, where I had remembered him as a quiet, hurried young man, thin and intense in his horn-rimmed glasses; he was working his way through school at Lady Bird Johnson's television station; he had stayed closely within the Johnson orbit in the 1950s. Our paths as young men with a flair for politics in the 1950s had already taken different turns. He was operating within the power structure in Texas and I was operating far outside it; he was learning its mechanisms while I on *The Daily Texan* was questioning its consequences. In the early 1960s I was the dissident editorial voice on a reforming provincial journal; he was helping set up the Peace Corps. He had handled the Johnson campaign for the Vice-Presidency, and he had been in Austin the day Kennedy was shot, trying to smooth out the perennial differences between LBJ and the liberals in advance of the President's trip there. When he heard the news he simply chartered a plane to Dallas, went over to Air Force One and sent in a note which said: "I'm here if you need me." In college I had always liked Moyers, and I had subsequently heard admiring things about his work as deputy director of the Peace Corps, but one would never have guessed then that here, at twenty-nine and only a few weeks into the new administration, he was already the closest advisor to a President of the United States. This remarkable young man, in early 1964, was at the very center of power in America.

I had always been obsessed by the workings of power in this country, not by its myths but by the way it actually worked at the source, not merely by its established institutions, but by the manner in which it manifested itself in human, personal terms. The give-and-take of advisors, the jockeying for position, the jealousies and ambitions and antagonisms at the center of things — these intrigued my writer's imagination and had once set me to reading everything I could get my hands on about the administrations of Lincoln, Wilson, and FDR, the ones who fascinated me the most. There was something about power in America, gargantuan, immense, yet at the same time plodding, accidental, and restricted, that must have distinguished it from every other nation on earth. As I sat waiting in the press room that day, on my first visit to the White House, I was unable to associate those surroundings with all the events that had taken place there; the midnight conferences, the fireside chats, the crisis meetings of cabinets, the notes and the telephone calls and the diplomatic messages that had gone out from there, the Presidents in their rages and solitudes and jubilations — all these seemed remote and mythic. And the longer I waited the more remote the whole business seemed.

Finally a secretary emerged from the inner-sanctum. Moyers, she said, had been in conference in the Oval Room with the President and the Prime Minister of Great Britain, and would meet me in the White House lunchroom. She ushered me inside, where we had coffee, and in a few moments Moyers came in to our table.

We sat there talking cordially about mutual friends from the past. We talked about the Administration, just then at its most effectual and respected in the gloomy, despairing days following Kennedy's assassination. Moyers joked about Lord Home, who a few moments before in the conference had said, "We want more miss*iles*." He asked my opinion on a number of the Administration's proposed policies, and I questioned him about the possibilities of his writing a book someday, an autobiography perhaps, a book about his experiences with the President.

"But what would I say?" he asked. "I don't really have much to say."

"Well, you've seen a lot, lived through a lot. You could write a great book several years from now."

"But I can't write very well. I'd have to get someone like you to help me."

"Sure I'd help, but I doubt if you'd need it."

"You know," he said, "I *was* in the hotel room in Los Angeles when he accepted the Vice-Presidential offer . . ." But what he really wanted to do, Moyers said, was to get away from here after a time, to go back to the Peace Corps, or maybe to teach government at the University of Texas. Well, I replied, I knew the people who were running things at the University these days and would write a letter about his desires, if he wished.

"Would you?" he said. "I'd appreciate that."

Another secretary came over to our table and told Moyers he

had a telephone call. She brought a phone, plugged it into the wall, and handed it to him. "Oh, hi," he said. "Listen, we sure did like the article. It was first-rate. In fact, the Man wants to see you tomorrow afternoon. Let me check the calendar and call you back."

All of a sudden, as he continued the telephone conversation, Moyers leaned over and gazed at something on the knee of his trousers leg, a dab of old scrambled egg, perhaps, or a drop of tomoto soup. "Hmmm," he said to himself, and started rubbing it off with his finger, talking all the while. It is curious how this trivial gesture impressed me, thinking as I did that it was somehow involved tangentially with conferences in the Oval Room, with being in hotel rooms where momentous decisions transpired for the very fate of the Republic. It was a gesture I had never made; I have always let eggs or other vegetable matter on trouser legs lie fallow.

Moyers hung up the phone, lit a cigar, and blew out the smoke. "How would you like to come to work for the President?" he asked.

"To do what?"

"We're putting together a staff," he said. They were looking for talent and writing ability, and also someone to help on speeches during the next Presidential campaign. "Would you be interested?"

It struck me on the spot that I would be most interested, to engage myself in a kind of experience I had never known before, to get down to the realities of power and try to understand it. And perhaps even do some good. We talked about the prospects. "I'll tell you what," Moyers said. "Let's set a date, and you and your wife come down from New York and have dinner with my wife and me, and we'll discuss this further."

"Come on," Moyers said, "I'll show you the office on the way out." We walked through the quiet corridors, where only two or three policemen were stationed; then Moyers opened a door and there we were. The first thing that impressed one about the Oval Room when no one was there was its strange, muffled silence; it was the very focus of power in the twentieth-century world, and yet on this day, on a gray January afternoon of 1964, it cast almost a dreamlike spell upon me in its deceptive quiet and isolation. I walked over to the Presidential desk and took a close look at the huge telephone with its rows of buttons, especially the amber-colored one that stood out over all the others; this, I naturally assumed, was the one that might begin to set in motion the "nuclear deterrent." "You know what these are?" Moyers said from across the room, pointing down at some marks in the floor. I went over to examine them. "Ike put those there with his golf shoes," he said. The white sofa was the same one I had seen in the photographs, when Kennedy sat in his rocking chair and his visitors sat there next to him. Next door in the cabinet room, Moyers pointed to the big chair where the President sat, the inscription in the bronze plaque on its back saying: "November 22, 1963." As we emerged again into the Oval Room, something unexpected happened to me: I got a weak feeling in the knees, a light, fragile feeling of weightlessness, much the way I had felt in the past before a big baseball game on an especially hot, humid day in Yazoo County; my confrontation with the appurtenances of concentrated power made me feel in need of a salt pill. Then again Moyers and I were walking down the hall, talking a little longer about the job he had mentioned. Two or three days later, back in New York, I had a dream: I was in the Oval Room alone. There were no doors to let me out; I kept looking for a door but there was none. Even the windows were shut tight. The telephone on the President's desk kept ringing, and I let it ring on and on; nothing would get me to answer it.

•

The next month my wife and I came to Washington. Moyers and his wife had arranged to pick us up at the Madison Hotel at nine o'clock in the evening; he had been with Johnson on a flying tour of some flooded areas of the Midwest that day and was again running late. As we sat in the lobby I saw the big black White House limousine roll up in front. The chauffeur opened the door and let us in the back, and then drove us to a plush restaurant near the White House.

It was a pleasant, relaxed evening. Again we talked of Texas, and of its fantastic political figures. We talked about Governor Connally. "You know the difference between Connally and Johnson?" Moyers said. "Connally wants to be lionized in the best country clubs in Fort Worth and Dallas. Johnson wants to be the best President in the history of the United States." We talked about professors we had known at the University, about what the Administration should or should not do on higher education, civil rights, Vietnam. At the next table a man drinking bloody marys leaned over to Moyers and said, "Didn't you use to work in the Senate Office Building?"

"Yes, I did," Moyers said.

"Where do you work now?" the man asked.

"Just up the street here," Moyers said.

It was near midnight when we got up to leave. "Let's walk over to the office," Moyers suggested. As the four of us walked down the broad boulevard he asked if I could arrange a leave of absence from my job. I said I thought I could.

"Have you mentioned to the President this business of my coming to the staff?" I asked.

"As a matter of fact, I brought it up just the other day," Moyers said.

"What did he say?"

"I asked him if he remembered you, and he said, 'Wasn't he one of those *Texas Observer* boys?' and I said yes."

"And what did he say then?"

"He said, 'Those *Texas Observer* boys haven't ever been good to me.'"

My wife Celia had had two martinis at the restaurant. I did not notice anything, however, until we were walking right past the completely darkened White House and she asked, "What's that building there?"

I thought she was joking. "That's a ball-bearings warehouse," I said.

"That's the west portico," Moyer's wife explained. We entered through the west gate, and when the guard asked my wife and me for identification, I showed him our Texas drivers' licenses. "These are good around here these days," he said. "The best identification you can have."

The west wing was deserted and almost completely dark, and as we walked down the hall Moyers flicked on a light here and there. A sleepy policeman sat in the hall next to the door. Then we were in the Oval Room.

Once again, for the same sudden and inexplicable reason, I got shaky in the knees. As the three others walked about, examining the books and the furniture, I sat down in the chair behind the President's desk and looked out onto the darkened lawn beyond. Then I pulled the big telephone over next to me and wondered what would happen if I pushed the amber-colored button. Maybe a voice would answer, "*Who pushed that button?*" "Willie Morris, from Yazoo City, Mississippi," I would say. And the voice might reply, "Are you serious, or was it a mistake? Do you really want to go through with it?" And then I would have to say: "Aw, I was just kidding."

On the other side of the round room my wife was looking at the portrait over the fireplace. "This is a Stuart of Washington," she said. "Is it an original?"

"I think it is," Moyers said.

As the four of us explored the west wing, wandering into the cabinet room again and the little rooms that bordered the big ones, an unlikely midnight stillness pervaded the place. Kennedy and Ike and FDR and Coolidge, Harding and Wilson and TR had walked these floors, but only Eisenhower had left a specific set of footsteps. We joked sacrilegiously about one landmark or another, like college kids out on some late night's lark, four young provincials enjoying these solemn surroundings before going off tomorrow to a lifetime of middle-class obscurity. Or was Moyers, our twenty-nine-year-old contemporary and classmate, trying to impress us?

We sat around in a smaller room for another hour, talking again about politics and inconsequential things. Then they took us in the black limousine to our hotel. I would not, however, get my glimpse into the workings of raw power. I never heard about that job, and it was the last time I would see Moyers, except on national television. As one of the *Texas Observer* boys, it was undoubtedly just as well. And once inside the Big Cave, as one grew accustomed to the dark, it was becoming more and more difficult to get out.

5

FOR IN THE city after a while, one got inured to the callousness, the senseless violence, the lack of simple courtesy everywhere, for these became a part of the very fabric of one's life. The provincial could even become inured, after a fashion, to the terrible claustrophobia — the claustrophobia of cramped apartments, the isolation of living on the same hall or in the same building for years without knowing the names of his neighbors and fellow apartment-dwellers. All I knew about the man who lived a few feet across the hall from my apartment was that he had a stereo, liked Bach, and subscribed to the *Saturday Review*. The positive aspect of this isolation was, of course, privacy, for in the city, indoors at least, one had the inalienable right to be left alone, free of the petty inquisitiveness, the totalitarian moralities, of the American small town. As I worked on a book, six or seven hours a day for several months, my desk was in an alcove in my kitchen. The view from the one window was the fire escape on the first floor, and beyond that a sort of concrete compound enclosed on three sides by brick walls. Even on a bright day the sunlight did not make it to my quarters; the sounds that drifted back to this place were the violent whir of the garbage trucks, the roar of the jet planes approaching Newark or Kennedy airports, the crash of colliding cars on West End or Riverside. I was in the middle of a great city, but I could not have been more isolated. On my first trip out of the city after months of living in it, I had my first awareness of that curious agrophobia which often seizes urban Easterners, so a few had told me, when they ventured into the hinterland. After a long time living in small places, traveling in murky subways, walking down cavernous and crowded streets, a sudden confrontation with open vistas makes one slightly fearful of what might be *going on* out in the distances; space itself becomes sharp, angular, the quiet too heavy, the light too glaring and unfiltered, the landscape too bare and unpeopled. Out in the country north of the city, where a traveler begins to encounter trees, hills, and open places, where the drab half-colors of asphalt and cement yield to the more intense lights and fuller colors of nature, I felt a small discomfort, and I recognized for the first time that a man's sense of space is acquired and takes practice.

On the Upper West Side in the city life was less crowded, less in a hurry; westward down the narrow numbered streets toward the Hudson there would be brief and unexpected glimpses of the Jersey palisades, and in the drab low-rent apartment houses and flophouses off the main drives and avenues there always seemed to be, at almost any hour of the day or night, the sound of the Puerto Ricans singing, and the heavy oily smells of their cooking. From Riverside Park, where there was a memorial to the Jews of the Warsaw Ghetto and where the apple trees blossomed in the spring, one could catch sight of some old barge moving up the river, slow as could be, or farther down an ocean liner coming in to dock, and perhaps a few seagulls on a maiden trip over the Henry Hudson Parkway. From here on some late autumn day the fading light reflected on the old brownstones and apartment houses of Riverside Drive, casting a grayish-orange glow; the river itself flowed with gold and purple, mocking its considerable pollution.

•

One also fell into the pattern of that most intransigent of New York's institutions, the "business lunch." Here all the aspects of one's trade were negotiated and refined. Sitting in some cramped restaurant in the East Thirties, you would mix the business and social amenities with a fine deliberation; it had taken me months to function in this institution. Worst of all were the days you were trapped with some hopeless bore or charlatan; the talk would run out, I would feel the sweat all over my face, and I would just gaze at the wall or the floor, embarrassed by the long and dreadful silences. Then I would start itching all over, and squirm around in my chair, and pray to some anthropomorphic Methodist deity that the next twenty minutes were over and done with.

One day my luncheon companion, a sociological writer from Washington, began the conversation by saying: "What I'd like to do in this article is explore the fluid contexts of the interrelations between the various power centers involved in some of the more pressing parallel concepts of public welfare."

"Could you be a little more specific?" I asked.

"Well, all these things are coming to fruition. There's a lot going on. But we haven't yet had the kind of public dialogue in depth which encourages all the interrelated interests, I mean *all* of them, toward some sort of genuine political fluidity."

"Fluidity of what?"

"Fluidity of *thought* — thought that mirrors the fluctuating bases of this generation. Up till now we've been positive without being futuristic, negative without being retrospective. Your publication would be doing a great service to provide real insights, both tangential and core insights, into the nature of these politico-social, if I may call them so, oscillations."

"*What* oscillations?" I asked. By now I was getting perturbed, and the clam chowder had not even arrived.

"Look," my companion said, "let me put it this way. A student of Confucius once pointed to a flag and said, 'See how that flag flaps in the breeze?' and Confucius replied, 'Only the mind flaps.' The structural changes under the social surfaces in this country are not the realities that are flapping. It's *we*, and we must move on that assumption, theoretical or otherwise."

"It's obvious *something's* flapping." I said.

The man stared at me in dismay, and we ate the clam chowder during an uneasy cease-fire. Then the talk started up again, in a great inevitable flow, over the corned beef hash. Finally the happy moment came, and I staggered back to my office, to the wonderful isolation of silence and the sports pages of the *Times*. On other days after lunches such as this, I might reach for my copy of Marianne Moore and read:

> Too stern an intellectual emphasis upon this quality
>   or that detracts from one's enjoyment.
> It must not wish to disarm anything; nor may the approved
>   triumph easily be honored
> that which is great because something else is small.
> It comes to this: of whatever sort it is,
> it must be "lit with piercing glances into the life
>   of things";
> it must acknowledge the spiritual forces which have made it.

Sometimes I would have lunch alone, and sit in the same restaurants overhearing the business conversations at adjoining tables. On these days, when the conversations were audible, I would feel the sorriest for the human race, for there were lines of work people pursued, and pursued with an enthusiastic gratification, that confounded even the most dog-eared sensibilities. I once overheard a forty-five-minute dialogue among three executives who manufactured toilet-paper dispensers. "It's going to be our best year yet in the Midwest," one of them said, full of undisguised jubilation for the dispensers. Over their third martini another of them prognosticated, "Gentlemen, you may think I'm mad, but mark these words: *by 1970 Chicago is going to be our biggest market.*" On other occasions in the restaurants of the East Thirties I listened to executives engaged in the making of calendars, hair curlers, and peanut butter, and public relations men representing thumbtack entrepreneurs, roach spray advertisers, and underarm deodorant manufacturers. From these I came away feeling that with the proper philosophical commitment, and if the structural oscillations and inter-relational fluidities were right, a man could sell anything in America.

Some days, after a business lunch in some dark and airless restaurant of the city, I would emerge coffee-logged into the smoggish glare and noise of Madison Avenue. On the walks back to my office I would be suddenly haunted by, of all the writers I had read, Faulkner, by his human beings, by the torrential flow of his prose, by the places he had written of that I had once known:

Soon now they would enter the Delta. The sensation was familiar to him. It had been renewed like this each last week in November for more than fifty years — the last hill, at the foot of which the rich unbroken alluvial flatness began as the sea began at the base of its cliffs, dissolving away beneath the unhurried November rain as the sea itself would dissolve away.

"Old man," she said, "have you lived so long and forgotten so much that you don't remember anything you ever knew or felt or even heard about love?"

For seven years now he had run his plow and harrow and planter within the very shadow of the levee on which he now stood, but this profound deep whisper which came from the further side of it he did not at once recognize. He stopped. . . .

"What's that?" the convict said. A Negro man squatting before the nearest fire answered him:

"Dat's him. Dat's de Ole Man."

It did not emerge, appear: it was just there, immobile, fixed in the green and windless noon's hot dappling, not as big as he had dreamed it but as big as he had expected, bigger, dimensionless against the dappled obscurity, looking at him. Then it moved.

It was the old Bear who took hold of my fantasies as I walked down Madison Avenue, obliterating the business lunches and the dispenser salesmen. The terrible reduction in humanity, the narrow scope of this life whose words meant such senseless grasping for the race — or worse, nothing for it — brought back the image of the Bear for me — "solitary, indomitable, and

alone; widowered, childless and absolved of mortality," inde-
structible in the woods and swamps, too large and mythic for
the mechanical terrors of Madison Avenue. I wanted to see
him walking up the dead center of the street, flaying his crooked
foot at an obnoxious truckdriver, ripping down street signs,
breaking restaurant windows, chasing the horrified junior executives and P.R. men straight up Madison and into Altman's, and
then watch with the same admiration of young Ike McCaslin as
the Bear "faded back into the wilderness without motion as he
had watched a fish, a huge old bass, sink back into the dark
depths of its pool and vanish without even any movements of
its fins." Such were one's daydreams after lunchtime in the
Cave.

•

Most of all there were the visitations from my own past, for
I found that the city in its frantic present thrust one backward
into himself as no other place where I had lived. My son one
day made fun of my Southern accent, and I knew some ir-
retrievable geographic turn had been made. The city obsessed
me with the unexpected memory of things I had long forgotten,
with old voices, with the indistinct faces of the dead, with the
lazy angling motion my father used in batting an outfield fly,
with the leafy smells of Jefferson Street in Jackson when I was
a child, with the grind and sizzle of the red water truck in Yazoo
a quarter of a century ago.

And always there were the Negroes, the white Southerner's
awareness of them — their voices and expressions and gestures.
I became attracted to the multi-racial scene on upper Broadway,
which recalled for me as no other street in America the Saturday
nights on Main Street in Yazoo. Everywhere there was the
sound of Southern Negro accents, the same words and inflec-
tions, the loose gestures and shouts of recognition — tangible

reminders of the great migrations northward of our time. Standing on Broadway in the Nineties on some warm Saturday night a Southern boy could shut his eyes and, like a fragment in some crazy Fellini film, he would be home again, outside of Tommy Norman's or Nelson's Red Front Department Store, eavesdropping as he had as a child on the wild delta talk.

Always the Negroes: and from the headlines the image of Meredith crawling across the highway south of Memphis, or the Negro child with the broken leg being beaten up by the mob in front of the school in Grenada, or the deputy sheriffs cheering on the mob in Neshoba. Nothing could blur these images, not Watts nor Harlem, not even the realization that in the 1960s the assignation of regional guilt was each day becoming a more subtle and complex question; they remained with me not in righteousness, but in simple horror; they obsessed me not merely on their own terms but out of the agonies I had seen in my own past. *I had seen them all before on the River*, Mark Twain had said; these images were a part of me; I could not say I was innocent of them.

There were many other things I had seen and known so often before; the virulent racism of the New York cabdrivers, who might give the red-necks in Mississippi a lesson in hate "I hate niggers," one of them told me. "I hate niggers so much I can't sleep good at night."

One rainy night my wild, uninhibited friend Larry L. King, the Texas novelist and political writer, and I were riding in a cab from Greenwich Village to the West Side. The cabdriver said: "It's good you're not niggers, or I wouldn't have stopped." My mind was elsewhere, but King listened solemnly as the driver launched into a broadside against "nigger brains, nigger noses, nigger character." He was engaging in a full-scale filibuster. "And I'll tell you something else," he said, "nigger men sleep with their daughters."

"You're full of bullshit," King said.

"What's that?" the driver asked, not expecting this from King's Southern accent.

"You don't know what you're talkin' about. You're full of shit."

This got me into the conversation. "What's your race and religion?" I asked.

"I'm Jewish," the driver said, "and I hate these black niggers."

King was getting mad. "Some people hate Jews the way you hate niggers," he shouted. "Why're you so full of hate, man?"

"Because they're taking over the goddamned city. They're taking over the *country*. That Martin Luther Coon is a demagogue."

"So are you, buddy," King said. By now he was shaking. When two converted Southern boys have right on their side and have a man cornered there are no limits to our rages; we are accustomed to being outnumbered.

"Coon is a Communist!" the driver yelled.

At this juncture I heard *myself* shouting. "We're Southern boys. We've lived with hate all our lives, and we're *goddamned* sick of it!"

Then King yelled, "And we're sick and goddamned tired of you Yankee cabdrivers knockin' our colored people! I've known colored people smarter than you and three times as good lookin'. When you knock colored people, you're knockin' us too. We all come from the same place."

"And we're *related*," I added.

King leaned over and shook his fist in the driver's face. By now the man was in noticeable distress. He trembled with rage, but the sight of my companion's bedraggled beard and beady eye, and my own visible anger, subdued him considerably. When he let us out at our destination King stuck his head through the window, handed the man a penny tip, and whispered: *"racist!"*

On another occasion coming home from a book party for Martin Luther King, I got in a cab driven by a Southern Negro — the kindest and most human of all the New York cabdrivers. I showed him the book Martin Luther King had autographed for me. "Ain't that sumthin'?" he said. "Now ain't *that* sumthin'?" When we arrived at my address he refused to let me pay: "Anybody who's met Martin Luther King and got him to sign that book," he said, "don't have to pay." One afternoon, in a crowded car on the Seventh Avenue subway, a pretty Negro girl sat holding hands with a Jewish boy. My gaze wandered to the other passengers; practically everyone was looking at the couple — some out of the corners of their eyes, the others more openly. Two Negro men were looking at them, a group of Negro teen-agers were looking at them, three Puerto Rican laborers were looking at them, two old Jewish ladies with shopping bags were looking at them, a Chinaman in a straw hat was looking at them, and I was looking at them. There the young couple sat, self-consciously holding hands, until after a while they dropped their hands to their sides and started reading the advertisements on the wall.

In 1964, after the Mississippi "Freedom Summer," I spent an evening with a group of young people who had been there with SNCC. Several of us, after dinner in an Italian place in the Village, lingered over coffee. I had been talking with a Negro girl; she was from the Mississippi delta, and she had come to New York to make money so she could return to college in Jackson. All of a sudden, for no apparent reason, she began sobbing; a few minutes later she left to go home. One of the white girls walked her to her apartment down the street. When she returned I asked what had been wrong. The white Snick girl said, "She told me you're the first Mississippi white person she was ever with socially. You made her nervous as hell. Her emotions got the better of her."

The Mississippi these young people talked of was a different place from the one I had known, the things they said were not in context with mine; it was as if we were talking of another world — one that *looked* the same, that had the same place names, the same roads and rivers and landmarks, but beyond that the reality was awry, removed from my private reality of it. After the riots at Ole Miss, I had written a magazine article in *Dissent* about Mississippi; in it I had called the delta "beautiful," a land of great romance and sorcery to me in my childhood. One of the civil rights activists at the table, a young Mississippi Negro, had written me a letter: "Your delta," he had said, "was not mine." Now he and his friends sat talking matter-of-factly about beatings in the jailhouses of delta towns — towns whose social graces and weekend celebrations I had enjoyed as a boy. They discussed a shooting in Greenwood, where I had once played baseball and gone to "Red Top" dances as a happy, oblivious senior in high school. They described the places of my youth, the quiet hill towns I had known — one was "tough," another "damned spooky," another "getting a lot better" — as if they were objects on some sliding scale to perdition. The world of a sensitive young person growing up remains fixed in one's emotions as it was years ago, it endures in the memory dreamlike and motionless, despite even what later knowledge discloses. The words of my companions intruded on this world of my past like harsh accusations, and made it complicated and unreal to me: I had changed a great deal, and yet in other ways I had changed hardly at all; although my mind accepted what they said, my emotional recollection of these old places and things was threatened and unsure. In America, perhaps more than any other place, and in the South, perhaps more than any other region, we go back to our home in dreams and memories, hoping it remains what it was on a lazy, still summer's day twenty years ago — and yet our sense of it is forever violated by others who see it, not as home, but as the dark side of hell.

I was confronted with this feeling even more vividly when, a few days later, I met a white girl from Texas, one of the first Snick workers who had gone to Mississippi. We had mutual friends in Texas; the talk was cordial. She was leaving for Mississippi again the following week. Near the end of the evening I said, "Think of me next time you're in Yazoo." This struck a raw nerve. "Think of it yourself, you son-of-a-bitch," she said. "It's your hometown, not mine." As I sat trying to think of what to reply, she got up and walked away, and I never saw her again.

•

Yet there was always that other, radically different experience of my home state: the first and original one. My mother and my grandmother Mamie made a visit to New York, the first time they had ever been East. It was an unusual thing, watching my eighty-six-year-old grandmother, youngest of those sixteen and the last remaining Harper, as she walked up Madison Avenue during a rush hour. As with the Snick workers' delta and the delta of my past, I found it difficult to *fit* her into New York City, this courageous and unconquerable old woman — niece of the first territorial governor of Mississippi, daughter of the editor whose printing presses had been dumped by the Yankee soldiers into the town well, product of that impoverished and defeated South of the post-Reconstruction. Much of her own humanity derived from the great qualities of that older South, of that deprived generation which came to maturity in the 1880s, before polarities were hardened, long before the latter-day defensiveness. The Mississippi of 1878, the year of her birth, and the Madison Avenue of 1964 were, in juxtaposition, too irreverent to bear sensibly. As she held on to my arm and looked up at the tall buildings I heard my mother say to her, "There sure are a lot of foreigners in this city." The ratio of white Anglo-Saxon Protestants on Manhattan Island, I remarked, was about 12 percent. "Twelve percent?" my grandmother said, laughing at the thought. "That ain't *much*." She had been uncommonly vexed by some of the recent happenings in our native state, especially by the activities of Governor Ross Barnett. "Well, what'll I say if anybody asks me where I'm from?" she asked me. "I'm ashamed of that old fraud." That afternoon in an art gallery she struck up a conversation with a man who sat next to her. Her accent caught his fancy, and he asked her where she was from. "I'm from north of New Orleans," she replied.

In our apartment that night she spoke again of her childhood, of those forgotten ghosts who had been the citizens of Raymond, Mississippi, when she was a girl. She spoke of these things, and of her brothers Winter and Sam and George, just as I had heard her when I was a child and lay drowsily in my bed at the old house in Jackson, listening to her voice and my great aunts' from the parlor and hearing the sound of the family clock on the mantel chiming the quarter-hour, inexorable as time itself. Here as she talked, with my son half asleep on her lap, not fully asleep because he was not wholly accustomed to words pronounced the way she pronounced them, I remembered exactly the way that old clock sounded, and my grandfather Percy's unusual snores, and his shy drawl when he told me stories; the memory of them competed with the mad traffic noises on West End Avenue, the sirens on Broadway, the shouting junkie waltzing down 94th Street, and some mad incomprehensible wail of anguish or pain or joy from one of the flophouses nearer the river. The city's exterior madnesses, its crashing echoes and reverberations, contrasted too violently with her soft, slow monotone; her stories of those vanished times haunted me now; I knew that one's life, one's spanning of years and places, could never be of a piece, but rather were like scattered fragments of old glass.

The next day my wife and I took my mother and Mamie to see the sights of Greenwich Village. We sat at a table in front of O. Henry's watching the crowds go past. Every time a Negro man and a white girl strolled by hand-in-hand I noticed my mother get tense and ball-up her knuckles. This was a big night for mixed couples. "I tell you," my mother said, speaking from a long and pent-up curiosity, "I've never *seen* the way these people carry on down here in the Greenwich Village. All these couples jumbled up this way, I don't know what's to *become* of it all. I can't understand these people carryin' on!"

It was just different from the place we came from, I said. Then Mamie broke in.

"Yeah, son," she said, "we come from a different place. You know that. You came from down there. You know we're just accustomed to doin' things different from all this. You know that." Then she paused for a moment, looking out beyond Sixth Avenue, at nothing in particular. "I don't know," she finally said, with a sigh just barely audible. "Maybe when we all get to heaven, they'll be white, and we'll be black."

•

Several years before, in Paris in 1957, I had been immersed in the novels and stories of my fellow Mississippian, Richard Wright. We went out to the Arab bar and had our talk about Yazoo and America.

Several days later a mutual friend delivered a message to me from Wright; Wright had been interested in me and suggested that we correspond. I did not take him up on the offer. Partly my reluctance had been due to a lack of self-confidence, that a "liberated" small-town Mississippi boy had anything unusual to offer this "liberated" Southern Negro writer of an older generation. But also I think it was due to my feeling that Wright, in many ways so admirable a man, was so different from me in temperament and loyalty and experience that we had almost nothing in common.

This was not to be the case when I got to know Ralph Ellison in New York eight years later. I first met Ellison at a cocktail party given by the *Paris Review* group in an art gallery on the Upper East Side. My wife, Celia, William Styron, Ellison, and I stood off in a corner and confessed to one another that the four of us probably had more in common than we had with all the other writers and authors and intellectuals and editors within hailing distance.

This original feeling was reinforced a few days later when Ellison and his wife, Fannie, came to our apartment for dinner. I recognized from the first his distinctive *Southernness*, and how similar his was to my own. It would have been naïve to ignore the differences, but it was the similarities — temperamental, intellectual, imaginative — which interested me. Ellison had just returned from Oklahoma, his first trip home in years; he fascinated us with uproarious stories about his homecoming.* We shared the same easygoing conversation; the casual talk and the telling of stories, in the Southern verbal jam-session way; the sense of family and the past and people out of the past; the congenial social manner and the mischievous laughter; the fondness of especial *detail* and the suspicion of the more grandiose generalizations about human existence; the love of the American language in its accuracy and vividness and simplicity; the obsession with the sensual experience of America in all its extrava-

---

* In his essay "The Southwest as a Racial Crossroads," Larry Goodwyn wrote: "If one had to write a cultural appraisal of the present-day Southwest, he would have to state that . . . Ralph Ellison of Oklahoma is the finest living novelist to emerge from the Southwest . . . *Invisible Man* is being read by young people in Texas, black and white, and he is influencing them."

gance and diversity; the love of animals and sports, of the outdoors and sour mash; the distrust in the face of provocation of
certain manifestations of Eastern intellectualism, particularly in
its more academic and sociological forms. And in both of us, I
felt, as in so many other Southerners in the East, there was a
pointed tension just below the surface of things, a strong and
touchy sensitivity — usually controlled but always there.* There
would always be one's own complicated experience as a white
Southern boy to come to terms with, yet during my first years
in the Big Cave it was Ralph Ellison and our mutual friend Al
Murray, also a Negro writer from the South and a former teacher
at Tuskegee, who suggested to me as much as anyone else I had
ever known the extent to which the easy *abstractions*, the outsider's judgment of what one *ought* to feel, had simplified and
dogmatized and hence dulled my own perceptions as an outlander in the East.

Does it seem strange, or a naive fantasy on my part, that a
Ralph Ellison and an Al Murray would have this kind of influence on me? They knew the evils of the South — as Negroes,
much more intimately than I ever had. They were men of mili-
tant integrity. Ellison, James Baldwin once said, "is as angry as
anybody can be and still live." Yet they tried to reduce their experience, not to polemicism, but to metaphor. They were
reading and understanding the work of Faulkner at Tuskegee
in the 1930s, when nine Eastern critics in ten were dismissing
him as another Southern Gothic of the blood-and-thunder
school. They tried to understand themselves in the light of their
own Southern and American experience. They refused to view

* In a portrait of Ellison in his superb book, *Who Speaks for the Negro?*,
Robert Penn Warren wrote this description: "[His] calmness has a history, I
should imagine, a history based on self-conquest and hard lessons of sympathy
learned through a burgeoning and forgiving imagination. Lurking in the calmness is, too, the impression of the possibility of a sudden nervous striking-out,
not entirely mastered; and too, an impression of withdrawal — a withdrawal
tempered by humor, and flashes of sympathy."

their own Southern past apocalyptically, as if it had all been disaster. They warned me, by word and by personal example, to beware of being "brainwashed" by a lot of accoutrements that could easily betray one's own unique consciousness as a white Southern intellectual from Yazoo City, Mississippi — accoutrements that could make an unwary Southerner a *rhetorician* rather than a writer. For a long time in my life, I had been ashamed of my Mississippi origins. Yet shame was too simple and debilitating an emotion, too easy and predictable — like bitterness. It was more difficult to *understand* one's origins, to discover what was distinctive and meaningful in them, to compare them with the origins of others, to give shape to them for the sake of some broader understanding of place and experience.

It was in Ellison's writings that I learned and acknowledged the difference between him and Richard Wright, and understood his own deepest feelings about the relationship between life and art. Why, he asked, was Hemingway more important to him than Wright?*

Not because he was white, or more "accepted." But because he appreciated the things of this earth which I love and which Wright was too driven or deprived or inexperienced to know: weather, guns, dogs, horses, love *and* hate and impossible circumstances which to the courageous and dedicated could be turned into benefits and victories. Because he wrote with such precision about the processes and techniques of daily living that I could keep myself and my brother alive during the 1937 Recession by following his descriptions of wing-shooting; because he knew the difference between politics and art and something of their true relationship for the writer. Because all that he wrote — and this is very important — was imbued with a spirit beyond

* This passage is taken from the brilliant exchange between Ellison and Irving Howe and is to be found in Ellison's *Shadow and Act* and Howe's *A World More Attractive*. Writers and critics should be reading this exchange a hundred years from now.

the tragic with which I could feel at home, for it was very close
to the feeling of the blues, which are, perhaps, as close as Americans can come to expressing the spirit of tragedy . . . But
most important, because Hemingway was a greater artist than
Wright, who although a Negro like myself, and perhaps a great
man, understood little if anything of these, at least to me, important things. Because Hemingway loved the American language and the joy of writing, making the flight of birds, the lop-
ing of lions across an African plain, the mysteries of drink and
moonlight, the unique styles of diverse peoples and individuals
come alive on the page. Because he was in many ways the true
father-as-artist of so many of us who came to writing during
the late thirties.

I admired Ellison as a writer and as a human being because
he remained honest to his own consciousness as an artist, and to
his own perceptions as a man. Especially in the 1960s he was
caught in a crossfire, between the activists, on the one hand,
who felt he should be more straightforwardly *engagé*, and some
of the critics, on the other, who felt he was not being true to his
experience as a Negro. The answer to both, I felt, was *Invisible
Man*.

"We are fortunate as American writers," he wrote in *Shadow
and Act*, "in that with our variety of racial and national traditions, idioms and manners, we are yet one. On its profoundest
level American experience is of a whole. Its truth lies in its diversity and swiftness of change." At Al Murray's apartment in
Harlem, on New Year's Day 1967, the Murrays, the Ellisons,
and the Morrises congregated for an unusual feast: bourbon,
collard greens, black-eyed peas, ham-hocks, and cornbread — a
kind of ritual for all of us. Where else in the East but in Harlem
could a Southern white boy greet the New Year with the good-
luck food he had had as a child, and feel at home as he seldom
had thought he could in the Cave?

•

Bundini Brown dropped by my office one day to show me some stories he had written. Bundini had come from Florida; at thirteen he joined the Navy, took to boxing, and eventually became Cassius Clay's trainer. It was he who originated Clay's old slogan for the first Liston fight — "float like a butterfly, sting like a bee." Now he was living in New York City, making a living selling rugs. He and Clay broke when Bundini refused to convert to Muslimism, although they would later join up again; Bundini's main trouble was that he was too full of love.

After a long and spirited talk, Bundini and I went up to my apartment for dinner. I introduced him to my son as "the man who taught Cassius Clay how to box." David Ray sat in a chair and gazed in admiration at our unexpected guest. Bundini got up and sparred with the boy, pushing him into a corner and trapping him in the ropes. David threw a wild right-cross, and retired to a neutral corner as Bundini fell over in mock pain. When Ralph Ellison and Al Murray came over, the conversation was about Florida and Alabama, and Clay vs. Patterson, and Clay vs. Terrell, and the great Jack Johnson. Then Bundini reached into his pocket and pulled out a letter he had written to Clay, explaining in the most charitable and human terms why he had not become a Muslim.

"Bundini," I said, "you should've been a preacher."

"Ain't you *somethin'*?" he said. His broad face burst into a grin, and he broke out into a stream of Southern rhetoric that would have shamed Martin Luther King at the March on Washington. David came over next to us with a paperback copy of *Invisible Man* and whispered, "The man who wrote this has a dog just like mine." Bundini turned away from Ellison and confided, "That *Invisible* book, ain't that somethin'? This fellow over here can *write*. He tells the *truth*. He makes my little stories sound like a bootlegger's. Them words in that *Invisible* book exhale and inhale." Bundini shook his great head in wonder, and then gave us all a lecture on Jack Johnson. David at this point started a sparring match with his dog in the middle of the room. "You stick with me, Dave," Bundini shouted, "and I'll have you fightin' in the Astrodome by the time you're fifteen."

A few days later I overheard from the next room a conversation between my wife and my son, who had just returned from his school. It was a progressive school on Bank Street in the Village; his best friend there was a Negro boy his age named Tommy Johnson. Unexpectedly David said, "Tommy is a nigger."

He had never said nigger before, and Celia asked him where he had gotten it. He said he didn't remember.

"Well," I heard her say, "it's not a good word to use. Don't you like Bundini? If you said that to Bundini it would hurt his feelings. Tommy too, and a lot of other people. I don't ever want you . . ."

"Okay, I *know*," the boy said. He turned red and looked away in silence. "I *won't*," he repeated; these last words he said with a touch of tenderness. He had been instantly abashed. I could sense he realized what "nigger" meant in terms of people he knew and cared about; for a six-year-old New York boy it was a word that conflicted with his own personal loyalties; I never heard him use it again.

•

Often, in the city, one encountered an *unexpected* racial madness — the ironies lurking under the epidermis, the old terrors leaping suddenly at the touch — so that even a Southerner accustomed to quick and passionate insanities might be taken by surprise, and respond unpredictably and without the code.

One evening my wife and I were at a small cocktail party. There was a book editor there whom we knew; he introduced us to his secretary, a handsome young German girl of about twenty-seven who spoke four languages and did translations. She had lived in New York for just over a year, she said; she had come full of excitement but she had been disappointed. No one gave a damn for anyone else, she said. She was very lonely and without friends, and she had decided to return to Germany the following summer. This was the sort of anguish I understood, this loneliness and disaffection in the cultural capital, particularly since she spoke of them with such intelligence and cosmopolitan sophistication. She was a lovely girl who was homesick; had my heart not gone out to her I would likely have consulted a cardiologist. "Why don't you come and have dinner with us tonight?" I asked. She accepted.

We returned to our apartment, and we drank martinis and continued the conversation. She deplored the subways, and the noise, and the violence, the transportation strike and the junkies and the night all the lights went out. We agreed with her, for perfunctory assent to such discouragements is one of the social formulas in the city. I sat there ruminating on these things, and my own curious experiences with them, only half listening to her as she continued in her rich Teutonic accent.

"The Jews," she said, "the New York *Jews*, they aren't as bad as the Jews in Germany. German Jews are much dirtier. They're the worst people I ever saw. The New York Jews aren't as despicable. But they're more ambitious; I think they're *crueler*."

"What's that?" I asked.

"The Jews in New York. They're more ambitious and more cruel. They're more money hungry. But I can still get along with them better than the Jews in Germany." She continued in much the same vein, citing an example here and there. "I suppose I feel uneasy around Jews," she said. "I've never cared for them, and I can't really trust them."

I paused for a moment, tempted to change the subject. I had never cared for lectures, or for sticky condescension, but I could not help myself.

"I think I've seen too many documentaries," I said. "It gets to me to hear talk like that in a German accent."

"Why does it?" she asked.

"It gives me a bad sensation."

"I'm sorry. It just happens to be the way I feel."

"I don't mean to be righteous. I come from the most brutal part of America. I know what racism is. But what Germany has done in the name of the things you're talking about makes the South a paradise by comparison."

"I didn't do them."

"I didn't do what the South has done, but I can't dismiss that they were done."

"So," she said, in a kind of whisper. "Where do we go from here?"

"I've never done this before in my life," I said. "But I'm going to ask you to leave. I'm sorry."

"Do you mean it?" the girl asked. She fumbled for her gloves and looked down at the floor. From the kitchen my wife was listening.

"I'm afraid I do."

I helped her with her coat and went outside with her to hail a cab. We stood on the street corner in silence. "I'm sorry," I said again, as she got in the taxi. She looked away and said nothing.

It is a comment on the tenacity of regional stereotypes, of one's regional narcissisms, that I felt a terrible remorse. I worried that I had indulged in a horrible exercise in bad temper and prep-school self-righteousness. The act of my booting that girl out of my apartment haunted me for days, even after my friend and fellow Southern exile Bill Styron, on hearing my description of it, said, "You should have kicked her out on her ass and kept your shoe for a souvenir."

Shortly after this incident a friend and contemporary of mine from Mississippi, a gentlemanly young lawyer and politician with a Princeton degree, came to the Cave on a visit. I told him of the confrontation with the German girl. "You mean you invited her out of your *house?*" he exclaimed. I said yes. He sat on the edge of his chair for a moment and then, ponderously, he began shaking his head. "That's just not done. I never *heard* of such a thing. You did *wrong.*" For an instant his judgment played on my own feelings of vulnerability. Then I got mad as hell at false chivalry, at empty gentlemanliness, at the old ritualistic forms that I had grown up with and that still suffused me out of mere force of habit. "To hell with you and your good manners!" I shouted at my companion. "They're as hypocritical as the *Southern Baptist Church.*" We both fell into an impenetrable Mississippi silence.

6

ON THE HUNDREDTH anniversary of Appomattox, *Harper's* published a special issue on the South of the 1960s. I had persuaded two of the contributors, C. Vann Woodward and William Styron, to come down from Connecticut to New York to appear with me on several radio interview programs.

There was no historian in America whose work I admired more than Vann Woodward's. He had come from a small town in

Arkansas, and now he occupied a distinguished chair in American history at Yale. He had been mentor, guide, and spokesman for a whole generation of uprooted young Southern intellectuals. As a human being he was, in the most legitimate way, someone to emulate. The humanity and honesty of his point of view, his humility before his own intelligence and before history, his lack of dogma and rhetoric, his great patience and tolerance of others both personally and intellectually — all these qualities in a man of strong conviction and intellectual courage contrasted sharply with much of the abrasiveness I had encountered in the East. He was a gentleman, in the deepest and best way. For myself, trying with considerable tribulation to remain true in New York to some honest sense of identity, his work had much in it that deserved heeding.

I had often suspected that, much as Faulkner had claimed to be a failed poet who had turned to the novel with the power of poetry in mind, Woodward was, in the best sense, a failed novelist, who brought to his brilliant histories — *The Strange Career of Jim Crow, Reunion and Reaction, Tom Watson, Origins of the New South* — the great narrative strength, the natural genius for the American language of the creative artist. In praising, as a Southern historian, the Southern men of letters, he spoke of "the vital relations between the crafts"; he was not, he said, asking for a relaxation of the limitations of the historian's discipline nor for his borrowing the novelist's license. But once the historian abandoned the false analogy with the natural sciences and admitted that history involves no special concepts or terminology, he will see that his task is to "explain" history in much the same way he explains events in ordinary life, and with much the same language. The Southern men of letters, who had advanced many of the historian's aims, have "helped us penetrate the romantic haze of an older generation as well as the cynical stereotypes of our own. They have endowed the denigrated and emotionally impoverished New South with a sense of tragedy and dignity that history had hitherto reserved for the Old Regime, and they have enriched our consciousness of the past in the present."

Woodward's essays, especially his collection *The Burden of Southern History*, were my favorites. In these, out of the "chaos and irony of history," he used more than the credentials of a great scholar and historian; in what I took to be both historical scholarship and acts of the creative imagination he addressed himself to many of the problems of consciousness besetting Americans of our day, especially but not exclusively Southern Americans. He quoted Ellen Glasgow's posthumous autobiography, but I knew he was speaking also of himself: "I had been born with an intimate feeling for the spirit of the past, and the lingering poetry of time and place." He did not seek to overlook the old scars, the monuments of the South's distinctiveness that were now disappearing; far from it. To seek identity in our faults, he said, was always easiest, for whatever reservations the South's critics had about our virtues, they had not been reluctant in conceding us our vices. At the same time, while the myths of Southern distinctiveness had been on the wane, the national myths had been growing more powerful and appealing. The danger, he wrote, "in the wholesale rejection of the South by the modern Southerner bent on reaffirming his Americanism is the danger of reaffirming more than he bargains for."

He wrote of the national self-image of innocence and moral complacency. The Southerner's preoccupation, on the other hand, was not with innocence but with guilt, not with the ideal of perfection but with the reality of evil. The Southerner's experience with evil and tragedy are as impossible to reconcile with the national myth of innocence and social felicity as the experience of defeat and poverty are to reconcile with the American myths of success and plenty. Amidst the "great assimilation" of modern America, two large minorities had remained as outsiders, the oldest and (with the exception of the Indians only) the most indigenously American minorities of all. Both were here before the Pilgrims landed on Plymouth Rock — the most durable of the "hyphenates" — "the Southern Americans and their ancient contemporaries, the Negro-Americans." And a certain stigma was attached to being both.

The shattering of the South's dreams, the frustrations and failures of its history, the lessons of living for decades with a great human wrong, with a quite un-American poverty and submission, could not be fit into any theory of divine providence. To Woodward these realities had provided Southerners with a different point of view from which they might, if they would, "judge and understand their own history and American history, and from which to view the ironic plight of modern America." In one of his most eloquent and perceptive passages on America's present role in the world, he wrote:

With all her terrible power and new responsibilities, combined with her illusions of innocence and her legends of immunity from frustration and defeat, America stands in greater need than she ever did of understanding her own history. Our European friends, appalled by the impetuosity and naïveté of some of our deeds and assumptions, have attributed our lack of historical sophistication to our lack of a history — in their sense of the word. America's apparent immunity to the tragic and ironic aspects of man's fate — that charmed and fabled immunity that once made America the Utopia of both the common men and the philosophers of Europe — has come to be pictured as Europe's curse. For a fear that haunts Europeans is the fear that America's lack of a common basis of experience and suffering will blind her to the true nature of their dilemmas and end by plunging them into catastrophe. But the Europeans are not entirely right. America has a history. It is only that the tragic aspects and the ironic implications of that history have been obscured by the national legend of success and victory and by the perpetuation of infant illusions of innocence and virtue.

I had also been an admirer of Styron's fiction, especially *Lie Down in Darkness*, which I had always considered the finest of the post-war American novels. This book had caused Malcolm McGregor such emotional pain that he could not finish the last fifty pages; another friend in Texas had bought thirty or forty copies just to give away to acquaintances; and still another member of the burgeoning Southwestern literati had tried, with the encouragement of several shots of Old Crow, to telephone the author long-distance on the occasion of Peyton Loftis' birthday. Styron was a Virginian, from Newport News; at Davidson College, North Carolina, he had a roommate who was destined to become sheriff of Bolivar County, Mississippi. Later, at Duke, yet another roommate was fated, in 1966, to be elected the first Republican governor of Florida since 1872, on a platform almost as reactionary in spirit as the Reichstag fire. Styron had been fired as a young man from a lowly position in a publishing firm in New York for blowing up balloons and letting them out the window, where they promptly blew back into the office-window of a senior editor. He had strongly advised his firm, before the balloon scandal, to turn down *Kon Tiki*. "Who wants to read about these scrubby Norwegians crossing the ocean in a dirty little boat?" he had argued. Later, at the age of twenty-four, he had written *Lie Down in Darkness* while living on government surplus canned goods (marked "certified edible" on the labels) in an old brownstone in the West Eighties. His poet's sense of ruin, guilt, and tragedy, his extraordinary structural genius for the progression of time in a work of fiction, gave Styron his own particular vision as an artist. He also had the advantage of a great streak of humor. Once, when an interviewer asked him if the young writer these days worked at a greater disadvantage than preceding generations, he replied,

"Hell, no. Writers ever since writing began have had problems, and the main problem narrows down to just one word — life. Certainly this might be an age of so-called faithlessness and despair we live in, but the new writers haven't cornered any market on faithlessness and despair, any more than Dostoevski or Marlowe or Sophocles did. Mark Twain was as baffled and appalled by Darwin's theories as anyone else, and those theories seemed as monstrous to the Victorians as atomic energy, but he still wrote about riverboats and old Hannibal, Missouri."

Now he was living in Roxbury, Connecticut, with his wife Rose, a rare and beautiful girl from Baltimore, in a big house that had once headquartered the Russian government-in-exile. He was finishing his ambitious and deeply understanding novel based on the Nat Turner slave rebellion on 1831; this book would be a moral act, an act of courage, on Styron's part, for in dealing with Turner in the first person on the level of his own artist's sensibility Styron was taking one of the largest risks in contemporary American fiction. The essay he had done for *Harper's*, a magnificent piece of writing called "This Quiet Dust," was a description of his writer's obsession with Turner, "that dim and prodigious black man who alone in the history of American slave uprisings achieved a certain triumph." He had gone back to Virginia to trace the landmarks of the rebellion. Driving around Southampton County with the sheriff, who knew all the old backroads and was, of course, perfectly aware of Nat Turner's identity, Styron had listened with mounting disappointment as his host queried various citizens of the county, white and Negro, as to who Nat Turner was. The sheriff found the country people's ignorance irresistible, and he kept asking slyly, "You heard about old Nat Turner, ain't you?" No one had, although an operator of a service station identified him as a celebrated old racehorse. Styron was discouraged by this tedious and fruitless search, and he and the sheriff finally drove back along the unpaved roads to town: "I had been gazing out the window, and now suddenly something caught my eye — something familiar, a brief flickering passage of a distant outline, a silhouette against the sun-splashed woods — and I asked the sheriff to stop the car. He did, and as we backed up slowly through a cloud of dust, I recognized a house standing perhaps a quarter of a mile off the road, so familiar to me that it might have been some home I passed every day." He had recognized it from the old photographs. "From this distance, in the soft clear light of a spring afternoon, it seemed most tranquil, but few houses have come to know such a multitude of violent deaths. There in the late afternoon of Monday, August 22, 1831, Nat Turner and his band had appeared, and they set upon and killed Mrs. Catherine Whitehead, son Richard, and four daughters, and grandchild."

On the day of the radio interviews, Woodward, Styron, and I met at a big radio station near City Hall. Here we were interviewed about the South, about race, about guilt, about demagogues, about the civil rights movement, and about ourselves. This was the pattern throughout the day, as we moved from one Manhattan radio station to another — to dissect, analyze, criticize, specify, defend, illuminate, and speculate upon our common region. We were interviewed by beatnik disk jockeys, news commentators, entertainers, and one announcer who sold tea. We were on the air citywide and coast-to-coast. We were piped into Canada and our servicemen may have heard us around the world. Why *is* the South the way it is, we were asked? Where does it head from here? Would you venture to make a prediction? What are your *true* feelings about the place? When an interviewer asked me "How did you get liberated?" I was so taken by surprise that I replied, "I'm not. I'm still tryin'." Over martinis at lunch that day, Woodward told us stories about the March on Montgomery, which he had just participated in; at one point he and several fellow historians had gathered in a circle and given three cheers for Martin Luther King. "There we were," Woodward said, "walking down that highway to Montgomery. I looked over to the side of the road, and I saw the red-necks lined up, hate all over their faces, distrust and misunderstanding in their eyes. And I'll have to admit something. A little part of me was there with 'em."

There were two interviews to go, and we got up from lunch to leave. "I'm tired of talking about the South," Styron said. "Let's talk about something else next time."

"Let's talk about the North," Woodward said.

"Let's talk about the New York subways," Styron said.

"I'd just as soon talk about Westchester County," I suggested.

As we walked up Park Avenue in the Fifties to the next engagement, the traffic was snarled, hopelessly and for miles. The sidewalks were crowded with officeworkers returning from the lunch hour; one practically had to stand in line before making any progress northward. I was in one of my Bear moods, and I thought of the haunting lines from Sir Thomas Browne's *Urn Burial*, which were the inscription at the beginning of Styron's *Lie Down in Darkness*. I had once memorized them and on this mild spring afternoon they came back in a great rush: "*And since death must be the Lucina of life, and even Pagans could doubt, whether thus to live were to die; since our longest sun sets at right descensions, and makes but winter arches, and therefore it cannot be long before we lie down in darkness and have our light in ashes . . .*" At that instant I was almost clipped by a taxicab, and the driver stuck his head out and yelled, "Aincha got eyes in that head, ya bum?" Woodward was caught on the traffic island in the middle of Park. "Come on, country boys!" he yelled. "Haven't you ever been in the big city before?" "*. . . since the brother of death daily haunts us with dying* *mementoes, and time that grows old in itself, bids us hope no long duration; — diuturnity is a dream and folly of expectation."* "What does that passage from Browne mean?" I asked Styron, as we waited for the light. "I like the sound of the words, but I'm not sure what he means."

"Well, to me he means we're all in it together, and we're all in for a pretty tough time," Styron said.

"You're the slowest country boys I ever saw," Woodward said, when we joined him on the traffic island. A few pedestrians, stranded there along with us, smiled among themselves, and two or three of them laughed, with a noticeable touch of condescension.

7

THE LITERARY WORLD of New York in the 1960s, perhaps more than any other time in America with the exception of the 1930s, was a harsh, cliquish, nervous world, a reflection of the great concentration of contemporary American writing in the cities. It was a world characterized by a fine abrasiveness, an impatience with the old regionalisms, and a disdain for intellectual insufficiency of any kind. It broke new records in wordage. It was mean as hell.

It was, on the other hand, a world of awesome brilliance, even when its brilliance was a little predictable, and except for three or four notable operators, not very colorful. Its stupendous articulateness was strong on polemic and broadside. It was given to extravagant claims and exaggerated dismissals. *Naked Lunch* was either the work of the greatest mind of our generation or it was a horrendous fraud, the only agreement being that the author did not write it on aspirin alone. *An American Dream* was either in lineal descent from Joyce, Pound, and Hemingway or it was simply a cruel and filthy book, in the generic and not the pornographic sense. It was a world of a roughly identifiable urban intelligentsia, about which more than a few detractors hurled the old accusations concerning conspiracies and shadow establishments. Being a populist who had always feared Eastern imperialism, I myself indulged in these thoughts when my blood was up, for such literary histrionics were good for one's emotional vitality, not to mention one's provincial ego. But more careful and extended observations revealed that if the literati of the city had indeed been engaged in a conspiracy, the initial consensus had broken down somewhere in the dead of night, for there were enough counter-, sub-, and intra-conspiracies to make any Eastern establishment want to dismantle and move to San Francisco. Or in the words of one critic, there was less back-rubbing than backbiting.

The city's intelligentsia directed much of its considerable talents and energies to the writing of articles, essays, and reviews. This was most emphatically a period in which the magazine or review "piece" came to fruition in this country, a form which showed a sophistication and an inventiveness that might have been thought impossible two decades before, and which even the best novelists of the time were attracted to. This may very well be a temporary phenomenon, indicative of the sheer strain and pressure of the age, of the writer's wish to get something into print fast and to reach the wider, hungrier audience the magazines and journals provide. And most of this "nonfiction" essaying, the best of it highly self-conscious and drawing upon the creative awarenesses and perceptions of the artist, came out of New York.

It was a period in which the language itself was becoming increasingly *American*, an expression of the linguistic tensions, of the daring to push the native idiom to its farthest and most imaginative limits. The best writers were engaged in mortal combat with the bland homogeneity of the mass media, which was making the language a kind of pale compromise bridging the dying regionalism and fading ethnic identification of modern America. Yet one had only to walk the streets of New York and *hear* the way the language was used — by the Jews, the Southern and Northern Negroes, the Italians, the Puerto Ricans — to appreciate its great richness, color and expressiveness. More than ever before television was the enemy; in the 1960s it had become so rotten in its violence, pettiness, and philistinism that reform seemed impossible, almost irrelevant. The country badly lacked a truly *national* magazine, unidentified with any intellectual clique or with any region, or city, or slice of a city, willing to fight to the death the pallid formulas and deadening values of the mass media. It needed a magazine young and courageous enough to carry the language to its limits, to reflect the great tensions and complexities and even the madnesses of the day, to encourage the most daring and imaginative and inventive of our writers, scholars, and journalists — to help give the country some feel of itself and what it was becoming.

•

In the period I was first introduced to it, the Manhattan mind was more than anything else an *intellectual* mind, precise, ideological, given to harsh empiricisms. There was not much civility in it — civility in its broad and human sense. *Ideas* — their sources, consequences, appositions, nuances — had priority; a regard for individual people with their flaws and weaknesses

and absurdities could not compete with the great ebb and flow
of ideas. The Manhattan mind, I suspected, would have been
eager to celebrate this lack of civility. Civility as a substantial
quality was not only unimportant, it was frivolous, the product
of a corrupt agrarian past, tending to get in the way of the dog-
fighting and ass-ripping so necessary to the life of letters in an
urban setting. It was immensely difficult on first introduction
to feel comfortable in this complicated, abrasive world of New
York letters. For the Southerner, in the words of Thornton
Wilder, "place, environment, relations, repetitions are the breath
of their being." These qualities, with all the things they implied,
seemed irrelevant and old-fashioned. There were other parts of
the Cave's literary life — less serious, at a remove from the older,
more substantial, more admirable intelligentsia. Here the intellectual fashions, hip, camp, black humor, pop art, came and
went, inexorable and temporary as the spring's rains, yet in these
quarters they demanded and got people's attentions. Reputations of young writers and critics were declared overnight, as if
by intellectual fiat. People talked unendingly, and all of a sudden, about Andy Warhol, or Timothy Leary, or some white
man's hip version of Black Power — a generalized intellectual
camp which eventually led me to believe that many of these
people were simply bored and out for easy kicks. The partisans of intellectual thrills, the "attitudinizers," seemed desperately to lack in *experience*. They had not been around people
different from themselves enough, there was an empty place
where some tolerant and forgiving human understanding should
have been. They seemed devoid of any serious concern with real
human beings in real human situations, in struggle with themselves and the world. Trying to understand something of life in
the twentieth century, in its own faltering and unsure way, was
difficult enough in itself without the devising of some phony and
momentarily fashionable measurement of "values." "The great

creative fight," I remember my friend Ronnie Dugger once said, "is with trivia." *

An emphatic distinction between the more serious, often Jewish and socialist intelligentsia (containing some of the country's best critics) and the swinging pop-art nihilists has to be made, yet the newcomer to the city on first exposure could easily be bowled over by either, or both, without quite knowing what had hit him, or why. There were so many *words* that one sometimes ceased believing that they meant much of anything. The high-powered intellection, the abstract and diffuse verbal exchanges, especially by the most dashing and "in" of the young academics, often went right by me — unidentified flying objects whose physical presence I acknowledged even as I doubted their reality. I feared being hit by some of those high-velocity volleys, and at first I would go to any lengths, to the extent of hiding in corners, to avoid becoming a stationary target of this social phenomenon which I did not fully comprehend. Three or four times, on friendly occasions, some agitated native would flush me for being a white Southerner; once a long-legged Eastern bluestocking with Gauloises smoke curling out of her ample nostrils blamed me for the institution of slavery, the Compromise of 1877, the Jim Crow laws, and the riots in Watts, and ended up, after two more drinks, identifying me as "poor white trash." One of her running-mates, a graduate student in sociology at Columbia and a member of the Village Independent Democrats, suggested I return South forthwith since I obviously suffered from *deracination;* she was angered further when I told her I took this to be a form of rat poison.

* Alfred Kazin, speaking of what he called the "fashion consciousness" and "success mongering" in the New York of our time, once said: "Everywhere many good young writers find themselves understandably backed up against the wall by the pressure of publishers, by the pressure of success; above all, by the fact that so many symbols that were once discovered by writers are now at the disposal of advertising, TV, and the rest of it . . . It is becoming increasingly difficult for the young writer to find a quiet place in his mind to write a book from."

One night at a small dinner party on the Upper West Side — it was my third or fourth month in the city — the guests sat around the table discussing a dozen intellectual matters with such a facility and a casualness, dismissing all the terrible complications abroad in the land with such a tempestuous argumentation, that suddenly and without warning I broke into a cold sweat. Every time they talked about something I knew better than they, which was rare, I discovered they did not know to any considerable degree what they were talking about, yet they embroidered on this argot misinformation with such hot and sweeping formulations that I could hardly keep track of the blow-by-blow fruits of their misdirections. They discussed the personal and day-to-day relationships between Southern whites and blacks, the political background of Lyndon B. Johnson, the politics of Populism, the decline of the American small town, the liberation of provincial American intellectuals, and half a dozen other items as if all the tribulations and madnesses in these human subjects had been devised to give some special substance to their own private language. Several things that I felt strongly and darkly in my heart they put through this linguistic wringer; some of my most contorted and painful emotional commitments came out like old work clothes gone through a dryer. Many of the words I recognized; I sensed the significance of a few of the clauses and prepositional objects, and an occasional infinitive used as a subject, but when they all came together in that great overflow of words and theories I was mystified. The mystification gave way to anger. At the end of the dinner, as the party retired to the main room, I cornered one of the combatants whom I knew. "Goddamn it," I said, tempted to grab him by the lapels, "I'm an American too. I talk the same language you do. I'm not *dumb*. But I couldn't understand ninety percent of what you people were saying. Is there something bad that's wrong with me?"

"What couldn't you understand?" he asked.

"Practically none of it. You could've been using High Norse."

"Well," he said, looking into the dregs of his drink, "perhaps we *are* a little idiomatic."

•

Eventually I discovered that in the matter of wordage, concepts, and meanings disguised from me, psychoanalysis played a role, for Freud was everywhere, from the drawing rooms to the funeral parlors. Sometimes it seemed that everybody got analyzed: one hour a day, five days a week for five years, at $30 an hour, not including tips. Many undergoing this experience liked to indulge in talk about it; inevitably some of the scare words slipped in. The spirit of the various psychoanalysts lurked in the shadows: "*He* said such-and-such" or "*He* thinks thus-and-so" were perfunctory references to these ubiquitous and unerring presences. Some people got to know themselves so well that questions concerning their inner turbulence became their favorite subject. They gave periodic weather reports on the barometric pressures and the warm-air fronts in their psyches. Since we, like the ocean, are 70 percent water, I wondered if an experienced water analyst, or a systematic humidification and purification program might not turn up additional flaws of a liquid nature, yet some people were so intimately aware of their tangible fissures that the human juices seemed to have dried up and lost all their mystery. Wives and husbands would split up and the respective analysts, like baseball umpires conferring on some knotty situation in the rulebook, would talk about the case to one another. Then the wife would telephone the husband's analyst, and the husband the wife's. Sometimes emotional compromises were negotiated that the U. S. Senate and William S. White would have done well to celebrate. The children would be prepared to go into psychotherapy at age ten, an urban substitute, perhaps, for the Brownies and Cub Scouts. "Know thyself, every heart beats to that iron strain, at $30 a beat." The stress of living in the great modern city, and all its traumas and fears, gave rise to a whole class of affluent and tormented people willing to unloosen with $5000 a year to map out their emotional tensions. The psychiatrists, who became minor deities, bought apartments on Central Park West and toured Europe during the psychiatric off-season, from August first to Labor Day. Meanwhile, however, the subways kept running, and there remained no better place to see the city's great unwashed and unanalyzed than the Seventh Avenue IRT at eight-thirty on a weekday morning, where the real world somehow went on.

For what one learned after some experience with the city was the considerable limitations of intelligence, intelligence per se and isolated: too many people who had it and were emotionally crippled, too many people who had it and cared little or not at all for human beings. Intelligence was not enough. One saw the extremely intelligent aging women, lacking in any fulfillment in their personal lives, isolated, lonely, and bristling with bitchiness. One saw all this elsewhere, but somehow the isolation, the intelligence in a human vacuum, was brought home more in the big city, this rootless, placeless, violent, and lonely society that we were becoming. Elsewhere there were more traditional roles to be lived, old unabstract forms to help give direction to unhappy lives, settled places which were a part of one's emotional commitment. Yet all these, where they still existed, were doing so on borrowed time, and would probably not last much longer. Sherwood Anderson and Eudora Welty and a dozen others had said this in the recent past; it was becoming more and more evident.

And finally, one learned something about the nature of New York friendships. They were unlike any other friendships I had ever known. In Mississippi, or in Texas, "friends" had been people whom one saw frequently and informally. Your children played with theirs, you went to movies all of a sudden and on a whim, you packed your families in a station-wagon and drove out to country places. You played tennis or touch football in some open space a few minutes from your houses, or if the mood struck you on some slow Friday afternoon, you would drop by a friend's office to flirt with his secretaries and to find out what he had accomplished or failed in during that week. Late in the day you could go to any one of three or four familiar spots, buy a pitcher of beer, and within ten or fifteen minutes people whom you knew on a first-name basis would be there at the table with you. You could organize a party on the spur of the moment, and you would have trouble getting everyone to leave. You shared certain things: a reverence for informality, an interest in what other friends were doing, a regard for geographic places, an awareness of a certain set of beloved landmarks in themselves important to one's everyday existence, a mutual but usually unexpressed sense of a community. I would not want to exaggerate, for there were drawbacks to this life, drawbacks that may have sprung from its virtues. Occasionally one got tired of the same faces, one wanted to meet and to know unusual people from somewhere else, one hoped to be in the middle of those remote outposts where the "real" activity was. But the friendships themselves connoted certain traditional qualities, qualities that people might reasonably expect of one another.

There was undoubtedly a higher concentration of talented, fascinating people in the New York City of our day than any other city in America, and perhaps in the world. One met them often in the mere course of business. Within a few minutes' walk from my apartment on West End Avenue lived a group of

writers, critics, journalists, artists, editors, and teachers who
were a credit not merely to the city but to the nation. Yet the
very absence of any homogeneity, the very diffusion of focus,
gave one's acquaintanceships in the city a fractured, fleeting
quality. One could call a person a "friend" if you saw him once
every four or five months, talked for a while, and got along.
Social evenings were often dominated by the glittering and famous people. Argumentation too often took the place of discourse, informality was discouraged by sheer social tension; in my
first months in the city, surrounded by all the famous names,
I half expected someone to notice me all of a sudden and shout,
Get out of this room! It was disconcerting to discover that the
political liberals and radicals, whose warmth of spirit I admired,
all had summer homes, as I myself would one day. The liberalism and radicalism of the intellectuals were argued and ex-
pounded in offbeat settings; the halfway social measures of the
Great Society were assailed on beaches and patios, and in the
proletarian glow of barbecue pits. The closest sense of community among the city's intellectuals and writers was engen-
dered not in New York but on Martha's Vineyard or Cape
Cod. The people whose friendships one most wished to pursue
were off on other tangents; everyone was simply too busy. It
was inconceivable to drop in on others without warning. "Business lunches" with one's fellow writers and editors in crowded
midtown restaurants took the place of family outings; martinis
on the rocks with slivers of lemon peels lubricated the wheels of
fealty. "We lunch twice a year," a native of New York once
said to me of a good friend of his, and without a trace of irony.
The terrible difficulties of personal relationships, even when
there was mutual admiration and sympathy, dissipated whatever awareness of place one had. Who gave a damn for the Big
Cave? So in the end one fell back on the city's standard customs and made references to "friends" previously seen last April.

One fall afternoon in 1966 I sat in a bar on Third Avenue with Norman Podhoretz, Midge Decter, and Marion Magid, who were then involved in editing *Commentary*, possibly the best and most uniformly intelligent magazine in New York in the 1960s. For three or four hours we sat talking about the places we had come from, about home, about people from our pasts. We told stories. We talked about editing, and about the things we were writing. I felt here, as I had perceived before, a certain electricity between Eastern Jewish intellectuals and white Southerners when the mood is relaxed and the pretensions gone, a certain *élan* in the casual talk about great characters, about comic moods, about Waspish Easterners more "inside" than we, and even, perhaps, an affinity in the historical disasters of our ancestral pasts. On this day I remembered the young writers I had read about in books, the ones who had come to the cultural capitals to learn their craft by working and by talking, by making friends with other young people also trying to learn. In the New York of my day this did not exist for me, or for any other young novice writer I knew of. James said of Hawthorne that he might have been even better if he had communicated with other writers working at the same sort of thing; Cowley said the same about Faulkner. They should have tried the city in 1966. "This is what's been *missing*," I suddenly said to my companions, cryptically and with a great flourish. I was so agitated I doubt if they had the slightest inkling what I meant.

•

Whatever was missing, the world of the young editor and writer, like other organized preoccupations, had a private rhetoric that at its worst bordered on bombast. Soon after I had settled in the city, a book editor, a large pompous fellow from a well-known publishing house who made one feel he had the inside track on everything written since Ecclesiastes, said at a business lunch otherwise filled with long silences, "I've got this book of mine coming out next month, and you've got to read it." I was naturally curious about what he had written, but it turned out he had not written a book at all! It was "his" book only because he had served as the editor of it. This was my first confrontation, and not my last, with editors who talked constantly of "my authors," "my books," and "my stable," as if writers existed only at their benevolence, or as if they themselves had written the whole Modern Library during summers on Fire Island. If there was any word I would have liked purged from the language of publishing, it was "stable"; writers may sometimes be horses' asses but they should not be confused with the whole animal.

The best editors, and there were a number of very good ones in the city, did not find it necessary to talk in this way. They were secure in their professionalism; they were of unquestionable help to the writer, especially to the young writer at work on his first book. Their encouragement, judgment, loyalty, and friendship, and their great patience in serving as sounding-board, were invaluable to any writer. But even the best ones acknowledged that they were brokers between the creative process and the total direction of that process, between the lonely and often agonizing work of the writer and the packaging, the merchandising, and the advertising of his finished product. They knew there was a limit to what editors could, or should, do, and they recognized without rancor or inferiority, the best of them, that the whole trade would go under tomorrow if writers stopped writing. The role of the editor essentially must be a quiet one, that of a passive co-ordinator; his relationship with the writer should be personal and private, not public. Much the same held true of the best magazine editors. The magazine editor must give tone and character to the magazine he edits. He must be above all a *catalyst* of good writing, he must provide sympathy, respect, and sometimes cajolery, he must understand and appreciate the great diversity of American experience. Sometimes, admittedly, the rewriting must go beyond the call of duty, but there was a trend in the Cave in the 1960s, a fertile period for the magazines, to glorify his role. The editor's position was one of tremendous importance, especially in shaping a broader and more civilized atmosphere and in making a certain readership available; for this reason alone it should not have required overexaggeration.

In the strange sub-culture of New York publishing, but particularly at its middle-levels where its practitioners, suffering perhaps from a certain insecurity, held a more celestial and cosmic view of the editor's life, I sometimes detected a *distrust* of the creative writer of our day, a distrust amounting almost to contempt. It was astonishing how much knowledge was had of the personal lives of our best writers, and the talk that went on of their broken marriages, their drinking, their irresponsibility, their psychopathic cruelty to animals and children. There seemed an extraordinary feeling that personal conduct and personal motive were everything in writing, and that the work of art itself was secondary. I also suspected there was far too much of the Eastern mentality in New York publishing; the Manhattan provincialism showed itself too often, as if anything much beyond the Hudson River was a vast and grassy steppeland populated by hillbillies and the descendants of the original Forty-Niners. One encountered too much super-sophistication, and too little enthusiasm for raw experience.

The best warning one could give the talented young writer serious about his work, willing to devote his lifetime to what Ralph Ellison once called "this very stern discipline," would be to get as far away as possible from the organized and official publishing world. A young writer's work rests in a very real way on his own private ego — on his own personal faith that what he has to write and the way he writes it are important in themselves, important to his own time and to future generations. Why else subject oneself to the miseries of writing? When one is too closely involved in the world of publishing, this private faith can wear very thin. There are too many *books*, too many reviews and too much talk about reviews, too much concern about books as commodities, books as items of merchandise, book quotas, book prizes, book sales figures, book promotions. There is too much literary activity and too much literary talk, having little or nothing to do with the intensely private and precarious act of writing. There is too much predictable flattery. All this is necessary to the trade, but it generates a total atmosphere which can be destructive of one's own literary values. Once, in talking with a book publisher, one of the most talented in the business, I remarked that as an editor and a writer I was glad I was a young American, that I was glad for "the basic pluralism of American life." "But the price we pay for that pluralism," he replied, "is too great." For the ideologue, for the polemicist, for the reformer, for the detached intellectual this attitude has a correctness, but for the young creative writer it is death.

8

ONE WINTER, for how can a Southerner with a growing son be without a big dog, I went up into the Hudson Valley and bought for my boy a black Labrador Retriever puppy by the name of I. H. Crane. Six months later he was the size of a quarter-horse, but without the discipline. My son began to call him "The Monster." The other people in our run-down old apartment building grew terrorized of our friendly and energetic beast. Coming hell-bent out of our first-floor rooms on his leash, I. H. Crane would quickly disperse the crowd gathered at the elevator; as they dashed and tripped in all directions they reminded me of the famous photograph of the people in the square at St. Petersburg the day the revolution began. On the sidewalks, whenever one of the neighborhood junkies came by howling or moaning or talking enthusiastically to himself, the dog, out of old misappropriated instincts, would freeze and point, and then let go with a bay ungodly enough to destroy a good fix. One morning, while I was waiting in front of the building with my son for his school bus, I was holding I. H. by the leash, paying little attention to his activities. A sharp-nosed woman with the beginnings of a mustache walked past us to the front door. Suddenly she swung on me and pointed at a respectable pile of dog shit on the sidewalk. *"Did your dog do that?"* she demanded. I had always had trouble when people shouted in my face; "No," I replied, "my little boy did." Even the building superintendent, a lovable Puerto Rican named Joe Gonzales who spent his leisure writing new verse to old Spanish songs, was compelled to call for discipline. In addition to this experience, and watching the boy and the monstrous black dog suffer from the usual claustrophobia of the Cave, I had read an article by Jason Epstein in *The New York Review of Books*, one of the most brilliant and acerbic of the city's journals in the 1960s. Epstein categorically advised the readers of the *Review* that it was impossible for people to live in New York City on less than $50,000 a year. I realized with this that it was time to get out, at least for the summer.

We found a big old farmhouse sitting on a hill overlooking a valley seventy miles north of the city; the oldest part of the house went back to the 1780s. I went into hock to publishers, magazines, bankers, and mortgagers, bartered my incorruptible soul for twenty years' labor, buying the house and its six acres, and depositing my family and dog in the old house for the summer. Against the full tradition of my boondocks background I became, of all the things I never thought I would be, a summertime commuter.

In the mornings I caught the train at 6:50 A.M., arriving at Grand Central at nine and at my office at nine-fifteen. This was duplicated in the afternoons. By my calculations my travel time from door-to-door, or "portal-to-portal" as the city's commuters said, was four hours and fifty-six minutes. Leaving my office at the end of a workday was an elaborate and highly contorted process. First I would wait ten minutes for the elevator to reach the eighteenth floor of our building, for we had moved out of the old building which housed the publishing firm into an anonymous skyscraper just across the street, then scramble against the dour insurance salesmen and businessmen from the adjoining offices for a place inside. Once downstairs I could make it easily into the subway on those afternoons when there had not been a tragedy at the unusual corner of Park and 33rd, that intersection where the mad cabs emerging from the secret tunnel wrought their havoc and offset the megapolis' birth rate. A wounded victim and the crowd gawking to see him might postpone my getting to the subway station by three to five minutes, but split-second timing would get me to Grand Central with two minutes to spare. Here I would bound up the two flights of stairs, fighting the strong torrent of Cave-dwellers descending the same stairways, and make it to the platform just as they were closing the gate.

It would be a long haul going home, more than two hours on some days, and I became obsessed with the mood of that commuter run. For three months I watched it as a loner, hardly speaking to anyone, sidling off to myself in the smoker or the bar-car, observing human nature in that unfamiliar moving culture. For some time, being an editor who was prone to experiment with exotic combinations, I had toyed with the idea of asking Norman Mailer, for $1500 and drinks, to travel for a week in the bar-car of the Harlem River line, standing nose-to-nose with the advertising men, smashing bottles, starting fights, pushing the women executives around a little, and then writing a piece of literary journalism, an article as art, a non-fiction short story, something about that modern American phenomenon of the commute-run that might Stand Up twenty years hence. I had also considered commissioning Styron to come along for a few rides and describe the landscape between Mount Kisco and Croton Falls, or the way the reservoirs beyond Golden's Bridge looked at sunset, but he was finishing the novel about slave revolts, which had traditionally been kept to a minimum in Thorndale, White Plains, and Pleasantville.

Coming into the city in the early morning mists was always a study in distances. The commuters who got on the train in Brewster, or those who connected up from the little towns of

Pawling, Towners, and Patterson to the north, were commuting not from suburbia but from a terrain approximating real country, though I knew that even this, in another decade, would be another extension of the city's lengthening suburbia. But now, in the early morning, through the woods and the purple hills shrouded in fog, riding by the reservoirs which could have passed for authentic lakes, one felt a thousand miles removed from Grand Central, from the East Thirties, from the intersection of Park and 33rd. Bleary-eyed, pulling out cups of coffee or egg sandwiches, the men who got on at Brewster talked about woodchuck, deer, and the elements. The thermometer in the barn, one would say, got down to forty last night. Somebody's spring was running low again. Another shot a rabbit at his back door and had rabbit stew. At Katonah, the first stop down the line, a few of the people who got on would start talking about crab grass. By Chappaqua crab grass seemed the biggest underhanded menace since Eva Braun. Even as early as Mount Kisco the atmosphere had become more distinctly businesslike. The men, brief-cased and meticulous in their expensive suits, shouted robust greetings to each other. Then the bridge boards would come out and the games would be underway. At Pleasantville, home of our modern cultural symbol, *The Reader's Digest*, the relaxed mood of the Brewsterites had been replaced by an aura of self-defense; seats were at a premium now, and there would be occasional exploratory elbow-jabs, and sometimes a few scattered oaths. If Pleasantville was a presage, White Plains was a boundary. From my window I would see the hundreds of passengers on the platform there, employing deft, executive-like stratagems which included not merely elbows but hips, kneecaps, and other joints depending on the situation and the lateness in the week. As the train moved, non-stop now toward the city, there would be little talk — only the quiet, earnest bridge games, a kind of post-breakfast seance to deaden perceptions in transit. We sped past the acres and acres of gravestones, the closer suburbs, and the Harlem River. We were a lily-white group moving across the narrow dark streets of Harlem; I would look out into Harlem, at the trash piled up on the corners, the old men standing against the broken buildings passing away the morning, the little storefront churches ("Jesus Salva," "Non-Denominational Protestant Church of the World"), so reminiscent of the Deep South. As we entered the bleak tunnel at 96th, a few minutes from Grand Central, swarms of passengers would get up and start walking to the front of the train. At first this curious exodus mystified me; it took me several days to realize that they were getting a head start before the train stopped to get two minutes closer to East 42nd Street.

Coming back in the afternoon would be slightly more relaxed; sometimes people would talk to each other. Occasionally the talk would be about the *New York Post*, the only afternoon paper available at the time, because of one of the city's periodic newspaper strikes; "it's a nasty little paper," I heard one man say. Kempton and Jules Feiffer and Pete Hammill seemed incongruous on a commuter run, but they had a captive audience. Once I sat next to a man who specialized in corkscrews, and he talked to me about what a new compound, a deceptive esoteric chemical without taste or smell, had done to his crab grass. Another afternoon I talked with a man who marketed a kind of tinfoil; he talked about the several nuances of the bank mortgage. The hum of the conversation these late afternoons would be of money — its sources, its complications, its fickleness, its wonders — a generalized high-level buzz about purchasing power, generating a rosy affluent glow among the tired men going home. Back in the bar-car, where the train drunkard would be on his fourth Scotch by Pleasantville, the boys would radiate an adolescent Boy Scout cheer, singing songs and

swapping sex stories. "Are you on Wall Street?" one of the Boy
Scouts shouted across at me at the bar one day. I said no. "Because you sure don't *look* like you are," he said. "Are you a
Democrat?" "Not just a Democrat, a *liberal* Democrat," I said,
and he and his companions looked at each other, shrugged, and
started in again on "Sweet Sixteen."

The car of the train seemed like a safe little island, removed
now from the threats of the Cave. Nothing atrocious or disrupting could happen here, with everything so homogeneous
and contained. Everyone rustled his afternoon *Post* and scanned
the headlines about Vietnam, about nurse-killers, rapists, sad-
ists; it was a particularly violent American summer, the incidents
of mass and impersonal homicide seemed everywhere, but we
were remote and moving, and I felt some secret, repressed glee,
at survival and invulnerability.

It was in such a mood that I learned a sniper had climbed to
the top of the Tower at my old university, the same Tower I
had stood at the top of my first day there as a freshman, and shot
down forty-nine people with a telescopic rifle. Sitting in a commuter car two thousand miles away reading about it, dwelling on
the landmarks of the campus I had known so well, filled with an
inexpressible horror; I could hear the other passengers talk of it
matter-of-factly, as if it were all a part of coming home. The
curious juxtaposition of violence and its incomprehensible
banality was becoming more and more a fact of life in America.
Who was protected against it? Where would it break out next?

For this man, whose name was Whitman, had also desecrated
the symbol of a specific place — The University of Texas — that
had once meant for me a liberation from narrowness and self-
destruction. He had climbed to the top of that Tower on a
hot, lazy summer's morning to try to destroy as many human
beings as he could sight through his three-power telescopic lense.
His victims lay strewn across the stretch of hill that I wandered

on at night, in my Wolfean moods as a college boy. His locus of terror enclosed trees, statues, buildings, and hidden walks etched on my memory. The dead and dying were struck down on that graceful mall where I had courted my girl, read poetry, and sat alone at midnight plotting my private hopes. The horrible act that killed or maimed his victims destroyed something in me. Night after night I would have dreams of that Tower — dark, desolate dreams about death and destruction. Whitman, so coldly rational in his madness that he had not even deigned to waste bullets on the tires of the armored car which tried to rescue the wounded victims, had impressed upon me that nothing — no human being, no symbolic place, no sanctuary of one's loyalty and liberation — was safe from the insane arbitrariness of total hate. One young man had looked around a stone walkway at the Tower, turned to others behind him, and said, "This is for real." Then he looked out again and was shot through the head. The woman receptionist he clubbed to death on the observation deck had pointed out the Balcones Hills to me on my first trip there in 1952. A friend of mine, along with a young boy and girl, was looking at the Tower through a small window of a building 500 yards away; suddenly the man next to him was shot through the arm. The sniper's telescopic lens missed nothing that looked human.

Reading of this now, in a commuter car of the Harlem River Line, I thought less of the terrible endemic violence of Texas than of the abjectness of us all before the mad capricious nihilism of our alienated and disaffected fellow human beings. I thought of the Tower, lit orange on some cold still Saturday night after the next football victory — the observation deck silent, dark, and unguarded. Then I looked around at my fellow commuters, talking of the sniper as casually as they might talk of some business associate, clinging to life not through terror, but through *dissociation* — a highly developed sense of detachment from the madnesses of our modern existence.

•

Sometimes on the train I would listen in on conversations between diehard commuters and outlanders who chanced to be riding to more remote outposts in the New England foothills. In these circumstances the talk would be about commuting itself. "Well, how much time do you *travel?*" the outsider would ask, and the cummuter would say, "Three hours and ten minutes" or "four hours and twenty, portal-to-portal." "But why do you do it?" "I do it for my family, especially for the kids." The city, you see, had become unlivable, and was getting worse all the time: crowds, noise, pollution, the subways, taxes, Negroes, Puerto Ricans. It was unsafe to go outdoors at night; drug addicts crawled the streets. "*I do it for my family, especially for the kids.*" I heard this phrase more than Mark Twain, in 1861, heard the story about Horace Greeley and Hank Monk in *Roughing It*.

There were the little bedroom towns with Indian names, the names as pathetic as the names one saw on the little lower-class houses in the working districts in England and artificial, so unlike the raw towns with Indian names I had once known in the Mississippi delta, with their grim and dusty exteriors, their closeness to the rich and humming earth from which they sprang. Could a man develop any feel for place along these tracks of the commuter run — identify with Pleasantville or Chappaqua, put roots in Valhalla? For always there was the agglomeration of split-levels and the thin patches of lawn, the rush to the train every day, the hundreds of stationwagons in the sprawling parking lots at the depots. I remembered my first train rides as a boy, the Illinois Central to Memphis and the

Negro conductor shouting: "Memphis-town is *heah!*"; and Thomas Wolfe's great expresses roaring through the cold American nights to Asheville or to the Fabulous Rock. This ride, by comparison, was only a daily chore. The world was making less and less room for drama, or for the possibilities of "grace under pressure." Was it possible to imagine anything less *heroic* than the life of the commuter?

Yet these were not "bad" people; they were not much better nor worse than the rest of us. The whole middle-class ethos had suggested to them that to be responsible to their families demanded a house with starched curtains and a piece of lawn as far removed from the disintegrating and ruinous city as possible. Did they want their daughters mugged in the streets? Their wives insulted by derelicts in supermarkets? Their apartments contaminated by the polluted filth sent forth by their city's own incinerators and by their monopolied utility Consolidated Edison? On a dozen occasions in the streets and on the sidewalks of the city I would see one of these middle-class commuters, having just emerged from the subway from Grand Central in starched white shirt, insulted and berated, out of mere chance, by the city's truckdrivers and cabbies. The men with the briefcases would never shout back; they would skulk around a corner avoiding an incident, or red-faced and sheepishly take the abuse as part of the risk involved in coming to work, confirmed even more in their desire to keep their children away.

In the 1960s the big cities of America were falling into extraordinary chaos and decay; New York, being the largest and most crowded, was becoming the worst of all. The middle classes reacted by retreating, as middle classes always had. Their instinct, far from being "corrupt," as some writers had suggested, was in human terms perfectly understandable. The man of the family ventured forth each morning into the bowels of the city, leaving his family in a secure and roomier isolation, and returned with the daily bread on the five-twenty-seven. As Pleasantville got pleasanter, the Cave grew darker and more forbidding; its devastation, for the commuter, became more perfunctory and unreal.

One afternoon in late August, as the summer's sun streamed into the car and made little jumping shadows on the windows, I sat gazing out at the tenement-dwellers, who were themselves looking out of their windows from the gray crumbling buildings along the tracks of upper Manhattan. As we crossed into the Bronx, the train unexpectedly slowed down for a few miles. Suddenly from out of my window I saw a large crowd near the tracks, held back by two policemen. Then, on the other side from my window, I saw a sight I would never be able to forget: a little boy almost severed in halves, lying at an incredible angle near the track. The ground was covered with blood, and the boy's eyes were opened wide, strained and disbelieving in his sudden oblivion. A policeman stood next to him, his arms folded, staring straight ahead at the windows of our train. In the orange glow of late afternoon the policemen, the crowd, the corpse of the boy were for a brief moment immobile, motionless, a small tableau to violence and death in the city. Behind me, in the next row of seats, there was a game of bridge. I heard one of the four men say as he looked out at the sight, "God, that's horrible." Another said, in a whisper, "Terrible, terrible." There was a momentary silence, punctuated only by the clicking of the wheels on the track. Then, after the pause, I heard the first man say: "Two hearts."

•

The old house on the hill reawakened one's awareness of the land; the yellowed deeds going back by more than a century, their property divides and their descriptions of noticeable landmarks existing yet, were enough to impress upon one that stretches of earth are ours for a brevity, in trust only, and would someday be someone else's, and someone else's again after that. The lovely hill with its hickory and maple and dogwood and apple trees, the ancient stone walls with each stone in its necessary place, the grassy slope tilting at a headlong angle into the woods, these were ours only for the moment, a mere temporary possession, and would one day return again to the commonality before some future bidder. In the winter the wind whistled down from the hollow, and the snow came in its great driven drifts from the taller hill to the north. The autumn here would be spectacular, its colors like none I had ever seen, and spring came forth so suddenly, in such contrast to the grim stark winter that its relief was more emphatic than the springs in the South, which had been a deeper and more fragrant green by far, yet had always been taken more for granted. An old photograph, from the turn of the century, showed an unidentified woman and a little girl in flowing dresses on the big front porch, and under the dogwood tree were two gravestones long since vanished. There was a photograph of the three fantastic figures, the Baldwins, who had once lived here. It was taken in the spring of 1914, the woman huge and phlegmatic, looking like a farmhand's Gertrude Stein, flanked on the same front porch by her two wild-eyed and stern-faced brothers.

The Burton twins, George and Charles, age seventy-eight, now lived down the road, carpenters who practiced their craft with such a skill, pride, and love that when I watched them at labor I felt I was *learning* something about my own work. They had grown up on "Quaker Hill," across the valley, now occupied by Thomas E. Dewey, Norman Vincent Peale, and a host of Wall Street lawyers, and others of the city's remote and well-greased executives in big country homes; they loved to talk about Dewey's hill as it was when they were boys. They had known the Baldwin siblings who had once owned our house: Jerome, one of the brothers, had been "mean as hell," and the sister Mary had suffered from asthma and was forced to lean her head out of a window every few minutes during the summer to catch her breath. Now the Baldwins were not only gone, no one knew their burial place, and their photograph in my study seemed their last and only tangible memorial. At Christmas one year, with all the presents scattered under the tree, and evidences of our own affluence everywhere, it occurred to me that the old house had never known such riches. The thought of the Baldwins with their two pot-bellied stoves, their hard existence as simple farmers — their old ledger which had "come with the house" recording their sparse barters and purchases at the country store in Patterson — seemed somehow forbidding; here we were, with a permanent apartment in the city and an eighteenth-century house with central heating, spoiled children of our age.

One day a woman drove by from New York City; she had been raised in the house as a girl, and her father was born in one of the bedrooms in 1865. It was a good old place, the kind of place Thurber had thought of to go away to and read *Huckleberry Finn* and *Tom Sawyer* again, or *Moby Dick* and the *Leatherstocking Tales*. Hound dogs barked in the distance on clear nights, and from the top floor there was a view of the purple range of hills, *mountains* to anyone who had grown up in the Mississippi delta. The locals of this countryside were laconic and self-contained. Faulkner and his friend Cowley had driven through these hills one matchless Indian summer day. They got lost; they stopped to get directions from two taciturn Connecticut farmers. "Does this road cross the mountain?" Cowley said. "Yes," the man said, with proper courtesy.

"Thank you," Cowley said, and they drove on for fifty yards. Then Cowley stopped the car and said, "Wait." He backed the car to the two farmers. "Can I get over it in this car?" Cowley asked. "No," the same farmer said. "I don't think you can."

In melancholy Southern moods I sensed that the great qualities of this country place were doomed; if so, the Big Cave would be the executioner. Often I would catch sight of the developers cruising up our hill in their Chrysler with the city plates, one a fat man named Michaels, his running-mate a thin fellow named Barco. They would get out of their car and unfold their prodigious maps, and then explore the hills and fields, talking and gesturing with great animation. One afternoon they stopped by to give me their business card and to talk with me about land values, for they were engaged in seeking out whatever land was for sale, to buy and re-sell at $2000 an acre. They had just bought a spectacular wooded hill down the road, sixty acres where the deer and rabbits roamed, to develop half-acre tracts and to contract for crackerbox houses at $18,000 apiece. They talked of the inexorable encroachment of the city's suburbia, seventy miles from Times Square, with a fanatical enthusiasm, and they planned to saw down the grand old trees a couple of hundred yards down the hill and put in a street. Up the hill you could hear the sound of their bulldozers and buzz-saws ripping out some tenacious natural obstacle. There is something agonizingly horrible to me in the rumblings of a bulldozer as it ravishes a lovely hill. Michaels and Barco were like their bulldozers. Rootless sons of the modern city, what did the land matter to them? On Saturday mornings you could see the two of them, stationed on some wonderful high place with their maps, motioning out into the distances. They wanted Thomas E. Dewey's land so badly they would have sprouted grisly mustaches to get it. Once I sat down and wrote Michaels a cryptic note to his office in the city: "Dear Michaels, *No wonder the ruined woods I used to know don't cry for retribution. The people who have destroyed it will accomplish its revenge.* (signed) I. McCaslin."

Yet from their growing suburbia we had a reprieve — five years, ten years? — and it was impossible not to become deeply attached to this old country of the Indians and the Dutch and the Yankees, to the quiet hills and farms of western Connecticut, to the great sweep and flow of the Hudson Valley — Washington Irving country: "A drowsy, dreamy influence seems to hang over the land, and to pervade the very atmosphere. Certain it is, the place still continues under the sway of some witching power, that holds the spell over the minds of the good people, causing them to walk in a continual reverie. They are given to all kinds of marvelous beliefs; are subject to trances and visions; and frequently see strange sights, and hear music and voices in the air." The reveries and superstitions had vanished, but reading such lines to a small boy on some windy night in November generated for the adult his own fantasies, and one was glad for the sake of the child's belonging that a real writer had lived in the neighborhood many years before. For country like this, its changing Yankee seasons, its unexpected shapes and divides, its neat eighteenth-century villages, could take hold of one's imagination, and even one's loyalties. The feeling grew upon me, not apocalyptically but slow as could be, slow as good sour-mash gets its mellowing or as a young man matures and finds balance, that in the great chaos of modern existence it was one's work that mattered, work in the broadest and most meaningful sense — this and being close to the people one loved. Here, in the country around this hill, and seventy miles away in the Cave, our fantastic cultural capital, was where one's work was, one's family, and friends — friends whose own work was important to the national life. The feeling had been a long time in coming: you did not have to go to your sources again to survive; one's past was *inside* of a man anyway; it would remain there forever.

9

ONE OCTOBER day in 1965 my son and I caught a jet at Kennedy Airport to go south, first to Texas, where I had been invited by the University to give a lecture, and then on to Mississippi. It would be my first trip to the South in three years, and the boy, sensing the drama in it, had talked his way into going back with me. He wore a navy-blue suit like mine, and carried a child's suitcase, and as the big jet took off and circled over Long Island Sound I looked at him in his wonderful excitement and marveled that at age five, going on six, he looked so grown-up, an innocent replica of the tousled and somewhat degenerate-looking thirty-year-old at his elbow.

From a jet at 30,000 feet the America of the 1960s was a beautiful, awesome, untouched place. On this clear autumn afternoon across vast distances I was as enthralled as I always had been by the massive contours of the earth, the big tangled rivers, the dark mountains and forests, the great geological changes that loomed up so unexpectedly, all giving one some suggestion, at such a remove from what it had become, of how this land had stunned the imagination and the dreams of its settlers 300 years before. My Greyhound ride in 1963 from San

Francisco had been a trip through reality, but on a high jet-ride America seemed made of its old incomparable dreams. As with every other time I had returned South, all my nerve-ends were strangely alive, and the boy kept looking out the window at some extravagant set of landmarks, asking incessantly what they were, or how big America was and where did it end, or whether we were flying over Pennsylvania or Maryland or Kentucky.

Just before we left New York I had read to my wife the lecture I had written. My son had been in the room, listening intently to the part which said: "My father had been born in those sulphurous hills south of Nashville, and had gone to the Deep South, at all times and to all places, during the Great Depression." Now we were over Tennessee, traveling with the sun's descent. The pilot's voice came on over the intercom and said: "If you'll look off to the east, folks, you'll see Nashville, and the hills south of it."

The sun gave to these dappled hills a flowing purplish texture, and the clouds wafted above the great dams, rivers, and lakes, inset there like mirages. "Daddy," the boy said, looking out his window, "did your father live down there?"

"Yes. A long time ago." There was a pause.

"Where is he now?"

"He's dead. He died in Mississippi." The little boy turned his head again, wordlessly, and looked out the window. Then the plane began to turn slowly westward, facing into the soft orange glow. In a few minutes we were south of Memphis, and over the great River near Greenville, where I had played baseball under our coach Gentleman Joe; and then Vicksburg and the bluffs where during the Korean War I had played taps for the best military funeral of them all; and the pine forests of East Texas which I had driven across in the moonlight as a college boy. Soon we were in Dallas, at the airport where Johnson had been inaugurated and where Kennedy's body had lain in the Presidential plane; here we changed for a smaller plane to Austin, and within the hour I was gazing down at the familiar divide of the Balcones, and the succession of lakes — and suddenly the same old Tower and the Capitol set against the night sky.

The next day we drove in Ronnie Dugger's convertible through the magnificent hill country, where I had been taken on my first "walk" as a freshman; then down the streets of the city, through the grounds of the Texas Capitol, where I had known my first confrontation with day-by-day politics. We drove to the University. Soon a new superhighway would come through near the barnlike building which housed the *Texas Observer*. The faintly ruined nineteenth-century homes nearby were being torn down for parking lots to service the campus — so huge and sprawling as to seem a different place altogether from the way I remembered it ten years before. The contractors had begun to destroy the splendid Austin skyline with dubious high-rise apartment buildings, emulating New York, and someone was even remodeling the old German beer hall. The Tower, the site of the sniper's mass murder, stood majestic and symbolic on this cold autumn day, and once again, for the thousandth time, I read the inscription on its stone which had so baffled and excited me as a homesick Mississippi boy: "*Ye Shall Know the Truth and the Truth Shall Make You Free.*" Down the street was the Slum Area, more respectable in appearances now than it had been, and the broad intramural field, and Brackenridge Hall, where the baseball players had once roamed in filth and nihilism.

I do not know what is so magical about a "New York editor" out in the provinces, but a crowd turned out in the auditorium that afternoon to hear my lecture: about my generation of young Americans, and about the University of Texas in the

1950s. We had been, I told those students of the 1960s, a very lucky generation; as far as the organized and official destruction of our age was concerned, we had been too young for the Second World War, just barely too young for Korea, just barely too old for Vietnam. We had come of age in the mid-1950s, whose only distinct ideology involved the struggle between Godless Communism and God's Free Enterprise Democracy. The later, more activist liberals and radicals would say we were a "vanished" generation, too much the children of the pervasive affluence and smugness of our silent coming to maturity to engage ourselves in social struggles that genuinely mattered — "children of the children" of the Depression, whose parents after their early deprivations had sought materialistic comfort as a first prerogative and as a matter of course, and who had given to us, their offspring, the easy comforts and securities they themselves had achieved with such difficulty. We had never known material want, and we probably never would. I told of having seen a film in New York, a documentary of the Spanish Civil War, and of how it had seemed merely sated on the familiar *celluloid* violence of the 1930s and 1940s, and how (even despite the books I had read of that period) it had seemed to me so remote and unreal. Could such unmitigated and recognizable evil return to haunt humanity again?

Yet, I said, we had been touched and moved, many of us, by the example set by Kennedy, despite the burgeoning Kennedy myth; we had seen briefly in those years some slight promise of modern America's true grandeur, its civility, and what its best and truest hopes might mean for the rest of the world. We were, the best of us, not taken in by slogans, easy answers, or dogmas; we were skeptics, and we were still very young. And some of us, at the University of Texas in the 1950s, were of another kind of society — the South, and of an upbringing that did not lend itself perfunctorily to the spreading homogeneity, the blandness, the blind sense of worth and superiority, of this age in America.

Then I described my own experiences as editor of the University's student newspaper in the 1950s — the attempt to stifle legitimate inquiry, the self-righteous desire to silence a few young people's search for something that differed from the norms and values of Texas in that day. I was living now, I said, in the middle of New York letters and publishing, and the events of 1956 had returned to haunt me there on the eighteenth floor of Park Avenue and 33rd Street. I had been working with some of the finest writers, editors, journalists, and publishers in America; the *Daily Texan* experience had, in the most basic way, shaped my attitude toward my own work, and the work of others, had shaped my own awareness of those things which must be fought the hardest in this country: the idea that anything could be *bought*, even culture, even loyalty. If I could, I said, I would have changed a lot of things in my conduct then, but I cared deeply for the University of Texas, and those days of my student editorship had stood out afterward as the proudest and most satisfying of my life. These words were received with sympathy and enthusiasm. Is there something in the mere natural passing of time, something involved in being ten or fifteen years removed from the vicious antagonisms of a painful controversy, that blunts and then dramatizes the edges of dissent in America? Is there some quality in the country itself, after all the passions of a moment or a period have faded, that accepts old dissent, and makes it heroic?

10

MISSISSIPPI. In the little frame house on Grand Avenue, where we were to stay one night, I showed my son the mementos from my high school: the framed scrolls and certificates and documents on the walls of my room, testifying still that I had once indulged myself in all the official trinkets and the glittering medals. Under the bed I discovered a whole shoebox full of love letters from the blond majorette from Belle Prairie Plantation; I took them into the back yard, arranged them in a neat pile near the place where my dog Skip was buried and where my father once hid from the visiting preachers, and put a match to them, gazing down at one phrase not yet burned: *"I'll meet you in front of the drugstore at 7:30 in my green sweater."* My mother and my grandmother Mamie fixed fried chicken and huge steaming casseroles, and chocolate cake and meringue pie, and while we digested this feast, spurning "Bonanza" on television, my mother played, on the grand piano, some of the old hymns: "Faith of Our Fathers," "Bringing in the Sheaves," "Living with Jesus," "Abide with Me." Outside, on the street, the teen-agers sped by, shouting and blowing the horns of their family cars, and the pecan trees in the yard rustled and moaned in the wind, stirring up too many ghosts.

Our plane for New York was to leave Jackson, forty miles away, at noon the next day, and since I had resolved not to see anyone, since old friendships suddenly brought together again had always embarrassed me, we got up at dawn to drive around town. The streets of Yazoo were so settled in my consciousness after all those years that the drive was unnecessary, for I still knew where every tree was, the angles on the roofs of every house, the hidden alleys and paths and streams. Coming around some bend I would know exactly the sights that would be there — and there they were, the memory of them even more real than the blurred shapes of reality. We drove through niggertown, some of its old dirt roads now paved and with curbs and sewers, past the grocery store where the colored men had seen my dog propped against the steering wheel of my car and shouted: "Look at that ol' dog drivin' a car!" Back again in the white section, every street corner and side street had meanings for me; I had sat on the curb at Grand Avenue and Second Street, near Bubba Barrier's house, one summer afternoon in 1943, wearing a Brooklyn Dodger baseball cap, dreaming of the mythical cities of the North, and bemoaning my own helpless condition. Grand Avenue, with the same towering elms and oaks, had changed hardly at all, and only the occasional new chain store or supermarket marred my memory of it. Driving down that broad boulevard, my mother pointed out the houses in which people I had known had died, by simple attrition or by violent, tragic causes; each house represented a death or more, and the knowledge of it, after my having been away so long, gave to the whole town a vague presence of inevitable death. My old schoolhouse on Main Street, where the ineffable Miss Abbott had taught my fourth-grade class enough Bible verses to assure our salvation, had a new coat of paint; the schoolyard where I had played football against the Graball boys still had its Confederate monument; the soldier on top with the gun in one hand and the other hand extended to take the flag from the Confederate lady had not moved an inch since 1939. On Main Street the Dixie Theater had vanished from the face of the earth, as had some of the smaller stores, replaced now by the Yankee chains advertised on national television; but many of the familiar places remained: the *Yazoo Herald*, where I had turned in my first sports articles at the age of twelve, the radio station where I had played Beethoven instead of Tennessee Ernie Ford, Tommy Norman's, Henick's Store, where my taps-playing colleague Henjie now sold tires and tire accessories. But most of the young people I had known here, in the 1940s, were gone long before, living now in the prosperous 1960s in the sprawling and suburbanized cities of the New South — Atlanta, Memphis, New Orleans, Birmingham, Nashville. Out on the edges of town, where the bootleggers had once flourished before Mississippi legalized liquor, I noticed that Yazoo had even developed its own suburbia. I was suffused with a physical feeling of lost things, with a tangible hovering presence of old dead moments; it was time to get out, and I drove as fast as I could up Broadway, that fantastic hill, for Highway 49 and Jackson.

We drove through the lush rolling hills toward Jackson. Along the highway a huge billboard had a picture of Martin Luther King, surrounded by throngs of Negroes, and the words on the sign said: "M. L. King Meets His Fellow Commies." Near Jackson I saw a more ambitious suburbia, sprung up fullborn from the pastures and cottonfields I remembered from my childhood, row after row of split-levels that seemed not much different from Pleasantville or Hawthorne on the Harlem River Line.

Mamie said, "Let's drive by the old house and see what they've done with it." We headed down Jefferson Street, and there was the brick house just as it was, the same magnolia tree, the sticker bushes where my great-aunts had gotten trapped in their endless peregrinations, the rickety garage where my grandfather Percy had built for me the miniature steamboats with names like *The Robert E. Lee* and *The Belle of Memphis*.

Then down the street Percy and I had walked to the Jackson "Senator" baseball games, past the old house where the man who "stole the money from the state" had once lived, to the old capitol building at the corner of Capitol and State. Mamie turned to my son, who had been looking at many of these unfamiliar landmarks with a Yankee's skepticism. "Son," she said, "you see that building there? My father — your great-great-grandfather Harper — was in the legislature there, and one day when I was a little girl my brother Winter took me inside and told the guards, 'She's Mr. George's girl, and I want her to sit in our Papa's chair.' See that balcony yonder? That's where your uncle Henry Foote — he was Governor of Mississippi many years ago — made a speech in 18-and-60, tellin' folks not to believe a word ol' Jefferson Davis said." The boy looked out at the object of these words, the graceful building that had been restored by the State to its previous grace and eminence, and then smiled sheepishly at me, still a trifle disbelieving.

We took the road out to Raymond and drove by the Harper house, also "restored" so that its picture now appeared in the travelogues, and then on to the town cemetery; neither my mother nor my grandmother had visited here in years. The old section was overgrown with weeds and Johnson grass, the iron fences rusted and fallen, the tombstones crumbled or vanished entirely. I parked the car on a ridge and the four of us, of our four different generations, got out and walked around. It was a bright, crisp October morning, but the terrain itself was damp and gray, casting an odor heavy with decay and ruin. We looked hard enough, but we could not find the Harpers, not a single one of them — not my great-grandfather nor great-grandmother, nor my great-aunts, nor even my grandfather Percy. We searched in the weeds and stickers on the hill where Mamie thought they had been laid away. "Well, I *thought* they were around here somewhere," she said. Fifty yards away was a well-kept plot of graves, soldiers who had been killed in some minor skirmish attendant to the siege of Vicksburg, watered and manicured now by the ladies of the town, and my son went over to look at these while we explored the countryside for our vanished kin. Finally we found what must have been the plot — the remnants of a fence, the unrecognizable stumps of gravestones, covered over now with the dank, moist weeds. "I guess they're here somewhere," Mamie said, "but you'd never know it."

I took Mamie by the arm and we wandered farther down the hill, stumbling occasionally over a stretch of barbed wire or what remained of a tombstone. I was impressed, even as I had been as a child my son's age, by her steady good humor. One of the old broken stones marked the grave of Miss Lucy McGee, born in 1820, died in 1850. "Mamie," I said, "this is where Miss Lucy McGee is. Did you ever hear of her?" "*Lucy McGee!*" she said. "Why, of course, son. I remember Papa and Mamma talkin' about the McGees when I was a girl. I believe she died very young for her age."

•

The airport was a new one, bright and shining and strangely quiet on this morning. As I confirmed our tickets back to New York, my mother and grandmother spotted some TV star on "Hollywood Circus" having coffee in the restaurant, and went up near to his table to get a closer look. Then we walked down the broad corridor toward the landing field, waiting near the door in that awkward moment that always precedes some long departure for me. The loudspeaker announced the flight, and we made our goodbyes. "You come back now, you *heah?*" my mother said, and my son and I walked down the ramp and got on the plane.

Why was it, in such moments just before I leave the South, did I always feel some easing of a great burden? It was as if someone had taken some terrible weight off my shoulders, or as if some old grievance had suddenly fallen away. The big plane took off, and circled in widening arcs over the city, over the landmarks of my past, and my people's. Then, slowly, with a lifting heavy as steel, it circled once more, and turned north toward home.

ALSO BY WILLIE MORRIS

MY DOG SKIP
Now a major motion picture

In 1943, in a sleepy town on the banks of the Yazoo River, a boy fell in love with a puppy with a lively gait and an intelligent way of listening. The two grew up together having the most wonderful adventures. A classic story of a boy, a dog, and small-town America, *My Dog Skip* belongs on the same shelf as *The Adventures of Tom Sawyer* and Russell Baker's *Growing Up*. It will enchant readers of all ages for years to come.

Memoir/Pets/0-679-76722-3

Available in hardcover from Random House and forthcoming from Vintage in Fall 2000

MY CAT SPIT MCGEE

Willie Morris never liked cats—indeed, he had a loathing of cats going back to his childhood. But the woman Willie married turned out to be a cat woman, and on their first Christmas together, a little white waif found starving in a ditch off old Highway 51 outside Jackson, Mississippi, crept out from behind their Christmas tree with a red Yuletide ribbon around her neck. Willie was horrified, but that kitten eventually became the mother of Spit McGee, who is the subject of this surprising and altogether winning book. The result is a story-filled celebration of the love that millions of others have for their cats. It honors, too, an abiding comradeship, and Willie and Spit's daily adventures as they try to fathom each other.

Memoir/Pets/0-375-50321-8 (cloth)

A DEATH IN THE FAMILY
by James Agee

On a summer night in 1915, Jay Follet leaves his house in Knoxville, Tennessee, to tend to his sick father; on the way back to his family, he is killed in a car accident. Forty years after its original publication, James Agee's novel seems, more than ever, an American classic. For in his lyrical account of a man's death and its impact on his family, Agee created a small world of domestic happiness and then showed how quickly and casually it could be destroyed.

Winner of the Pulitzer Prize
Fiction/Literature/0-375-70123-0

ALL GOD'S CHILDREN NEED TRAVELING SHOES
by Maya Angelou

Maya Angelou's lyrical and acutely perceptive autobiography explores what it means to be an African-American on the mother continent, where color no longer matters but where American-ness keeps asserting itself in ways both puzzling and heartbreaking.

Autobiography/0-679-73404-X

BIG BAD LOVE
by Larry Brown

Larry Brown is one of the fiercest and most powerful voices in Southern literature, and in *Big Bad Love* his passionate regard for ordinary people shines through on every page. Brown's heroes have a fatal weakness for beer, fast women, and pick-up trucks, and even when thwarted by state troopers or the women that drive them crazy, they find salvation in the reckless pursuit of love.

Fiction/Literature/0-679-73491-0

ELLEN FOSTER
by Kaye Gibbons

"When I was little I would think of ways to kill my daddy. I would figure out this way or that way and run it down through my head until it got easy." So begins the tale of Ellen Foster, the brave and engaging heroine of Kaye Gibbons's first novel. Wise, funny, affectionate and true, *Ellen Foster* is, as Walker Percy called it, "as much a part of the backwoods South as a Faulkner character."

Fiction/Literature/0-375-70305-5

THE OPTIMIST'S DAUGHTER
by Eudora Welty

Laurel McKelva Hand has left the south only to return, years later, to New Orleans, where her father is dying. After his death, she and her young stepmother travel to the small Mississippi town where she grew up. Alone in the old house, Laurel finally comes to an understanding of the past, herself, and her parents in this moving work by a modern American master.

Fiction/Literature/0-679-72883-X